touchpoints

BOOKS BY T. BERRY BRAZELTON, M.D.

On Becoming a Family
The Growth of Attachment Before and After Birth

Infants and Mothers
Differences in Development

Toddlers and Parents
Declaration of Independence

Doctor and Child

To Listen to a Child
Understanding the Normal Problems of Growing Up

Working and Caring

What Every Baby Knows

Families, Crisis, and Caring

Touchpoints
Your Child's Emotional and Behavioral Development

with Bertrand G. Cramer, M.D.

The Earliest Relationship
Parents, Infants, and the Drama of Early Attachment

Janice Fullman

Steven Trefonides

Dorothy Littell Greco

PHOTOGRAPHY

Steven Trefonides
Janice Fullman
Dorothy Littell Greco

Capture The Magic Of The Swan Princess!

Exclusive Portraits From Photography by JCPenney!

the Swan™ princess
Now playing at a theater near you!

FREE 8x10
With Portrait Package at $7.95!

DAKIN

Exclusive Swan Princess props and background — new at -
Photography by JCPenney. Create memories for a lifetime!

©1994 Nest Productions, Inc.

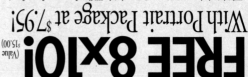

touchpoints

YOUR CHILD'S EMOTIONAL AND BEHAVIORAL DEVELOPMENT

T. Berry Brazelton, M.D.

A MERLOYD LAWRENCE BOOK

ADDISON-WESLEY PUBLISHING COMPANY

Reading, Massachusetts   Menlo Park, California   New York
Don Mills, Ontario   Wokingham, England   Amsterdam   Bonn
Sydney   Singapore   Tokyo   Madrid   San Juan
Paris   Seoul   Milan   Mexico City   Taipei

The author and publishers would like to thank Lynne Meyer-Gay for skillful, perceptive, and tireless help in the preparation of this manuscript.

Many of the designations used by manufacturers and sellers to distinguish their products are claimed as trademarks. Where those designations appear in this book and Addison-Wesley was aware of a trademark claim, the designations have been printed in initial capital letters.

Library of Congress Cataloging-in-Publication Data

Brazelton, T. Berry, 1918–
    Touchpoints : your child's emotional and behavioral development / T. Berry Brazelton.
      p. cm.
    "A Merloyd Lawrence Book."
    Includes bibliographical references and index.
    ISBN 0-201-09380-4
    ISBN 0-201-62690-X (pbk.)
    1. Child devleopment—United States. 2. Infants—United States—Development. 3. Child psychology—United States. 4. Infant psychology—United States. I. Title
HQ792.USB725   1992
305.23′1—dc20   92-23004
                                         CIP

Cover design by Diana Coe
Text design by Karen Savary
Copy edited by Sharon Sharp
Set in 11-point Times New Roman by ComCom

1 2 3 4 5 6 7 8 9-VB-97969594
First printing, October 1992
First paperback printing, January 1994

To Alfred, Rosalis, and their grandmother

contents

introduction   xvii

---

one **TOUCHPOINTS OF DEVELOPMENT**

1   **PREGNANCY: THE FIRST TOUCHPOINT**   **3**
2   **THE NEWBORN INDIVIDUAL**   **23**
3   **NEWBORN PARENTS**   **37**
4   **THREE WEEKS**   **53**
5   **SIX TO EIGHT WEEKS**   **68**
6   **FOUR MONTHS**   **83**
7   **SEVEN MONTHS**   **105**
8   **NINE MONTHS**   **119**
9   **ONE YEAR**   **132**
10 **FIFTEEN MONTHS**   **151**
11 **EIGHTEEN MONTHS**   **166**
12 **TWO YEARS**   **180**
13 **THREE YEARS**   **200**

---

two **CHALLENGES TO DEVELOPMENT**

14 **ALLERGIES**   **219**
15 **BEDWETTING (ENURESIS)**   **227**

16 **CRYING**   231

17 **DEPRESSION**   239

18 **DEVELOPMENTAL DISABILITIES**   243

19 **DISCIPLINE**   252

20 **DIVORCE**   261

21 **EMOTIONAL MANIPULATION**   269

22 **FEARS**   276

23 **FEEDING PROBLEMS**   286

24 **HABITS**   293

25 **HOSPITALIZATION**   298

26 **HYPERSENSITIVITY AND HYPERACTIVITY**   305

27 **ILLNESS**   312

28 **IMAGINARY FRIENDS**   323

29 **LOSS AND GRIEF**   328

30 **LYING, STEALING, AND CHEATING**   336

31 **MANNERS**   343

32 **PREMATURITY**   350

33 **SCHOOL READINESS**   355

34 **SELF-ESTEEM**   362

35 **SEPARATION**   367

36 **SIBLING RIVALRY**   374

37 **SLEEP PROBLEMS**   380

38 **SPACING CHILDREN**   390

39 **SPEECH AND HEARING PROBLEMS**   398

40 **STOMACHACHES AND HEADACHES**   405

41 **TELEVISION**   409

42 **TOILET TRAINING**   414

three ALLIES IN DEVELOPMENT

43 **FATHERS AND MOTHERS**   421

44 **GRANDPARENTS**   428

45 **FRIENDS**   437

46 **CAREGIVERS**   443

47 **YOUR CHILD'S DOCTOR**   451

bibliography   463
useful addresses   467
index   471
about the author   481
photography credits   483

introduction

After forty years of pediatric practice in Cambridge, Massachusetts, participating in the parenting of 25,000 patients, I have developed the map of infancy and of early child development that I have laid out in this book. This map of behavioral and emotional development is designed to help parents navigate the predictable spurts in development and the equally predictable issues that they raise in virtually all families.

Unlike yardsticks of physical development (the heights, for instance, that parents take such pride in marking off on door-frames), this map has several dimensions. There are regressions as well as spurts. Psychological growth takes place in many directions, not all at once. The cost of each new achievement can temporarily disrupt the child's—and even the whole family's—progress.

Underlying the map, and indeed this whole book, is the concept of "touchpoints," which I have refined over years of research at Children's Hospital in Boston and in other sites around the world. Touchpoints, which are universal, are those predictable times that occur just before a surge of rapid growth in any line of development—motor, cognitive, or emotional—when, for a short time, the child's behavior falls apart. Parents can no longer rely on past accomplishments. The child often regresses in several areas and becomes difficult to understand. Parents lose their own balance and become alarmed. Over the years, I have found that these predictable periods of regression can become opportunities for me to help parents understand their child. The touchpoints become a window through which parents can view the great energy that fuels the child for learning. Each step accomplished leads to a new sense of autonomy. When seen as normal and predictable, these periods of regressive behavior are opportunities to understand the child more deeply and to support his or her growth, rather than to become locked into a struggle. A child's particular strengths and vulnerabilities, as well as temperament and coping style, all come to the surface at such a time. What a chance for understanding the child as an individual!

Part 1 of this book is organized around these touchpoints in the areas of behavioral and emotional growth, showing how they affect decisions about all areas—sleep, feeding, the independence that comes with walking, communication, discipline, or toilet training. Issues are laid out just as they emerge in office visits with parents, from the prenatal visit with an expectant mother and father to the checkups for the infants to the annual visits with the older child. Parents' questions appear at predictable times. Their concerns about how to handle these disruptive regressions make our visits focused. If I can help parents understand the mechanisms in the child that contribute to troublesome behavior, each visit becomes more valuable. A caring professional can use such times to reach into the family system, offer support, and prevent future problems.

Part 2 takes up those specific issues of child rearing in the first six years that can challenge normal development. "Problems" of sibling rivalry, crying, tantrums, waking at night, fears, emotional manipulations, lying, or bedwetting begin when parents attempt to control situations that really belong to the child. I try to show how parents can see these various kinds of behavior as part of the struggle for autonomy, and how they can remove themselves from the struggle and thus defuse it.

In writing part 2, I have drawn on articles I wrote for parents on the same issues in *Family Circle* and earlier in *Redbook*. The topics are perennials, raised in urgent tones by parents both in my office and whenever I speak to groups. In part 2 these topics are put into the context of my touchpoints concept of development. These chapters, written for parents who see themselves or their child getting stuck in an issue, are designed not only to help them avoid getting locked into destructive patterns or incapacitating anxiety but also to know when to seek help if their efforts fail. Certain chapters, such as those on depression, developmental disabilities, or speech and hearing problems, are not meant to be comprehensive. They are intended only to help parents distinguish between normal variations in behavior and problems that require expert help.

Part 3 examines the ways in which children's development is affected by those around them. Each close relationship— with fathers as well as mothers, with grandparents, friends, other caregivers, and the child's doctor—contributes to the child's emotional and behavioral growth. The more that parents can enlist these contributions, the more allies a child will have on the journey toward autonomy.

In my experience, no developmental line in a child proceeds in a continuous upward course. Motor development, cognitive development, and emotional development all seem to proceed in a jagged line, with peaks, valleys, and plateaus. Each new task a baby learns is demanding—it requires all of the baby's energy, as well as that of family members. For instance, when a year-old baby is learning to walk, everyone pays a price. The baby is up and down at the side of the crib all night, coming to full waking at every light-sleep cycle, crying out for help every three to four hours during the night. Everyone's sleep is disrupted. The child's doctor is sure to hear about it. In the daytime, the baby cries out in frustration every time a parent or sibling walks by. When a parent turns her back, the frustrated baby collapses into a frantic heap. A child's learning to walk is costly to everyone's peace of mind. The child who has finally learned to walk becomes a different person, face aglow with triumph. Everyone in the family settles down. The next phase in development will be spent in consolidating and enriching this last achievement. A toddler will learn to walk holding a toy, to turn around while walking, to squat, to climb stairs. In this phase, the child won't be so unpredictably volatile. The pressure is off—until the next spurt.

Each of these spurts and the regressions that precede them are touchpoints for me as a pediatrician interested in playing an active role as part of the family system. When parents come with concerns, I can share my observations of the child's behavior and expect to be heard. Insights into this behavior become our shared language. I can use my experience with the family to help them uncover their underlying anxieties. By pointing out the reason for the turmoil and the predictable outcome in development, I am able to share their concerns in a positive and helpful way. Parents are likely to meet a child's regression with anxiety and an attempt to control the behavior. At a time when the child is searching for a new sense of autonomy, they add pressure to conform. This can reinforce any deviant behavior and set it as a habit pattern. These touchpoints are opportunities to prevent such difficulties from getting locked in. At such times, I find that I can offer parents choices in behavior. If their own strategies have ended in failure or in anxiety, they are ready to look for alternatives. Someone outside the situation can suggest these before the family becomes fixed in a failure pattern.

Neither allowing a child autonomy nor relinquishing unproductive habits of child rearing is a simple, rational matter. We are all likely to become mired in situations that call up ghosts, or powerful experiences, from our own nursery. Patterns of parenting learned from our own parents loom over us, pressing us to respond irrationally. As I pointed out in my book *The Earliest Relationship,* written with Bertrand Cramer, by bringing these ghosts to consciousness, we are able to strip them of their power. We, as parents, can then make more rational choices about how to handle our child's disturbing behavior.

Parents don't make mistakes because they don't care, but because they care so deeply. Caring revives issues from the past. Passion creates determination, which may supersede judgment. If parents can understand the child's powerful need to establish his or her own autonomous pattern, they may be able to break a vicious circle of overreaction and conflict.

Learning to parent is made up of learning from mistakes— not from successes. When something goes wrong, a parent must reorganize in order to remedy the situation. Mistakes and wrong choices stand out and grab you; successes do not. Rewards for "right choices" are deep and quiet: having a child cuddle in your arms to be crooned to, or announce proudly, "Look, I did it myself!" In any case, what parents do at any point may not be as critical as the emotional atmosphere that surrounds their action.

In recent years we have been learning more and more about the importance of individual differences in children. As I wrote in my book *Infants and Mothers,* babies' individual temperaments, or styles of interacting with and learning about the world, can influence heavily the way they pay attention and absorb the parents' guiding stimuli. Their temperaments also profoundly influence the parents' reactions to them from the moment of birth. While a child cannot be seen as born with a fixed nature, neither is the environment all-important in shaping a child. These inborn individual differences mean that the chronology suggested by the ordering of topics in the following chapters must be adapted to the reader's own child.

Each parent's own style and temperament must also be respected. Two parents cannot be expected to react the same way at the same time to the same child—nor should they. Their own differences in temperament and experience should make their reactions different if the parents are true to themselves. Hence, each situation demands a custom-made decision if it is to be a "right choice"—that is, right for the child and right for each parent.

Parenting today can be lonely. Most new parents are insecure and wonder whether they are doing as well as they can with their children. As a pediatrician, I have always felt a responsibility to anticipate the issues that I know will arise, and to help parents find opportunities for learning to understand their children. I want to be an active part of each family as a system, as it interacts and readjusts to stress or to each new level of learning in any one of its members.

When I began to practice, I found I was bored by the routines of shots, weight and height checks, and physical exams. For me, the excitement lay in the developmental issues that the child presented and that the parents raised with deep concern at each visit. Such concerns as nightlong sleep, food struggles, or bedwetting were uppermost in parents' minds when they brought a healthy child for a checkup. If I was ready to probe and to share ideas with them, they were eager and grateful to discuss their side of the issues. While we talked, I observed the child's play and way of handling my examination. Through many such observations, I learned to form an idea of each child's temperament and stage of development. Then, I could predict for the parents the issues that might arise in each of the areas we discussed—feeding, sleeping, thumb sucking, toilet training, and so on. When I could predict their conflicts, and when I could help them understand the child's issues, our relationship deepened. Each visit became more exciting for me and more rewarding for them.

Shared experiences such as these are valuable both to the parents and to the physician. When parents bring the child for a later visit, they and the doctor have a chance to reevaluate any earlier predictions. If the predictions have held, they know they are on the right track. Unpredictable outcomes are also revealing. Parents and physician can then examine (1) the biases that shaped the predictions in the first place; (2) the strength of the defenses of the family, which may have hidden certain vulnerabilities and underlying issues; and (3) the relative strength of the physician–family relationship, which determines how much a family can trust the physician and reveal their concerns openly. At each subsequent touchpoint, these will become clearer, and the ability to predict will grow.

When I discuss the concept of touchpoints with parents and describe the role a pediatrician, nurse practitioner, or family physician can play in interpreting the regressions and spurts of development for parents, many tell me that their own doctors are more interested in assessing physical growth and dealing with illness. This problem, which I discuss in the final chapter, is due to the nature of pediatric training. In this training, based largely on the medical model with its emphasis on disease, there are two major gaps. One is a lack of emphasis on the importance of examining and strengthening relationships. Pediatricians have a unique opportunity to listen to new parents and support the birth of new families. In our program at Children's Hospital in Boston, we try to fill these gaps. A large part of our time in training is spent examining how to interview, how to share observations of the children and each one's development, and how to encourage parents to share the feelings that are part of learning to nurture.

The second gap in pediatric training is knowledge of child development. This field has grown remarkably, with new research in areas such as cognitive development, parent–child attachment, the abilities of the newborn, genetic influences, and temperament. Pediatric training has lagged in assimilating these advances. Understanding the issues and challenges with which all children are concerned at each age gives pediatricians rare insight into the uniqueness of *each* child. They are then more able to convey these observations to parents, in a shared "language" that solidifies the parent–physician relationship. I have found that parents who know I understand their child can forgive me for all kinds of delays or frustrations in our work together. They see me as their ally in providing the best environment we can for their child. They share their own mistakes, their own concerns. We are a team.

Knowledge of the map of development in each of the developmental lines—motor, cognitive, and emotional—makes a "compleat pediatrician." For one who can appreciate the

powerful, universal forces behind the struggle to learn to walk, or the passionate conflict between "yes" or "no" in the second year, which leads to temper tantrums, pediatrics becomes a delight. Every office visit is a window, offering the perennial excitement of watching each child grow and master the great tasks of the first few years. Not enough pediatricians are yet trained to understand and enjoy this aspect of their practice. Through our work at Children's Hospital in changing this training, and through this book, I hope to transmit these shared joys, the rewards of a lifetime of caring for parents and children.

one

TOUCHPOINTS OF DEVELOPMENT

1

PREGNANCY: THE FIRST TOUCHPOINT

In the last few months of pregnancy, expectant parents become aware of the reality of pregnancy, of the activity of the baby-to-be, and of the huge adjustment that lies ahead. The seventh month is the ideal time for a first visit to the physician who will care for the baby. By now, parents know they will need a pediatrician and advocate for the baby and are eager to share their hopes and concerns. Later in the pregnancy, I find mothers-to-be more concerned about the ongoing experience of delivery and less available to talk to me about the baby. Fathers will become involved in childbirth education classes by the eighth month. Their role in the delivery process will then be uppermost in their mind.

At seven months, parents are still dreaming of the baby. They wonder who this child will be. I can uncover and share their anxieties with them. I see this as the first "touchpoint," an opportunity for me to make a relationship with each parent before there is a baby between us. The visit can have lasting effects. When I can see fathers in my office at this time, even for ten minutes, I can be sure that 50 percent of them will be present at each subsequent visit throughout the baby's first year. Eighty percent will come in for at least four visits. A father who feels wanted in a pediatric office is allowed to feel important to his baby's well-being. Fathers say to me, "So far, no one else has really spoken to me about this. They talk only to my wife. But it's my baby, too. When you asked me to come in and to be a part of the interview, I knew you realized that." A father's vulnerability, his hunger to be included, makes this visit a valuable touchpoint for both of us.

When mothers-to-be call for an appointment in pregnancy, some who are exceptionally busy will say, "My obstetrician says I should come to meet you *before* I deliver. Is that really necessary?" This question often shields a number of anxieties, which may be interfering with her interest in getting to know her pediatrician in advance. I can honestly answer, "Yes, it is very important for us to meet before we have a baby to concentrate on. I want to know you and your concerns ahead of time so we can share them." "Oh well, then when can I come?" she will say cautiously. At this point, I express my interest in meeting the baby's father as well. If she hesitates again, I simply suggest that she ask him before making the appointment.

When the parents-to-be do come in together, the father tends to retire to the background. Since I feel strongly that we should be urging fathers to be equal participants in their babies' care, I ask him to pull his chair up to my desk. As he does, he looks to his wife for permission. I point this out and use the opportunity to introduce the notion of "gatekeeping"—a new name for very old feelings. All adults who care about a baby will naturally be in competition for that baby. Competitive feelings are a normal component of caring for a dependent individual. Each adult wishes that he or she could do each job a bit more skillfully for the infant or small child than the other. This competition is based on wishful thinking and is energy for attachment to the child. Such feelings are present in other members of the family. They can unconsciously influence grandparents' behavior and lead them, without intending harm, to criticize the sensitive new parents. Doctors and nurses felt the same way when they kept parents out of children's hospitals, as was formerly the case. Schoolteachers and parents are likely to compete with one another. All this gatekeeping is predictable and represents caring on both sides.

If the competition does not interfere with the child's best interests, it can fuel passionate caring. But as we will see later in this book, the urge to exclude the other parent can create friction in the family, if parents aren't aware of it. For instance, as a new, vulnerable father begins to diaper his new baby, his spouse is likely to say, "Darling, that's not quite the way you do it," or when he settles in to give a bottle for the first time, she may say, "Hold her this way, and she'll be more comfortable"—innocuous remarks on the surface, but ones carrying an unsettling message to a vulnerable new father. If fathers are to participate, both parents must be prepared for this subtle competition. For the same reasons, when a new mother starts to breast-feed, fathers and grandmothers are likely to say, "The baby's crying again! Are you sure you have enough milk?"

First-time parents have universal doubts and questions: "How will we ever learn to become parents? Will we have to be like our parents?" With these questions come concerns about the baby. "Suppose we have a damaged child? Will it be our fault? How can we ever face such a thing?" All parents-to-be dream of the various defects that they have ever seen or heard of. Part of dreaming during the day and most of the dreaming at night concerns this fear. The dreams stir up attachment and help to prepare prospective parents for the possibility of a less-than-perfect baby. A pregnant woman and her spouse dream of three babies—the perfect four-month-old who rewards them with smiles and musical cooing, the impaired baby, who changes each day, and the mysterious real baby whose presence is beginning to be evident in the motions of the fetus.

Preparing for Birth   The work of the last part of pregnancy is to prepare parents for the crisis of birth. Anxiety, coupled with the parents' efforts to reconcile their three dreamed-of babies, generates a kind of alarm reaction in them. An alarm reaction energizes one's system: adrenalin flows, blood pressure rises, and oxygen circulates to prepare the brain. All this inner turmoil loosens up old habits, opening parents to the job of rebalancing their lives.

In the short interview we have together, my questions are simple ones. I am looking for the feelings below the surface, which will give me an opportunity to know this family better.

"How do you plan to deliver your baby?"

"We are going to childbirth education classes. I want to be in control as much as possible. I don't want any medication, if I can help it; I want to deliver my baby naturally—without anesthesia."

At this point, the mother-to-be may have questions about how medication and anesthesia affect her baby. I explain that labor seems to alert the fetus and serves to awaken the baby after delivery, whereas many types of medication have the opposite effect. The longer medication can be postponed, the more alert and responsive the baby will be. She knows this already, so what we are really sharing is our mutual concern for the baby. I hope she sees that I will join her in wanting a responsive baby above all, and that I am ready to address any other concerns she might have about labor and delivery.

This is where a father can be a real help. He can help his wife follow the lessons of the childbirth classes in managing her pains and support her in postponing medication. Depending on the approach of the obstetrician, the father may have to help the mother be firm in declining offers of medication. Well-documented research shows that actively supporting persons, such as fathers or labor companions (*doulas*), can shorten a woman's labor and help her postpone or avoid medication, one of the main goals of childbirth classes.

While explaining this, I try to listen for any sign that they may want to ask more questions. "What will a cesarean section do to the baby, if it becomes necessary?" "What are the effects of epidural anesthesia?" "Will I feel like a failure if I have anesthesia?" By discussing these questions with me, parents-to-be can become clearer about their goals and the depth of their fears.

The effects of a cesarean section on the baby are not yet well understood. In the past, infants delivered by cesarean section without labor were watched in a special nursery for twenty-four hours. They were expected to be sleepier and less able to cough up their mucus. We now know that the premedication given to the mother during labor and before a cesarean section crosses the placenta to affect the baby's behavior for several days after birth. So, the effects that were previously seen clinically might be attributable to maternal medication. In studies using my Neonatal Behavioral Assessment Scale (NBAS) on babies born by cesarean section when medication was carefully managed, there are only very transient effects on the baby's behavior compared to a group of babies who were delivered from naturally laboring mothers. These effects of mild depression were gone after twenty-four hours, and the baby's subsequent courses were no different.

Medication given more freely during labor may have a more

lasting influence on the babies' behavior. Medicated babies are sleepier, more difficult to rouse. They stay alert for shorter periods, and their responses to human stimuli are also more short-lived. If a mother is aware of these effects, she can make up for them by working harder to keep her new baby alert. If she's not, she may see her baby as quiet and dopier than otherwise expected. This early image might become self-perpetuating. I urge a mother to postpone medication as long as possible and to have as little as possible. If medication becomes necessary, she must plan to rouse the baby more vigorously—at feedings and for play—until the medication will have worn off several days later. (See Abrams and Feinbloom in the Bibliography for an explanation of the difference between various pain medications as to their effect on the newborn.)

While the rising rate of cesarean sections is a national concern, they have also been of benefit. The fact that we can detect a baby's difficulty during labor by using fetal monitors, either external or internal, placed on the baby's scalp after the mother's membranes are ruptured, means that we detect more distress signals and earlier ones than we were able to before the use of monitors. As a result, obstetricians feel responsible for intervening before the baby suffers any real brain damage. While the resulting cesarean section is harder on the mother physically and psychologically, it also certainly protects the baby from brain injury caused by too little oxygen (hypoxia) during a stressful period of uterine contractions and a poor oxygen supply from the placenta. This may prevent some cases of cerebral palsy, although the cause of this condition now appears to be complex. A physician's job is to help parents understand the reasons for a cesarean section and to assist them with feelings of disappointment if it becomes necessary.

Breast or Bottle

When I ask about feeding the baby, I listen for the reasons behind whichever choice the parents will make. Until recently, I expected parents to choose breast-feeding. I added my strong support, and we discussed the preparation for it. More recently, mothers-to-be who are going back to work after a few months have been choosing bottle feeding. Logistics are a concern, but when I have inquired further, some have expressed their fears of getting too attached to the baby, whom they will have to leave in someone else's care. When mothers are open with me in this way, I can help as they sort out their goals. My role as the baby's advocate gives them the safety to explore their decision. I can help them make either choice more effective.

However, I also make clear that I am prejudiced about the value of breast milk and the importance of breast-feeding in strengthening the parent–infant relationship. Breast milk has so many advantages—it's perfect for a human baby. No babies are allergic to breast milk. The ratio of protein and sugar is ideal, and breast milk is loaded with antibodies that will boost the level of immunity with which the baby is born. Babies receive immunity from their mothers across the placenta, but this will diminish over the next few months unless breast milk keeps the level up. Because of this, the dangers of infection are lessened by breast-feeding. In addition, the closeness in communication between mother and child via nursing is ideal.

At this visit, I mention to women who plan to breast-feed that it may hurt when they begin. The baby's suck reflex can be amazingly strong. Also, breast milk ducts can go into spasms at first and hurt until the milk starts flowing. I reassure mothers-to-be that after a few initial feedings the spasms will stop, and the resultant feeling will be pleasure.

There are conflicting points of view about whether mothers-to-be can prepare their nipples ahead of time. They would do well to buy a good book on breast-feeding (see Huggins in the Bibliography) and also consult their physician. In my own experience of having helped mothers over the years, I have found that blondes and redheads are likely to get sore and to have cracked nipples unless they toughen them up beforehand. To do this, a woman should wash her breasts and hands with mild soap, then gently massage the nipples between the fingers twice a day. She should get a little tougher as time goes on but *not* hurt them. Infection could easily begin, and when the breast is engorged, the infection could spread. It's better to avoid cracked nipples than to have to treat them afterward.

While I respect the concern of working women about the

difficulties of breast-feeding when returning to their jobs, we might still discuss ways to keep that option open. We can discuss the possibility of having the father or another caregiver use a bottle of supplementary feeding and the possibility of pumping breast milk while at work. It is so nice to come home after a hard day's work and to put the baby to breast—to get close again. But, at this time, we can also discuss the fear of separation that accompanies this attachment to the baby. Meanwhile, as we talk, the parents and I are establishing a closer relationship. They see that I want to support their choice and their attachment to the new baby.

For the mother who wants to breast-feed, I can offer other practical suggestions, such as being prepared to wait for the milk for several days after delivery and feeding for short periods at first until her nipples toughen up—all the while offering my support as she prepares for the new job. Meanwhile, I hope she will express any concerns about her ability to feed, as well as to tend the baby in all areas. By discussing feeding now, we are making it easier to face feeding problems together as they come up later on.

Circumcision

I always ask the father at least one question, directed to him. The most common one is, "If it's a boy, do you plan to have him circumcised?" This is a sure way to bring out his involvement. If he asks my opinion, I can give him the pros and cons, while encouraging him to take responsibility for that decision. I want him to feel that it is his and that we can make it work for him and the baby. The decision to circumcise or not should be a personal one. Particular studies can be used to prove that either alternative is safe for the baby. Each study supporting one point of view can be balanced by a study supporting the other. Certainly a painful procedure, circumcision is necessary for physical reasons in only one percent of boy babies. In that one percent, a very long foreskin can conceivably interfere with future urination, but this is very rare. The decision about the need for a circumcision can be made immediately after birth.

I address the arguments on each side. A painful circumcision can disrupt sleep, EEG (electroencephalogram) patterns, and other behavior patterns for twenty-four hours. Now, we can inject local anesthesia at the base of the penis quite safely to prevent much of the pain and disruption seen previously. The well-known study that demonstrated more cancer of the cervix in wives of uncircumcised males was probably not well designed, and it has not been replicated. In a later study reported in the *New England Journal of Medicine,* researchers found that uncircumcised males are more likely to have urinary tract infections, and the authors recommended routine circumcision to prevent a very low incidence of such problems in the future. This study, too, needs replication before it can be used to support circumcision with any certainty.

Most important is the father's role in participating in his child's future. I think a father should make the choice for his son. The choice will be likely to reflect the father's own experiences, and it should. This may be the first time that he experiences a deep possessive feeling about the baby-to-be. Most fathers want their boys to be like themselves. In the future, when a little boy compares himself to his daddy, differences can feel hard to explain. However, comparisons of size will call up questions in any event, and a difference in foreskin could be explained as well. I feel this question is of deep significance to a male, and the father's choice needs to be based on his emotional reactions rather than on the fairly inconclusive studies that have been done so far. This discussion and his decision will draw the father into more thinking about his future baby. If I show my support for him, he will feel freer to turn to me for advice later on.

The Physician as Advocate for the Baby

At this visit, I am likely to hear about the family constellation. There are many new kinds of families. I want each one to feel respected and backed-up by me.

If the mother is a single parent, she will need extra help in her new, demanding role. As she raises her fears, I can assure her that I will assume a more actively supporting role than I usually do. Raising a child alone is likely to be difficult, but it can be done well, and I assure her that I will be ready to guide her whenever she wants me to. Often, I will be more dogmatic than she may like, for I will play the best role I know of— being the baby's advocate as she makes her decisions.

The hardest part of single parenting seems to be letting the baby become independent. At each stage of autonomy, when babies are still vulnerable, it is easy to overpower their search for their own way of doing things by showering them with too much attention and too much direction. All of this comes from caring, which is critical to the child, but a single mother will need someone to say, "Let your child go. Let her get frustrated. Let her work things out for herself. In the long run, if you can do this, it will be *her* achievement, not yours." No parent really wants to hear this kind of advice, so I warn a single parent that I will be saying it for the child's future benefit, and I know how painful it may be for her to hear. But I will support her in other, more welcome ways. For example, discipline is hard for a parent alone. The child teases incessantly, and a whole day can feel like one long struggle. In the second, difficult year, I will need to offer firm advice and support. I urge her to surround herself with any family who is nearby. If there is none, I suggest that she find a support group of other single parents who can offer emotional backup for day-to-day crises.

Families in which both parents work full-time outside the home deserve special attention at a prenatal visit. I want them to be aware of my backup in seeking what they, as parents, need from the workplace. I also want to provide for the supports they'll need to do the best job they can for this baby. Have they provided themselves with the kind of supplementary care they'll need when they must return to work? As we said, I will try to help them work out breast-feeding, if they decide to do that. Are there grandparents nearby who can help in a crisis? What are the pressures of their jobs, and how will they share the baby's care? Will one or both parents be able to stay at home long enough to give the baby a good start? Are they aware of the importance of the first few months as a time for adjusting to the changed way of life, for the mother to recover from any postpartum letdown or depression, for them both to accept the deepening responsibility to the new family?

Learning about a new baby—her individuality, depen-

dency, and remarkable responsiveness—will take time and energy. As the baby's advocate, I will be pushing the parents to immerse themselves in adjusting to this initial period. Their own development as nurturing adults is as critical to the baby's future as is their adjustment to the baby's need for them. Parents today who need to maintain their jobs in the workplace need to plan. I want them to fight to stay home with a new baby for the first precious months. While I don't see myself as directing their decisions, they may need my help in laying out priorities for care and determining the times when the baby will need them most. We know now that the first three months are a critical time. Can they free up this time? Will the price at the workplace be too great? They need to face this decision *now*.

Parents-to-be find it hard to face the issues, often because of the pain of separation, which they can experience ahead of time. We need to face that pain so they can be free in this period when their energies are needed in learning to attach to the fetus and baby-to-be. In my experience, helping parents recognize their ambivalence and their tendency to deny the future pain of separation makes these issues more manageable when the time comes.

While it may seem almost magical that parents and a doctor can form a close relationship in such a short time, they can. The parents' hunger to understand what is ahead creates an openness about themselves that cuts across the usual barriers. Their hunger and openness, the results of a tumultuous inner transition, make possible a wonderful burst in the adults' development. This giant step toward their own maturity is the main focus of this first touchpoint between parents and their baby's physician or nurse practitioner.

Drug Exposure   Today, parents are very aware of the dangers to the fetus of medication, alcohol, narcotic drugs, and infection. During our first visit I try to learn as much as possible about any exposures, so that I can guarantee the parents that I will evaluate the baby with these in mind. I also can promise to share any concerns with them from the very first exam. The now-widespread knowledge of the risk to the developing fetus of poor nutrition, drugs, smoking, infections, and so on raises deep concern among pregnant women and fathers-to-be. Many couples indulge before they are aware of a pregnancy. Then, they are bound to worry that indulgences at the critical early stages of fetal development may have caused defects. Fortunately, the most severe exposures, when they occur very early, will result in an aborted fetus. A healthy pregnancy is our best way of predicting a healthy baby. When parents are able to share their concerns, I can usually allay them now or at birth. At least we can address them together.

Heavy exposure before birth to alcohol, tobacco, or narcotic drugs can cause a great variety of problems. In particular, exposure to these substances can lead not only to a decrease in the number of brain cells due to interference with cellular replication in critical periods of growth but also to damage to the connections between parts of the brain. A smaller brain can result. Cocaine and crack raise the blood pressure, close off small capillaries, and damage brain substance in developing areas of the brain. In addition, an addicted mother tends to eat poorly, and malnutrition in the developing fetus adds to its vulnerability to these insults. If an addicted person continues to ingest these toxins toward the latter part of pregnancy, the baby is likely to have mild or major interference in the transmission of messages from one part of the brain to another. The fetus will then be either hypo- or hypersensitive to stimuli (see chapter 2).

At birth, the baby's behavior will reflect these disorders in neurotransmission through slowness to respond to stimuli, unreachableness, and apparent attempts to maintain a sleep state. When such babies do respond, they may shoot to an equally unreachable crying, thrashing state. They can be so volatile that they appear to have no state in which they can take in information from the environment, digest it, and respond appropriately. These babies can be at high risk for abuse or neglect. They are not only unrewarding to their already depressed, addicted mothers, but they give back only negative or disorganized responses. They are extremely difficult to feed and to organize for sleep. Their potential for failing to thrive is enormous. If they survive, they are likely to be disabled in their capacity for attention and for future learning. These are very high risk infants.

If we can identify babies born to addicted mothers or suffering from other intrauterine deprivation, we can institute a program of early intervention. The long-term follow-up studies done so far suggest that a nurturing environment, one sensitive to the easy overload or damaged nervous systems, can bring about an amazing recovery in most of these babies. This, we have learned from many studies, is true of other kinds of insults in the uterus. But we need to start intervention as early as possible.

If I can establish a trusting relationship with parents-to-be in this first visit, they are much more likely to share any such exposures or untoward events with me. We can discuss their fears of having damaged the baby. For withdrawal from any of these addictions, we can institute a program that will protect the baby. Even the last two months free of drug exposure can provide babies with a chance to reorganize their disordered nervous system and be readier to adapt to the outside world. If either parent will share such fears with me, we can discuss this healing adaptation and can plan for any necessary intervention after birth. I realize that few addicted parents are likely to "confess" to an addiction on such short notice, but by asking in a sympathetic, understanding way, I am at least making clear my readiness to participate with them in intervention, if it turns out to be necessary. I assure them that I will not only look for and let them know of any deviant behavior I see in the newborn period but also work with them to help the baby.

Parents deserve to know about any deviation or behavior that will make parenting their new baby more difficult. I do not believe in protecting them from such awareness; they know anyway. A physician who cannot or will not share such information is creating a base for distrust amd implying that parents are not accurate observers. I feel that the rehearsal all parents go through in fantasy for the impaired baby prepares them for any problem they will encounter in their baby. When I meet parents during pregnancy, my role is to encourage this sort of preparation and to explain as fully as possible what I will watch for in the baby.

One of my major goals with expectant parents is to begin to establish the notion of the individuality of each baby and that baby's behavior. To do this, I press parents to talk more about how they experience the fetus as a person. "Have you a picture of this baby as a person in your mind?" Mothers who have noticed whether the fetus is particularly active or quiet will wonder whether, if a fetus is active, it means an active baby, or if quiet, a quiet one.

There is some correlation between fetal activity and the baby's behavior. The way a fetus responds to stimuli may be significant. Some startle more easily. Many parents report that the fetus gets very active when they go to bed at night. There does seem to be an inverse relationship: when the mother is active, a fetus is likely to be quiet. When she quiets down, the baby's activity increases. This tuning in to cycles of rest and activity is a preparation for the rhythms a baby will follow later. Already, the fetus is learning to cycle between sleep and active states (see chapter 2). A fetus has short cycles of rest and activity. The mother's own cycles of activity and sleep are already entraining the fetus to longer cycles of rest and responsiveness. This entrainment is reflected in the baby's cycles at birth.

Mothers-to-be have long believed that they are influencing the unborn baby by what they do and how they do it. This can lead to concerns. "If I'm tense, will I have an anxious baby?" While I can't answer that question, I point out that all pregnant women are tense and anxious. It wouldn't be normal otherwise. Moreover, evidence from fetal research shows that fetuses adapt to tension in the environment and may even learn from it, some becoming quiet and controlled, some more and more active. The main job for a mother will be to adjust to whatever kind of baby she gets.

Parents work in the last trimester of pregnancy to understand their baby-to-be. They pay conscious and unconscious attention to the movements and the behavior of the fetus. Parents today realize that the fetus can hear and does respond to stimuli around the mother. Many fathers talk to and sing to their baby in the last three months, in an effort to get close

The Developing Fetus

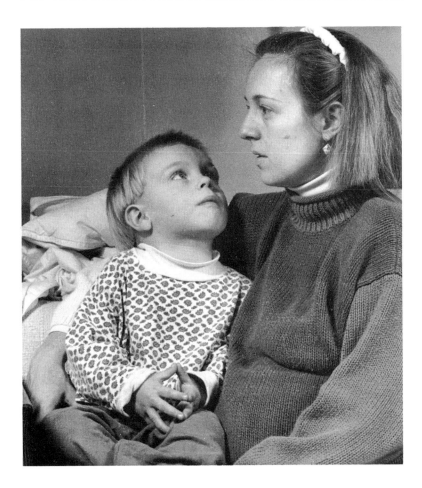

to her before delivery. One mother who is a pianist told me, "I knew my baby could hear because she seemed to dance in rhythm with my music. What I didn't realize was that she was learning from it as well. I practiced a particular phrase in a Chopin waltz over and over the last few months of pregnancy. She always seemed quiet in the uterus when I played it. For some time, after she was delivered, I had no chance to play. When she was three months old, she was lying in her playpen by the side of my piano. I started practicing again. As I played through the waltz, she was playing on her back, looking at her mobile. When I got to that particular phrase, she stopped playing, and turned to me, looking surprised, as if 'There it is again!' I know she recognized it and remembered it. I was amazed. Now, I hope she'll be a musician."

I have been working to develop an assessment scale to be used in the last trimester of pregnancy to judge the well-being of the developing fetus. The behavior of a fetus that is well nourished and is not being affected by maternal drugs, medication, alcohol, and so on will be complex and predictably rich in responses. When, on the other hand, the fetus is being stressed by malnutrition, toxins, or a poor placenta, its behavior will reflect this by becoming restricted. Such a fetus will not show the same complex responses to auditory, visual, and kinesthetic cues that a healthy fetus does. We have known for some time that the nature of the fetus's movements can help to diagnose stress. For example, when there is too much activity, or if the fetus is not responsive to the mother's movements or demonstrates too few movements with no response to external stimuli, one needs to worry. These aberrations should be reported to the obstetrician for assessment of the fetus's well-being.

Heart rate and the respiratory movements made by the fetus can be measured. They, too, can reflect stress. If the fetus is stressed by too little oxygen, the heart rate will become too active or invariable, or it may become too slow, the respiratory movements gasping. An obstetrician can tell by these signs whether the parents-to-be need to worry. If these stresses are judged to be endangering the fetus toward the end of pregnancy, we can deliver the baby prematurely and possibly do a better job of nurturing her outside the uterus. As we learn more, we hope that parents can be alerted to some of the danger signs and can become even better observers of the fetus's well-being.

We have been slow in recognizing the amazing complexity of the fetus, just as we were previously slow in respecting the newborn's amazing capacities. There are several researchers in France and the United States working now to determine the fetus's capacity for learning, in particular from auditory messages. Anthony De Casper, at the University of North Carolina, has shown that babies store complex songs and stories when they are repeated in the last three months of pregnancy. As the mother in my practice observed, after delivery babies recognize them and respond with increased attention to the familiar ones. Babies do seem to have memory.

A few can learn and make choices even in the uterus. In our research at Children's Hospital in Boston, we visualized fetuses with ultrasound machines. We found we could tell when they were asleep or awake. We could also identify at least the following four states of consciousness (see chapter 2 for such states in the newborn).

1. In *deep sleep* the fetus is predominantly quiet. If there are any movements, they are in the form of discrete jerks. In this state the fetus is unresponsive to most stimuli.
2. During *light sleep,* or *REM (rapid eye movement) sleep,* writhing or stretching movements predominate. Movements are rare, but they are smoother and a bit more organized. Still pretty unresponsive to stimuli, the fetus can be roused, but with difficulty. Periodically, there are jerky movements—kick-kick-kick or bang-bang-bang of one arm or respiratory efforts repeated in sequences of four to eight movements.
3. The *active alert* state is felt as the fetus climbs the uterine wall. This state occurs at predictable times during the day, usually when the mother is resting and is tired. If the fetus reacts to stimuli from the outside, the response will be that of quieting. Afterward, the high activity will be resumed. The most common time for this state occurs at the end of the day. Parents know when it is coming and know what will change it—for instance, if they go out at night, the active period may be postponed until they get home. If the mother doesn't eat properly, the active period can occur earlier in the day, probably due to low blood sugar.
4. In the *quiet alert* state the fetus will be inactive, as if listening. Movements are smoother and more organized. In this state fetuses are especially responsive to outside stimuli.

In our research we presented six- and seven-month-old fetuses in the quiet, alert state with various stimuli. Using a loud buzzer placed eighteen inches from the abdominal wall, we sounded a short buzz six to eight times. This caused a predictable set of reactions in the eight fetuses we studied. The first buzz caused the fetuses to jump, and their faces looked strained. The second buzz resulted in less startlement. By the fourth buzz, the fetuses had stopped startling and had become immobilized. A few had respiratory jerks of their abdomens, but no other response. Their faces continued to look strained. By the fifth buzz they would often bring one hand up close to the mouth, sometimes to insert a thumb or finger. Then they would turn away from the buzzer to relax. No more responses. We thought these fetuses had adapted, or "habituated," to these negative stimuli.

Next, we shook a rattle next to each mother's abdomen. We thought the uterus might be too noisy for the fetuses to hear it. But as soon as we rattled it, the fetuses would turn in the direction of the rattle, as if waiting for the next signal. As we continued with discrete rattles, the fetuses would continue to be quietly attentive. They were already showing the capacity to attend to positive stimuli and to turn away from negative ones.

We also tried a series of very strong light stimuli, flashed in each fetus's line of vision. We first determined which way each fetus was facing as it lay with its head engaged in the mother's pelvis. The first few stimuli caused slow startles, then the babies would bring their hands up to their mouths and faces. They'd turn the head away from the stimulus and again, all movements would cease, as if they had habituated to the strong light and gone into a sleep state. Using a pinpoint light on another part of the mother's abdominal wall over the uterus, we noted that the fetus moved slowly to turn in the direction of the pinpoint light, as if focusing on the spot where the light stimulus came through. When one baby became active and seemed upset, my colleague Dr. Barry Lester placed both hands on the mother's abdomen around the fetus. He started rocking the fetus, which calmed it down. At this point, the mother expressed the thoughts of all of us: "I didn't know babies were so smart so early!"

When I quote this research to parents-to-be, they begin to tell me stories of how they'd noted this already. When I confirm their observations, they give them more attention and credence. As one mother said to me, "When I went to a Bach concert, she danced in rhythm with the music. When I went to a rock concert, she danced entirely differently. She got wild. *I* knew she could hear already. It has just taken you researchers a long time to catch up with what parents have known all the time."

My dream is that the assessment scale we have been developing can become much more sophisticated in assessing fetal behavior. If we knew the average expectable responses, we could be alert to unusual behavior as soon as a fetus is being stressed. Each mother-to-be could routinely observe and record the behavior of her fetus. Then, if things weren't going right, they could tell us when to worry. In any case, they would enjoy their baby-to-be's responses long before she arrived. They'd get the feeling of "knowing" the fetus and of participating in its care. Nearly all parents say to me, "I don't care whether it's a boy or a girl or even what it looks like, just so it's normal."

A New Alliance   Once the expectant couple and I feel close enough to each other, I ask more about pertinent medical history. As they tell me about diseases or congenital defects in the family, we know we are sharing fears that are bound to surface. If there is a baby with a problem in another part of her family, any caring pregnant woman will fear a replication in her baby. If a father has a parent or relative with heart disease or a chronic disease, he is bound to wonder whether this can be a tendency in his baby. Irrational fears can erupt in the middle of the night. If parents tell me of these, I can become part of the defense system they use to cope with fears. If I am aware of the pertinent family history and the parents' anxiety, I can address these openly when I examine the new baby later on in their presence.

When we have discussed these hopes and fears common to all caring parents-to-be, and when I have established my role as that of a concerned participant, we have established an important initial relationship. I want new parents to know ahead of time when and how I can be reached for routine calls, for emergencies, and of course for news of the baby's birth. I ask to be notified as soon as possible, in order to examine the newborn in the first twenty-four hours. It is important for me to share the baby's behavior with both new parents before they leave the hospital. Often I can help when a mother starts breast-feeding, or when she will be feeding the baby with a formula. After they are at home, any calls parents make at my routine call-in hour every morning as well as their first visit to my office at two to three weeks will give me a chance to participate actively in their adjustment to the new baby.

Ideally, the visit during pregnancy will leave each one of us with a feeling of trust and of intimacy for facing the next important touchpoint. While this first meeting need not take very long, it is the most valuable opportunity I will have with any new family.

2

THE NEWBORN INDIVIDUAL

The second touchpoint—the second time I have a chance to participate in the growth of a new family—is the exciting moment when, together with the parents, I examine their baby soon after birth.

Evaluating a Newborn's Responses

Evaluation of a newborn by the physician has long been a routine part of pediatric care. An initial physical assessment of the baby's color, breathing, heart rate, muscle tone, and activity, known as the Apgar score, is done moments after birth. Assignment of two points for each of the five items if they're optimal or one if they're okay leads to a total score (with ten the highest). This is an assessment of the newborn baby's ability to respond to the emergency of labor, delivery, and the new environment. As such it does not predict the baby's future

well-being but reflects more what the baby has encountered in delivery. To evaluate the baby more thoroughly, a physical and behavioral assessment is done within the first days by the pediatrician or other specialist in newborns on the staff of the hospital. At this time, the baby is evaluated for physical health and for his responsiveness to being fed and nurtured.

As mentioned in chapter 1, the Neonatal Behavioral Assessment Scale (NBAS), now used in hospitals worldwide, is designed to evaluate the kind of person the newborn is. It assesses the baby's behavioral repertoire as he responds to human and nonhuman stimuli. The way he uses states of consciousness to control his responses reveals his capacity to adjust to his new environment. With the help of a number of colleagues, I developed this scale, which provides a basis for scoring responses and reflexes in a twenty- to thirty-minute interaction with the baby. Unlike other medical tests, our assessment treats the newborn as an active participant, and the score is based on *best* (rather than average) performance. We have been refining the NBAS for twenty years and have been adapting it to evaluate premature and small-for-date babies, and most recently, we have used it to reflect intrauterine influences in fetal development.

The most important use of the NBAS has been to share the baby's behavior with parents to sensitize them to the abilities and amazing variety of responses already present in their baby. Every parent worries, Is my baby okay? When we can elicit the baby's best performance, parents' anxieties can be dispelled and the possibility of communication enhanced. We have found in nearly a hundred studies that new family bonds can deepen during this rich, though brief, encounter. A newborn's behavior seems designed to capture new parents. His tiny, strong grasp, the way he nuzzles deliciously into the angle of a neck and shoulder, and the way he looks into a parent's face with his searching eyes all reach out to a father or mother hungry to hold and learn to know him.

In the NBAS, I like to start with a sleeping baby so that I can test his ability to maintain a deep sleep state. I try to examine the baby in each of six states of consciousness: deep and light sleep, semialert, wide-awake alert, fussing, and crying. As the baby moves from one state to another, I look for his ability to respond to stimuli, both positive and negative, in each state. The stimuli I use include a soft rattle, a bright light, a bell, a red ball, and the human voice and face.

The first step, while the newborn is still asleep, is to test his response to a light, a rattle, and a bell sounded several times in his ear during sleep. The purpose of this is to measure his capacity to shut out disturbing stimuli. This tests his ability to habituate, that is, to decrease his level of responsiveness when negative stimuli are presented repeatedly. It lets me know whether this baby will be able to shut out unnecessary environmental stimulation. Some infants have a "raw" nervous system due to stress before birth. These infants cannot shut out stimuli and must respond over and over, mercilessly. They will need a very protected environment similar to those we are developing for premature infants.

The first stimulus is a bright flashlight shone for two seconds through the baby's closed lids. After his initial startle or movement subsides, I shine the light a second, a third, and finally, a tenth time. The first few times, the baby will demonstrate responses by startling and moving his whole body; his arms and his legs will jump, but each time these movements should decrease. By the fourth light stimulus, there is usually little or no movement. His breathing becomes deep and regular again. His face softens. His whole body returns to relaxed sleep. The baby has habituated to the light. Next, I try a rattle about ten inches away from his ear. Again, he rouses with a startle, and his whole body may move. The second rattle might produce a second big startle and a whimper. But by the third or fourth rattle there is likely to be a diminished response with very little movement. Later, subsequent rattles cause only a flutter of his eyelids and a grimace, then he subsides. Soon, he is no longer responding and seems to be in quiet sleep with deep breathing again. If the bell is used last, in consecutive, one-second bursts, it may produce only a couple of responses initially; then the infant subsides into a successful, deep sleep. He has proven his ability to maintain a sleep state even in a chaotic environment. A baby who can habituate this way has built-in resources.

Premature or Stressed Babies

When babies are premature or have been stressed in the uterus, they cannot shut out repeated stimuli. They respond to each rattle, each bell, or each bright light. One can observe how costly this is for them. They will frown and their color may even change, for their heart rates and respiration speed up with each stimulus. They may make attempts to quiet themselves by arching away or by bringing a hand up to their mouths. If they can't manage the repetitious stimulation by going into sleep, they may have to build up to a crying, thrashing state. Crying also can serve to shut out stimulation, but it, too, can be costly for a fragile baby (see also chapter 32).

When I find a baby who has real difficulty in shutting out stimuli, I let the parents know and plan to follow him for a period. If he becomes more proficient over time, the problem may have been due to a stress at delivery, which many babies undergo, or it may be from the effects of medication or anesthetic given to his mother at delivery. If the hyperreactivity persists, I worry about whether he will have a difficult time later, overreacting as he tries to assimilate information from the environment. The ability to shut out unimportant stimuli is necessary for all of us in order to focus on the particular information that matters to us. Hyperactivity can become one way a baby discharges the overwhelming overload of too many incoming stimuli.

Parents of a hypersensitive baby can help him develop an effective threshold for screening out unimportant information. They can cut down on stimuli; they can arrange a quiet room at home, with subdued light, and use low-pitched, soft voices or visual or tactile stimuli, especially at feeding times or when they want to play with him. We have even found that some babies can tolerate being looked at *or* touched *or* picked up— but only one of these at a time. By waiting until the baby subsides, another modality can be added. Gradually, all of them can be put together at once, but in a low-keyed way and with respect for the baby's easily overloaded nervous system. A baby's behavior will show when he feels bombarded. With patience, parents of a hyperreactive baby can teach him how to take in and manage information in short bursts and how to manage by taking time out. Knowing of their baby's needs early will help them respond appropriately to that baby. Over time, he'll get better and better at managing for himself.

I then begin to undress the baby gently, observing his reactions to being handled. I want to observe and score how long he takes to go from sleeping to rousing. As he rouses, I will assess and record his pattern of coming to a semialert state, and to fussy and wide-awake states. The way a baby moves from one state to another is likely to be a predictor of his style or of his temperament. A baby who moves slowly from one to another, and who can hold onto an alert or a sleep state, is already demonstrating a marvelous capacity to manage his world. If he moves rapidly, shooting between states, unable to stay in any one, he will need a patient parent's quiet help to learn to develop his own controls. It will take time—a year or more. A pediatrician can help such parents chart the baby's progress and can support them in their demanding job. Holding and carrying him, swaddling him, or encouraging thumb sucking or use of a pacifier may help him learn to master these transitions from one state to another.

A baby who cannot control state transitions is at the mercy of a raw, immature nervous system. Some easily irritable newborns are recovering from maternal medication. Women who smoke, drink alcohol, or expose their babies to narcotics in pregnancy can expect irritable babies as the babies recover from the effects of these drugs and experience a period of withdrawal. Babies whose mothers have had to use medication at delivery can be quiet for the first several days but then react with irritability after that. This period of irritability is likely to be short-lived, and it won't really reflect the baby's future personality. To help him, a parent can provide a quiet, nondisturbing environment. While an irritable baby will be trying for new parents, they won't benefit from blaming themselves. Instead, recognizing this as the baby's response to his immature, raw nervous system can help parents to learn techniques that help him gradually learn ways to calm himself.

Once the baby is undressed, I can assess his state of nutrition and hydration. I look for good skin color and the amount of fat underneath his soft, slightly fuzzy skin. A baby who has been stressed in the uterus will have wrinkled, peeling skin and a worried look. He will look like a weary, little old man, as if his time in the uterus was too tiring. Once he's rehydrated and fed after delivery, he will gain weight and lay down fat, his skin will improve, and his drawn face will fill out to look pudgy, babyish, and beautiful.

Now that the baby has been awakened, I can test his reflexes and all of his waking responses. As the baby lies in front of me undressed, I watch for smooth movements of his arms and legs. I watch to see whether he can maintain good skin color even though he's unprotected. At the end of each stretching movement, he may have a short period of jitteriness of both legs, and his arms may come together in a startle. I stroke his feet to produce reflexes. When I stroke his inner sole, he grasps my finger with his toes. When I stroke the outer side of his sole, he spreads his toes out in a *Babinski reflex*. I test him for active knee jerks and for firm body tone of his muscles.

Checking a Newborn's Reflexes

Given a forefinger to grasp in each hand, a newborn can be pulled up slowly to sit. As he comes up, his head will lag, but he will make a real effort with his shoulders to bring his head up to the midline. When he is sitting, his eyes pop open like a doll, and he begins to look around. At this, parents will gasp with admiration. If a newborn's head continues to hang backward and he is unable to right it, I check further into the tone of his musculature. I know from the reflexes that I've tested whether the baby's muscles are intact and strong. But his shoulder girdle's response as he is pulled to sit tells me how responsive he will be to being handled by his parents.

To elicit the *walking reflex*, I lean the baby's body forward across one hand, planting his feet firmly on the bed. He will begin to step first with one foot, then with the other, in a kind of slow jog. Not only is this great fun to watch, but it offers parents a sense of the potential for the future, compressed into this perfect little being. Nothing I as a caregiver can say will be as convincing to parents as this powerful, wordless repertoire.

A baby who has had a hemorrhage or an episode of too little oxygen at birth may not be able to produce all of these responses. So, it is a relief when parents can see them all performed. If they are delayed or weak, or if they are *too* active, I will need to examine the baby several days later to see whether they are changing over time. If the reflexes appear more normal by then, I won't worry. Many infants, in the period after the birth, perform sluggishly, as if having to recover from the stress of labor and delivery. If they continue to do so, we must look for a reason, such as a depressed nervous system, for which there can be help. But I want to start it early. Now we know that early intervention for a disorganized or an impaired baby can make a significant difference in how much he recovers. From the earliest age, he can learn either patterns of success in overcoming his difficulties or patterns of failure, which will add to his problems. Parents who worry about their child's development should pursue a competent assessment and join into an early intervention program. This can not only help the baby develop his best potential but also offer worried parents the support and understanding that will encourage their participation in his recovery.

When I lay the baby down on his back again, he will begin to squirm and to startle. A baby on his belly can dig into the bedclothes. On his back, he's at the mercy of startling and flailing legs and arms. While he's in this position, I can test for the important *protective reflexes.* If I place a soft cloth over his eyes and nose, holding it gently by my fingers on each side of his nose, he will thrash. Though his airway is not obstructed, he will arch his head, turning it from side to side to throw off the cloth. He will bring one hand, then the other, up to his head, swiping across his face to push off the cloth and keep his airway clear. Babies are not likely to smother, unless heavy bedclothes are pulled over their face and airways. Only a sick infant will not resist having face and nose covered. Sudden infant death syndrome, or SIDS, not yet fully understood, isn't likely to be due to smothering. It is more likely to occur because of some imbalance of a baby's heart or respiratory apparatus which depletes him so that he doesn't struggle to breath properly. At the time of this writing, many studies are being done in regard to the cause of SIDS, but none are yet conclusive.

The head arching and the hands coming up to push off the

cloth are both examples of an intact nervous system in a full-term baby. As we pointed out, if the baby is too sedated by maternal medication, or if he is premature, all of his motor patterns will be markedly diminished. If he has had brain damage, his motor activity will be disorganized, and the kind of ineffective attempts to perform all these behaviors become clues to the fact that he's in trouble. We must go to work to help him recover!

The *rooting reflex* appears if you touch a newborn on either side of his mouth. He will turn in the direction of the touch, searching for the "breast" with his mouth. When you give a newborn your finger to suck on, you can tell a lot about his *sucking* coordination. You can feel at least three different kinds of milking reactions. The front of his tongue laps on the part of your finger nearest his mouth. The back of his tongue begins to massage the middle of your finger. Finally, he will begin to pull on the tip of your finger with his esophagus. All three mechanisms become quickly coordinated in a healthy, alert newborn baby. If he is immature, they are slow to become coordinated. Nurses know that such a baby may not be ready to suck on a bottle, so they must feed him with a tube. As he matures, these three necessary sucking reflexes start to pull together and the baby is able to suck on the breast or bottle.

A sleepy baby may not coordinate his sucking unless a parent or nurse gets him started. First, the caregiver must awaken him, then stroke around his mouth, and finally, give him a finger to suck on. After jiggling it in his mouth gently to elicit all these responses and then feeling them becoming coordinated, the parent or nurse will know he is ready to go to the breast. If the mother flattens the areola so the nipple protrudes between her two fingers, it will go into the *back* of his throat to set off an effective sucking mechanism. The most potent such reflex is at the back of the tongue. When all three reflexes begin to pull together, the mother's milk will let down, and the process is on its way. After a few helping efforts, the baby will learn how to do it for himself.

When I turn a newborn's head to one side, he produces a *tonic neck reflex*—a fencinglike response in which the baby arches away from the face, the arm on the face side stretches out, and the other arm flexes up by his head. Flexion on one side of his body and extension on the other help him lateralize his movements in the future, that is, make them one-sided instead of symmetrical. Interestingly enough, reflexes are useful in labor. As the newborn turns his head in response to contractions, he sets off a series of writhing reflexes, which contribute to delivery by stimulating the mother's uterus. Later in infancy, this same reflex will again be useful as it helps him use one arm to reach out for a toy and to suppress the other arm. The development of a dominant side for coordinated activity is helped by the underlying tonic neck reflex.

Another of my "toys" in this assessment is a shiny, red ball about two inches in diameter. When I hold it about twelve to fifteen inches in front of an alert newborn's eyes, he will fix on it slowly and follow it back and forth and even upward for as much as a thirty-degree angle. He follows it with jerky movements of his eyes, his head turning slowly from side to side. This tells me that he not only can see but also can maintain an alert state for himself and respond with appropriate motor activity to follow the ball. His whole face brightens and his whole body participates in this state of attention to the visual stimulus. Vision is already important to him.

If I then present my face at the same distance, his face will become alert and mobile. He can follow my face back and forth. The newborn follows the human face differently from a nonhuman stimulus. Not only is he likely to be more intensely involved with the face, but his own face becomes active, too. With a red ball or the rattle, his expression will be static and

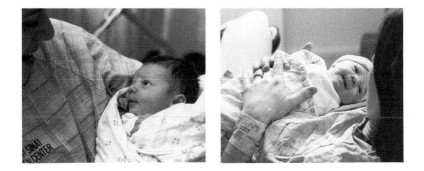

"hooked." With a human face, his mouth and his own upper face will wrinkle and move slowly, as if in imitation. In such an alert state, some babies will indeed imitate what they see. They will open their mouths to stick out their tongues when you put yours out. This has been documented by several researchers, especially Andrew Meltzoff at the University of Washington in Seattle. He sees this as a first sign of the way the baby's behavior can be shaped by the important people around him.

If I talk gently, the newborn's interest in my face will increase. Some babies can follow me smoothly backward and forward, up and down for several excursions before losing interest. As the baby does so, his mouth and face move in rhythm with my voice. By this point in the assessment, if he is responding and even sticking out his tongue, most parents are ecstatic. The newborn's many skills, and especially his clear preference for human faces and voices, fill them with anticipation.

There is an important mutuality here. Parents seem to have an expectation for the kinds of behavior with which a newborn is equipped. When the baby's skills and preferences are confirmed, they gain more confidence in their own ability to understand and care for their infant. Our studies have shown that after such a shared assessment, the mother and the father are significantly more sensitive to their own baby's behavioral cues at one month, and they remain more involved throughout the first year.

Sooner or later during this examination, of course, a baby is likely to become upset. At first, it may be just a whimper, but when he is left undressed and not held, his activity will begin to increase. As he moves, he begins to startle. These startles, or *Moro reflexes*, consist of his throwing out his arms, arching his back, grimacing, and then crying out. When there is nothing to grab and hold, or no one to hold the baby, each startle sets off more startles. Soon, the baby will be very upset, with constant flailing activity and a persistent demanding cry. When parents watch this, they can hardly contain themselves. They feel a great urge to help him, as do I. At this point, I explain that I want to see what it takes to help him contain himself. I like to know him when he cries as well as I know him when he's quiet. In this way, the parents and I can learn to help calm him when he needs it.

The baby may try to turn his head to one side to get his thumb up to his mouth, suck on it, and quiet himself. If I talk firmly and soothingly in one ear, he may stop the frantic thrashing to listen briefly. Then he may begin to cry again, but less insistently. I hold both hands on his chest to contain the startling movements. This time, as I talk to him, he is more likely to quiet himself. His body will soften and he may bring his hand up to his face, turn his head slightly, perhaps insert one finger in his mouth, and attend to my voice, his face alert.

If he doesn't quiet to my voice and my containment, I pick him up to hold and rock him. If that doesn't work, I might give him his finger or a pacifier to suck on. At each step, we learn how this particular baby can be consoled and how much he will contribute to consoling himself.

A baby who can't get himself under control or can't use help in controlling himself will be difficult for his parents. A baby who is irritable and easily upset may need to be placed on his belly to sleep, or he may need to be swaddled or carried or rocked. These maneuvers help contain his startles, which would throw him into an anguished state otherwise. When he is contained, he can pay attention and can learn to manage to calm himself over time. Meanwhile, he will need to be handled with a smooth, gentle approach.

Among the other reflexes that are exciting to see and to understand are the Babkin, Gallant, and crawling reflexes. When you stroke a newborn's cheek or put your finger in his palm, he will bring his fist up to his mouth and try to insert a finger. This is the *Babkin,* or *hand-to-mouth reflex* that serves him later to suck on his fist or fingers. If you stroke along the side of the newborn's spine while he is held under his belly over your hand, he flexes his whole body to the side that is stroked; when you switch to the other side, he flexes to that—a swimming reflex results. We've inherited this reflex, known as the *Gallant response,* from our amphibian ancestors. In the *crawling reflex,* when the newborn is placed on his abdomen, he flexes his legs under him and starts to crawl, picking his head up to turn it and to free it from the bedclothes. He is likely to bring his hand up to his mouth to suck on it and to settle down in a cozy position.

As I share a newborn's responses to the rattle, the bell, the red ball, and various kinds of handling with his parents, I describe the states of consciousness we are seeing and what they represent in terms of the baby's internal organization. We look for clues to his style of managing this new world. Parents who can understand the cycle of six states that we mentioned earlier (deep and light sleep, fussiness, crying, and two alert states) as the baby's way of controlling his internal and external world are already able to understand their baby. The cycling of these states over a twenty-four-hour period becomes a window into the predictable behaviors that parents will encounter as they take care of the baby. Understanding the way a newborn actually manages his own environment gives caregivers and parents respect for his competence.

Learning Your Baby's Style

The major goal for sharing all these responses and reflexes is to identify a newborn's particular temperament. There are wide individual differences in the style in which a baby handles responses to stimuli around him, in his need for sleep and his crying. Babies differ in how they can be soothed, as well as in their responses to hunger and discomfort, to exposure to temperature changes, to handling, and to interaction with caregivers. The task for parents is not to compare these characteristics with some other baby's, but to watch and listen for their own baby's particular style. As we saw in the last chapter, the parents may have had a preview of this style before birth.

One part of the outside world that the baby has already experienced is the sound of his parents' voices. With a quiet, alert baby, we can test this during the hospital visit. I hold the baby up with his head in one of my hands, his buttocks in another, while he is looking at the ceiling. When I talk gently to him, he turns to my voice and searches to find the source. When he finds my face and mouth, he brightens. Then I get his mother to stand on his other side and to compete with me, talking to him gently on the other side. Any baby will choose the female voice, turn to her, find her face, and brighten. Each time I do this, a new mother will reach for her baby and cuddle him closely, saying, "You know me and my voice, don't you?" This predictable but powerful newborn response cements their relationship.

When fathers are present, I try the same procedure with them. In most cases (80 percent) the baby will turn to his father's voice instead of mine. Whether the baby senses his father's urgency in eliciting their attention, or whether the baby actually recognizes his father's voice, I cannot tell. (If he doesn't turn to choose his father's voice, I may tip his head toward his father.) For fathers will then do just what mothers do—reach out for and grab their new babies, exclaiming, "You know me *already!*" as if it were a miracle.

Adults who are trying to get a baby's attention automatically pitch their voices at a higher level. Babies are probably conditioned in the uterus to the female pitch of their mothers. Hence, they are more responsive in that high-pitched range. In every sensory modality, the baby will have a preferred range. When you stroke a baby slowly and gently, you soothe him. When you pat him rapidly, in a staccato way, he alerts or startles. The same goes for visual responses. If you move slowly, he can follow your face. If the movement is too abrupt and the stimulus is more than eighteen inches away, he can only stare, not adjust or focus.

Many parents will not need these explanations to help them understand the wonderful complexity of their newborn. Nevertheless, sharing the first assessment of their baby with a professional gives them an opportunity to ask questions and to unload concerns they may have. As I examine the newborn's behavior with parents, my goal is, therefore, twofold. One goal is to alert them to the magnificent map of behaviors with which the newborn is equipped. I know that they will observe his behavior with new eyes and will experience each response as his language for communication with them. This prepares them for our future work together in monitoring his development. The second goal is to alert them to my interest in their reactions and interpretations of their baby. If they can accept me as an active observer and participant in their development together, their need for defenses with me is likely to be

diminished. In future visits, they will want to tell me about his development. Through this brief viewing of the newborn as he takes in, shuts out, and starts to master his world, we find a shared language, a true touchpoint of opportunity for our future relationship. Later, parents will call me or visit me, saying, "You remember what you showed me that day? Well, now he's doing this! I knew you'd be interested."

A mother I hadn't seen for thirty years once stood up in an audience of 1,500 parents to tell me that I'd seen and played with her baby and she'd never forgotten it. She went on to tell me that I'd made a prediction when he was only two days old. Because he was so feisty, I'd predicted that he would definitely be negative in the second year—and (surprise!) he *had been*. After all those years, she still remembered that someone had joined her in her job of understanding her new baby.

3

NEWBORN PARENTS

The newborn baby is not the only member of her family facing a new world; her mother's and father's lives have also changed. These days, doctors and nurses have finally learned that parents need as much care, as much "mothering," as their baby. A new mother and father have made one of the greatest adjustments anyone can make: taking on a mysterious new charge who will be their full responsibility for the next eighteen or so years. As the renowned child psychiatrist D. W. Winnicott wrote:

> So here you are with all your eggs in one basket. What are you going to do about it? . . . Enjoy letting other people look after the world while you are producing a new one of its members. Enjoy being turned-in and almost in love with yourself, the baby is so nearly a part of you.

Together with this delight will be a natural anxiety. All parents who care deeply will be anxious. Anxiety serves a vital purpose: calling up energy to help parents meet new responsibility. Anxiety can open them up to the baby and to others who can help them.

If anxiety is overwhelming, it can close off new parents or lead to depression. A depressed new parent is no longer available to the many cues the baby offers. Since nearly all new mothers, who have labored hard and have had to come down to earth after the initial euphoria, are somewhat depressed in the first few days, one of the roles of a supportive professional is to differentiate between this natural letdown and a more deep-seated one. The former can allow the new mother to slow down and to recover physically from the stressful labor. It is common, normal, and adaptive.

In the Japanese islands of the Gotō Archipelago, where we have studied families for several years, a new mother is expected to stay in bed, wrapped in her quilt, for one month after delivery. Her baby is wrapped up next to her. For one month, grandmothers, aunts, and relatives come in to take care of her, feeding her and helping her to the bathroom. She is expected to do nothing but feed her baby and to recover. While her relatives help her to regress and recover, they speak to her in a form of baby talk. In response, she answers them in a high-pitched voice. For one month, she is a child in their eyes. At the end of this time, she must return to her heavy-duty chores of managing the household and helping her fisherman husband tend his nets. A postpartum recovery period is accepted and treated as normal in this culture.

In the United States we expect a new mother to rise swiftly to the demands of her new job as a full-fledged parent. She is expected to "bond" in the delivery room, before she may have fully recovered herself. Nowadays, she is rarely kept in the hospital long enough even to recover physically. If she has had a cesarean section, she may have five days at most of nurturing and recovery. For normal vaginal deliveries, forty-eight hours represents a long admission. Implicit in this is the message that a new mother should be ready to handle her own recovery and attachment to the new baby. Since our ability to depend on an extended family and on the older generation has become more difficult, the new father may be her only support. He has his own new adjustment to master. If he has taken his role seriously and is ready to back up the family adjustment to the new baby, he is offered a unique role today. But, with this opportunity for him comes a heavy responsibility. Having generally had no role model in his own past, a father, too, can be anxious and overwhelmed. A professional who recognizes this can be a major source of support. In my own work, I make an effort to "touch base" with each new father, both in the hospital and at home over the phone in the first week.

Bonding   The pediatricians Marshall Klaus and John Kennell were the first to describe the bonding that takes place between parents and newborn and to emphasize the importance of the first few days. They also pointed out how the needs of new parents were neglected in modern hospitals. As a way of enhancing the new parents' closeness to the baby, they recommended a period in the delivery room during which each parent could touch, hold, and communicate with the newborn. They recommended that the brand-new baby be placed skin-to-skin on the mother's chest, and then allowed to suckle at her breast. The father was encouraged to hold and examine his new baby. Their research indicated that this could be a sensitive time both for channeling all the eagerness that parents had generated in pregnancy and for allowing them to become attached to the real baby. More recent research from Drs. Klaus and Kennell demonstrated that the presence of a *doula* (an encouraging woman who assists the mother throughout labor and at birth) can significantly reduce the length and complications of labor and delivery. Such continuous support helps the parents have the best possible birth experience and be ready to nurture and reach out to their infant (see the Bibliography).

Certain childbirth educators, however, took the implications of the bonding research too literally. Some went so far as to place a sign on the closed door of the parents' hospital room: "Do not disturb—Bonding in process." This interpretation misses both the variety of approaches among individuals and the long-term nature of the bonding process. In my research in other parts of the world, women don't all want the new baby with them immediately. Some seek to recover their own energy for an interval after hard labor. Then, they are ready to receive the new baby. This makes me skeptical of any routine practice of giving the baby to the mother "to bond" right away. I like to give parents a choice, plus the chance to recover and feel eager and hungry to be with their new baby.

If parents are overwhelmed, it is important for a supportive person to be available to them as they get to know the baby. This should be on their own timing. The individual choices of each parent must be respected, if we want to make the best of the initial introduction to the new family member.

Instances in which the baby's condition demands that she be whisked away to the intensive care nursery, and in which there is no opportunity for the parents to greet the baby immediately, have demonstrated that attachment to a baby is a long-term process, not a single, magical moment. The opportunity for bonding at birth may be compared to falling in love— staying in love takes longer and demands more work. When the first greeting must be postponed, parents can still become fully attached to their baby. It is very important that expectant parents and those who assist them in childbirth know not only that each family has its own timetable but also that strong, long-term attachment is the goal.

When I examine the newborn and share her behavior with her parents—the second touchpoint—we get to know their baby together. I like to remind them of the baby they dreamed of and of their predictions during our prenatal visit. Since they are now trying to fit that image to the real baby, it serves us both to be reminded of the adjustment they are making. If, for instance, they've dreamt of a quiet, gentle baby and this one is vigorous, impulsive, and difficult to quiet, the new parents have a lot of work ahead. If they can be conscious of the adjustment, it is liable to be easier. Their feelings of disappointment can give way to the challenge of understanding this particular baby. If we discuss how they feel, they can see me as an ally.

"She has your nose." "He has my father's eyes." "Her voice sounds just like Aunt Hattie's when she's mad." Such com-

Discovering the Re Baby

ments represent attempts to make the baby into a familiar person, and to identify the kind of person she will be. The infant psychiatrist Bertrand Cramer, in the book we wrote together, *The Earliest Relationship*, speaks of how the parents must reconcile the real baby with an imaginary one that represents important experiences from their own past. Their attempts to label or characterize her are part of the work of getting to know this stranger. Like theatrical directors, they cast the baby into many roles—"little empress," "whiner," "out to conquer the world," "angel," and so on—as they reach into their own family history in trying to understand her. If the baby is miscast, adjustment will be much harder and the parents may need help.

Examining the Baby

As parents examine their new baby, first gingerly, then inch by inch, every detail catches their attention. They often worry about the shape of her head, which may be a little pointed and lumpy. The head must mold for labor and delivery. It can become elongated and shrink in diameter as much as an inch. However, it will round itself out in two or three days. This doesn't hurt the brain. The only kind of lump that will last is a big, soft, blood-filled swelling on one side or the other. This is called a cephalhematoma, and it will be reabsorbed in three to four months. Even this kind of swelling does not reflect an injury to the brain, which is cushioned. The soft spot in the top of the head, called the fontanel, allows the skull to mold for delivery. If the head gets a bang, the skull will give. It's an important protection.

Bruises do not mean the baby is damaged. If one side of her face droops and doesn't move when she wrinkles up her expression, this could be due to facial paralysis, sometimes seen after forceps are used during delivery. This is likely to be temporary and will go away in a few weeks. Bruises and swelling go away quickly.

A baby's eyes will be swollen from a combination of the pressure used to instill the medication and the silver nitrate, which is still given in many hospitals to all babies to prevent gonococcal infection in a few. It is an abrasive substance and causes swelling. Some states now allow the use, instead, of an antibiotic ointment, which causes less swelling. In any case, a baby can see through the little slits, even if her eyes are swollen.

Other people worry about the needle sticks done for screening blood tests. While this seems a dreadful attack on tiny, tender feet, it is necessary. They'll heal miraculously. These tests are done to identify jaundice as well as a series of congenital disorders—thyroid difficulties and phenylketonuria, or PKU, a disorder that affects a baby's brain unless it's treated as soon as possible. Thyroid difficulties can be handled, too, but we need to start early. Sticking babies' heels for blood to identify these diseases is an important preventive measure, although very few babies test positive for any of them.

Many newborn babies begin to get yellow (jaundiced) by the second or third day. Jaundice is caused by immature blood cells, which carry oxygen in the uterus and are fragile in the presence of normal oxygen outside the uterus. In the uterus, more cells are needed to carry the oxygen than outside. After birth, there are too many cells. These break down, and the breakdown products produce bilirubin, or jaundice. A newborn's immature liver and kidneys don't discharge the bilirubin very easily. If the bilirubin begins to get above a certain level, which changes from day to day, it is necessary to intervene. Bilirubin lights will help to break it down. These lights are used as a form of phototherapy. The baby's eyes must be covered, and she is undressed. A newborn hates all of this. While she is under the lights, she will be jumpy and jittery and hard to feed. But she will recover. This behavior will pass in time, and it does not represent any brain damage. Since jaundice and brain damage are often equated by parents, I want to reassure them.

A vital task for new parents is to learn to identify the different cries of the newborn. Any cry on her part is interpreted as a call for help. Parents automatically feel that they must respond and must find the problem that is making the baby cry. This will take time. There are at least six different cries: pain, hunger, discomfort, fatigue, boredom, and tension discharge. As we encounter them in our exam, I attempt to describe them—their tone, their quality, their duration and intensity. I also try to help parents observe any self-calming efforts the baby makes, for all of these observations can be used later as they learn how to respond to her cries. When they can begin to see the baby's own efforts to calm herself and can differentiate between different cries, they will be able to understand their role.

Research shows that parents can tell their own baby's cry from another newborn's by the third day. By the tenth to fourteenth day, they can differentiate among cries. The rapidity with which they learn can be enhanced if a caregiver shares this information with them. Instead of a frantic effort to stop all crying, they can learn the more realistic goal of helping the baby calm herself and regain control.

Each family needs to work out its own routine for changing, feeding, burping, cuddling, carrying, and rocking the baby or crooning to her. They will gradually learn what works and when the baby needs to be given a period to calm herself and settle down. Learning to parent is a long-term process. We all make mistakes. From the start, I try to emphasize to parents that learning to parent results from learning from one's mistakes. You learn a lot more from mistakes than from successes.

Early Care   When there is an opportunity, I like to observe a feeding. This is also a touchpoint for us. If the new mother is trying to get breast-feeding started, there are many tricks that I can suggest to help her. Such simple maneuvers as holding the baby, certain ways or flattening out the nipple so it can get far back in the baby's throat to set off the suck reflex, as well as the measures we mentioned in chapter 2, can alert a sleepy or fussy baby toward organized sucking.

There are two kinds of sucking: (1) nonnutritive, or positive, sucking, which a baby uses to keep herself comforted and under control, and (2) nutritive, or negative, sucking, which she uses for feeding. You can feel the difference by inserting a clean finger into her mouth. The first type uses the front of the tongue and a kind of licking motion. In the second, as we described earlier, the end of the tongue starts lapping, the back of the tongue begins to milk the finger, and finally there is a real pull from the back of the throat. All three components start independently, then become coordinated into an effective sucking motion. Parents can feel these differences for themselves. When the first kind of sucking is being used by the baby, she can be ready to be alert and be talked to. Parents can use these times to talk to her and to play with her. A baby's day should be more complex than just sleeping and feeding.

Regarding feeding, new parents often ask me, "How do I know when she's had enough?" A baby will start out with a short burst of constant sucking. Very quickly, she resorts to a burst-pause pattern. A burst of sucks will be followed by a pause: suck-suck-suck-pause. Psychologist Kenneth Kaye and I studied the pauses to try to understand their significance, for we were aware that babies tended to look around and to listen in these periods. In a pause, a mother often will jiggle her baby, then look down at her to urge her on to more sucking or touch her baby's cheeks as she speaks to her. Fifty percent of the pauses are accompanied by a maternal response, and fifty percent go unnoticed. We asked mothers why they jiggled or touched or talked. The answers were along these lines: "To get her back to eating. She seems to be dreaming or to have forgotten about eating, and I want her to get full." In our study, the baby's pauses when the mother didn't respond were significantly shorter than were those when she did. In other words, the baby seemed to prolong her pauses to capture social stimuli. We point to this burst-pause pattern in babies to help emphasize the importance of playing with and talking to a baby at feeding time.

As we talk about the opportunities for play, I like to point out that diapering and bathing can also be important times for communication. Talking to the baby and kissing her stomach are irresistible accompaniments to diapering. Parents can make it a fun time! Many babies hate to be undressed for a bath. If this is the case, parents can swaddle her in a diaper after she is undressed in order to keep her feeling safe. They can then lower her into the warm tub, holding her head up with one hand. While her body is submerged, the diaper can be taken off. She will become active, but not upset, when she's submerged in warm water. While she's kicking and scrabbling,

the parents can talk to her and play actively with her. New parents may need permission to feel free enough and encouragement to see that play with a baby is just as important to her as are the more sober forms of care.

"How will I know when to feed her?" Parents wonder whether to follow a schedule or to go entirely by the baby. Here's the advice I offer them. At first, feed her when she cries. If that doesn't work, you'll learn which cry means hunger and which ones indicate other things. If she's really hungry, it certainly will be hard to miss it. She'll keep on fussing and squirming until you feed her. When you first take her home, follow her cues to feed her whenever you think she wants it. Wake her after four hours if she doesn't awaken herself. That way, you'll begin to work toward a schedule. Later, in a week or two, you'll know her cues better and you can begin to push her to wait a bit for each feeding. In about two or three weeks, she should be able to wait two to three hours, but she should also be eating at least six times a day.

When a baby spits up or gags, you may worry that she is choking. It's very hard for newborns to choke, because their breathing reflexes are good at keeping the airway clear. If, indeed, your baby should really begin to choke, put her over your lap, head lower than body, and smack her gently on the back. That will help to clear her trachea so she can breathe. You—indeed, all parents—should have a first aid guide such as is found in Boston Children's Hospital's *New Child Health Encyclopedia* (see the Bibliography). You should also have emergency numbers by each phone. Then, in an emergency, you won't have to think; you can just react.

If the baby spits up after each feeding, it's probably because she's been taking it down too fast. If you can hear a gulp with each swallow, it has air in it. Prop her gently after a gulping feeding before you bubble her—that is, prop her up at a thirty-degree angle for twenty minutes, letting gravity push the milk down and the air bubble up. Then, when you sit her up, the bubble will come up without bringing milk with it.

Nothing in parenting is as rewarding as a big, wet burp after a feeding. To burp a baby, put her up on your shoulder. Pat her gently on the back as you rock and croon to her. She may not have a bubble at each feeding if she's very efficient. If she's a gulper, she will have bubbles. Every gulp carries air down. But bubbles won't hurt her, and she can always pass them on through to the other end if you miss them. It's not very likely that they'll cause her stomach pain. If you have tried for five to ten minutes and she won't bring up her burp, leave her propped up on her back at a thirty-degree angle; then she'll probably bring it up herself.

The first hiccups can seem like a cataclysm to a new parent. Relax. They'll go away. You can always give the baby something to suck on—water or sugar water. But they'll go anyway. Hiccups can often be a sign of too much stimulation, so don't add to it.

While I try never to issue categorical rules to a parent, there is one question to which I give a very firm answer. If parents ask whether to leave a baby with a propped bottle, my answer is *absolutely not*. Every baby deserves to be held for a feeding. Communication at feeding time is as important as the food.

Breast-feeding mothers always wonder whether the baby is getting enough milk. If the baby seems satisfied after a feeding, that's the most important sign. Does she wait for a few hours? Is she urinating several times a day? Also, she should regain her birth weight in the first seven to ten days of feeding. All babies lose a portion of their birth weight in the first few days—sometimes as much as a pound while they wait for the mother's milk to come in. Breast milk may not really come in until day four or five. Meanwhile, the babies' own stores of extra tissue, which they have laid down at the end of pregnancy, protect them. Colostrum precedes breast milk by one to two days and is very valuable—rich in protein and antibodies against infection.

A baby's bowel movements are rather alarming at first. They are black, known as meconium. This is made of stored up and ingested cell-breakdown products from nine months in the uterus. By the third day, the stools change to greenish and are mucousy. By the fourth or fifth day, they may begin to be yellow and mushy. This is the first sign that the baby is beginning to get milk. They can happen with every feeding or even once a week in a newborn. With a breast-feeding baby, they are not smelly. Often, they are a gaudy yellow and green. (For information about breast and bottle feeding, see the Bibliography and chapter 23.)

Mercifully for parents, much of a newborn's life is spent asleep. Most babies have a strong preference about what position they like for sleep, and they let you know it. Nurses in hospitals often tell you to prop them on their sides. This is done to prevent aspiration of milk or of the secretions after birth, but doesn't really seem necessary after the first few days. Once a baby is active, she'll roll over one way or the other. On her belly, she can pick her head up to free her nose and mouth, *if* there aren't too many bedclothes. She may also be quieter on her belly. She won't be able to startle, for her arms will be restricted by the bed. So, if she's very active, try that position. On her back, if she likes it, she will find a cozy, curled-up posture, her hand up by her mouth. You'll know, for she'll tell you.

"Should I use a pacifier?" Some babies absolutely need one to help them calm down. They are babies who can't or won't find their thumbs. But I'd certainly prefer a thumb. It is always there, and she can use it whenever she wants. Most babies need a self-comforting pattern. If they're active or easily aroused, they certainly need a way to fall apart and to relax. I'm always relieved to see a baby who can comfort herself. She'll be an easier baby to parent.

When a baby is extremely overstimulated, her eyes may seem to float, her arms and hands may go limp, her face may frown, or she may avert her gaze. Spitups and bowel movements can be a sign of stress. They can come at unexpected times, along with whimpering, high-pitched cries. These responses are signs that the baby needs time out to recover and reorganize. If you do too much to try to help her, you might just add to the overload. When you've tried everything and it doesn't work, you may need to step back and just watch her. From her behavior, she'll tell you what she needs.

The Baby as the Teacher

As I said before, learning to parent a child is learning from mistakes as well as successes. As you try things out, I tell new parents, let the baby tell you whether you are right or not. When you're on the right track, her face will be placid and content, her body will be relaxed, and her responses will be organized and predictable. When you're on the wrong track, she'll be disorganized and unreachable. She will avert her face from yours. She'll thrash around and be unable to get calm. Her color will change to either very red or slightly blue. Her limbs will stiffen out, and her cry may be piercing and breathless. You may not know what to do, so try everything, including leaving the baby alone to reorganize, as we just said. Over a surprisingly short time, you will learn what her behaviors are trying to tell you.

Many new mothers have said to me, "I wish I could stay here in the hospital where I know my baby is safe." Everyone feels that way. But think of all the klutzes over the centuries who have made it with a new baby. I assure each new mother that she will learn what to do, with her baby's help. Her nurse or pediatrician can help, too, but her best teacher will be the baby, whose special language—behavior—can be observed and trusted.

Starting Out with Premature Babies

When the baby is born early or is stressed by intrauterine conditions that deplete her, each parent feels responsible. Mothers feel they could have done something differently. Whether it's rational or not, the mother feels she has endangered her baby. A concerned father will feel responsible in his own way. With this sense of responsibility comes depression. Parents blame themselves, feeling angry and helpless: Why me? What could I have done differently? A rational answer does not help; such feelings go too deep.

The birth of an extremely premature baby, or one who is at risk or is handicapped in some way, will elicit three predictable defenses:

1. *Denial*—Parents may deny that the problem matters, while sensing how fragile this defense is. The denial tends to distort the reality in one way or another, portraying the situation as too rosy or too grim. This denial helps parents keep going but eventually needs readjusting.
2. *Projection*—The fault is seen as belonging to another person, who is imagined as causing, or in some way

worsening, the problem. Doctors, nurses, or others in charge become targets of this defense. Their assistance becomes suspect, and relationships are endangered.

3. *Detachment*—Parents can pull away from a baby who is at risk, not because they don't care, but because it is too painful to care deeply and to feel so helpless.

These grief reactions and defenses are natural and even adaptive. They must be accepted. Those who care for parents and newborns should understand that such defenses are necessary ones and need not be destructive if they are understood. A caring professional can see them as a part of parents' attempts to recover, and to relate to a baby who does not fit the one of their dreams.

After delivery, all babies go through a period of recovery. A premature baby or one who has been stressed in the uterus will behave in a way that shows her physical fragility. As her autonomic (respiratory and cardiovascular) system recovers from the shock of having to take over prematurely, and as her neurological system matures outside the protection of the womb, a baby will be very vulnerable to auditory, visual, and tactile stimuli. Every touch, noise, or even change in light will be reflected in a change in her color, breathing, and cardiac control. Her motor behavior will reflect her immaturity either in weak muscle tone and few spontaneous movements, or in uncoordinated, jerky movements, which come at unpredictable times and occur after any stimulation. These movements are upsetting to the baby's fragile system. Her state control is poor, and although she tries to stay asleep to avoid overwhelming stimuli, she may shift from sleep to brief awake states within very short periods. In an awake state, she is more often crying than quietly alert and may avoid being looked at or talked to or touched. She may give back nothing but negative responses. For fearful parents, hungry to communicate, such behavior in their baby increases their anxiety about whether she is intact and whether she will be able to recover.

Parents need patient support as the baby recovers. If they can visit her, can learn over time how to handle her, they will be ready for the job of caring for her when she is discharged. Doctors and nurses can help by demonstrating the baby's behavior and responses to them before discharge. Such a baby can tolerate only stimuli that are at a very low level. They can be held *or* rocked *or* looked at, but only one of these at a time, and very gently. If you respect this low threshold for taking in information, a recovering baby can gradually take more and more.

Over time, each system—motor, autonomic, state, and attention—will begin to show sturdier responses. As the baby becomes less fragile, she can begin to pay attention to auditory and visual stimuli, but still at a low level and for short periods. When she begins to fix on the red ball or her parents' faces, or to turn to their voices or toward a rattle, you can see what a great challenge this is to her nervous system. Her movements will become jerkier or her extremities limp. She may turn away from the voice or rattle instead of toward it. Her eyes may begin to float in her head, her face become slack, her color drain, and her respirations increase. Hiccups, yawns, spitups, or b.m.'s can all be signs of stress and overload. Parents may need to understand these symptoms, too, in order not to overreact.

By decreasing the noise, the light, and the stimulation in our preemie nursery, my colleagues and I have attempted to respect the fragile nervous systems of these babies. They have recovered sooner, have gained weight more quickly, and have needed less oxygen and less incubator time. Also, they have been discharged home earlier and in less fragile shape. Parents who continue to provide a low-key environment at home will help their babies begin to thrive.

As premature babies or those who are born on time but are small for their gestational age (known as SGA babies) mature, their states begin to last longer. They become able not only to pay attention longer but also to suck and eat more effectively. They can be handled and played with for longer and longer periods. However, catching up to a full-term baby's behavior may take longer than parents expect. It is destructive when parents constantly compare their baby's progress to that of a full-term baby. If, instead, they can carefully attend to their own baby's individual behavioral responses, they can fix on appropriate goals. When the NBAS, described earlier, is done together with parents, the particular capacities of these babies to see, hear, and pay attention are evident, along with their weaknesses. Their need for special handling or early intervention can then be explained in a helpful manner.

A baby with an impaired neurological system can benefit from very early remedial programs, learning to substitute other systems for impaired ones. A blind baby, for instance, can learn to utilize auditory and tactile cues to make up for her blindness *if* these cues are given to her at her own speed. If they are offered one by one as quiet, slow, nonintrusive stimuli, it is possible to watch the baby's behavior to see whether she is utilizing them. We have followed several blind babies. They are hypersensitive to touch and sound, so one needs to reduce one's voice and to handle them more gently and slowly. Parents of a baby with any type of impairment or developmental delay need a trained professional to identify the baby's positive responses, the ways to help her learn control, and the signs of having overloaded her threshold (see chapter 18).

Over the years, I have been impressed with the remarkable ability of babies to recover from insults such as prematurity, and I can be optimistic as I work with the parents of such a baby. There are two pitfalls that parents can learn to avoid as they adjust to a fragile baby. First, anxiety and disappointment can lead a parent to hover excessively. Even the most delicate, stressed baby can achieve more by learning to achieve each step by herself. It is difficult not to continue to hover long after a fragile baby actually needs protection. Letting her have enough space and time to learn each step by herself is difficult but pays off as her sense of autonomy and self-competence develops.

The other pitfall is one we have already mentioned. While all new parents compare their baby to every other baby, the parents of one who is delayed are even more likely to want the baby to measure up to others. "When will she catch up and be like other babies her age?" parents will ask me. "What age should he be? I'm so scared he'll be slow. Whenever he doesn't make each step on time, I'm afraid he's got brain damage." These questions are an honest reflection of the fears that go with parents' adjustment to a delayed or disabled baby.

The baby's individual responses and her own temperament are the best antidote to such fears. At each visit, parents should ask the doctor to explain the baby's progress and level of development. Even when the months of prematurity and the weeks in the hospital are subtracted, each new step takes twice as long, for it may cost her nervous system that much more to organize itself in order to accomplish each step. For example, the fussy period at the end of the day can start later and continue later, and smiling and vocal responses can take longer to appear in a fragile baby after a difficult recovery. When parents know that this is likely to be true, they can keep their anxiety from interfering with the job they have of helping the baby recover. Patience and an optimistic, sensitive approach is the goal. These are difficult to achieve, and parents deserve all the help professionals can offer. In each chapter in part 1 of this book, the age levels mentioned must be adjusted and, in any case, should not be taken as rigid yardsticks (see chapter 32).

4

THREE WEEKS

When parents bring their baby for the first three-week visit, they are both likely to be exhausted. New parents come to my office for comfort, for understanding of their overwhelming new role. Sometimes, a grandparent, a nanny, or an au pair comes with them. I watch to see who carries the baby. If the grandparent or nanny does, I wonder how much the new parents have relied on the more experienced caregiver, and how much actual experience they have had with their newborn. I am also looking for evidence of support systems for these new parents.

Many new mothers will be in the midst of some degree of postpartum depression. Such a depression can accompany the physical recovery and rebalancing of hormones from labor and delivery. But it can also be part of learning an overwhelming new role. A mother who is depressed is usually working hard at becoming a parent. Often she looks bedraggled, while her baby is carefully dressed in delicate, impractical little outfits and pastel receiving blankets. A new mother will clutch her baby tightly, as if afraid to trip or drop her precious bundle.

The new father hovers protectively in the immediate background. After taking the mother's coat, he may help her get settled by offering to hold the baby for her. If she gives her baby up momentarily, he will look down hungrily, longing for the baby to wake up and look back at him. From his handling of the baby, I can tell how much he has been participating in the care. Mothers who dare not share the baby's handling will sit down awkwardly rather than handing over the baby. Every gesture of new parents reveals where they are in making this major adjustment.

As we talk, a new mother will look down at the bundle in her lap after each sentence. If the baby begins to move, she is likely to look at me anxiously, as if to say, "What do I do now?" If the baby cries, I can expect the new father to jump to help. Both will begin to try to comfort the baby, adjusting from one position to another, offering a pacifier—if they've decided to use one—looking at me somewhat beseechingly for help. A mother's last resort is to try to breast-feed. Although women are less inhibited today than when I began my practice, the new situation of being in my office and of being under my scrutiny can be daunting. I may have to suggest it. As she puts the baby to breast, she will look relieved. A few fathers will take the fussy baby to comfort and try to spare their wives, demonstrating a shared relationship with this baby.

I have come to expect this tenuous, rather childlike behavior when new parents come into my office. Rather than a sign of incompetence, it represents their ability to accept me in a nurturing "grandfather" role and to let down their defenses. All new parents need a supportive figure who can sort out their questions and concerns. I am grateful for their trust, and I try to indicate this in my voice and comments.

By three weeks most parents have done an enormous amount of work in adjusting to the new baby. Many phone calls have been made between parent and physician or nurse practitioner. While they are beginning to feel in charge of their lives again, this new adjustment is physically and emotionally overwhelming. A postpartum depression can be seen as a way to conserve energy after delivery. I have always urged new parents to conserve their resources in every possible way. Visits from outsiders should be limited to a few helpful, supportive people, excluding, for the time being, all the well-wishers who consume time and energy. If this is awkward, parents can say that the baby's doctor asked them not to have visitors for two weeks. Until their immune system is fully active, newborns are vulnerable to germs from visitors. A period as free of outside pressure as possible provides new parents with the space to become a family. Often, the higher the elation of parents after birth, the lower the slump after they return home. The reality of being responsible is awesome to thoughtful parents.

In this first visit, I try very hard to include the father, urging the parents to make the appointment at a time when he can come in. Early in the visit I ask him what his impressions are and what he has noticed about his baby. After he's opened up once, I know he'll communicate throughout the interview. I look for an opportunity to observe him with the baby and to comment on the interactive behaviors that he and the baby show me. By about four weeks, new babies have learned special behavioral patterns for each parent. For a mother, the baby's extremities, movements, and facial behaviors are smooth and rhythmic in anticipation of their low-keyed, rhythmic interaction. With the father, the baby's facial features all go up, the extremities tense and waiting, as if the new baby had already learned that his father plays with him. When I can see behavior that starts to show this recognition in the three-week-old baby, I describe it for parents so that they can observe and enjoy it, too. These different responses to each parent are an exciting sign of early cognitive development.

Fathers who can take time from work not only learn to diaper, to feed, and to play with the baby but also help their wives in the enormous shift of focus toward caring for a new, dependent individual. If gatekeeping by a new mother or a grandmother makes the father feel shut out at this time, the likelihood of his feeling involved later is significantly reduced.

While I'm talking to parents, learning about them and their adjustment, I am able to observe the baby's temperament. Temperament is a concept of style—how a baby sleeps, how difficult he is to soothe, how intense his movements become, how he tries to comfort himself, and how alert he becomes as I handle him through the exam. All of these observations can be shared with his parents from the first so that they know I am seeing the same baby that they are living with. Once parents sense this, they feel much more confident and relaxed as they ask for information and support.

On our map of touchpoints, of these times in a child's life **Feeding** when certain issues are bound to arise, feeding questions are inevitable at three weeks. Once the subject is opened, I can expect a deluge of questions: how often to nurse, how to know when a baby is hungry, or how long to feed at one time, as well as questions about burping, spitting up, or bowel movements, and about the father's attempts to give the baby a bottle—especially if the baby is breast-feeding. At first, formula feeding may seem easier because each parent knows how much and how often the baby has fed.

Often parents will call, greatly concerned because the baby "spits up the whole feeding." I explain that, after a gulping, noisy feeding, they can expect a big bubble and a gush of milk to follow. A feeding that goes down like an elevator, comes up like one. As we said in the previous chapter, learning how to bubble the baby is one of the major achievements in the first weeks. Often, small practical suggestions from an experienced mother or a pediatrician bring reassuring success. After such practical questions, parents will often move on to deeper concerns about the feeding. For breast-feeding mothers, the primary concern will be, Is he getting enough? We discuss the ways they can tell:

1. Does the baby seem satisfied after a feeding?
2. Does the baby sleep one to two hours between feedings?
3. Does the baby urinate often? (Wet diapers mean the baby is getting fluid.)
4. How many bowel movements does the baby have? (I warn parents that the pattern for b.m.'s may change drastically in the next weeks. A baby on the breast may have eight or ten a day at first, and then may change to a pattern of once a week. If, after a week, the b.m. is soft and curdy, this is not constipation. Breast milk can be completely digested, and without any residue. Many

babies have this pattern on breast milk and until they start solids or more formula. Then, the pattern will change.)

5. Has the birth weight been gained back? (As mentioned before, babies lose stored-up fluid right after delivery. They can lose as much as 20 percent of their body weight in the first four or five days, before breast milk or formula can be expected to rehydrate them. Most babies are discharged from the hospital at less than their birth weight. The transition to home is stressful, and a new mother's milk may not come in until as late as the fifth day. Hence, the possibility of gaining weight may not even arise until the second week. By the third week, babies should be gaining their weight back. Every mother and father is relieved to see that the baby is gaining.)

Parents usually see feeding as their most important responsibility. The more intense this feeling of responsibility, the less likely parents are to recognize the child's contribution. At this first visit I try to elicit or point out the behavior around feeding time that gives us insight into a child's particular temperament and the importance of the intensity of the baby's participation. I try to stress cues from the baby that parents can use to enhance the development of the baby's autonomy in the feeding situation. We talk about the burst-pause pattern in sucking, which gives parents the opportunity to talk to the baby and to play during a feeding.

Communication   Our discussion of feeding leads into the most important point of all: Getting the baby fed is only half of the job. Learning to communicate with the baby—touching, holding, rocking, talking, and learning to synchronize with the baby's behavior—are as important as getting him fed. Often at this stage, both the new mother and father are likely to be too caught up in the "instrumental" job of learning how to feed. They aren't yet able to hear me talk about the "softer side" of feeding a baby. But I bring it up, as I do at each subsequent visit.

Meanwhile, there is a good opportunity to watch the way parents communicate with the baby right in my office. I observe the patterns parents and baby have learned. Does the baby brighten when they look down to talk to him? Have they learned how to hold the baby and where to place him in relation to their faces, so they can hold his interest? In the job of learning attachment the first two steps are to help the baby pay attention and to prolong that attention in a face-to-face situation. The special low-keyed rhythm of speech and of facial behavior, which is necessary to attract and keep a baby's interest, must be learned over the first weeks.

All these little clues reveal how much time this new family has spent in learning about each other. Many anxious new parents devote their first weeks to feeding and sleeping, with no time for communication. If I see evidence of this, I look for an opportunity to model play with the baby. I take him in my hands, hold him out in front of me, and with gentle rocking, bring him to an alert state. Then we communicate in slow, gentle cooing. The baby's responses capture the parents' attention, and they take in the rhythms, the low voice, and the slight rocking needed to alert a small baby. If a particular baby is intense and overreacts, I swaddle him and contain his arms before I try to produce an alert state.

If the baby is fed in my office, I try to point out the burst-pause rhythm. As mentioned earlier, a baby starts sucking initially with regular sucks. After thirty seconds or more, he will fall into a different pattern—a burst of sucks followed by a pause. It is helpful for parents to know that pauses that are rewarded with a smile, a touch, or another social signal from the caregiver are prolonged by the baby, as if he actually wants social communication—as well as the feeding. Just food is not enough!

eping and Waking   The next most important task for a baby at this time, one that is full of issues for the parents, is to gain control of his states of consciousness. Readers will recognize these states from the description of fetal behavior in chapter 1 and from those pointed out in the discussion of newborn assessment in chapter 2.

Deep Sleep In this protected state, the infant can shut out disturbing stimuli from the environment around him. He breathes deeply, regularly, and heavily. Eyes tight shut, he is motionless. If he moves at all, his movements are slight, short-lived, and jerky. The self-protective nature of this state is reflected in the infant's curled-up, economical posture, with the hands up by his mouth, all of his limbs in flexion—closing out the world.

Light, or REM (rapid eye movement), Sleep In this state, breathing is shallower and irregular. From time to time, the infant sucks with or without a finger in his mouth. He periodically moves in a writhing way. He may startle once or twice. In this state, he is more vulnerable to outside influences. When roused, he will either awaken sleepily and fussily or struggle to sink into deep sleep.

Indeterminate State This short-lived state is one that occurs frequently as the infant rouses or returns to sleep. In this state he squirms and moves jerkily. His eyes open dully and close again sleepily. He may whimper or cry out, but without focus. He will often try to curl up into a comfortable position, but startling, jerky movements interfere. He looks disorganized, and his frowning face shows the uncomfortable attempts he makes to reach a more organized state—either of deep sleep or of an alert state.

Wide-Awake, Alert State The baby's bright face and shining eyes demonstrate his open receptivity. His movements are contained. If he moves, he moves smoothly and can even achieve a goal, such as bringing his hand to his mouth or holding one hand with the other. His breathing fits itself to the stimulus. With an exciting stimulus, his breathing is deep. For a negative one, it is shallow and rapid. One can see his responsiveness on his face and in his entire body as he attends to an interesting noise or a familiar face. His face, his breathing, his body's posture—all convey interest and attention, or else a desire to withdraw and turn away from an overwhelming stimulus. Parents look for, and learn to help him to prolong, this wonderful alert state, for this is the time they can communicate with him. An attentive parent soon learns his signals for "I've had enough" when he's tired or for "I want attention" when he's feeling overlooked.

Fussy, Alert State This state often follows the alert state. The baby's movements become jerky and his respirations irregular. He turns away from stimuli, fussing or whimpering from time to time. He makes ineffective attempts to control himself. As he thrashes around in his bed, his face reflects his feelings of ineffectuality. In this state he cannot control his movements, his autonomic system, or his ability to take in stimuli from around him. Helping him to calm down is rewarding for a parent, but he may go into an uncontrolled crying state. Then, parents feel they have been ineffective also.

Crying Many different kinds of crying can be demonstrated: (1) a piercing, painful-sounding cry; (2) a demanding, urgent cry; (3) a bored, hollow cry; and (4) a rhythmic, but not urgent, cry that occurs when a baby is tired or overloaded with too many stimuli. His movements are thrashing, yet somewhat organized, in spite of his constant activity. He may quiet

briefly as if to listen. He is likely to quiet when picked up, rocked, or fed. This state demands parents' attention, and they learn which comforts relieve it. It serves many purposes.

The way a baby moves in and out of his states of consciousness becomes predictable to parents. His style of moving from one to another is one of the best indicators of his temperament. If he is active and intense, he will move in and out quickly. If he is laid back, he will move slowly in and out of the six states. By now, parents are likely to know that when he is in an intermediate, fussy state, he will begin to cry if they do certain things or will quiet if they do others. His states and his mode of participating in the cycles of states every three to four hours are their best window into an understanding of their baby. The new parents' first job is to learn their baby's most important language—his state behaviors.

If they understand this language, parents can push a baby to organize the states into cycles of behavior. A predictable pattern is now possible because the baby's nervous system has matured and because the parents know more about him. At three weeks the brain's electroencephalogram (EEG) tracing shows a spurt in maturity, and sleep records are significantly more mature. Tests also demonstrate a new stage of predictability in heart rate responses to visual and auditory stimuli. At this point, the baby's heart beats faster in response to a negative stimulus and more slowly in response to a positive one. These physiological changes lead to a spurt in development. By three weeks the baby begins to be able to wait longer between feedings. He is ready to pay more and more attention to his parents, and this attention will lead to cooing and smiling.

At first, feeding the baby whenever he wakes is the most appropriate response. In this way, parents can learn at which times the baby is hungry, plus which feedings are successful and which are not. Often these less successful feedings are times when the baby is not ready. Starting in the third or fourth week, feedings can be postponed for a bit of play. New parents often ask, "How do I know when to stop and play?" The only way to find out is to try. It won't hurt the baby to wait a bit. The baby will gradually learn that playful interaction can be as exciting as feedings. Once parents are confident that a baby is getting enough food, they can begin to stretch out a baby's alert states between nursing and sleeping. A mother has more and richer milk after a two- to three-hour stretch than after hourly feedings. Her breasts are likely to develop a better let-down pattern if there's an interval between feedings.

The goal is to "stretch out" the baby's waking moments to three to four hours between feedings and a long sleep at night. Certain new babies have already reversed day and night. They are up all night and sleep during the day. In order to change this pattern, parents can try to keep the baby awake at the end of each cycle of light sleep during the day. They can then awaken the baby in the evening for a real play period and gradually introduce the last feeding earlier and earlier. Over time, the baby will start to stay awake longer each evening, learn to sleep longer stretches at night, and learn to awaken in the day.

The adjustment of the new baby's cycles of sleep and waking is the parents' first attempt to fit him into his new world, to bring his rhythms into harmony with theirs. This process, as all experienced parents know, takes years, and because we raise individuals and not clones, it is fortunately never complete.

The Fussy Period Between three and twelve weeks of age, **Looking Ahead** most babies will develop a fussy period toward the end of the day. Because this will arise before my next visit with the family, and because it can be one of the most upsetting hurdles parents face, I make sure to raise the subject during this, our three-weeks, visit. The chance to anticipate this trying behavior, to understand its value for the infant, will spare parents some unnecessary panic and anxiety. If they can understand the infant's need to fuss at the end of each day between three and twelve weeks of age, they won't have to feel so responsible for the fussing.

In the past, many of us in pediatrics called this inconsolable, fussy period "colic," and we joined parents in their efforts to stop it each day. We tried sedatives or medications such as antispasmodics, and we urged mothers to carry their babies around, to nurse them constantly, and so on. All of these things helped temporarily, but they didn't get rid of the daily fussing and crying. Curious about this, I planned a study in which I asked eighty mothers to collect data for me on when and how their babies fussed. All but a few of these normal babies with healthy parents did about the same thing. They had a predictable fussy period that began at the end of each day—just as their mothers were exhausted and their fathers were coming home. (This was back in unliberated days.) When they fussed, it was a kind of cyclical crying, not at all like the cry of pain or hunger. When these parents picked them up or nursed them, the babies would stop, but they'd start in again after they were put down. If they were carried a lot, this reduced the quantity of crying but didn't stop it. There seemed to be an inevitability to it in 85 percent of the babies. Just before the period began, these babies were jumpy, and one could predict when it was about to begin. After it was over, parents reported that their babies slept better and longer and more effectively.

Whenever a certain behavior is so predictable and widespread, we assume that it is adaptive and look for the purpose it serves. This fussing began to look like an organizing process. An immature nervous system can take in and utilize stimuli throughout the day, but there is always a little bit of overload. As the day proceeds, the increasingly overloaded nervous system begins to cycle in shorter and shorter sleep and feeding periods. Finally, it blows off steam in the form of an active, fussy period. After this is over, the nervous system can reorganize for another twenty-four hours. It's almost clocklike in its predictability.

After I have explained this, mothers often ask, "But how can I stand back and let him cry?" That is not what I recommend. Instead, I give them the following advice. Go to the baby. Try out all the maneuvers you know to find out whether he needs anything. Pick him up and carry him. Feed him, cuddle him, change him. Give him warm water to help get a bubble up. But don't do too much. Once you've reassured yourself that he is not wet, in pain, or hungry, either use soothing techniques or let him be. The normal one to two hours of fussing can easily be prolonged into a four- to six-hour ordeal if parents get too anxious and barrage the already overloaded nervous system with too much handling and stimulation.

At this point in my explanation, many parents ask for an explicit routine. As one father put it, "I'm sure my wife will feel he's hungry and worry that she hasn't given him enough milk." Of course he is right; she will. That's the reason I suggest feeding him first. But if he doesn't really eat well, if he just nibbles off and on, parents can be pretty sure it's not hunger. I suggest that after they have tried all their maneuvers, they give the baby ten or fifteen minutes to "let off steam." After that, they should pick him up to give him warm water and to bubble him; he'll have gulped down air as he cried. Then they need to let him have another cycle of fussing, after which they can repeat the same maneuver. This routine is rarely needed more than three or four times. After it's over, the baby will probably seem better organized—sleeping, eating, and staying alert in more regular rhythms.

This is the extent of our discussion of the fussy period at this time, for it will not yet seem real to parents. By discussing the likelihood of the baby's developing this regular fuss period every day, and by giving parents an understanding of it, I hope to reduce their anxiety. When he does develop this rhythmic pattern at the end of each day, they will be less likely to overreact and to overload him. Now I find that babies in my practice cry for one to one and a half hours rather than the three-hour stretch I used to hear about. Such results make the discussion an important touchpoint.

What about babies who cry more and more? Shouldn't they be taken seriously? Absolutely. If parents find that this fussy period increases in timing and intensity despite their restraint and low-keyed efforts, I would want to hear about it. I would want to search for other reasons for this crying—such as a mild allergy or a reflux of acid from the stomach into the esophagus which can cause pain. There are other reasons for crying that I need to search for when it is intense and unrelenting.

Thumb Sucking and Pacifiers The three-week visit is none too early for parents to sort out their feelings about thumb sucking and pacifiers. I often ask parents whether the baby gets his thumb in his mouth yet. Can he comfort himself? Occasionally a mother will quickly reply: "I don't let him. I don't want a thumb sucker. I've been taking his thumb out of his mouth. If he needs anything to suck on, he can have me as often as he wants. Otherwise, I'll give him a pacifier." Or a father might remark: "I'd rather he'd suck his thumb than be wheeled around with his mouth plugged up." Sometimes parents will disagree on this issue and will ask me which is better.

Before outlining the pros and cons, I try to hear what the parents themselves feel about thumb sucking and pacifiers. Some will remember dreadful childhood battles. "My mother did everything to stop her, but my sister would sneak off to hide just so she could suck her thumb. She sucked it until she was seven or eight years old." I might ask, "Is there a reason why your mother felt so strongly?" Sometimes parents see a thumb as dirty; others worry that a pacifier will ruin a child's

teeth. To calm this latter worry, I am able to tell parents of a study done by dentists at Children's Hospital on children who suck their thumbs or pacifiers and those who don't. There was little difference in their need for braces. Apparently, it is tongue thrust that deforms upper teeth. In any case, the most important reason for the need to straighten teeth is likely to be a genetic tendency. The exception may be children who are withdrawn and who suck most of the time, or children who go on sucking intensely after age five or six. But the problems of such children are in the area of socialization rather than in the area of sucking.

To give parents a little perspective on this issue, I explain that thumb sucking is a healthy self-comforting pattern. A fetus sucks his thumb. As noted in chapter 2, a newborn is equipped with the hand-to-mouth, or Babkin reflex. When he's upset or trying to settle down, he will resort to this as a way of controlling himself. The pattern seems to be built in. Babies who make use of it are easier to live with. As I mentioned in chapter 3, if parents ask about the relative merits of thumbs versus pacifiers, I point out the obvious: a thumb is always available. After saying this, however, I turn the issue back to the parents. Preferences and feelings on thumbs and pacifiers have deep roots in family history and culture. "But won't he grow up sucking on his thumb? It will be easier to take the pacifier away," some mothers and fathers will ask.

Very few people go to college sucking their thumbs or pacifiers. The children who keep on as late as kindergarten or the early grades are those in whom the habit has been reinforced by parents who interfered with it. If you want to set a stubborn pattern in a child, just try to interrupt it at a time when he needs solace. It's true of many other "habits" that would be transient unless adults tried to stop them. This is why I suggest to parents that they evaluate their own feelings about thumb sucking as early as possible. A parent who objects to a child using his thumb is bound to let him know it sooner or later. Parents who are bothered to see a child sucking his thumb should consider a pacifier. It's a stressful world for small children. They are likely to seek some sort of self-comforting as their way of managing the stresses. I see this as a very healthy sign of competence, not as a dirty or shameful habit.

One mother in my practice put into words the real issue underlying the struggle over thumbs and pacifiers: "I feel that if only I could do everything for him and do it right, he wouldn't need such a crutch." A child's own self-comforting pattern calls up feelings of inadequacy in parents—maybe even jealousy. For this reason, they see the habit as dirty and embarrassing. One father, after hearing his wife and me go through all this discussion, looked over at his baby who had started to fuss. The baby thrashed a bit, whimpered, then turned his head to one side, pulled his thumb up to his mouth, and settled down. "Well," said his father, "I think he's decided it for us."

This father's wise observation is the answer to a perennial question from new parents: "How do I know when I'm being a good parent and when I'm not?" The only sure way is to watch the baby. Only the baby—not the doctor or a book—can tell you when you're on the right track. When you are not, you'll learn from mistakes and won't lose anything in the process. The job of a physician (or pediatric nurse or nurse practitioner), as I see it, is to alert parents to the developmental steps that are likely to unsettle them. Anticipating these times gives parents choices that they can make on their own.

5

SIX TO EIGHT WEEKS

At the next office visit, six to eight weeks after a baby's birth, the mother often comes alone. When the father accompanies her, I feel he and I are off to a good start, and I take this as evidence of how much he wants to participate in each milestone with his baby. Later, parents who are both very involved may alternate visits. By now, the mother, who is usually still on leave from her work, may look a bit less tired. She may have dressed up for this visit, as if it were an important occasion, a chance to get out of the house. Since we probably have been in touch several times by phone, she may greet me as if we were old friends. Generally, the first thing she may do is try to show me how her baby is learning to smile and to vocalize. Rarely will the baby cooperate, but that makes me know that they are enjoying each other. If she gives the baby to the father to hold as she concentrates on her questions with me, I learn something about the way they are sorting out their roles. If, on the other hand, the mother hovers over her baby or the father dominates the question period, I wonder how

much they are sharing, and I may need to reach out to each of them to hear their concerns. If the mother is pale, exhausted, and jumpy, I must be alert to the possibility that the very common postpartum blues are deepening into depression.

At this visit, my goals are simple. First, I want to assess the baby's development. Is she normal neurologically? Has she been gaining weight as expected? Is her behavior normal? Does she react by smiling and vocalizing? Does she move her arms and legs vigorously? If she is placed on her belly, will she elevate her head and free her airway? When pulled to sit, does she keep her neck straight? Is the time between feedings spreading out? Does she have a fussy period at the end of the day, or is she crying all day long?

I am also eager to hear the parents' concerns. If they need help with feedings, we can concentrate on that. Do they understand the concept of states and the way these states cycle during the day and night? Can they tell the difference between their baby's cries? Do they feel more confidence about handling these, or is the crying too much for them?

Together with the parents, I watch again for signs of the baby's temperament. Is the baby active or quiet? Is she easily overloaded and hypersensitive? If so, have they learned how to help her calm down, and how to handle her without overloading her? We share these observations as I undress the baby and examine her. Parents often find it easier to voice their worries and their questions when I'm commenting on the baby's behavior during the course of the actual checkup, rather than when we are sitting still, face-to-face.

Feeding   Most parents still worry about whether their baby is getting enough to eat. After I have ascertained that the baby is gaining weight appropriately (about a half pound a week), I can assure her parents that she is well fed. Her body should be filling out; she should be stretching out the intervals between feedings. If the baby is being breast-fed, fifteen to twenty minutes at each breast is more than enough for sucking and for adequate milk. Even a few minutes on each side will stimulate milk production. If she is formula-fed, six to eight ounces is plenty.

Too much spitting, frequent bowel movements between

feedings, or a dry eczematous face rash can be an early indication of intolerance to a formula. If the baby shows any of these symptoms, the parents should check first with their physician. She may be sensitive to milk protein. Breast-fed babies are not prey to these sensitivities. It is important to identify a milk allergy as early as possible. Eczema can be avoided if milk is eliminated early. There are formulae made from soybean products that do not contain milk yet are just as nutritious. They do not challenge a milk sensitivity, and they are safe for milk-sensitive infants. If parents can avoid milk, the allergic baby will outgrow her tendency to react to it. As she gets older, the danger of allergic eczema and intolerance is decreased.

Before solid foods are started at four to five months, it is important to recognize and take care of any sensitivity to milk. Otherwise, the chances of other foods setting off allergic reactions are increased. An allergic child is rarely intolerant or sensitive to one food product alone. Milk and other allergens are more potent if given together. Avoiding allergies is an important goal for families that have this genetic tendency. Breast-feeding mothers who are allergic to certain foods should avoid these, for their own sake, and also because the baby may inherit these allergies. (See also the discussion of allergies in chapter 14.)

By this time, feedings should have become expectable and more routine. Breast-feedings should now be easy and pleasurable. If the father feeds the baby with a bottle, a routine for this can also be established that will not interfere with breast milk production. One bottle a day will never reduce a mother's milk and will give him a real sense of participation.

If the baby is a regular spitter, the parents and I have no doubt discussed this over the phone already. I estimate that 15 percent of normally thriving babies in my practice spit up. They spit small amounts from one feeding to another, and they always bring milk up with a bubble. They spit whenever they're handled or whenever they get upset. They seem to have a weak valve at the top of the stomach, and milk spills out when they are handled at nearly all times. As long as they're gaining weight and are contented between feedings, it's not a serious concern. I try to reassure parents that it's common and that they don't need to worry. Slowed-down feedings with the baby held in a semiupright position can help. Nursing mothers tell me that their babies spit up less when they lie down to feed them. As we suggested before, after a feeding, a spitter should be propped at a thirty-degree angle without handling her for twenty to thirty minutes. That will enlist gravity to hold most of the milk down. Then, the caregiver can bring up a bubble gently if it's still there. These maneuvers tend to reduce the spitting, but they may not eliminate it. Breast milk doesn't smell, but formula comes up with a pungent odor. When I walk into a house, I can tell from its characteristic odor that there is a spitting, formula-fed baby there. Baking soda sprinkled on the spitup will help to counteract the smell. When parents know that the baby is healthy and gaining weight, a sour lapel may not seem like the end of the world.

Breast milk or formula is all that a baby needs at this age. Solids are not needed and probably are not digested before three to four months. An infant's swallowing mechanism isn't mature before that: she just sucks food down, as if nature didn't mean for her to get solids too early. Milk is the perfect food for babies. Allergies to other food can be hidden at this age and don't show up until later. I don't recommend solid foods at this age for all of these reasons.

A breast-fed baby may not have a bowel movement each day. Many babies who are getting adequate feedings and are gaining weight will digest breast milk so completely that they have only one b.m. every three to eight days. This never happens with formula-fed babies who usually have one or more b.m.'s a day. Breast-fed babies may change abruptly from a pattern of one after every feeding, to one a week. I've had two in my practice whose pattern was one every tenth day. In between, the babies are happy. Toward the end of their cycle (for I do see it as theirs), they strain and act like the stool is bothering them. If parents use a rectal thermometer as a stimulus, their baby will produce a movement at any time, but this is not necessary. If it is her normal pattern, the movement will be soft and *not* constipated. Parents, of course, tend to get anxious. They feel this is constipation and rush to use suppositories or to manipulate the baby rectally to produce regular stools. This is completely unnecessary and interferes with a normal rhythm. A constipated baby is one who has hard, large, difficult movements. Those of breast-fed babies are soft, not hard, and often have greenish, bile-stained mucus in them. Although the baby may cry out as she passes them, she is not constipated. Breast milk is a perfect milk and can be burned up almost completely. Parents who know this in advance are saved from interfering with the baby's normal pattern.

Formula-fed babies may have b.m.'s every other day, but they are not likely to postpone their stools. Formula is never as completely digested. If a formula-fed baby has either hard stools or more than five or six green, mucousy, watery stools, parents should check with their physician.

Crying

A baby's cries should be clear to most parents by now. Cries of boredom, pain, discomfort, hunger, fatigue, and letting off steam are all distinctly different from each other in most babies. New parents learn to tell them apart by trying out all the comforting maneuvers: feeding, changing, cuddling, swaddling, and so on. By finding out what works, they then find out what to try the next time. But they shouldn't be surprised when the method that worked last time won't help. Learning to parent is a process of trial and error.

As we saw in chapter 4, a regular fussy period, usually at the end of the day, is both common and adaptive in children of this age. It helps the baby let off steam so that she can adjust to a four-hour cycle of states. Gradually, the baby will learn more mature ways of self-quieting, such as using her hand-to-mouth reflex or listening to voices or being propped up to watch light and color.

The way parents learn to handle normal, fussy crying in their baby can be a particularly important touchpoint—a time not only for them to grow as parents and adjust to a stage in the baby's development but also for a physician to support this growth. Parents who can understand the different cues and what works to soothe each cry—as well as what won't work—may not be as frantic over their apparent failure when the regular fussy crying continues at the end of each day. The studies I have done on average babies indicate that this fussy crying peaks at six weeks and decreases gradually over the next few, to be gone by twelve weeks.

Parents want to know whether they can spoil a baby by rushing to her every time she cries. They ask, "If we carry her around during this fussy period, or if we feed her a lot, are we spoiling her?" I reassure them that this is not spoiling. In fact, I don't believe "spoiling" is possible in the first year. Parents should try out whatever helps, up to the point where everything they do is just adding to the fussiness. Then, it's time to slow down. They should either carry the baby very quietly and calmly or put her down for brief periods of fussing. Five to ten minutes at a time will help her get it over with. After such a time, they can pick her up to calm and even to burp her, then put her down again.

In my experience, a "spoiled child" is an anxious or driven child. You don't make a child spoiled by attending to her needs. Hovering over her all the time and attending to her with anxiety and anger might lead to an anxious, whiny child. But picking her up to play with her or trying things out to satisfy her will not. Parents and babies learn about each other this way. Mothers and fathers may learn different things about the same baby. A different style of response in each parent is fine for the baby (see chapter 16).

Sleeping and Waking

The baby's pattern of sleeping and feeding should be more and more predictable. As we saw, she should be stretching out the time between feedings. At least a three-hour break between feedings gives parents a chance to plan the baby's and their own day. Depending on birth weight and other factors, babies of two months have longer and longer stretches asleep each night. I urge parents at this time to wake the baby and start her day when they are ready. At night, parents can get the baby up before they go to bed to feed her one last time. A schedule helps everyone adjust to the baby. It doesn't need to be rigid, and it certainly should follow her demands, but she's ready to fit in by now. She is more likely to adjust to her parents' environment if they expect her to.

In addition to the prolonging of the intervals between feedings, which will occur as the nervous and digestive systems mature, the baby continues to perfect her own patterns of self-comforting. Thumb sucking, rooting around in bed, and rocking the head are among the ways a baby calms herself. After feeding the baby in their arms, then rocking and soothing her, parents can lay the baby down in her crib when she's quiet but not asleep. They can sit beside her to croon and to pat her gently. If she has a difficult transition from their arms to the bed (as highly active babies do), it seems even more critical to "teach her" early how to console herself at night. As she scrabbles to find her pattern of self-comforting, parents can gently help her discover her thumb or a pacifier or a position in bed that she can seek each time she rouses. As we said in chapter 4, not only are these self-comforting patterns nothing to worry about, but parents will be helping her build on independent strengths for the future.

Communication

Of the baby's many powerful ways of reaching her parents, perhaps none other is as effective as her smile. In these early weeks, parents will have learned what they must do to produce one, and the baby is learning what an extraordinary and reliable response this gentle signal can bring. Parents learn to cuddle the baby, contain her arms, rock her, hold her at a thirty-degree angle, and talk gently to her, with infinite variations for each loving couple. Too great a response from an eager parent can be as much of a turnoff as too little. You can turn off her smile by overreacting too noisily to it!

By now a baby can watch a parent's face for long periods. As she watches, she will get more and more interested until she breaks into a broad smile. Smiling back is likely to prolong the smile. As she wriggles with glee, she may make a brief cooing sound. If the parent imitates her sound, she will stop moving, and a surprised look will come over her face. She may work hard to coo again. Unable to do so, she may give up in frustration. Such frustration is evidence to me that she knows what she has done, that she recognizes the adult's imitation, and that she wants to repeat it. She disintegrates when she can't live up to her own expectation.

At our office visit, I watch carefully to see whether parents and baby smile and communicate with each other. Most parents will want to talk about this enchanting new dialogue. Some others even report that all other activities pale beside this new delight. "My problem," said one, "is that I can hardly do anything but look at her and play with her every minute she's awake." Some, especially parents who have very little time at home from work, will get a baby up just before bedtime or before they leave in the morning to play with her. Many parents also report that the baby sleeps better after such a play period. As the parents and I talk together during a checkup, I take this opportunity to point out how the baby is trying to intercept their attention. When she manages to engage them, her face lights up, her shoulders rise, and she may even squeal with pleasure. She knows *she* has done it!

New parents, who can find a way to worry about almost everything, sometimes ask if they can "overdo" play. "She is so delicious when she smiles and gurgles. I keep her at it until she breaks down and starts to cry. Am I pushing her too hard?" they may ask. The only advice I need to give is, No! Have fun. This is such a great time for learning about communication. The baby can take care of herself by falling apart. Then, she can even come back for more. Some babies will reflect overload with a kind of small shudder or with hiccups.

These, too, are nothing to worry about. Babies reach a point where they can't go on. They seem to wish they could do more, but they can't. Frustration is a powerful force for learning, and the baby can be allowed to handle the frustration herself.

Some parents of a two-month-old will ask, "Has she learned to cry for attention already?" Certainly she has. Babies develop an expectancy when parents respond readily. Parents can see this as a welcome sign of learning and early attachment. Who wouldn't yearn for another person who comes to make you giggle, who sings, rocks, cuddles, and smiles—one who is already passionately in love with you?

Temperament

During this second office visit, the baby's characteristic ways of reacting to handling will be more apparent. I try to enlist the parents in watching the baby's activity with me: the way she responds to touch, to sounds, to being undressed, and so on. By this age, quiet babies can be distinguished from more intense, driving babies. A certain temperament has revealed itself by now. Each of these kinds of babies, especially the extremes, demands a particular adjustment from parents. In my book *Infants and Mothers*, I discuss these adjustments and the marked individual differences between babies over the period of the first year.

As the parents adapt themselves to their particular baby, observations about her intensity, her threshold for utilizing stimuli, and her motor style, competence, and ways of self-soothing can be helpful to them. If I watch carefully and speak about the baby's language—which is her behavior—to the parents, they will more readily share their questions about her and about themselves as parents. As we play with the baby together, deeper concerns often surface.

For example, a hypersensitive baby poses a tough challenge to any parents and can arouse painful doubts about their ability to nurture. A baby who responds to playful attempts to elicit a smile, or to cuddling, with frantic activity and crying can be terribly frustrating, even to experienced parents.

When her parents try to play with a hypersensitive baby, she may arch away, avert her face, spit up, or have a bowel movement. In every system of her tiny body, she is saying, "I'm overloaded." With such a baby, parents must learn subtle techniques of containing, swaddling, and gently playing in a quiet, nondistracting atmosphere. A hypersensitive baby can be approached through one modality at a time—*either* speaking softly *or* looking in her face *or* rocking her gently—but only one. As she begins to assimilate each modality and to respond warily, another modality can gradually be added, until finally all three are together and she is able to respond to them. Learning to take in and combine all three modalities is a big achievement for such a vulnerable infant.

Sometimes I can help by asking the parents to watch me handle the baby, respecting her very low threshold for taking in and utilizing stimuli. I begin by simply holding her, not looking at her face or talking to her. Whenever I move even slightly, she will probably startle and stiffen all over again. I must wait until she is relaxed, *then* look down at her. She will stiffen briefly. When she begins to relax again, I can talk quietly to her in a crooning, soothing way, until she gradually relaxes to look up at me. Perhaps, as I talk *and* look *and* rock her gently, she will begin to smile or to coo gently. If this is successful, I suggest that parents run through the same slow steps, with me or at home. I encourage them not to add any other stimulus until the baby tells them that she is ready. When her body stiffens, then relaxes, that tells them she's processing information and reminds them how hard it is for her not to get overloaded. With only one new stimulus at a time, parents can gradually teach a baby to take in her world *without* shutting it out.

While discussing ways to connect with a hypersensitive baby, I also try to explain to the parents that the concern and eagerness to nurture, which show what devoted parents they are, can be the very qualities that overload such a baby. If they can recognize her fragility and respect it, adapting their deep desire to reach and play with her, a new rapport can gradually build between them (see also chapter 26).

A quiet, watchful baby can also frighten parents. She frowns at you whenever you try to reach out for her. If you talk too loud, she turns away as if you were not anyone she wants to listen to. Every attempt to reach her seems to end in failure. This can make an eager new parent feel rejected.

When talking with parents of such a baby, I give the following advice. Approach your baby slowly and without talking. Look away from her face as you contain her by her buttocks. Gently touch her legs and let her grasp your fingers with her hand. When she relaxes her grasp, then you can dare to look her in the face. If she stiffens and averts her head, you have gone too fast. Wait and try again. When she'll let you look at her, wait until she's relaxed again. Then, start cooing softly to her. If she brightens and tries to coo back to you, you can start a rhythm between you—of your cooing and of her cooing, back and forth until she overloads to turn away. Don't feel rejected. Realize, instead, that she is a very sensitive baby who needs to be introduced to one thing at a time. When she can take one, add another very gently. Over time, she'll learn how to handle stimuli without withdrawing. Then, she'll be so rewarding—quiet, observant, even grateful for your respect for her. Our goal is to have her grow up with the feeling that people respect her quiet shyness for what it is—an easily overloaded nervous system. Jerome Kagan, of Harvard University, has done interesting research by following shy, sensitive children into their school years. Many turn to intellectual and artistic pursuits.

Motor Skills

At six to eight weeks, most babies have begun to control their reflexes to a limited extent. Instead of startles, which have interfered earlier with attempts to move, a baby can now control her legs and arms. She can lie in bed on her back, cycling her arms and legs. If you touch her hand with an object she's interested in, the touched hand may jerk out toward the object. Long before she can reliably reach for an object, the ingredients that make up a reach are there. She is now successful in turning her head to a preferred side and inserting her fist to quiet herself. This control over her movements has taken two months, and parents can see her practice as she lies in bed in the morning.

When a baby this age is pulled to sit by her extended arms, her head lags only briefly. She can now maintain it in a sitting position for a minute or longer. When placed face down, she can pick her head up off the bed to look around to free her airway. In a standing position, her walk reflex is still present, but it's harder to elicit than it was at birth. Parents can watch as the reflexes that are present at birth gradually go underground and as more voluntary behavior develops.

Cognitive Skills   Being human, parents get great excitement at the first signs of intelligent learning in their babies. By six to eight weeks, babies have already developed all kinds of expectancies. For instance, when you rock a baby gently to bring her up to a thirty-degree angle, she knows that this is a position for interaction. She alerts predictably. As I examine a baby, I like to see when she produces smiles and vocalizations. I want to observe her ability, by eight weeks of age, to differentiate between her mother, her father, and a stranger.

In our laboratory at Children's Hospital in Boston, we can watch a baby on videotape for a two-minute stretch. By observing her fingers, toes, hands, feet, and facial behavior, we can actually tell to whom she is reacting. In front of her mother, her movements are smooth and cyclical. Her hands, feet, fingers, and toes extend toward the mother and withdraw at a rate of four times a minute, in smooth cycles. Her face brightens softly. As the mother looks, the baby looks away gently at intervals of four times a minute. With her father, every part of her body reacts differently. Her body gets tense and jerky. Her face brightens; her eyebrows go up, her mouth opens in a grin; and her fingers, toes, arms, and legs jerk out toward her father as she expects a playful interaction from him. With me as a stranger, she will brighten at first. Then, she will turn away or will look at me as if she recognized me as a stranger, in the same hooked, fixed stare that she saves for objects. In this way, observed carefully, a six- to eight-week-old baby can be seen to differentiate between the three of us. I like to point out these subtle differences in behavior to new parents, so they can learn to watch their babies.

At this age, too, objects become more fascinating. A mobile becomes a source of great pleasure, and she will watch it for longer and longer periods, even trying to stay awake to do so. At this age, babies also watch their hands, turning them over and over in front of their eyes. This way they learn hand–eye coordination, which will help when reaching begins at about four months. She will then quickly learn to reach a target accurately, having practiced. By four to five months, when a baby reaches successfully, she will be able to keep her hand in peripheral vision to make it work accurately for her.

Back to Work? "I'm having to think about going back to my job. My leave will be up in four weeks. I can hardly stand it. They have offered to let me stay out another month, but without pay. Is it worth it?" Before this visit is over, I will hear this question in one form or another. The timing of the mother's return to work raises many important issues. If she plans to leave her baby with another caregiver, we need to address her feelings about separation, as well as our concern about the care that the baby will receive. If the father is to share the care, they will want to discuss this arrangement. If there is to be a secondary caregiver at home, I should, ideally, meet this person as well.

Looking Ahead

Depending upon the parents' circumstances, I am likely at this visit to encourage at least four months at home for the mother. Four months gives her time to get through the fussy three-month period and enjoy a month of pleasure, with the baby smiling and gurgling at her. If she must share all these new steps with a substitute, it is awfully hard on her. Sometimes, parents who had well-laid plans set in motion for day care or a nanny/sitter/caregiver at home will find their feelings changed. "I just can't bring myself to think about it," said one mother. "Every time I think about leaving the baby, my mind goes blank and I feel overwhelmed." Parents must weigh these strong and important feelings against their need for two salaries or pressures from employers. It is one of the toughest of all decisions. When parents face both the pain and the opportunity that a return to work represents and discuss them openly with me ahead of time, I know we have reached a vital touchpoint in our relationship and in their growth.

If parents feel that they both must work full-time, I then encourage them to take time to look for the right caregiver.

They need someone they like and can trust, and they should always watch her with other babies. It is important for them to consider how they will feel if this person takes care of their baby and shares her with them. I remind parents that the nicer and more appropriate a caregiver is, the more jealous they will be. I urge them to get someone they can be jealous of. But they should also try to find someone who cares about them and their adjustment. Parents must be able to participate in decisions about their baby, whoever is caring for her. In my book *Working and Caring*, I go into each of these issues in depth.

In day care, the ratio of babies to adults is absolutely critical—not more than three babies to one adult. It is expensive, but it's critical to the baby and critical to parents' peace of mind.

Sometimes parents ask, "How long would you recommend I stay at home if I had a real choice?" If this choice appears possible, I suggest one year. By the second year, a baby can handle playmates, so a group situation is not so stressful. Before that, the optimal solution is for one or both parents to work only part-time, so that one parent is available to the baby for a large part of each day. I see this opportunity as one that is almost as important to the parents' development as it is to the baby's.

If a family just can't afford this option, I still try to help them work things out. If a mother can figure out how to keep nursing, by pumping her breasts at work and perhaps nursing at lunch, both she and the baby will benefit. It's wonderful for a mother to be able to put the baby to breast when she gets home from work.

For mothers (or fathers) who plan to stay at home for a time, I nevertheless encourage them to respect their need for time to themselves. After the huge changes of new parenthood, they need to re-cement their relationship with some time together. This may be a very good time to think about a sitter and some time away from the baby. A short time will do. It is vital that parents find a sitter they can trust.

The parents' difficulty in separating may be the most significant hurdle in leaving a new baby. The baby may miss them, but parents will surely feel lost without the baby already. Parents need the baby more than she may appear to need them. Caring new parents need to prepare for these feelings, for they are common. A short time away can be a real help in mastering these feelings of loss. When they first leave, most mothers prefer to return for each feeding. If necessary, however, a mother can pump her milk beforehand to leave it with the sitter.

Sometimes, a mother will ask me: "Will she know me if I go back to work and have to leave her?" I assure her that the baby will. She'll show this by the special movements and rhythms they have learned together. A mother can watch for these so that she won't feel so separated.

At this six- to eight-week visit, parents often ask whether they can take their baby with them when they go out or to their offices. I assure them that they can and mention that the only problem with crowds of people is that many of them will have infections that the baby could pick up. It is a good idea not to let unknown people or runny-nosed people hold her or lean over her to play games. Everyone wants to hold a small baby. When we'd travel with one of ours, all the dear old ladies (and some gents) would try to hold her, and they'd eventually sneeze in the baby's face. I'd have to say to these well-meaning invaders, "I'm sorry, but I must protect you. My baby is under surveillance for a serious infection—syphilis or encephalitis, we fear." No one wanted to hold her then.

6

FOUR MONTHS

Over many years of practice, I remember looking forward especially to the four-month visit. Parents and baby are now "an item." Bonds of affection are weaving them tightly into a family. Even brand-new parents are likely to be more self-confident at this visit. Either parent may carry the baby, tossing him about like a package. When they sit down, they place the baby out in front of them to coo and gurgle over him. If he is sleepy, they wake him to perform. They watch other people to check whether they are noticing and admiring this remarkable offspring of theirs. Innocent bystanders in the waiting room are regaled with his latest achievements. It's likely that friends and co-workers find them a touch boring.

Once in the office, both parents tend to tickle him and to coo in high-pitched voices—anything to elicit one of his adorable responses. When I must undress him, they hover over me to be sure I'm handling him properly. When I give him an inoculation, they wince and grab him away from me. They *know* him now and are at a peak of their love affair with him. All this is very good news to me, and I enjoy observing him as he reacts with them. He will have even more clearly different behaviors with each of them than at the last visit—smooth with his mother, jerky and playful with his father. He will grin and coo to me across my desk but will break down into wails if I come too close, or if I lean over him to examine him. My office and I are strange to him. This represents the beginning of stranger awareness. It comes at a period when the baby is taking a real spurt in cognitive development. He is sizing me up for comparison with the familiar figures of his world—parents, siblings, sitter.

The passionate new feelings of parenthood may be overwhelming to some parents. "I can't talk or think about anything but my baby. My unmarried friends are sick of me. When I walk around with her, I just want to show her off. Am I narcissistic or something?" I can reassure parents that this storm of feelings is called falling in love. Parents are so in love that they feel the baby is a part of them. Every achievement the baby makes feels like it's their own. With it goes the wonder of watching someone learn a task for the first time. Watching him learn in such detail is awesome. Of course they are wrapped up in that baby. Everyone who has ever had a baby knows the feeling. From a pediatrician's point of view, it is the best thing that could happen. These deep attachments will become the anchor for a secure childhood.

So much else has happened, as well. In just four months the family has been reorganized. By now, each member knows his or her role. The difficult adjustment to understanding the baby as an individual has been mastered. The fussy periods at the end of the day are being replaced by a period of intense communication. This formerly dreaded time becomes the most exciting period of play. If crying or "colic" is still an issue, we need to discuss the underlying reasons.

After sharing the parents' exuberant delight in their baby, I may hear concerns expressed in the areas of feeding and sleeping. The baby's development will create choices for parents in the way they choose to handle feedings and sleep cycles. I use this touchpoint to help parents understand the baby's side of the issues that will arise. If they can understand his developmental needs, they can make the choices they must make to prevent problems in feeding and sleeping.

In the feeding area, easy routines will be upset by competing

interests—the baby will want to look around and listen. He will not stay at the breast or bottle. He may even become difficult to feed. Parents may feel it's their failure. If they can see this brief period (one to two weeks) as an exciting cognitive burst of interest in the environment that competes with the feeding, they won't confuse it with failure on their part.

In the sleep area, it is now critical to set up rituals that will help the baby learn to get to sleep in the first place, and to sleep through an eight- or twelve-hour stretch without waking. At this stage, the central nervous system has matured enough to allow a longer period of sleep. Helping parents understand the baby's sleep cycles will prepare them to push him toward an independent sleep pattern. As we will see in what follows, these new feeding and sleep issues are touchpoints that the parents and the physician can address before they arise, rather than after problem behavior has set in.

Feeding   The now-predictable schedule makes normal life possible again for new parents. No longer does the baby need to choose his own feeding times. He can be awakened in the morning to fit the family schedule. Then, parents can plan the other feedings every three to four hours, with morning and evening naps. Five feedings a day are the average at this age. The last feeding can be set by parents just before their own bedtime. If the baby is regular, a parent will know how to recognize when there is a new change occurring. If he is irregular, it is harder for them to figure him out. For this reason, I encourage parents to press the baby toward some sort of steady schedule. If he is gaining and thriving on his formula or breast-feeding, they can be sure it suits him.

A mother who is already working outside the home can pump her breasts once or twice to bring breast milk home to her baby. She can leave the person caring for her baby with her milk from the day before. She and the baby can enjoy three good feedings—in the morning before she leaves, in the evening when she returns, and one more before her bedtime. It is important to her milk supply to waken him for this third feeding at the end of a working day. It is wonderful for them both if she can come home to gather him up for an intimate breast-feeding. That's "quality time"!

It's always amazing to me that the breast can adjust to a baby's increasing demands. As he grows over these first few months, he will have more than doubled his birth weight and will have grown four to five inches. The breast as an adaptable organ is nonparalleled. It will keep up with what the baby demands of it. After feedings have settled to a regular, predictable three- or four-hour pattern, there will still be off days when the baby wants to eat every two hours. These represent bursts when his needs are out of proportion to the balance that the breasts have achieved. By eating more often, he stimulates them to respond with richer milk and more of it.

When these periods of demanding more and more feedings continue for a week or more, and if the baby is over four months old, it is time to consider solid food. Around this time, most babies begin to need a supplement to milk feedings. The American Academy of Pediatrics considers four months a good age to start solids. Starting solid feedings earlier, which was in vogue twenty years ago, has been abandoned. The belief was that by starting early, parents could avoid the refusals of solids that were felt to occur in older babies. However, the baby's sucking apparatus is not well suited to the voluntary act of swallowing until after three months.

Swallowing solid foods, fed by spoon, is a real transition for a baby. When solids are first introduced, most babies frown, sputter, drool, and extrude them. Parents say, "Shouldn't I start with something sweet? He seems to hate this new taste." Of course, the first solid should be fluid and milky, but it probably isn't the taste that is at fault. Learning to swallow rather than to suck, an already familiar act, is the challenge for the baby. Any new achievement takes time. I would expect a baby to fuss over solid foods for the first week. A parent can forget about how much gets in and see this as the time the baby is learning to swallow. Her job is to teach him patiently and slowly. Of course, he needs to be propped in an upright position; otherwise, he might breath the food in. His hands will get into the food. He will bat away the spoon and use his fingers to help suck the food down. Hands are an important part of exploration at this age, so I would never tie them down—I'd wear a raincoat and let him explore.

Parents should introduce one new solid at a time. An interval of a week between each solid food is important as a way to find out whether the baby is allergic to any of them. Before six months, a baby may not always show immediately that he is sensitive to a food. His intolerance, usually in the form of eczema or a gastric upset, may not show up as soon as a food is introduced. As he gets closer to six months, he will demonstrate his allergy within a few days. This makes the introduction of solid foods much safer after six months. Before that, a week or so may be necessary to identify an intolerance. Parents can prevent allergies to foods by being careful at this age. Avoiding sensitivities prevents allergies. After an allergic reaction is set off, it is more and more difficult to treat. If he responds negatively within the week, the food can simply be eliminated. (See the discussion of allergies in chapter 14.)

A good idea is to start with a one-grain cereal in the evening. Mixed cereals are risky, for they contain three or four challenges. Parents should use cereal alone for the first two weeks until the baby has learned to swallow. If it is given in the evening, before his milk, he is more likely to accept it, and it may help him sleep longer at night. Next, a fruit can be given in the morning, and a week later, a vegetable at noon. Finally, beef or chicken at noon can be started a week later. Each food should be pure, with no other ingredients, so parents need to read the label. If the baby should break out with a rash after any of these foods, parents should stop using them and then try one new food after that. If he should break out with a new rash, whatever food was just started should be stopped.

When new foods are introduced, such as peas or carrots, they can be seen right away, bright green or orange, in the baby's stool. Parents needn't worry. These foods are not completely digested at first, as the intestines must get used to each new one.

By five to six months, a typical feeding schedule might be as follows:

7:00 A.M.	Milk feeding
8:30 A.M.	Fruit
12:00 P.M.	Meat, vegetables, and milk
3:00 P.M.	Juice or fluid
5:00 P.M.	Cereal
6:30 P.M.	Milk feeding
10:30 P.M.	Fourth milk feeding

By separating out the meals of solids and milk at each end of the day, the baby can get accustomed to four milk feedings.

The spurt in awareness of things around the baby that will occur at four and a half to five months will interfere with smooth feedings. This will bother parents and frustrate them if they have not been prepared. I try to make it a touchpoint, an opportunity to help parents see this change as normal and exciting. The good news is that each feeding can be a time for play and communication. The baby's newfound reaching will make each feeding a lively game. He will want to help with the spoon. He will need to smear the food over his face and in his hair, and if you are holding him, he'll smear it over you. That kind of exploration is as satisfying for him as being fed. While it makes feeding more difficult, it is a sign of growth.

At this point, many breast-feeding mothers tell me that their baby is "ready to wean." When I remind them that they wanted to breast-feed through the first year, they reply, "I did, but he doesn't want it anymore. Whenever I start to feed him, he pulls away and won't stay at the breast. Every sound or motion distracts him. He just won't take enough at any one feeding. I think I'm losing my milk." The nursing mother is running headlong into this same new developmental spurt—in cognitive awareness. The baby is suddenly aware of sights and sounds in a brand-new way. As each new noise or sight distracts him, he is difficult to feed. He pulls the breast around with him. Each new stimulus demands his attention. For example, babies become more excited about new toys, literally panting with anticipation when they see something new.

Mothers who have been savoring the warm, uninterrupted intimacy of breast-feeding often feel deserted at this time. The baby's new independence and focus away from her feel like a desertion. Until now, it has been possible for the mother to think of herself and her baby as a single unit. No longer. In fact, psychoanalysts such as Margaret Mahler have spoken of babies beginning to "hatch" at this time, or of a "psychological birth" several months later than the physiological one. If mothers do not recognize what is happening, they can become sad and frustrated. They feel as though they are losing the wonderful love affair they've developed. They don't recognize the separation as a spurt in the baby's autonomy. Some even become pregnant to fill the perceived emptiness.

When mothers seem to me to be experiencing such feelings, I can point out that the baby isn't losing interest in the breast. He just has a whole new set of competing interests. They are *temporarily* more important than the familiar gestalt of breast-feeding. This spurt of interest in the world lasts one or two weeks. Then, babies will return to the breast with renewed vigor. There is no reason to give up. The mother can let the baby look around and explore, and can even give him a toy to handle while nursing. During this time, daytime feedings may not stimulate the milk supply sufficiently. The baby may be too excited to eat properly in the day. Morning and evening, the feedings should take place in a quiet, dark room where there are no competing stimuli. That will keep the breast milk coming through this period. Babies often prefer solids right now, because the situation for feeding them is more complex and they can be more involved while being fed. Nursing at the breast may be too passive at this time—babies this age are anything but passive! The quiet, cooperative little infant has become a whirlwind of activity. It is more and more exciting to take in and conquer a whole new world.

Feedings are no longer simple events for parents. The distractions can be a real threat to the instinct that all mothers have. They feel they must get food into the baby. If parents can understand what is behind the baby's distraction and refusals at feeding time, they need not feel they are failing. Supporting the child's excitement in learning is also a vital part of parenting.

As solids are started, some babies wait for them and demand less milk. Sometimes, I've wondered whether this competition isn't reinforced by a breast-feeding mother who is jealous of feeding anything else besides breast milk. That spoonful of rice cereal is the first step away from the complete, idyllic union of a breast-feeding mother and her baby. "I really feel sad that she needs anything but me," said one mother. "It's been so delicious to have her completely dependent on me." In this situation, many mothers find it best to nurse first, then try the spooned-in solids.

Other mothers have quite a different set of feelings: "At last, I can start solids. All my friends started months ago, and their babies are way ahead of mine." When I ask what a mother means by "ahead," she might reply, "Well, they weigh more, and they must know more different tastes. They don't gag with the spoon like my baby does." My answer to this is that fat babies are not healthier, and solids can put extra fat on babies. In addition, the gagging is a normal reaction to a new kind of mastery. The real question for parents is whether they want to raise their baby with a competitive, keeping-up-with-the-Joneses attitude. I try to raise this issue while respecting the universal desire of parents for their baby to be "the best," the most perfect of all. This natural part of caring fuels all the strenuous adjustments a parent must make. But when parents seem too driven, lacking in any humor over this competition, I need to point out the price for the baby in too much pressure from competitive parents.

Sleep   By four months, many babies no longer need a late-night feeding. For a baby to sleep through the night, he must be ready to cycle between deep and light sleep several times. Understanding this is our first touchpoint for avoiding sleep problems. Sleep experts have found that all of us cycle between deep and light sleep, coming up to a state of light sleep called REM (rapid eye movement) every ninety minutes. Every three to four hours we come into a more active state, closer to waking. A REM cycle is characterized by very highly individualized patterns of activity. As a baby comes up into light sleep, he is likely to cry out, to become disorganized, and to thrash around in bed. If he's on his stomach, the resistance of the bed generally subdues this disorganized activity. On his back, he is likely to startle, throw out his arms and legs, become upset, and cry. As he cries and moves around, he gets more upset. If he has a pattern of self-comforting, such as finding his thumb or a blanket, or if he can get himself into a comfortable "nesting" position, he will settle down again. Some babies scrabble their way into the corner, apparently seeking the pressure on the top of their heads that they had in the womb. An active, intense baby has a more difficult time settling himself down. Thrashing around, more and more upset, he shoots up to being wide awake and alert. Then he wants to be held and comforted. He hasn't yet learned to quiet himself. Parents of such a baby will feel compelled to dive in and offer the baby the comfort he needs to quiet down.

Most babies can settle themselves over these 90-minute cycles. But the more pronounced three- to four-hour cycles of arousal are more intrusive. At these predictable times, behaviors are more vigorous and difficult to get under control. At these four-hour cycles, babies come to a wide-awake state. Many cry out as if in pain or fear. They aren't awake, but they may awaken themselves by their own thrashing, uncontrolled behavior. Parents find these periods very difficult. They feel they must go in to help the baby settle. Feedings at 10:00 P.M., 2:00 A.M., and 6:00 A.M. are predictably based on these arousal periods. However, if parents become part of the baby's arousal pattern, they will have to be there to help him settle himself every three to four hours. If they pick him up to feed, change, and settle him, he will not learn to quiet himself back into deep sleep. Understanding these patterns and the effect of their response on the baby will help parents stay out of a cycle that the baby must handle.

At this important touchpoint, when parents express their distress over the nightly waking, I must first make clear the difference between helping a baby learn to settle down and leaving him to "cry it out." I don't think any baby *ever* needs to "cry it out" over anything. Being left to cry it out doesn't teach a baby anything except that his parents can desert him when he needs them. The task for parents is to develop a supportive bedtime ritual and to learn not to jump at the first whimper. When a baby is put to bed in the evening, parents can sing to him or feed him and croon to him in a way that's different from the daytime feedings. Then, the baby can be put to bed before he's completely asleep, while the parent sits there and pats him calmly but firmly. If he has a "lovey" or pacifier, this can be used to help him. A baby who is always allowed to fall asleep at the breast is not learning to get himself to sleep. He's learning to use his mother for that purpose. As a result, every four hours at night, when he comes up to light sleep, he needs her as part of his pattern.

"Sleep problems" are most likely to be parents' problems (see chapter 37). Many parents are reluctant to leave a child to be independent at night. I can understand that. But parents who find it hard to leave a baby until morning will make themselves part of his self-consoling pattern when he wakes through the night. This can set a pattern that is likely to last into the future.

Working parents in particular find it difficult to separate from the child at night, because they have been away all day. A warm, intimate ritual in the evening and time to cuddle in the morning before work can help them deal with this feeling. But many working mothers find they need their babies at night. We discuss their issues and the risk that separation will grow more and more difficult for the baby later on. But it must be their choice, and I will support it.

Some families believe strongly that the whole family should

sleep together in a "family bed." If new parents are considering this, they must realize that such a decision will affect the family for many years ahead. An open discussion of this issue can become an important touchpoint between parents and their physician and prevent unanticipated crises. Although it may not seem apparent at the time, cosleeping is a *parents'* issue. Learning to sleep through is the child's issue. If he can be helped to adjust to it early, it needn't become a "problem" later on. Parents will want the child out of their bed sooner or later. Then, they may become punitive at the child's normal resistance. Anticipating these issues can prevent the confrontation later.

Our culture still expects children to sleep away from parents, and many psychiatrists worry about the long-term effects on children who stay in their parents' bed at four and five years. Once babies are allowed to sleep in their parents' bed, they cannot be evicted whenever the parents feel that they want their bed to themselves. The transition will take time and may be much more difficult than giving the baby his own crib from the first.

In many cultures, parents and children sleep together because of lack of space. In Japan the arrangement is called *kawa,* or "river." The mother is one bank, the father another, and the children in the middle are the river. The father moves out of the bed when there is more than one child and when there's room for him to move out. The mother continues to sleep with the children until they are five or six years of age. In parts of Africa and southern Mexico, a mother and father sleep with the baby between them until the woman gets pregnant. Then, the child is put out for the next baby. This seems like a double insult to me.

In our culture, where there is a choice, it is not fair to push a child out abruptly later. No child should be left to cry it out in order to "break" him. So, the decision should be made in advance. There are other things to consider in our culture. Most of us have deep-seated taboos from our own past about cosleeping. Child-abuse experts are generally opposed because of the threat of sexual abuse—in the child's fantasy as well as in reality. All this is part of our culture's bias against cosleeping. Parents must examine their own biases before they decide.

If they do decide to cosleep, they will want to watch the child for autonomy issues in other areas of his development. Many parents have reasons to feel compelled to respond to fussing at night. Single parents, who may be lonely themselves, will find it particularly difficult to let their child work out his own pattern. Parents who have felt deserted by their own parents want not to repeat this pattern. They find it impossible to leave a baby to find his own means of self-comforting. Parents who work full-time and are conflicted about the time they are giving the baby or who have had difficulty in separations and in developing independence in their own past may not be able to acknowledge the baby's readiness for independence at night.

Students of infancy have shown that, in about four months, a baby's nervous system matures enough to make him able to sleep for a twelve-hour stretch with only one awakening at night. An eight-hour stretch of sleep means that the baby must get himself back down into deep sleep at least twice. In order to sleep through twelve hours, he must be able to settle again at least three times. If he is to sleep independently, he must learn patterns for self-comforting each time. For all these reasons, the period from four to five months is a crucial time for parents to make decisions about their role in helping the baby learn to sleep.

Teething

Most babies begin to get primary teeth after the age of four months, usually at six to nine months. There is an old-fashioned saying that babies should have a tooth for every month from four months on. This is not to be depended upon. The time of teething is genetic, and late-teething parents are likely to have late-teething children. None of my children even began to get teeth until they were nearly a year old. Neither did I, my mother said. There is no known disadvantage to late teething.

Permanent teeth begin to form in the gums in infancy. Allowing milk and milk sugars to remain in the baby's mouth for long periods (four to eight hours) can cause "nursing bottle cavities," which in turn can affect permanent teeth. Parents should not leave their baby with a bottle of milk in his bed!

Teething becomes a catchall to explain every upset at this age. Every time a baby whimpers or squirms, "it's his teeth." By blaming everything on teeth, parents are likely to miss other reasons for the baby's behavior. Frustration at not being able to do what he wants to do is one reason. He may want to reach or to move or to pay attention. Boredom and other forms of discomfort are other reasons for "teething" complaints.

Teeth bother babies because they are like a foreign body in the gum. They probably feel like a splinter in a finger. The tooth causes swelling around it. When the baby sucks, more blood rushes into the already swollen gum. So he squirms, whimpers, and refuses to suck. If a parent can rub out the initial swelling before she offers him the chance to suck, he can suck painlessly. Whether a child is teething should be easy to determine: if you press on his lower gums in front, he will cry out. A parent should wash her finger and rub vigorously before each feeding. After the first cry, he'll love it. The lower front teeth, the incisors, are usually the only ones that interfere with feedings. After the first two, the baby is used to the dull ache of other teeth as they break through. Teething pains probably don't last more than a few weeks. All of a sudden there is a clink against a cup or spoon. A ridge of tiny white dots has cut through the gum, and it's done! But the timing varies from one baby to another.

Communication

In the fifth month babies begin to play games with their new achievements. They learn to cry more deliberately, to wait to see whether anyone is coming, then to cry out a second time. This is a big step toward a cognitive process known as causality: If I do something, I will get this result.

Parents tend to blame this kind of manipulative crying on teething, on fatigue, or on "being spoiled." Each of these may certainly play a role. If parents think their baby's teeth are the reason he's complaining, they can test it out, as we just suggested. If it's fatigue, the baby can be soothed to rest. He may have to cry a bit before he can relax. If nothing works, maybe his parents have become *too* available and need to try sorting things out.

With the development of this ability to manipulate, an exciting new dialogue has begun! Coughing, sneezing, gagging, and squealing all start out as exploratory behaviors. Gradually, the baby learns to master them, to produce them at will. Eventually, he will learn that "da-da-da-da" calls up his father's face. When he whiningly says "mum-mum-mum-mum," his mother comes running. Soon after, he learns how to master these vocal games and how to use them to manipulate people around him. The ante is raised.

Parents wonder, How do I know when he's manipulating me? It may not be clear at first. But when it happens over and over, there will be signs. Does he cry out, then wait to see whether he gets a response? Does he show in his facial behavior that he's "learned" to get a response? He may even look self-satisfied afterward. This marks a very important achievement—the baby has learned not only to expect responses but to produce them. For the parents, too, this will be a turning point. Instead of automatically responding to the baby's cries and signals, parents must pull back to figure out how far they want to go in responding. At the point where they feel manipulated, they must make a decision. Much of the time, this new dialogue will bring a deeper relationship and new pleasures; nevertheless, the parents' and baby's needs will take some new balancing.

Learning

Motor and cognitive learning are inseparable at this age. The efforts of a four- to five-month-old baby are spent in trying to learn to sit and to use his hands to transfer objects. Both of these activities open up new worlds to explore. Whenever a parent pulls a baby up to sit by pulling on his arms, he will strain to get himself up. By five months, he'll work so hard that he'll come up on stiff legs into a standing position. Standing, he'll look up at an adult as if for approval. Already he is in a hurry to get upright.

Babies at this age can't wait to get going. Some fuss and fuss until a parent sits them up in a chair or lap. But frustration is a powerful force for learning. Parents can show a baby how to pull himself into a sitting position, but it will take a long, frustrating month or so for him to learn to do it. Parents can do what they can to help, but they mustn't feel that they *have* to go to the baby all the time.

If parents get a chair or a swing, the back should be tilted so that the baby is not too upright. He can strain his back if he is slumped forward in it for too long. The motorized swings do soothe a baby and reduce his frustration, but I don't think they are necessary.

Learning to transfer objects from one hand to another is a great step toward playing with objects. A baby at four months should be trying to play with and handle an object. By five months he usually can hand it back and forth. I'd tie several handy objects on a safe string across his crib, as a cradle gym. They should be available to him for handling and exploring. Mouthing, touching, and fingering them all become his way of finding out everything he can about objects.

I am always thrilled when a baby explores my face as I hold him at this age. This is such a tender gesture, and it demonstrates a keen sense of exploration in him. This learning will eventually lead to a sense of "person permanence"—the awareness that persons are real and continue to exist even when out of sight.

Rolling over is an unpredictable milestone for many babies. Many normal babies never roll over. They are contented on their backs or stomachs and don't care whether they turn or not. Fat babies have too much to move and are likely to be inactive. The first time that a baby turns over may be a reflex response. When babies happen to writhe and turn themselves over, the suddenness is coupled with a strange new posture. This frightens them and they cry out. A parent rushes to find them in the new position. But they are overwhelmed, and they may not try it again for weeks.

Parents who hear that other babies are already rolling over wonder whether to teach their baby this skill. I do not recommend it. This motor milestone is the least reliable one. There is no particular time that is appropriate for a baby to be rolling over. It's much too individual. When a parent asks about this, I take the opportunity to discuss the reasons for not comparing one baby with another. Comparisons and competition can put parents under pressure, leading them to push the baby to "catch up." It is much more important to get on his wave-length and value him for what he can and wants to do. When parents value a baby, he'll value himself. Of course, it is very hard not to compare, and that is one way to learn what to expect. But babies know when parents are not happy with them.

When a baby spends all the time on his back, parents wonder how he'll learn to crawl. I assure them that he'll learn to crawl when he's ready, at seven or eight months. If he's on his belly, he can already begin to try to crawl, and he will strengthen his back. If the baby seems frustrated, parents can get down on the floor at his level and make life interesting down there with little games and toys to watch. But this is not necessary. He will learn to crawl eventually and will have learned to do this *himself*.

Looking Ahead

Feeding The exploratory behavior we have spoken about will increase in the next few weeks, so I give parents the following suggestions. The baby will want to hold his own bottle. Hand it to him with the bottom first. Watch him look at it quizzically, then realize that he can turn it around to get the nipple in his mouth. He will have learned something about fulfilling his own expectancy. But you should always sit and hold him when he's eating. Feeding time is much more than food. Communication with the baby is also essential. Studies show that the necessary fluids for digestion (hydrochloric acid in the stomach and duodenal juices in the small intestine) are not activated unless a baby has a pleasant time at a feeding. There is a syndrome called failure to thrive, in which the baby does not gain or grow, despite adequate feeding, when he is not in a nurturing relationship with his environment. At this age, a baby will pause during a feeding for you to talk to him, to look at him, to cuddle him. Then he'll resume his sucking with a pleased look on his face.

When you continue to try the baby on solids, postpone mixed foods, eggs, and wheat until after nine months. As we mentioned earlier, those are the most likely to set off allergies in an infant. When you feed solids, the baby will want to hold one spoon while you feed him from another. Expect him to drop the spoon, look down for it, then look up at you to pick it up. He is learning about object permanence. When you start feeding him from a cup, let him help you. The play and experimentation that accompany a feeding are to be enjoyed and encouraged.

If you are bottle feeding, twenty to twenty-four ounces of formula are adequate for this period. Milk does count before solids, so if the baby is hard to nurse or feed with a bottle, drop back on solids to be sure he gets his milk. You can nurse or give him his bottle twice a day in a dark, quiet room. That way, he'll get the milk he needs to grow and gain. A baby won't gain weight unless he's getting an adequate amount of milk.

Babies will continue to spew out solids at times. They must learn how to eat them. Up to now, they have been sucking only. Many babies put their fingers in their mouths to suck on to help them swallow solids. Parents sometimes feel as if the baby were teasing them by spewing out food. He is not. A strong reaction will only reinforce this. Often, he's already full and really doesn't want the solids. It's a good idea to stop feeding him when he does that. If the baby makes a big mess, wear a raincoat and feed him in a washable chair, but don't restrain his hands. Let him play with feedings in his own way. He must have time to make the transition from sucking. Also, he's just learned to reach and wants to participate by touching his food. If you interfere, you may set up resistances in him about feeding that will make him negative and hard to feed in the future.

Sleeping If a baby has established a going-to-sleep pattern, parents can expect him to continue to stretch out at night. He will still come up to REM sleep, scrabble around in bed, cry out, and then find his pattern to get back down. These patterns for self-comforting and for getting himself to sleep will become even more important to the baby over in the next two months. On a day when a baby has been overstimulated or exposed to many strange events, he is likely to awaken all over again at night. He may need several nights of comforting in order to resume his former pattern of sleeping through.

Making Time for Play The continuing burst of cognitive awareness will affect every part of the baby's day. Not only feeding time but diapering and bath time will become chances for exploration. He'll want to turn one way, then the other, scrabbling around in your slippery hands. This means additional vigilance from parents. A wriggly, slippery baby needs every bit of attention. It is vital *never* to leave a baby alone on the changing or bath table. *Always* keep one hand on a part of him. At some point, when he's sitting, you can bathe him sitting in a little tub or in the sink *if* you have your hot water heater turned down below 120 degrees. Many serious burns occur when a baby turns on the hot water spigot accidentally. One delicious way to bathe a baby is to take him in the tub with you.

Parents wonder how vigorously to clean a baby's genitals. My advice is, Don't be too vigorous—it isn't necessary. For a little girl, secretions from her vagina will help keep her clean. When you immerse her in a bath, she'll get clean once a day. *Never* use bubble bath or detergents with a little girl. They cut the protective mucus in her vagina. Then irritating fluids (detergents) can creep up into her bladder, and bacteria can seed into the unprotected orifice and create cystitis and renal infection. In both sexes, bubble baths and detergents can cause sensitivity rashes and dry out the skin. They should be prohibited for babies. For little boys, there is no need to retract the foreskin.

Don't be too fussy about cleanliness. Bathtime can be a lovely, amusing time to get close to your baby. If you're out working all day, try to fit the bath in when you have time at home for fun. Diapering can be an additional time for games and communication. If necessary, get up early so you can have a leisurely time with the baby in the morning before you leave. Plan to have another as soon as you walk in at the end of the day. He will fall apart and fuss at you when you arrive. He has missed you and saved up his protest all day. But after this period of disintegration, you can have a lovely reconciling time together. Rock him and sing to him. Let him "talk" to you about how awful his day was without you.

Motor Skills In the next two months, the baby will be learning many new and exciting skills. When pulling him up to stand, you can see the excitement on his face. A five-month-old baby *loves* to stand up. He looks around for your approval. Even when he is crying, when you stand him, he gets excited and stops. His long-term goal, after all, is to get on his feet and become upright.

He will try to master sitting in the next two months. At first, he'll sit with a rounded back and a tripod made from his arms. At six months, he'll sit with a stronger back, but he'll still use his arms to balance himself. He can't and won't let go to reach for an object while he's sitting.

Reaching, transferring objects, and mouthing them to explore them will continue as vital parts of learning. The baby will play with one hand by fingering it with the other. If you provide him with a jungle gym, he'll work at it for long periods.

On his stomach, or when he collapses from sitting, he'll be likely to get the concept of moving around. He will conceive of creeping on his belly. He will first learn by pushing himself backward, *away* from his goal. He will cry out with frustration. It is difficult for a parent to watch this frustration. A hand held firmly against the bottom of the baby's feet may help him learn he can push himself forward. In any case, he'll learn from his frustration. I can't emphasize enough that nothing is as powerful as frustration to push a baby to learn—as long as it's not overwhelming for him. Watch him try a new task, get frustrated, but then finally achieve it. He will be so thrilled with himself when *he* finally achieves it! He has done it *himself.* When parents can understand the drive and the intensity in the baby's attempt to learn all these new achievements, they are paving the way to become allies in his development and not sabotaging his inner drive. If they come to me with worries about the baby's frustration, we can make this discussion an important touchpoint.

Stranger Awareness The new burst of awareness in sights and sounds can affect a five- or six-month-old baby's readiness to accept strangers. Before this, he may have been happy as he was handed from one person to another. Parents of four- or five-month-olds proudly tell me that their baby likes everyone and will enter a crowded room without a whimper. This is likely to change soon. I see a new recognition of strangers in my office at the five-month visit. Across my desk from me, he gurgles and goos, smiling invitingly as his mother talks to me. If I let myself be seduced and take him up out of her lap, or if I look him in the face when she puts him on my examining table, I know he will start crying. He will cry relentlessly throughout the entire exam. If, on the other hand, I look past his face and talk softly past him, if I can get her to hover over him while I examine him, I can do an entire exam without upsetting him. I can even give him the necessary inoculation without real upset if I urge her to hold him tight on her shoulder, then quickly shift him and distract him with something to look at. The new field of visual exploration is so powerful that it makes him disregard unpleasant sensations.

A stranger presents a baby with too many new, unfamiliar stimuli. He wants to be able to conquer each one. At this time, grandparents or sitters can cause real upset if they rush at him too quickly or look him in the face when they first meet him. He needs time and space to handle each new sight and sound. This new sensory awareness and the motor achievements of reaching and handling accompany and fuel each other. No wonder life is so exciting and overwhelming!

The new awareness that leads to stranger anxiety also leads to an increase in the baby's ability to protest separations. More than ever, he needs a stable caregiver. If one parent is at home, the baby will still protest an evening baby sitter, and if both parents work away from home, any changes in day care or live-in caregiving will upset the baby.

This change can come as a surprise to parents. "She cries every time I leave her with someone else. This is new. She never used to mind it," said one mother. This is one of those bursts of development when babies get increasingly sensitive to change and appear to be suddenly much more dependent. The acute phase of this sensitivity may last only a week or two, but the need for a steady caregiver will remain.

Often this new dependency coincides with a mother's return to work or with a new caregiver's arrival. If the changes can be made carefully and gradually, the whole family will benefit. The parents will want to leave the baby with someone he knows and is used to. If possible, the parents should let the baby get used to a new caregiver while they are still nearby.

They must know they can rely on any caregiver to understand this new fear of strangers and not get angry about it. This reaction is not easy for anyone. Leaving the baby with a new person for short, gradually lengthening times will ease the transition.

When parents return, the baby can be expected to fall apart and fuss at them. He's saved up this behavior *especially for them*. Parents are usually relieved to hear this. A new parent often tells me, "Every time I leave him with someone else, he cracks up when my husband (or, my wife) or I walk in. The caregiver always says, 'He never cries like that with me!' It hurts to hear that." If parents can take this as reassurance from the caregiver, but also as a sign that *they* are the most important people in their baby's life, the baby's outbursts will be less painful. The reason parents feel all this so deeply is that the wrench of leaving their baby makes them feel vulnerable and guilty.

Parents who must return to work often have deep fears that their babies might be damaged. I can say with conviction that, as long as they find a really nurturing, caring person for him, the baby can adjust without permanent trauma. It will not be the same as having one parent all day, but that can be pretty conflicted for the baby and parent, too. In *Working and Caring*, I describe the qualities to look for in a caregiver at home, or in a center or family day care. Training, as well as warmth and a calm personality, is necessary to understand the needs of a four- to five-month-old. I am very worried about babies in group care where there are more than three infants or four toddlers per well-trained adult.

Together with colleagues, I have studied four-month-old babies in day care chosen for good quality. They seemed to cycle through waking and sleep states over the eight-hour day in a very economical way. They never got too excited or too invested in the caregivers, even though these were trained and good people. But the babies seemed to be saving up. Then, when the parent came to get them, they burst into violent wailing, saving their passion for the people who mattered most to them.

After this crying period, they became alert and intensely interactive with their parents. Babies seem to be able to take in, and adjust to, more than two people. When parents can save some of their own energy for the end of the day and take advantage of this intense reunion, the separation will seem less painful. Sometimes, I encourage parents to sit and rock and sing to the baby when they get home—to talk to him, ask him about his day, and tell him how much they missed him. When parents wonder whether the baby can understand, I explain that he certainly will glean the spirit of it, and they both will be starting a ritual for all the years to come.

7

SEVEN MONTHS

As a seven-month-old baby sails into my office on a parent's arm, I can see that she already participates in being carried. She clings actively. If I come to meet them in the waiting room, she expects to be picked up and holds up her plump arms as her mother or father says, "Come on. We're going in to see the doctor." At this age, most still welcome me at first, grinning as I play with them. They perform and chortle with glee. If a baby looks wary as I come up to her, I ask her mother to hold her. I examine her in her mother's lap. Stranger anxiety is cropping up again. Usually, however, this visit, without inoculations, is a cheerful one in which I can point out to a confident mother each milestone in development. The baby literally overflows with self-importance at this age. She shows off for me across the desk as I talk to her. She hides her face, turning to look back at me. She giggles and squeals in an attempt to attract my attention. If she can't break into my conversation, she will even bounce up in front of her parent or put her hands over his or her mouth in an attempt to interfere. She wants both of us to focus on *her*!

At seven months, babies look around as if they owned the

world. It is a picture-book age. A baby can sit up now, chortling and playing with one toy after another, with a triumphant look. A baby this age will pick up a toy, examine it carefully, mouth it, turn it over and over, then drop it over the table edge. She then looks up expectantly, making some peremptory sound. The parent stoops dutifully to pick it up. If this retrieval game goes on for a while and a parent says, "Don't drop that, I won't pick it up," the baby will look up, sizing up her parent's determination. She may give up her game and recognize that her parent is indeed involved with me, or she may try a few more games—calling "da," "ma," then laughing out loud. If her attempts to compete with me fail, she may give up gracefully and start to play alone with the toys on the table in front of her.

By this age, a baby's personality seems to be predictable—for her parents and for everyone else around her. The tendencies and signs of temperament—a child's style of dealing with her world—that we saw at six weeks are now fully expressed. I like to share my observations about a baby's temperament with parents at this point, so that we both can better understand what is normal for this particular child.

There are several attributes that are incorporated into the concept of temperament. These elements set a constellation of expectancies for how she will cope with new and old events, how she will deal with stress, and they give her parents a frame in which they will work to understand her. Temperament is an important concept for parents, for they can judge a child's reactions within this expectancy. They know when she is her "usual self" and when she's not. When she's not, they can evaluate her for illness or a reaction to stress, and they can begin to recognize transitions just before a spurt in her development. When she deviates from her usual self, a parent must decide which of these events is taking place. If it's a spurt in her development, they may want to understand that spurt before making decisions.

The nine elements we watch for in assessing temperament were pointed out by Stella Chess and Alexander Thomas (see the Bibliography). In brief, they are:

1. Activity level
2. Distractibility

3. Persistence
4. Approach–Withdrawal—How does she handle new and stressful situations?
5. Intensity
6. Adaptability—How does she deal with transitions?
7. Regularity—How predictable is she in sleep, bowel habits, and rhythms during the day?
8. Sensory Threshold—Is she hyper- or hyposensitive to stimuli around her? Is she easily overstimulated?
9. Mood—Is she basically positive or negative in her reactions?

With these as a base, a small child can be characterized, as can the challenge she poses—for herself and for those around her. My first book, *Infants and Mothers*, attempts to map the progress of three different babies—active, quiet, and moderate—as they and their parents progress through the first year. After the first half of the first year has passed, parents and the baby's other caregivers would do well to discuss a baby's emerging personality to make sure they are experiencing the same baby as they prepare for the many decisions ahead.

Sitting alone is a major milestone. As we saw earlier, at five months, a baby must sit up by leaning forward propped on both arms—in a tripod fashion. She is immobilized and unable to change her posture, except by toppling over. At six months, she will have learned to straighten her back and to manage the backward–forward balance. But her arms are still propping her on each side. If she tries to pick up one arm, she will topple to that side. Sitting alone is still very precarious. The baby depends on her steady arms to maintain balance. She still cannot get herself into the sitting posture.

By seven months, a baby no longer needs her arms as props, and can briefly maintain a straight back. She still must not use her arms in any way that is too free, or she will fall to one side. She can dare to play a bit with toys in front of her, but if she falls, she knows she cannot get herself back up to sit. She still plays gingerly and attempts to maintain her exciting new posture. By eight months, she will be assured of freedom in a sitting position. A baby that age can twist around and can lean forward or to one side. She has mastered sitting and is free to experiment with it. Even if she falls, she can probably struggle up again.

Residents in pediatrics and experienced parents can tell how long a child has been sitting by the complexity of her body behavior as she sits. If she is immobilized, she is still a recent achiever. If she can rotate, lean to each side, she's been sitting for at least a month. At the point where she can get into sitting from a flat position, she is demonstrating a familiarity with handling her body in sitting and crawling that speaks of at least a two-month achievement.

Small motor achievements are developing in parallel with this progress in sitting. As a child becomes freer in handling her body, her hands become more and more exciting to her. At six months, her fingers still act in a package. When she grasps an object, she literally rakes it into her palm. By seven months, her dexterity is increasing. As she transfers an object from one hand to another, she begins to explore it with her fingers. In the process, she is gradually separating her forefinger and thumb for more skilled activity. By eight months, she will be

Motor Skills

able to use thumb and forefinger to make a pincer for picking up small objects. As she explores this new achievement, she picks up every small bit she can find. Fuzz on the floor, a dropped aspirin tablet, a small piece of dog food—all become exciting to her. She carries everything to her mouth for further exploration. This is a time for careful cleanup of a baby's entire environment, with no dangerous bits left around.

The pincer grasp, the separation of the thumb and forefinger for skilled behavior, is one of the distinctive human attributes separating us from the great apes. "The hands," said Maria Montessori, "are the instruments of human intelligence." Speech and our skill in manual dexterity mark us for more complex achievements. No wonder a baby is so excited by this skill. She practices it all day.

Soon she begins to explore her world with her fingers. Pointing at objects to engage adults around her, putting a forefinger into every orifice, including electrical outlets, she finds marvelous new uses for her separated fingers. The thumb and forefinger are used to explore the faces of her beloved adults, to explore every possible hole or hidden area. They have become powerful extensions of her eyes and her mouth. Before this, only her mouth was used to evaluate the world of objects and people. Now, she can extend this exploration with her hands.

By this time, nearly all babies show a reliable preference for one hand or the other. They have probably been demonstrating a pattern in the months before, but by now they suck on the less dominant hand in order to free up the dominant one for exploratory behavior. At this seven- to eight-months spurt in small motor achievements, the preferred hand can be easily determined. If an adult offers a toy in the midline, a baby's dominant hand will come forward first. The two major fingers of the dominant hand will be utilized most for exploration. We unconsciously push a baby to be right-handed. When we hand an object to a baby, we almost invariably hand it to her right side. If she is left-handed, she must reach across her midline to grasp it.

Curiously, a child begins to lose interest in her feet at this time, for the baby spends less of the day on her back, watching her toes. As she learns to stand, her feet will actually even become less agile, less like fingers.

Learning to crawl offers another thrust toward independence. By seven months, most babies start to creep on their
bellies. Toppling from sitting or rolling over from the back, a
baby of this age shows her determination to get going. She
learns to get herself onto her abdomen so that she can practice
moving forward on her belly. *Creeping* is the name for wriggling along on one's stomach. At eight months, as a baby
achieves forward creeping, she will begin to add to it. She is
likely to get up on all four extremities, rocking backward and
forward, to flop on her face and body at the end. Although
this may hurt, very few babies cry out when they have brought
it on themselves. The urge to achieve is too powerful and
counterbalances any discomfort.

As the baby first attempts to coordinate her legs and arms,
she recaptures the reflex swimming behaviors seen in the first
few months. She begins to crawl backward like a crab. *Crawling* is the name for moving on elbows and knees. Each child
who crawls has a distinctive way of doing so, but many children never crawl. There is a myth that unless a child crawls,
he'll never be coordinated and she'll have learning problems
later. This is groundless. I have seen many children who never
crawled, but who walked and learned in perfectly normal
sequence. Many children go from sitting to standing to walking, never creeping or crawling. Crawling is not a necessary
milestone.

When a baby does begin to crawl, her parents can see the
consternation in her face as she gets further and further away
from her desired goal. Her frustration mounts. She may
scream out as her newly coordinating legs and arms carry her
backward. As we mentioned earlier, a parent can place a firm
hand against her feet. She will press herself forward against
this hand. The surprise and joy that she feels may well fuel her
to learn how to adapt her movements to be able to repeat the
forward motion on her own. But she is likely to have a month
or so of repeated frustration. Parents can comfort and support, but they needn't try to spare the child these tortured
efforts as she begins to learn a new skill.

As mentioned earlier, parents at this stage need to protect
a child from her own inquisitiveness. Well before this age, all

parents should inspect their houses for potential dangers to an exploring, ingenious child. They should look for uncovered electrical outlets, stairs that need gates, and poisons or medicines in or out of cupboards. Babies find everything. The next months will be made up of unexpected surprises, and parents must be prepared for them. Parents should get ipecac to induce vomiting in case of an ingestion, and they should record next to each phone the phone numbers of the nearest poison control center, the emergency room of the nearest hospital, and the ambulance. Being prepared is important. After an emergency has happened, parents are too overwhelmed to function properly.

Feeding The new motor skills of sitting and exploring, and of the fascinating pincer grasp, are major touchpoints of development affecting all aspects of a child's life. In particular, they change the feeding scene radically. A parent who can use these skills to enhance the child's sense of her own independence in the feeding area will ward off many problems. Learning to play with a cup and to handle it herself is one exciting goal for the baby. Although she certainly isn't ready to gulp very much from a glass or cup, she will want to try. When a parent is drinking from a glass, he can offer her a sip. Imitation is always a force for learning. If she wants to try to master the cup, the parent can let her have an empty one to play with, while feeding her from another. As she gets into a practicing phase, she can try her cup in the bathtub. She can drink and pour bathwater and have a great time sloshing about, all the while learning to master the cup.

The baby needn't be expected to be a step ahead too often, however. Even if parents fill both the baby's hands—a piece of zwieback in one hand and a spoon in the other—she will drop her things to grab the parents'. Or she'll get diverted to play with her toast or her spoon. Parents need to respect this. Feeding is just not as important now as exploration. Parents who forge on with the usual boring routine may be successful, but they are likely to set up vibes of resistance. It's just not worth it. Expecting the baby to explore in her own way for a little while and letting feedings go are okay. She'll come back with renewed interest when she's mastered her new skills.

This is an arena where a parent's goals and the baby's may conflict. It is also an arena in which she will always win. Parents can step back and enjoy her new skills. She'll return to a rounded diet after she has mastered them, but her burst of learning will supersede everything else. Fortunately, a child's food needs can be met if she has two to three good milk feedings (morning, noon, and night). If necessary, she can be awakened for one more at 10:00 P.M. before her parents go to bed.

Although solid foods have become a major part of most babies' feeding schedule, they are not as important as milk and vitamins. If the baby is refusing solids during this spurt, I would emphasize fortified cereal or meat for its iron. Parents can offer them at whatever feeding she will accept them. Two or three teaspoons of solids will tide a baby over a twenty-four-hour period at this time. Feeding her a "rounded diet" is often a parental goal, but it isn't necessary.

The new pincer grasp, of course, leads to splendid new fun at feeding. A parent needs to offer one or two soft bits of food at the beginning of each feeding. As these go down, she can be offered another. She won't be able to chew for a long time, but she can gum up soft bits. Little bits of banana, of cooked potato or vegetable, soft parts of toast, even bits of soft hamburger or a scrambled egg will do.

As the bits get eaten, explored, fingered, dropped, smeared, or otherwise demolished, two more can be put in front of her. If someone offers too many bits, she'll just mash them or sweep them over the side of her feeding table. Parents should be prepared for some bits to be extruded back at them or drooled down the side of her chin. The goal is to enhance this new adventure. She may be so intent and excited that she'll let someone feed her regular sloppy food while she is trying to master the lumps on her tray. But she may resist being fed at all. Parents shouldn't persist; otherwise, they'll compound the resistance. This is likely to last only a week or so; she wants to be in control.

Sleeping   Although the baby may have been sleeping eight to twelve
hours a night prior to this, the excitement and frustration of
learning new skills, such as sitting, creeping, crawling, and the
new fine motor tasks, carry over into the night. Her naps may
be disrupted, too, as she practices her new skills in bed. She
may be harder and harder to put down. This new disruption
is frustrating to parents who have just begun to enjoy some
quiet evenings.

Like other touchpoints, this change is a step back that
precedes a big stride forward. I try to help parents by offering
the following suggestions.

Renew your bedtime ritual to let your baby know how
important that is to her and to you. She still needs two naps
or two breaks in the day—midmorning and midafternoon. So,
whether she sleeps or not, she should go into her bed and
room. If necessary, you can sit quietly by, not responding or
telling her to settle down to rest. Pat her quietly and rhythmically, but without looking at or responding to her. She may
not like it, but she'll soon learn that you mean business—that
this is the bedtime ritual and not a game.

If you are away all day, be sure her daytime caregiver gives
her a long afternoon nap. Then, she'll be ready to stay up
longer in the evening. But at the point where she begins to get
too high or shows signs of disintegrating, remember that she
needs to go to bed. It's awfully easy to forget that she needs
to go down at a certain point. Your firmness and your regular
routine will help her. If you are still ambivalent, your baby will
sense that and push you. Then she'll build up with more and
more disintegration, desperately unable to give up. Once in the
bedroom, you may have to try rocking and soothing, but with
the firm conviction that she is going to bed.

Sometimes babies this age start waking again at 2:00 and
6:00 A.M. They cry out pitifully but don't really seem awake.
Sometimes, they're up on their arms and knees, rocking away,
not even awake. Parents wonder whether to wake the baby,
feed her, and then put her back down. Since this is the REM
or light sleep behavior that we've described earlier and that

occurs rhythmically every four hours in most people, I advise parents not to get her up. I would advise parents not to wake the baby and not to take her out of her crib. In fact, I wouldn't reinforce this frustrated behavior in any way. At most, I'd help the baby get herself back down by soothing, patting, and softly crooning, or by offering her pacifier or lovey. Even if she comes to full waking with a parent there, I'd try to do as little as possible but encourage her to find her own pattern for returning to deep sleep. Parents who get her up at this stage may have to be part of her sleep pattern for a long time to come.

Parents who have been away all day have the hardest time with this night waking. It is really more their problem than the baby's, and one I can surely understand. But parents with heavy work schedules also need sleep, and eventually the night waking will wear down the whole family.

Communication

At seven to eight months, a baby not only uses syllables with a consonant and a vowel ("da," "ma," "ba"), but she practices them. She will trill and use them in scales in the morning while she lies in her bed. She will try them over and over, using them to call adoring adults to her. Rarely will she assign the proper syllable to the proper person. Babies this age can probably understand "no," but they do not respond to it.

All the bursts in motor and cognitive development make games and play more fun for parents. Each parent should play with the baby in an active way that suits his or her own temperament. Mothers at this stage will warn fathers that "they're too rough." Fathers may say, "You are too soft with her. You give up too easily. Can't you see she's asking for more?" Parents should respect these differences and use them. In this way, a baby learns that each parent is a separate and distinct individual. There is no need to treat her alike.

Learning

In her play, the baby will be testing her new cognitive skills. She will hide a toy under a cloth, pull the cloth off, and gleefully greet it with an "ooh" and "aah." A sense of object permanence—knowing the object hasn't gone just because it has gotten out of sight—is beginning, and she wants to explore its facets. As she learns to creep or to crawl, she struggles to reach a coveted object. If she does, she explores it and then begins to lose interest in it, shoving it just out of reach. Then, as she strives once again to get to it, its value to her is newly heightened.

Mirrors have been an interest for a month or more. As she looks at herself, she seems to try to get a response from her image. She may even reach out to try to touch herself in the mirror. When she gets a response, she may even startle with surprise. At about seven to eight months, if her parents come up from behind her, she may first try to react to them in the mirror. Then, she will turn around to see where the familiar people really are. She is learning about space and spatial relationships.

Stranger awareness accompanies the bursts in cognitive development that continue dramatically. She hunts for lost toys and will lift a cloth or a box to find them. She experiments with person permanence by playing peekaboo games. She is imitative in games involving facial expressions, plus sputtering and other sounds. In the next two months her cognitive development will be thrilling to watch and enjoy. Parents shouldn't get too caught up in her frustrations. She can master them—and she will.

In this period of rapid learning about clues from those around her, a baby will wait at the end of the day for a noise that lets her know a parent is coming home. Her sensitivity will need to be respected in many ways. Exposing her to noises that are too loud or changes that are too abrupt, or even leaving her in a familiar environment or with someone who has been familiar before, will likely bring out the fragility that accompanies this period of rapid learning. All the baby's energy is going into mastery and exploration of these new cognitive capacities.

Person permanence is beginning to follow the same course as object permanence. What does this mean? For parents who want to avoid a traumatic episode, I give the following advice. Don't let strangers or family rush up to the baby to hold her.

Warn grandparents that they'll do well to wait until she's looked them over and begun to lose her initial wariness before they pick her up. Expect necessary separations, such as those at day care or substitute care, to be painful and noisy. Always let her know when you're leaving, and be sure she's in caring hands. When you return, let her know you've missed her. Reduce any unnecessary separations and changes to a minimum for a while.

Parents can play peekaboo and other games that play out this anxiety about separations and leaving. Go around the corner and come back. Let her explore your face, your clothes. Play mirror games with her. And have important strangers enter her life so that she can learn about them. You don't need to overprotect her. But you do need to realize that she's in a major and demanding spurt in her development—a touchpoint in these cognitive and social areas.

Looking Ahead   **Feeding** The issues around feeding will continue to be those
of the child's wanting to explore and to be in control. These
intensify. When she refuses to be fed, be ready with finger food
or a breadstick or zwieback to let her play with. Don't hover
over her. Move around the kitchen, tending to your business.
If you concentrate on her, she'll tend to show off and tease you
by dropping food or by refusing it. Try the spoon. Let her play
with it while you feed her from another one. She may accept
all you offer her while she's distracted. But she may not. If not,
quit. Once again, don't try to control her play or feed her when
she's refusing. It's not worth it.

   If she doesn't eat, will she get hungry later? If you haven't created a feud, she probably will, but her desire for mastery is as strong as any instinctive urge at this time.

Sleeping Before a baby crawls or tries to pull up to stand, or as she learns about strangers, she may awaken all over again. Fall back on the routines you've used before to help her get herself back down to sleep.

During the day, when she's frustrated with a new learning task, help her learn how to comfort herself. Reinforce her with *one* special toy or a blanket. If she has learned to suck on her fingers or a pacifier, help her find them when she's upset or is falling apart. When she settles, tell her how well she's done.

Safety This is the period when a playpen may help, because it means she's safe when you leave her. If you don't use one, be sure you have a safe room in the house for her. Her new-found mobility and the need to satisfy her inquisitive cognitive burst will lead her into any available trouble. Be prepared!

Spoiling At this visit, many parents again express worries about spoiling a child. If they are worried about giving a baby of eight or nine months too much love and attention, that is a needless worry. My concept of a spoiled child is that of an anxious child, searching for limits. If no one provides them, she must keep searching, testing. In the coming months, you will see behavior that is clearly a bid for such limits. When a child first crawls up to the TV set and looks around to be *sure* you are watching, this is what is going on. You can remove her and/or distract her. But make the limits clear from the start. Discipline is a parental responsibility: to provide small children with firm limits that they can then incorporate for themselves takes years to achieve, so don't get frustrated.

8

NINE MONTHS

A nine-month-old baby rarely spends the visit at my office in his mother's or father's lap. He is just as eager to slip to the floor or heave himself up to standing at a chair or table as his parents are to show off these amazing accomplishments. Most of the questions at this visit will have something to do with his motor development. With a baby so driven to move around, everything—feeding, sleeping, diapering—will be different. New issues of safety, discipline, and anxiety pop up daily as the baby wriggles, rolls, crawls, creeps, pulls, and topples his way from dawn to dusk.

The new dramas and conflicts bring a rebalancing of the family routine and lead parents to reach out for support. The motor spurt and the regression in sleep and feeding that usually occur make this period a perfect touchpoint, an opportunity for me to reach out to support parents.

One or the other of the parents of this nine-month-old powerhouse will arrive ready to burst. "Well, how are you?" I ask, waiting for the opening blast. "Awful," says the mother. "Oh?" "Yes, Alexander has totally fallen apart. He's either charging around, bawling, or sucking his thumb and glaring at me. He refuses the food I try to feed him. He just won't eat for me, and if you want the whole works, I'm not getting any sleep. He drives all day and all night. He wakes up at least once or twice every night. He's a mess, and so am I!''

After listening carefully, I hope to help the parents appreciate their child's side of all this. Perhaps, I suggest, he is difficult and disorganized because he's working on new skills. As he does, feeding and sleep, in particular, are likely to become difficult.

Learning to stand begins at this point. Given anything to grab—any chair or table will do—a baby will begin to pull himself up. Legs wide apart, body arched forward, he'll grunt and strain against gravity. He'll teeter as he clutches the table edge. When he gets there, he'll stand for long periods. In my office, if I try to interrupt him by offering him a toy, or by picking him up to examine him, he'll fix me with a withering look that says, "Leave me alone. Can't you see I'm busy?" If he starts to fuss with frustration on my table, he can easily be stopped by supporting him to stand in an upright position. Once up, he will grin with pleasure. His goal is obvious, and his focused intent is so strong that he vehemently protests any interference.

Motor Skills

Babies at this age will stand as long as they can, then they will cry, but in frustration rather than in pain. If they fall, they wail. The fall doesn't hurt, but the thrill of standing is gone and that's what hurts.

Thank goodness for flexible skulls and the soft spot on babies' skulls. Obviously, nature meant their heads to be cushioned for falls. For the first two years, the skull in a baby is pliable and gives with each blow. The brain isn't bruised, as it can be when adults fall or hit their heads. Nature has prepared. The soft spot (or fontanel) doesn't close, and the bones of the skull don't cement until after babies have achieved a safer balance and are walking well at eighteen months.

Despite this protection, parents must be watchful. If a baby doesn't cry right away after falling, or gets knocked out, it could be the sign of a concussion. I'd be sure that you have a rug under him at the places where he practices standing. A

baby can probably take a knock on the head from a wooden floor, but not a concrete one. After a few falls, a baby begins to learn how to fold in the middle. By poking out his bottom, he gradually learns to balance and to let himself down slowly, with a sedate plop.

Movement is the ultimate goal. When standing and clinging, a baby is pretty immobilized. But he is already yearning to go forward. Given an upturned chair or a stroller, he will learn very quickly how to push it forward as he hangs on. Early American antique chairs are flattened on their back surfaces where Pilgrim toddlers pushed them ahead as they learned to walk. The drive to be upright and to get going is built into the human infant.

Parents often ask at this visit whether to buy the baby shoes. I don't recommend it. If he's barefoot, the toes grip the ground and help him learn to balance. In shoes, he'll slip and teeter more. After he's walking, stiff, solid shoes are good because they make him grip the sole to flex his foot. That will give him a stronger arch.

A baby this age can often get from his belly into a sitting position and then pull on up to standing. What a complex set of motor skills he has mastered in only nine months! All this has given him a sense of being able to conquer his body and of achieving everything he wants to achieve. Now comes the world from a standing position! He is bound to work at such a plum all day and all night. He will have it as a goal as soon as he wakens in the morning, and he'll relive it at night, his unconscious pressing him into action during every light sleep cycle. No wonder he's "falling apart."

As he stands, holding on, he finds all kinds of ways to test his new trick. If music comes on, he tries to dance to it. Everyone around gushes with approval. Dancing is fun! Next, he might try to walk sideways along furniture. That works, too! He can get from one place to another. Now, the forbidden objects on tables become accessible. The world is no longer flat. He has added a third dimension.

Early Discipline   The world of parents has changed, too. Instead of simply applauding every new trick, they must decide about "no's."

Should they remove previous objects, or should they forbid certain things and try to restrict the scope of the baby's new excitement? Stoves, lamps, washing machines, TVs, and personal computers have become fair game. Houseplants, the leaves of which may be toxic, are so attractive all of a sudden. How can a parent decide when to remove temptation and when to discipline? In my experience, the fewer conflicts, the better. The most important issues, such as not touching the stove, are better learned if they aren't diluted by too many piddling ones. So, I would remove the attractions that are easy to move and block off the dangerous, large ones with a chair or furniture, leaving very few for conflict.

Although a parent can divert the baby's attention at this age, his negativism is coming soon. Distraction works only for unimportant issues and can too easily turn into a game. Now is the time to prepare for the negativism of the second year, for everyone's sake. Parents ask me how early discipline begins. The first time the baby crawls to the TV or to the radiator and *looks around* to be sure you're watching, he is asking for discipline. He demonstrates his awareness of the forbidden, and his need for limits. It is now time for parents to recognize the baby's bid for their participation in learning how to stop himself (see chapter 19). This is the first touchpoint in learning when and how to discipline. Parents must decide how to face it and start practicing. It's a long road!

Another heart-stopping surprise in store for parents of nine-month-old babies is to find them halfway up the stairs. Unless they can be there all the time to help the baby, they need to get a gate for each end of the stairs. Later, they can teach him how to go up and down, but it's too early for that now.

The bathtub is another scene of joy and danger. The first and vital rule is: *Never* leave a baby alone in the tub, even for a moment. He could fall down and breathe in water. It would frighten him at best, and it could be serious at worst. If a child will be anywhere near a swimming pool, now is the time to be sure it's either covered safely or completely fenced in. As a pediatrician, I've seen too many children with brain damage from nearly drowning in pools not to feel adamant on this point.

As for the rest of the house, the surest thing is to baby-proof it. If parents can't do it all, they should do one or two rooms and make sure that is where the baby stays.

Sleep As we said earlier, a baby who is learning to get up to standing will practice at night, too. This becomes another touchpoint, as I emphasize the decisions parents must make to reinforce sleep as *his* issue. At every REM cycle, his new motor goal will emerge as the baby moves into light sleep. When put to bed, a baby will stand up in the crib as soon as the parent leaves the room. If you put him down, up he comes again—up to ten or more times.

Here's what I tell parents. To overcome this, each time you go back, put him down firmly and tuck him in tightly. After the second or third episode of standing, just stay there holding him down and soothing him to sleep. He'll fight and struggle and screech. But don't fight back. That's too exciting. Be firmer than he is. He certainly will need his lovey to help him down, but he won't accept it gracefully. He needs to know for certain that you mean it's time for bed.

A sleep ritual assumes new importance at this time. I'd suggest that you use the breast or bottle as part of the routine in putting him down to sleep. Do not leave him in bed with milk in a bottle, however, as we said earlier. This will damage his baby teeth. Feed him in your arms, rocking and singing to quiet him. But don't put him to sleep in your arms. Put him into his crib while he's still awake. Give him a blanket or a toy to cuddle as a lovey. Sit by him and pat him down. Once again, your goal is for him to develop his own pattern for getting himself to sleep. It may take time, but it's worth it.

For some babies, self-comforting takes the form of rocking. They rock vigorously, often making the crib bang on the wall. They seem to enjoy the noise. Since this rocking calms the baby down, I wouldn't stop it. The loud noise (or destruction to the wall) can be handled by putting the crib posts in rubber casters that don't move. Then, the baby can rock and squeak to his heart's content, but his bed won't move. Of course, the screws on the crib will need tightening from time to time.

Usually, after the child starts to walk and has become successful with large motor achievements, he'll be less frustrated at night, and the rocking will slow down. But some children rock at night as part of a pattern of relaxation for several years. This isn't a sign of anything serious. Perhaps introducing a special toy or blanket to cuddle will replace the rocking, but if it doesn't, I wouldn't worry. He needs his own pattern if he's to be independent at night, and for some babies, this is what it takes.

Each new spurt in development will have set off a new chance for learning to get to sleep. Each time it should get easier, especially if parents are determined. As the child gets older and more sophisticated, he'll try more and more interesting ways to divert them from the task of putting him to sleep in the first place. But he is also learning richer and richer self-comforting techniques, and he's learning new limits for himself.

Often parents will tell me that their baby seems to get "higher and higher" at night. I suggest that he's telling them something. He *needs* to crash. Few children can crash on their own. Most need a push from their parents. At the point where he's had enough and is getting less and less organized, that's a sure sign that he needs someone to calm him and put him down. When both parents are away at work all day, it's difficult to be firm and leave the child at night. If they watch for the time when the baby usually needs to give up, and they make bedtime into a cozy, regular routine, everyone in the family will learn to rely on it. The caregiver should avoid having the child take a long nap in the afternoon.

Sometimes a mother will say to me, "But he gets absolutely desperate! I *have* to help him get down. He gets stuck at the side of the crib and can't get down. He's frightened." When I ask whether the baby can get himself down when he stands up on furniture during the day, she usually replies, "Oh, yes! He's great during the day. He can let himself down very gently." This is my cue to suggest that the baby probably doesn't completely forget at night. Why not go in and give him a little shove to see whether he won't fold in the middle? A reminder like this, with a few soothing words, may be all it takes. After a few nights, he'll know he can do it for himself. Babies learn very quickly to incorporate a learned task into their REM cycle. If they call out for help, parents can call back to say they're there. But it is the baby's job to let himself down and curl up to go to sleep.

An occasional parent will wonder whether to strap a baby in bed to prevent this. I don't like the idea of straps or harnesses at all. A little patient teaching will result in learning patterns that will be important to the child for years. This touchpoint is an opportunity for parents to learn how to help him toward independence, in this case, at night.

Feeding   Mealtime is not exempt from the tyranny of the new motor prowess. "He won't let me feed him anymore," a mother will announce. "He refuses almost everything I offer him. He just bounces up and down in his chair." As usual, the best policy is not to fight but to join. I offer parents the following tips. Enlist the baby's fingers and curiosity. The more feeding he can do for himself now, the better. While you're working around, leave a variety of important foods—including protein (eggs, cheese, meat), cereal, fruit, and vegetables—in front of him. Give him a few soft bits at a time and stay out of the feeding. He'll love to make his own choices and to do all his own feeding. He may let you feed him soft foods while he's involved in feeding himself with both hands; but then again, he may not. By now, he needs to do most of it himself.

Instead of struggling with him to keep a cup of liquid upright, let him have a cup. Since he will usually turn it upside down, put only a sip in it at a time. He'll be excited about drinking by himself, if he can. Babies enjoy cups or little plastic thermoses with spouts as a transition to a real cup.

While mastering a spoon is not likely to happen until well into the second year, learning to imitate with one, or clank and clatter, is fun for babies of nine and ten months. Again, let him have his own, while you wield yours.

All the new distractions make parents think of weaning. Some worry that if they wait too long, the baby will get too negative about giving up the breast or bottle. I don't agree. When a baby shows signs of wanting to give them up, parents should by all means follow him. But there's no real reason that

I know of, otherwise. Certainly, there isn't a critical time when weaning is easier, a moment that will never happen again. There are many points in a baby's development when he'll be more interested in learning about other things than he is about being fed by bottle or breast. Food will take second place many times. As a background to all these forays into independence, it may be critical to hang on to the lovely, warm, secure ritual of feeding him milk. All the self-feeding of solids is independent. Why not let him regress for milk—and be sure he's getting enough that way. Apart from nursing or bottle feeding, meals for a nine-month-old baby cannot be long and leisurely. When he starts bouncing up and down and stops eating, he's saying he's bored. Parents need to put him down out of the feeding chair right away and not keep pursuing him with more food. Also, he shouldn't be fed between meals. By letting him wait until the next feeding time, he'll learn the mealtime routine.

When parents ask about weaning a baby, my advice is, Start with eliminating the breast-feeding in the middle of the day. Save night and early morning for the last. Be sure he gets enough milk from the cup (sixteen ounces) as you wean from the breast, for once you start weaning, your own milk will decrease, and you won't be able to depend on it. If you want to keep the nursing routine at night and in the morning for the sake of closeness, don't hesitate. It's such a nice way to start and to end the day. Again, I wouldn't advise that you put the baby to sleep in your arms: put him down when he's quiet but not yet asleep, and let him do the rest. (For detailed advice from experienced mothers on weaning, see Huggins in the Bibliography.)

Learning

New motor independence brings the need for learning about danger. For instance, soon after he learns to crawl, a baby learns that he can endanger himself by crawling over the edge of a surface. The eminent child development researcher Robert Emde and his colleagues used this awareness of a cliff to devise a fascinating experiment to test the concept of "referencing." They demonstrated that when a baby makes a decision, he uses cues from his parents—he "references" their approval or disapproval. If he is allowed to crawl across a transparent plastic surface with a visual "cliff" below it, he stops at the edge of the cliff. Although he could keep crawling safely, he takes note of the drop off of the table top and stops himself on the plastic surface. If his mother is stationed across the table, giving him facial clues, he watches for them. If she smiles at him, he keeps crawling across the perceived danger. If she frowns and looks warningly, he stops and won't keep going. This experiment dramatizes a baby's capacity to use his parents to help him make important judgments. He takes in all sorts of cues from them—facial behavior and gestures, as well as speech—to help him recognize attitudes and their meaning for him.

Peekaboo and other repetitive games—such as banging foreheads over and over—are a way a baby begins to test and to develop expectancies. If you play at gently banging a baby's forehead in a rhythm, he'll close his eyes for each bang. Then, if you change the rhythm slightly, he'll close his eyes on time, expecting you to come. When you don't, he'll look up at you and giggle. He's developed an expectancy and loves the violation of it.

Understanding of object permanence ("The object is still there even though I can't see it") is changing to understanding of person permanence ("If mommy and daddy go in another room, they'll still exist"). Peekaboo and games that involve hiding an object or a person explore this concept. By playing with these repetitions over and over, the baby learns mastery. He learns he can control them, can produce them. He needn't be frightened of giving something up, because it will return. He learns this with objects that are neutral. Peekaboo and hiding games are more exciting because they involve people. The development of trust in your own environment is intimately tied to mastering object and person permanence. A baby will test rhythms in these games, as well, breaking the rhythm to laugh. If you break the rhythm, he looks at you, grinning and waiting. This involves a sense of timing. These games prepare the way for communication, for speaking and sharing the rhythm of conversation later on.

Showing-off games—clapping, "so big," "bye-bye,"and so

on—all provide the baby a chance to play with adults. The excitement of these games comes from adult approval. These are grandparents' games! They tap his newfound skills in imitation—one of the most powerful learning modes a baby of this age has at his disposal.

The baby will try out lots of new sounds, like "ga-ga," "ma-ma," "ba-ba," "bye-bye," but they may not yet attach to specific meanings. Speech sounds are explored. In bed, he can trill, use inflections, or try out a new sound or syllable over and over. He uses them to call his parents to him. Crying out is not his only ploy now. He can enlarge on it by using gestures and syllables as he begins to try to manipulate his parents.

Causality is a new concept for a nine-month-old and is just surfacing. How do things work? What makes a truck run? At this age, exploration is confined to such efforts as pushing on a truck to make the wheels turn. The child may push it ahead of himself to go after it. This is already an example of testing out his space, mastering it. But, at some point, he will turn the truck over to examine its wheels. It is as if he wants to know how the truck goes—just when he's learning how to make himself go.

Expectation of Success or Failure By nine months, we can tell by a baby's behavior whether he expects to succeed or to fail at the tasks he sets for himself or that others set for him. We often have to assess babies at Boston's Children's Hospital about whom we know very little. As we offer a nine-month-old a task on the infant assessment scale that we use, we observe his behavior, for that is his language. For instance, we can tell a great deal about a baby by such a simple test as handing him two blocks the same size. The baby who expects to succeed with new tasks will grab them, mouth one, rub it in his hair, and then often drop it to see if an adult will give it back. Finally, after lots of testing and exploring, he will put the two together, showing that he knows they are the same size. Then, he'll look up at the person examining him with a delighted, proud expression. He expects to be praised.

In contrast, a baby who expects to fail may dutifully take the two blocks. He doesn't do much with them, as though he realizes that no one will care. He brings the two blocks close to each other, showing that he is able to see that they are the same size, but then slides them right past. He gives the observer a dull look, as if to express his sense of failure, or as if to say, "Hit me. I can't do it. I deserve to fail." Later on, at twelve months, the same baby might knock down a block that he has piled up on another, as if by accident, and look up with the same cowed, hopeless expression. At 15 months, when such a child trips, he looks up with a cowed look of failure. He doesn't expect success.

At nine months, we don't know whether this expectation to fail comes from within the baby or from his outside environment. If he comes from a chaotic household that never rewards him, we know that it is environmental and that he's never been encouraged to succeed. If not, parents and pediatrician should look at him more closely. He may be showing that he has problems in integrating information for learning. He may have a learning disability and be unable to take in cues, integrate them, and respond to them without cost. Or he may be hypersensitive and attentionally disordered. A child who can't stay at a task long enough, or one with mild neuromotor problems, can be saying through his behavior that any task is so difficult that he expects to fail. Such children need long, patient, respectful help. Their disabilities can be overcome in time if they are understood. The most serious deficit for a learning disabled or minimally impaired child is not the disorder itself; it's the poor self-image and the expectation to fail. If we can identify the disorder early, maybe we can prevent these serious consequences. I always watch a child at this age for evidence of inner excitement or recognition of success as he tackles a problem.

Looking Ahead   **Feeding** From now on, the baby will need to have more and more control over feeding. When I stress this with parents, mothers especially will say, "But I *need* to get a rounded diet into him." Parents must remember that, at this age, food is not the main issue. The baby's need to imitate, to explore, to begin to learn to refuse takes priority. By a year, he must be able to control the situation. I would urge both parents to reconsider any attempts to dominate meals and, instead, to make it a period of interplay and of learning. When our first child was a year old, her antics, refusals, and explorations at the table nearly gave me an ulcer. We learned to let her feed herself. Then, she could either join us at mealtime or she could play near the table, but not on it. You can't expect too much in the way of manners or of a "rounded diet" at this age. It's too important to the child to begin to learn to feed himself. The difficulty for most parents is that food was overemphasized in their own past. It's hard not to perpetuate that pressure.

Sleeping With a nine-month-old, I tell parents, expect the baby to start awakening at night with each new motor task— standing, cruising, and walking. Learning these is so exciting. As we saw, the excitement, as well as the frustration, carries over into the night, surfacing in light sleep. Be ready to keep reinstituting a comforting but firm pattern, helping the baby to put himself back to sleep at each cycle. I would use the same ritual you use for any impending separation. Warn him that nap or bedtime is coming. When he protests, comfort him, but let him know you still mean it.

Toilet Training You may already recognize one of the causes of problems in the area of toilet learning: pressure on parents from outside to train the baby early. Since the goal will be to train himself, there is absolutely no reason to start now. If you did, you'd be training yourself or training the baby's sphincters, as people did in the old days when they didn't have diaper services. As I warn parents, you may get a potty seat in the mail for your child's first birthday from one of the grandparents. This present will make you feel guilty that you haven't thought of it yet. The present will come with the unspoken message, Now's the time to get started. It's not. When the "present" arrives, thank the senders for the seat and tell them you do have a plan. When the baby is two years old, he'll be ready to do it for himself. You plan to wait until then, when it will be easy and nonproblematic. When further suggestions are made, ignore them or point out that you have plenty else to worry about.

Separation In the next few months, separations will get more difficult. Be sure to prepare the baby whenever you must go away. At first, leave him for only brief periods with someone he knows. When you return, let him know you're back. Gradually increase the time. This stage will pass, but it can be pretty horrendous. At this stage of development, he is developing the concept of becoming independent and moving away. As he does, he will become more *dependent*.

All transitions are bigger now, because they are fraught with more implications. When the baby is in day care, morning leavings will be hard. This is a precursor to the baby's growing independence. It's a good time to evaluate how the caregivers are handling the baby. Drop by at unexpected times. See whether he's happy or not. Look to see whether the day-care people are sensitive to his rhythms or not—sleep, play, feeding, and so on. Also, when he looks at them, are they sensitive to him, do they offer respect and a caring look? If so, it will help with your own separation. If not, it may be time to change.

At the end of the day, continue to have a close time with him, perhaps in a rocking chair. Your anguish at being away from him will convey itself, but it's part of your caring. Recognizing these feelings will bring you closer.

Safety Review your safety precautions periodically. With each new developmental stage, especially these new motor triumphs, you'll need to reevaluate all you've done before. Most children's hospitals and toy stores have safety booklets to remind you of all the traps you might have forgotten (see also Boston Children's Hospital *New Child Health Encyclopedia* in the Bibliography).

9

ONE YEAR

Getting through the first year deserves a celebration. Every baby album usually has a photo of a chubby one-year-old about to demolish the cake with its one candle. This birthday may also be worth savoring as the quiet before the storm. All of the baby's behavior is likely to go into a period of disorganization soon, before the next spurt. Just before she walks, the toddler-to-be starts waking every four hours at night. She screams every time a parent walks away from her. Under the surface is a realization that she wants to be the one to walk away. Every task may bring on a burst of angry frustration, as does every confrontation or request. All this turbulence is stirred up by the new goal—walking, and on to independence!

I remember a family, whom we'll call Lowry, coming for an appointment with their one-year-old daughter. From inside my office, I knew they'd arrived. When I walked out to the waiting room to greet them, I was met with screeches of protest. "Dana always used to like to come," said the Lowrys sheepishly, "but now every new thing brings on this kind of storm." Once they put her down, she subsided. She had seen the fish tank and was off like a rocket. Her father felt he should take off some of her outer clothing. He rushed after her, which made her crawl even faster. He dove at her. She screamed, half gleefully at her success in drawing him in. But as soon as she realized he was about to "do something to her," her screeches of protest resumed. After he'd pulled off her cap and her outer coat, he let her go and she started out again. This time she pulled herself up at the fish tank. In her excitement, she toppled over backward and hit her head with a thwack. She screamed. The Lowrys zoomed over, sure that she was hurt. As I saw this happen, I could tell by her watchful face and alert eyes that she was not. She was frustrated. I pulled her back up to stand. She quieted completely, looking pleased with herself.

When she saw I was a helper, she looked at me to check whether I was looking her in the face. I was prepared for this and knew that I must look the other way. On the brink of independence, a one-year-old's fantasies about being invaded are peaking. Intruding into her personal space by looking at her is bound to raise self-protective feelings. I looked just past Dana. She gurgled. I thought this was a response, so I said, "Hi, Dana." I felt her stiffen, and she began to whimper again. I knew I'd gone too fast. I moved away. This intrigued her and she started to follow me. By now, I knew we could go into my office without a firestorm.

In my office, when I want to examine a child of this age and want to keep her happy through it, I ask a parent to hold her in the parent's lap and undress her there. I let her stay unapproached until I see her begin to relax and to play with a toy on the desk next to her. At that point, without looking her in the face, I can approach and settle cautiously on the floor in front of her parent's lap. I sit and look beyond her. She will have stiffened as I approach. Meanwhile, I continue to talk to the parent behind her. I bring along the child's lovey—a blanket or doll. If she has none, I bring her a doll from my office to hold. As she accepts it and begins to relax with it, I dare to start the exam. I put my stethoscope on her parent's hand, then on the parent's arm, then on the doll. If she is not too threatened, I dare to put it on her briefly. Then I shift very quickly to the doll or to the parent again. I play this game of approaching her through her parent and the doll with repeated passes until she begins to relax. As she does, I can gradually examine her chest, her heart, and her abdomen. I never let her catch me looking in her face.

Examining a one-year-old's ears can be a major trauma. I examine the baby doll's ears first and then her parent's ears. Finally, I ask the parent to turn her to one side, holding onto her outer arm. I show her her parent's ear being examined. I examine her ear quickly. After showing her on the doll again, I get her parent to turn her around. I look at the second ear. Then I show her how to open her mouth wide. I ask her parent to "open wide" and to say "aaah" and to stick out his or her tongue. Many, many toddlers will imitate me and their parents. If imitation fails, I ask the parent to sit the child in his or her lap facing me, then to put an arm under each of the baby's arms. With the child's head locked between her parent's arms in a full nelson hold, I can open her mouth quickly with a throat stick, examine it, and get out quickly.

When all this goes as planned, toddlers don't need to protest. They accept my maneuvers and realize that I respect their fear of being invaded. The use of imitation with their mother or father and with the doll becomes interesting enough so that it captures them and diverts their fears. These maneuvers add no more than five extra minutes to my exam. They are more than worth it, for I have kept the child happy about coming to see me. When she is happy, I get to see the quality of her play and can estimate her developmental progress while her parents and I are conversing. Having watched in the waiting room for motor skills, I already know whether I should suspect motor impairment. Having watched the parent with her, I can estimate the quality of their relationship. By the time I turn to her physical exam, I know a great deal about her and her parents and how they interact.

Often, the first question at this visit is about the baby's sudden new "irritability." "Every time we want to do anything, she gives us grief. She needs to make all the decisions. We can't." If this is the case, I see that feelings of independence are dawning. Looking back, the first year seems easy as the baby enters a whole new phase. When a baby is resistant, parents are taken by surprise. "You mean all year-old babies are like this? None of our friends have hit it yet. We felt we had created a monster." When parents express concerns about this new turmoil, it is obviously a relief to them that I can place it in the context of the baby's development.

Not all babies get independent suddenly and dramatically. But when they do, I am always glad to see it. This is a real touchpoint if parents can see the progress it represents. Though it means the love affair of the first year is over, the burst of autonomy is normal and healthy. A baby's struggle to express herself and to find out her own limits will take many years. This kind of baby shows us that she'll do it openly. That becomes easier in the long run, believe it or not. A baby who is too compliant will have to rebel eventually, and it may well be harder when it happens. An easy, compliant baby lets parents sail through the first year almost without problems. The shock of early negativism then comes all the harder.

When this new independence comes, parents inevitably worry about spoiling. An independent one-year-old is not a spoiled child. As we saw earlier, a spoiled child is one who doesn't know when to expect limits. She has not been disciplined and has not learned what her own limits are or when to expect limits from others. The behavior we call spoiled is her way of asking for limits, which she instinctively knows she

needs. Firm handling and limits will help such a child, but they won't do away with the normal turmoil of the second year. When the child has overcome the ambivalence and fears brought by this new independence, she will be more reasonable. The turmoil will subside. But the need for discipline will not go away. We will discuss this in more detail as we look at the months to come.

Somewhere at the beginning of the second year, occasionally **Motor Skills** sooner, a baby becomes a toddler. The world opens up—the world of independence. With the urge to walk, a child begins to experience a tumultuous ambivalence. Will I be on my own, and do I really want that? Do I want to walk away, or don't I? Must I do it my parent's way, or can I do it my own way? No other period in a child's life is as fraught with these wrenching questions—not even adolescence, although it is a similar kind of turmoil. The conflict between "Will I or won't I? Do I or don't I?" is so intense that it will not be sorted out for at least a year and a half. At a time when no one else cares, a toddler will lie down to have a rip-roaring temper tantrum over whether to go through a door or not. Temper tantrums will peak somewhere in the second and third years, as part of this struggle. Parents invariably blame themselves. They needn't. A temper tantrum reflects an *inner* struggle. The parents may have triggered it, but their actions are not responsible for the turmoil, nor can they settle it for the toddler.

This surge to become independent and the negativism that accompanies it start with walking. These mark a particularly intense touchpoint, an extraordinary growth spurt for the child and a trying challenge for all parents. When they understand what lies ahead, many a crisis can be defused. The close interaction between motor achievements and emotional development becomes apparent. Mothers of toddlers immobilized in a cast, for instance, tell me that the babies were compliant and eager to please and be pleased—until the period of immobilization was over. As they got to their feet, the toddlers' concepts of their world changed. No more compliance, no more easy ways to be pleased. By walking, a toddler says, "I can walk away and I can come back. But what will happen if I do? I am in control of my destiny, but what do I want?''

Walking actually does not happen all of a sudden. All through the year, a baby has been practicing and trying out the components of walking. As noted earlier, the walk reflex is present at birth and lasts for the first few months. It incorporates many of the motor skills that surface again. As voluntary mobility becomes a possibility in the second half of the first year, the walk reflex goes underground. Creeping and crawling take over. Before it disappears completely, at around five months, if you pull a baby to sit, she will often stiffen her body up to stand, a wide grin on her face acknowledging the built-in excitement of standing. She is learning the control over her trunk muscles that will be necessary in standing. As creeping, crawling, standing, and finally, cruising, occur sequentially, the ingredients of the process are mastered one by one. Finally, they are ready to be put together. Cruising on furniture has prepared the pretoddler for moving her legs as she maintains upright body posture and balance. When she finally feels courageous and dares to let go with both hands, she teeters and collapses. But she keeps trying, undaunted until she finally puts all of her sensory and motor achievements together to walk unsteadily. The new sense of mastery glows on her face. She walks, walks, walks with a grin of ultimate satisfaction. She has done it!

Before this great moment, all of her energy, both day and night, goes into this new step. Seeing someone walk can make her scream. Whenever a parent walks away from her, she cries out in frustration. She falls again and again in her attempt to keep up with a walking sibling. At night, this frustration boils up at each cycle of light sleep. She stands at her cribside, crying out in revived desperation every three to four hours, as she remembers her attempts to master this new task. Sleeping through the night becomes impossible for her and for her weary parents.

A baby's struggle to learn a skill as important as walking demands all the family's energy. She might be sitting happily in her high chair when the urge to stand and to walk comes over her. You can see her eyes change suddenly. Her hands, busy with finger feeding, become immobile. Sweeping the leftover food off the tray onto the floor, or her parent's lap, she reaches for the back of her chair and squirms around to free herself of the tray. She stands in her chair, ready to topple. Standing and walking are her first priority. Food and hunger are second.

All of the daily tasks of living are turned into scrimmages. Trying to lay her down to diaper her becomes hopeless. She is sure to flail, kick, and scream even at the thought. A parent must learn to diaper her in a standing posture. Suddenly, just immobilizing her to take off her clothes is more interference than she can tolerate. Having her eyes covered to slip off a shirt or jersey means that she must lose sight of her goal. She is likely to have a tantrum over any restriction on her mobility—visual or motor.

Parents whose child isn't walking at a year will worry and wonder why she is delayed. Although I tell them they are lucky to have a few more months of grace before the siege of toddlerhood, they are not reassured. There are many reasons why a year-old child isn't ready to walk. Children who are more low-keyed may simply not be in a hurry to walk. For Caucasian children in the United States, the average is twelve to fourteen months. A second or later child may walk later. It takes twice as much courage for her to dare to let go, if she has older siblings whirling by and endangering her newly found balance. Children who are heavy tend to walk later, as they must learn to master their bulk.

Big children are also likely to be flop-jointed. A child who has highly extensible joints may be delayed in walking by six months. When I can bend a child's knees or elbows beyond an 180-degree angle, I can assume that she has extensible ligaments and more flaccid musculature around each joint. This need not be a defect, but it makes it difficult for the child to start walking. As time goes on, such a child develops extra muscle strength to master these unsteady joints.

Frustration builds up in a flop-jointed child. She will need the extra drive to walk that comes from this frustration. But it may also bring crankiness, demands, and anger at her inability to get on her feet. A low tolerance to other sources of frustration can last for several months in such a child. Unless parents understand what is going on, they are likely to be daunted. Most of these flop-jointed children have been very good, very quiet, and easy in the first year. The sudden reversal of temperament feels like a failure to caring parents. "What have I done wrong? When I try to pull her up to help her and to show her, she just goes limp. It's hard to believe she really wants to walk!" A parent's help will not work, because she wants to do it herself. Frustration will drive her to learn. Many of these children who take longer to master walking and running grow up to become athletes. It's almost as if the drive toward mastery presses them even farther later on.

The agitation that accompanies learning to walk can lead some parents to worry about whether a child is "hyperactive." The drive to become mobile and upright makes her keep going constantly—cruising on furniture, crawling frantically, even rolling to get places. Once she's there, she starts out toward something else. This does not mean that the child is hyperactive. She just wants to learn how to be mobile and on two legs.

A truly hyperactive child can be diagnosed at this age because she is distractible. She can't stay with any task because she is too sensitive to every sight and sound. She can't stick to any one task. Each new sound or new stimulus takes over. If she is alone and without distraction, she can focus and learn. But if she hears a sound or sees a change, she is at the mercy of her response to it. For instance, even something so simple as a block falling down can make her lose concentration. The sound or the visual image diverts her. At one year, a truly hyperactive, hypersensitive child expects to fail at any complicated task. This sense of failure pervades everything she does. This is entirely different from the single-minded drive of a child learning to walk (see chapter 26 on hypersensitivity and hyperactivity.)

Sleep   The drive to master standing and walking upsets all the daily rhythms. Two naps, which have been predictable before, become less so. At naptime, a baby may spend all of her time up and down in her crib. I often recommend that a parent still put the baby into her crib for a short time in the morning and afternoon, but not to worry if she doesn't sleep.

As we saw earlier, whenever a child who is learning to walk

rouses at night, she will be driven to stand in her crib. In the process, she may awaken herself, but she may not. She may stand and cruise around her crib half in her sleep. But as she does, her frustrated screams wake the household. This phase needn't last too long. As I discussed in chapters 7 and 8, she must keep on learning how to get herself back to sleep. Each new daytime achievement, or the struggle leading up to it, will surface in these cycles of light sleep. Parents can help by reacting calmly and firmly and by reinstating all the familiar rituals. They should pat her for a while, then leave. If parents reinforce their child by staying or playing, they are telling her, "If you fight hard enough, I'll give in!" Parents who have chosen to keep the baby in their bed should expect these same cycles of disruption, and they too will need to find some firm way of avoiding a wide-awake family gathering every three to four hours.

Another helpful measure in encouraging a full night's sleep for everyone may be that of parents waking the child at 10:00 or 11:00 before they go to bed. They can love her, even feed her if necessary, and help her down again, saying, "Mummy and Daddy are right here, and we love you. We'll be here when you wake up." For some reason, breaking into her sleep rhythms *before* she wakes is like magic. The chances of her awakening at 2:00 A.M. will be much less.

When a twelve-month-old baby wakes in the morning, she is ready and capable of entertaining herself. If parents do not run in at the first peep, they may be treated to chirping monologues and little songs. It can be a cheerful way to start the day.

Feeding

Parents who have not yet instituted finger feeding will find that their child is resistant at this point. One mother told me she could feed her child only if she distracted her. One way she'd tried was to turn up the television so loud that the child opened her mouth as part of a startle. Her mother stuffed in food, until she shut her mouth firmly. She'd then turn down the TV for a minute and turn it up again to stuff in another bite. Clever as this was, it was hardly addressing the real issue.

At this age, the control of feeding must be the child's. Getting the food in by dubious manipulations is beside the point. Not only should all feeding become finger food, but parents must not set their sights high for feeding a toddler. A "rounded diet" cannot be a goal for the second year. By the fourth year, a child may be ready to eat everything and to imitate her parents with table manners, but the second and third years will be full of quirky experimentation.

One week the toddler will eat eggs or meat, another week, no eggs but all milk foods. Occasionally, she will even explore vegetables. But there is no way to count on this, and the more persistent the parent, the less success. Over the course of a month, a baby may well consume a rounded diet. But whether she does or not had better not be a parent's concern. A toddler is extremely sensitive to adults' reactions around feeding. This is probably a sign of the importance of autonomy in this area. In order to help parents turn the feeding choices over to the child, I have searched to define a minimal daily diet. For the second and third year this can consist of the following:

1. One pint of milk (sixteen ounces) or its equivalent in cheese, yogurt, or ice cream
2. Two ounces of iron-containing protein (meat or an egg), or cereals fortified with iron
3. One ounce of orange juice or fresh fruit
4. One multivitamin, which I use to cover for uneaten vegetables

When conscientious, idealistic mothers hear this from me, they ask, "You mean, that's all she needs in a twenty-four-hour period?" I reassure them that this will cover the basic nutritional needs during this period of intense negativism. When an older child is eating well, vitamins may not be necessary. But, by using them, parents can forget about pushing vegetables. "Not even green vegetables?" mothers will ask. "Not even yellow vegetables?" I find I must stress that vegetables and a rounded diet must wait until this period passes and the whole drama of making choices about food is less charged. Even when I get mothers convinced, grandmothers will worry.

Feeding is an area in which independence and the negativism that surrounds it hit a parent at a vulnerable spot. These are what make it a valuable touchpoint. Parents feel that feeding a baby is their responsibility. To leave it to her gives them an empty feeling—a feeling of having neglected the baby. The parents' job is to understand and deal with these feelings.

When I talk with parents, here's what I recommend. The moment a child of this age loses interest and starts to tease by smearing or dropping her food, or by getting up to stand in her high chair, put her down immediately. End the solid feedings with a bottle or the breast. After that, let her go. Don't try to prolong the meal for "just a bit more." When her meal is over, it is *over* until the next meal. If she gets hungry, she'll learn to respect mealtime. She'll eventually learn to eat when it's offered. But don't hold your breath. Children's hunger at this age is easily submerged in the more exciting game of parent teasing. If you do try to feed her in between, or if you have food where she can get it, you are not only devaluing the importance of mealtime, but you are using not-too-subtle pressure to eat. And you will invariably lose. These are quick ways to set up feeding problems. Her need to control you and her intake will supersede hunger and any desire for food.

If she starts to hold food in her mouth, or to spit it out, or to gag or vomit, she is telling you very clearly that she views feedings as a pressured situation. You are consciously or unconsciously putting her under pressure. Sit back and reevaluate your behavior.

During these months, parents sometimes are so concerned about getting milk into her that they let a child walk around all day with a bottle. They are likely to find that the toddler will drink even less milk if they give her the bottle all the time. I don't like this, for it devalues milk as a food and uses it for comfort, or as a way of teasing parents.

Once this habit starts, it is not easy to stop. A child may beg for a bottle, even have a tantrum to get one to carry. Parents will have to be patient and firm, telling the child that she can have her lovey during the day and that she can have her bottle at mealtimes. Then, they can tie her empty bottle to her doll, a stuffed animal, a blanket, or any other lovey for a period. When she has transferred her attachment, the bottle can be dropped from the lovey, with her permission. Meanwhile, milk shouldn't be put in the bottle. If she doesn't drink enough milk, parents can use yogurt, ice cream, or cheese (one ounce of cheese is equivalent to four ounces of milk). Then, when she does get her bottle, they can make it part of an important ritual, holding and loving her while they give it to her.

The interminable smashing and squishing of food that goes on at mealtimes will also get to parents. The toddler does it as a part of exploration, but soon also realizes a secondary gain—that of teasing her parents. Once upset, parents might as well give up on the feeding, put her down until the next meal, and not make an issue out of her playing with her food. Negative reinforcement will fuel her teasing.

While a child this age will enjoy playing with a spoon, she will usually lose the food. Not until fifteen or sixteen months will she have real success. Meanwhile, she is learning how to manipulate utensils—valuable play.

If a pacifier has become a habit, now is not the time to take it away. Nor would I talk about it. Any attention parents pay to it will heighten its use as a teasing issue. In the second year, a child deserves to have a crutch she can use to help her soften the struggle of being a toddler. When she loses it, or drops it over the side of the crib to make her parents come to find it, this is part of the fun of torturing them. Parents can tie it to her wrist with a ribbon during the day or to a lovey she cares about at night, or tie it to her crib with a *short* ribbon, too short to get around her neck. She can then retrieve it for herself, if shown how. She doesn't need to use it for manipulation.

Teething In the second year, toddlers begin to get molars. Chewing on things that soothe their back gums helps to rub out the swelling in the gums. They chew on everything. This is the time to worry about toddlers eating toxins, such as lead paint, for many children begin at this age to develop "pica," the tendency to eat everything. Lead paint tastes sweet, and smaller children will eat flakes of it. The danger of having lead paint in your house should be less common now, because no modern

paint has lead in it. It's present only in old houses. If you live in one, have a lead-level blood test done on your child. Most city health departments will do one free.

Signs of learning receptive speech are present at this age. If **Speech** you ask a child to get a toy or a diaper, she will show that she knows what you are asking, either by doing what you ask or by showing clearly that she refuses to do it, even though she knows what you mean. One-step requests, rather than more complex ones, work better. Productive speech is getting more and more exciting. She will stand in bed, one arm aloft, declaiming with the inflections and rhythms of a speechmaker. Very few words are distinguishable, but the base for future language and speech is proceeding. Usually a few words can be made out like "goggie," "mama," "babee," and "no." Names get connected with the correct person. She may use pointing and gesturing. At any rate, she'll use her eyes and facial gestures to accompany her words.

Pointing and gesturing become clear communication signals. When she wants to get or keep your attention, she'll use pointing and a vocalization. If her vocalization is not quite clear, parents will always correct her with the word. In this way, they give her the message that they expect her speech to get more and more distinct. She may even repeat it more distinctly right after her parents. She is eager to learn to speak.

Learning   The concepts of object and of person permanence still dominate a child's day. She will go around a corner, call to you to be sure you are still there. If you are out of sight, she may make a noise or try out a forbidden task in order to push you to respond and to come to her. All of a sudden, after she's been ominously quiet, the television may start blaring. When you come to her, your presence is her reward. No amount of censure counteracts her delight in drawing you in. Being left—during the day, as well as routine separations at bedtime—become significant all over again. She may have been very

good at leave taking until she reached this stage. Now, she protests vigorously and tearfully. She wants control over leave-taking. She will leave you, but she won't let you leave her.

To help a child through this period, I advise parents, always tell her you're leaving. In fact, talk about it ahead of time. Before she's into the upset of the actual leaving, prepare her and tell her you'll be back soon. As we said in earlier chapters, if she's having a very tough time, just leave her for fifteen minutes the first time. When you return, remind her that you'd promised her you'd come back. Each time she'll learn to trust you. She'll gradually master her feelings about leave-takings. Meanwhile, protesting is the healthiest thing she can do. If she's with a familiar caregiver who loves her, she knows it and will turn, sobbing, to that person to be comforted. After you are gone, she will soon be fine. Each time, she'll learn a bit more. When you come back, always remind her that you promised to, and you have.

Storage This is a new concept. If you offer a child younger than a year two objects, she will grasp one with each hand. When you offer a third, the younger baby will drop one to take the third. By a year, a toddler will try to figure out how to keep all three. She may put one in her mouth to take the third. Or, she may store one or two in the corner of her arm in order to take the third. If the objects are small enough, she will grasp two in one hand. She has learned to store.

Block Building A child this age will put one block on top of the other. If it falls, she will show her frustration and will turn to some other game quickly. As she learns to build, she becomes more and more precise.

Imitation Peekaboo or gesturing games become more exciting and engaging at this age. A child will imitate parts of the game, even if she can't perform it entirely. This shows that imitation is becoming a source of major interest to her. This is the age when a toddler begins to learn so much from her older siblings. They will teach her, and she will work at learning from them. She will imitate hunks of behavior from them that she'd never learn from a parent or an other adult. Small children are much more intrigued by an older child than they are by an adult!

Causality Before a year, she will push a windup car along to make it run. By a year, she knows that you did something to make it run. She may turn it over to look at the underside. But she will hand the toy back to you for you to make it run again.

Fears Because of the rapid increase in the size of her world, a toddler's personal space suddenly has become even more precious to her. This awareness is coupled with her rapidly increasing sense of independence and the dependence that balances it. The two are different sides of the same coin. A one-year-old baby will let you pick her up, but when she realizes that she's allowed herself to be dependent, she'll squirm to get down. She both wants it and doesn't. Any closeness or approach endangers her sense of personal space and control over her world. If she can look strangers over and digest their features as she clings to her safe parent, she can gradually take them in. The most threatening "stranger" will be an *almost familiar* one— such as mother's sister or father's brother or a grandparent who comes only rarely. In order to give her the sense of control she needs as she sorts out the subtle or obvious differences, such a visitor must be patient.

Looking Ahead **Negativism** The thrust toward independence will be flourishing and growing stronger in the next year. "No" becomes a favorite word. Shaking her head from side to side while saying "no" with a glower will become the toddler's most common behavior. Any request will be met with sullen or unrepressed negativism. Parents need to be prepared. If I can use the one-year visit as a touchpoint to alert them to the reasons why a compliant infant will turn into a stubborn, resistant toddler, they do not feel so guilty and helpless. Otherwise, they take her negativism personally and try to restrain or control it.

Temper Tantrums These are characteristic in the second year, and they make all parents feel that it's their fault. As we said earlier, they're not at fault. The intensity and passion that a toddler feels about each and every decision are reflected in her tantrum. You can try, but you can't always keep ahead of these peaks of negativism. Often, a firm, uninvolved approach helps the most, for it says, "I wish I could help you, but I can't. You decide what you want, and I'll either go along with it or I'll say no. Either way, it will help you to make up your own mind." I know it feels cruel to ignore a tumultuous tantrum, but anyone who's tried knows how a parent is likely to prolong the turmoil by trying to help. Walking away until it's over or using time out will often help.

Parents sometimes ask why toddlers have tantrums in public places. For one thing, they're overloaded by the excitement. They also realize their parents' attention is diverted from them, and they want it back. They know they can embarrass mom and dad, who are more flustered in public. Parental consternation and attempts to smooth them over a tantrum are likely to prolong it. My best recommendations both will seem impossible: (1) Gather the child and give up on the shopping. Go back to the car, and let her have it out safely in the car. Let her know calmly that you can't stay at the store. (2) Act as if she's not yours and ignore her. She'll stop very quickly. *Then*, sit down and hug her, saying "It's terrible being so upset, isn't it?" (For more on temper tantrums, see chapter 10.)

Discipline Even when parents can divert a busy toddler by changing her diaper standing up or by removing valuable, fragile treasures, discipline will become necessary. Parents should continue to save it for important things, so that it will be more meaningful when they do use it.

The toddler needs to hunt for something that will get to her parents. As I warn parents, it is easy to predict which times of day she'll be at her worst: at the end of the day when you are both tired, whenever you have an important visitor, when you get on the phone, or whenever you go to the grocery store.

This newly aggravating behavior will drive parents to seek solutions. It becomes an important touchpoint if they can realize what is actually going on.

At this age, when a toddler asks for attention, she needs a hug or a short bit of recognition, but not anger. Physical punishment such as hitting or spanking will mean two things to her: one, that you are bigger than she and you can get away with it, and two, that you believe in aggression. In talking with parents, I suggest the following approach. Find a way for time out or a hug in a rocking chair to break the cycle of buildup. It will help you, as well. As you stop her, say, "I'm sorry. I love you, but not what you are doing. I'll have to stop you until you learn to stop yourself."

Discipline is the second most important thing you do for a child. Love comes first, and discipline second. Discipline means teaching, not punishment. The goal is for the child to incorporate her own limits. Each opportunity for discipline becomes a chance for teaching. Hence, after a brief disciplinary maneuver, sit down to comfort and hold her, saying, "You can't do that. I'll have to stop you until you can learn to stop yourself."

Toilet Training If the subtle and not-too-subtle suggestions from friends and relatives for you, the parents, to start toilet training have not begun, count yourself lucky. *It is still too soon.* Toward the end of the second year, the toddler may be ready to do it herself. Think what we are asking of a toddler: to feel a urine or bowel movement coming, to hold onto it with pressure, to stagger to a place that *we've* designated, sit down, and finally produce. Then we ask her to give it up for good as we flush it away. Isn't that a lot to ask at a time when a toddler is working so hard on the task of becoming her own person? I guarantee that if you do wait to let her get the idea and choose to conform to it herself, you won't end up with soiling, smearing, wetting, or withholding. If you start too early, you might well have any of those as reactions to your pressure. It's got to be her achievement. Be patient and wait!

Biting, Hitting, and Scratching These will soon surface, along with other unpleasant behavior, in the normal course of development. Though mortifying, they are expectable in this period. They start out as exploratory—testing her skills, you might say. They are associated with periods of overload when the toddler is out of control. If you lose control, too, you will frighten her and reinforce the behavior. So, expect such things to happen. When they do, gather her up to contain her, but don't reinforce them—negatively or positively. Say as calmly as you can, "I don't like that and neither does anyone else. You just can't do it. I'll stop you each time until you can stop yourself." Knowing that babies everywhere have shown such behavior will help you say this convincingly.

10

FIFTEEN MONTHS

Parents of toddlers have little chance to read the magazines in my office. From the moment they arrive in the waiting room, they are on the alert, watching their whirlwind to be sure he's safe, to divert him before he gets into trouble. Their questions to me and the way their attention is constantly divided show me how their days are spent, preventing their toddler from destroying himself and his environment. During the appointment, they are in minimal contact with me.

The toddler, too, has divided attention. He keeps one eye on his parents, to be sure they're watching, and one eye on the toys. During all this he maintains a wary sense of what invasive ideas I might have in mind.

As I observe him playing, my main concern is not only about his neurological and physical development, but also how effective he is as he tries to master various tasks. Does he expect to succeed? Does he keep trying? When he succeeds, does he expect approval from those around him? Or, does he give up easily? Does he try to divert attention from a task that he knows he can't master? Does he realize he's failing and look to you for disapproval? If a toddler is overwhelmed by the strangeness and the threat of my office, it is much harder for me to make a judgment about his behavior and his development. For this reason, I try very hard to encourage him to want to come to see me, so I can be of value to his parents in helping them foster his well-being. Providing physical exams and inoculations is not enough in a pediatrician–patient relationship.

If the child is now walking, I sometimes ask the parents to come with me into my office and let him follow. This does not always work, but the earlier we respect the toddler's independence the better.

When parents announce to me that their child is going to be frightened by me, I know that the wrong cues have already been given. He will comply dutifully—by screaming whenever I approach him. Of course toddlers dislike being examined and hate the necessary inoculations. Of course they have a memory of both of these from past visits. But parents can underestimate the child's ability to live up to the occasion. All children like being the focus of attention. If their anxiety is respected, we can work around it. New toys in the office and rewards after the exam are also things they don't forget from one visit to the next. When a toddler can master his anxiety, he will feel an inner sense of success.

As the toddler plays in the office, I can see all his new achievements. To get up from sitting, he will push his buttocks high in the air, balancing on both arms. When his legs are straight, he straightens up, a bit unsteadily. Spreading his legs apart, he regains his balance. If he has just begun to walk, he will hold his arms out to keep steady as he toddles along. A wide-based gait is another a sign of having just learned the task of walking. As he gets more adept, his base will narrow. When he's really secure in walking, he can place his legs together and reach up to take a toy over his head. Earlier, that maneuver would have been sure to unsettle him and destroy his balance. You can date a child's walking by watching for these maneuvers.

All the new cognitive abilities at fifteen months also come into play as I try to enlist the toddler's cooperation. When I need to measure his head (a baby's head growth is as important as his linear growth, both for the gradual growth of the brain and for a baseline measurement in case of a brain injury), I measure my own head. The toddler will look at my tape measure and laugh at the absurdity of seeing it on my head. Then, he may allow me to measure his. The otoscope goes first into a doll's ears, then mother's or father's, then into the child's ears. To weigh him, I ask a parent to step on the scale without him, then with him, and I subtract the parent's weight. Sometimes this tempts the toddler to step on the scales out of curiosity, sometimes not. With luck, we can complete an entirely satisfactory exam without a whimper.

In any case, I get to observe the toddler under a series of conditions. I see how independently he can relate to me. If he is pushed, he'll rebel. This is appropriate. He shows me that by using a new cognitive acquisition—symbolic play—he can transfer his anxiety about himself to a doll and can receive reassurance from watching the procedures with the doll. Imitation of his parents is usually strong at this age. So, as I use them as models, I watch to see whether he is willing to imitate them. All of these are burgeoning cognitive processes. Meanwhile, I can assess how much equanimity he can muster in the face of an invasive examination. If he can meet and manage stress, using his parents, a doll, and me to help him, he has had a good start.

When I have to give the measles-mumps-rubella shot at the end of the visit, this will be a big blow and seem like a betrayal. I ask a parent to hold the toddler. I prepare him by telling him about it and by showing the shot with a bear or doll. I ask a parent to squeeze him just as I give it and, then, to dance around to distract him as soon as the shot is finished. After it's over, I offer a reward. Often this is refused. I explain that I know he is angry and I surely understand, but that the shot is to keep him healthy. I want to be his friend *and* his doctor. A doctor is someone who wants to keep children healthy so they can play. A doctor loves them, too. Sometimes my present is then accepted. But the more important issue is that the parents and I have not ridden roughshod over the child's fears, over his wonderful but fragile new sense of himself as an independent person.

Discipline becomes important in year two. However, it must **Discipline**
be seen as a long-term teaching project. Understanding the
child's need for learning limits is the most important step for
parents, the basis for discipline decisions. What a parent does
for discipline at any one time is less important than long-term
attitudes and expectations. For this reason, as I said before, I
would choose only important issues to confront. The inevitable parental concerns about taming their fiercely independent
toddler make this a vital touchpoint for us.

Many couples, particularly those who have their first child
late, don't want to have to change their way of living. They
want to teach the child that he can't touch precious objects
around the house. While this may be possible to teach, parents
will spend a lot of energy and time at it that might better be
saved for more important issues. Why not put them away for
now? Then there are fewer issues to confront each day. The
child will still learn self-discipline and respect for others' rights
in all sorts of other ways. Every time parents model thoughtful
behavior, he'll be learning from it. But it may not show up
immediately.

Parents of a fairly easygoing child sometimes actually ask
me how to tell when a child needs discipline. All they need to
do is listen to the child. When he touches something forbidden
and looks back to be sure you're watching, or when he's
building up to more and more provocative behavior, you
know he's asking you to step in and say, "Stop, that's
enough."

At this age, parents wonder whether to continue or start
using a playpen. The answer is no. But a toddler does need a
safe place where he can be left to explore. If parents can't set
up his room to be safe or can't organize part of the kitchen,
they may have to confine him in a playpen. But I hope not. It's
an insult at this age, when experiencing of freedom and movement is at a peak. I would certainly rather he had freedom to
explore. But letting him be free *does* mean that someone must
be on hand all the time.

Temper tantrums have usually made their unwelcome appearance by the time a child is fifteen months old (see chapter 9). They are horribly embarrassing to parents when they

happen in public. Everyone gathers around, looking at the parents as if they were certified child abusers. In such a situation, parents might turn to the onlookers and suggest that they handle him themselves. They'll melt away quickly after that.

When distressed parents report to me about the first tantrum, it becomes a touchpoint, a key opportunity for me to point out that these are a normal part of a toddler's behavior. A feisty child is almost bound to have them sometime in the second year. A child who never throws a tantrum in year two or three may well become a volatile, hot-tempered adolescent or adult who must work out all of this turmoil at a much later date. As we said before, although parents' behavior or a request may well have triggered the tantrums, they come from the child's own inner turmoil. Only he can resolve the indecision that is behind them. It's the toddler's basic struggle between dependence and independence. After he has learned to handle this struggle, he'll be a stronger and more secure child.

I remind parents of some steps to take. First, remember your options, all directed at leaving it up to the child. Either pick him up to hold him quietly, gather him to carry him to a safe spot where he can work it out himself, or walk out of sight momentarily. When he can't see you, the tantrum will lose force. Then quickly return to say, "I'm sorry I can't help you more. I'm still here, and I love you, but this tantrum is your job." Giving the child space to resolve his own turmoil is not the same as deserting him. Do it in a way that lets him know you want to help. But you and he know that your efforts to help will just prolong the tantrum. Firm limits will reassure him that he will not be dangerously out of control.

Some parents find it hard to leave the scene because they are afraid the child will hurt himself. When he thrashes violently or bangs his head on the ground, it is frightening. However, it is unlikely that he'll hurt himself. If he seems too violent, he can be removed to a rug or a crib. Fortunately, in most cases, he will stop before he loses control.

Years ago in Oregon, I spent a week with the two-year-old Anderson quintuplets. One of them had a violent temper tantrum. The other four crowded around to try to stop it. Their efforts made him more violent. One tried to hold his arms, another lay down beside him to croon to him and soothe him. Another yelled at him. The fourth threw cold water on him. Nothing worked, so they all gave up. As soon as they did, he stopped crying. He got up quickly and started to play with them, as if nothing had happened. This experience was a vivid demonstration to me that tantrums are a reflection of inner turmoil. Support, but not interference, is the only help. After it's over, parents can find ways to convey that they understand how hard it is to be two years old.

Finding safe, simple ways to discipline, ways that cannot lead to abusing the child, is an important goal. Using time-outs works for many parents later in the second year. Firmly holding the child and putting him in his crib or room are ways of briefly breaking the buildup of teasing behavior before he loses control. When the cycle is broken, parents should make clear that a certain behavior made them act, and then they can offer plenty of hugs.

With the surge in independence and the comprehension that exploring brings, a toddler is bound to develop fears. A fear **Fears** of the bathtub is common. At this point, a parent might take him into the tub for a joint bath, being careful not to leave him alone to slide in the tub or to feel precarious about standing in it. Washing his hair will bring on ear-splitting screeches, so it needn't be washed often. When it is, the child will need to be supported. The toddler's fear of losing his balance, of being tilted back for a rinse, is worst at this time.

Motor Skills When the child first learns to walk, he will walk all day long, swayback, stomach jutting out in front, with the wide-based gait we discussed earlier. He will look like a duck with feet splayed out. As he gets familiar with walking and managing his balance, his feet will begin to turn in and become parallel. Only when a toddler has been walking for some time will he be able to do other things when he walks. If he can carry a toy in one arm while he walks, he's had a month of experience. If he can reach above his head or look up when he walks, he's been at it for at least two months. When he can turn and can squat, he's had two to three months' experience.

As mentioned in chapter 9, learning to walk barefoot is ideal. Shoes become necessary as a support later. As a toddler learns to walk, his toes will grip the ground and build up his arches. Shoes are necessary only to protect against cold or sharp surfaces. Walking barefoot is the best exercise for his feet.

Once again, it is important to note that stairs need to be gated at the top and bottom. He will be intrigued with climbing. He needs to learn, but with someone in attendance. Carpeted stairs are easier and safer.

Feeding At this visit, my main concern is that the toddler be independent about his own feeding. Does he make choices, and can his parents leave them to him? I reiterate the minimum diet, for I know how difficult it is for his parents (especially his mother) to leave it to him.

Parents often feel that they must at least shovel in some

mushy baby food. But a baby this age does not need mushy foods. Everything fed that way could be fed in finger bits or in substitutes. When a mother protests that "I can't stand to go to all the trouble of making something special for him, just to have him refuse it," I tell her not to bother. She is blaming the situation on the feeling that her cooking is rejected, but the truth is usually that she feels the need to control what the toddler eats. The solution is to stop cooking for him and respect what he's trying to say: "I want to do it all myself." Parents' hints—like "Look what Mommy went to the trouble to make you" or "Want some of these delicious green beans off Daddy's plate?" or "Look at your big sister; she *loves* her vegetables"—are blatant pressure and are sure to turn the toddler off and lead to feeding problems. Unless parents are tense and pushing him, he is likely to eat. They just need to be sure that what they offer him is in line with the minimum discussed earlier: iron-containing meat, egg, or cereal, milk, fruit, and vitamins (see chapter 9).

For the few toddlers who won't take milk, yogurt, cheese, ice cream, or other substitutes can be given. When a baby wants to try the cup but spills most of it, parents can either put down a tarpaulin around his chair and let him spill on it or give it to him in the bathtub. They'd best give up on cleanliness for a while. Other, more important things are at stake.

This nondirective approach to feeding is genuinely difficult for many parents, especially mothers. Feeding becomes equated with the maternal instinct. While malnutrition is a terrible world problem, it is not likely to affect the families who are reading this book. When parents cannot handle this critical area of independence, I watch for what the psychoanalyst Dr. Selma Fraiberg called "ghosts in the nursery." Mothers tell me dreadful stories about having been left at a table for hours to finish food. The extreme result of long-term coercion can be seen in a condition called anorexia nervosa. This usually appears in adolescence and starts with an early feeding problem. Parents shouldn't take the chance. The best insurance against perpetuating eating problems is to get out of the picture and leave it to the child. He'll find his own balance and keep a feeling of independence. Any adult knows that the food you choose yourself tastes better.

The cup and spoon can be mastered about this time. If this is made to be fun, the use of these utensils can add to a sense of mastery. Meanwhile, simple finger foods are enough.

Sleep   The same issues of self-comforting rituals that have been discussed already need to be raised again at this age. Usually, after walking is achieved, a child is ready to sleep through the night again. One nap may now be enough, early in the afternoon so as not to affect bedtime. Waking the child at the parents' bedtime may continue to be an effective way of ensuring a good night's sleep for everyone.

Parents who have chosen to keep the child in bed with them may be reconsidering this decision now. A child in bed with parents is more likely to rouse at 2:00 A.M. and 5:00 A.M. or thereabouts and expect to be nursed or rocked or comforted. Sometimes this causes a rift between the parents. "My husband hates it," a mother might say. "He feels shoved out. But what can I do? I can't let her cry it out." I couldn't either, and I wouldn't suggest it. But I don't think it's very good for a family to get into a split over something like this. When I point out that this situation could last for several years, "Oh god," the mother might then say, "he'd flip if he thought this would last." One possibility is to set up a crib next to the parents' bed as a transition. Parents can then still roll over to pat the child down when he comes up to light sleep. Parents who have had losses in their past, or who have had sleep and separation issues in childhood, will invariably find it difficult to give up the child at bedtime. Then, each peep or whimper becomes a signal for rushing in to offer comfort. Any child will fight for this kind of reinforcement.

Play   A toddler's main purpose in my office will be to distract me from interacting with his parents as he plays. Going from one toy to another, he is likely to elicit our response by saying, "See? See?" Even though his attention span is still short, I like to be sure that he examines objects with real interest. Can he be enlisted to play with toys at any length, or does his anxiety consume all of his attention?

At this age, the difference between a toddler's enormous energy and normally short attention span, on the one hand, and genuine hyperactivity, on the other, begins to be evident. A hyperactive child will have a split-second attention span, moving from one toy to another. He can never allow time for close inspection or for any sustained play with toys. His distractibility interferes. Any sound or visual stimulus grabs him. His threshold for taking in information is short, hampered by this distractibility. He moves constantly, in an effort to handle his hypersensitivity. Usually, his face has a worried expression. He has slight tremors of his hands as he tries to pick up a toy. If someone claps repeatedly, a truly hypersensitive child will startle each time. He cannot shut out incoming sights and sounds. Hence, he is at the mercy of all stimulation around him. His hyperactivity seems to be a response to a hypersensitive nervous system.

When we can identify such a child early, I can help parents reduce stimuli around him. At particular times, when he needs to pay attention to a learning task or eat or sleep, this will be critical. Over time, he can learn ways to control himself as he overloads—by frequently taking a time-out, by clutching a lovey, or by finding active ways to shut down on incoming stimulation. If parents do not recognize his problem, they may see him as a spoiled or acting-out child. Their overreaction then adds to his, and the buildup within the family reaches chaotic levels. Parents of such children need support at each visit, or perhaps even a referral for early intervention (see chapter 26).

At this age, most children are able to stack four blocks. They are generally able to find a hidden toy, if you demonstrate that it is hidden under one, then a second, cloth. We call this "two displacements." This test of object permanence is a delightful game, but also a very telling cognitive task. Symbolic play also starts early in the second year. Does he feed a doll a toy bottle? Does he croon to the doll or carry it in a way that his parents carry him? Does he make a garage out of blocks—a symbolic representation?

When you play a rhythmic game with a toddler—for example, "This is the way the ladies ride, . . ."—does he anticipate the denouement? Does he laugh when you hold his hands and clap, then stop? Has he a concept of breaking into a repetitious expectancy?

Causality is beginning to be better understood. With a windup toy, rather than hand it back to you when it runs down, the toddler may now try to wind it himself. Every aspect of play—which, as Montaigne said, is "a child's most serious action"—reveals the toddler's stage of maturity. In it we see the leading edge of learning, of motor skills, and of emotional development.

Speech   The gobbledygook of sounds continues, mostly at night and in the crib. Inflections and the practicing of words and phrases show that a toddler is readying himself for speech. Adults feel compelled to correct and model speech after each attempt. In this way, parents lead children on to the next stage. Most of the time, nouns are the goal, not verbs, adjectives, or adverbs—"me," "Mommy," "Papa," "cookie," although an occasional "more" and, of course, "no" will appear. At this age, toddlers begin to show a real frustration in not being able to talk. They gesture very clearly and do understand almost everything you say.

Looking Ahead   The second year is a time for learning all over again how to parent. In the love affair of the first year, the baby's behavior was predictable and usually rewarding. The parents' efforts met an immediate response in the baby's behavior. No longer will this be true. From now on, the toddler will make his own choices. "Is he deaf?" a parent will ask. "Is he hearing me but not reacting? What do I have to do to maintain control?" The "terrible twos" are terrible for parents, but not for babies. The second year is made up of an enormously rapid kind of learning. The spurt toward independence carries with it a kind of energy for exploration and for learning about the world that is truly remarkable. Learning to parent in the second year is made up of learning from mistakes. The rewards of the first year have fueled parents as they followed the child for direction. Now, they must find their way at an entirely new level.

The principal touchpoint at this age is one of control. Who will call the shots? When parents feel the need for control, the child meets it with negativism and resistance. Parents are likely to feel like failures. Constant reorganization to find a new way to handle the resistant child becomes the experience of parenting in the second year. For parents who are not flexible, it can indeed be a terrible year. Faced with a sense of humor, the second year can be tremendous.

Of course, keeping a sense of humor during this period is easier said than done. "Every time I ask him to do something, he resists," a parent will tell me. "Even his posture says no. He's either a limp rag or a beast, arched away from me." This negativism arises because every suggestion or request from the parent poses a dilemma for the toddler. "Will I or won't I? Do I or don't I want to do it?" As I advise parents, if you really want him to do something, telling him not to do it may work. But, if it's important, I'd push on through. If it's not, I'd let it go. The fewer confrontations you have, the better. Then, you'll find the ones that you do have are important learning experiences.

Toilet Training At each visit during this year I reiterate the importance of waiting until the end of the second year to start toilet training. Parents who are in a hurry may say, "But he's already conscious of his b.m.'s. He pulls at his pants afterward." Or, "He runs off to hide when he goes in his diapers." These are especially clear signals, and they simply underline that when the time comes, he will want to be in control of his own toilet habits.

Allergies As we've seen in earlier chapters, the best way to deal with allergies is to prevent them. Many of us have a genetic tendency to show them at certain times—under stress, when the pollen is flying, or when we've eaten or inhaled the wrong thing. But the tendency rarely shows itself, because it may take several triggers to set it off. Up to a certain point, several mild allergens may not bring out the symptom. But, when you add a cat, fur, dust, molds, feather pillows, hair mattresses, eggs, fish products, stress, or any of the common allergens, the system cannot take it; and wheezing, hay fever, or eczema may result. One trigger may work one time, another the next. An emotional stress or a separation can bring on symptoms. Parents fear these psychosomatic triggers and begin to defend themselves against the fear that they've done something terrible to the child. Denial can keep them from acting to get rid of the many possible triggers of recurrences.

There is a second reason for early prevention of allergies. The older a child gets before his allergy expresses itself, the harder it is to set it off. I recommend working very hard in early childhood to prevent an allergic reaction, and I direct parents to take the following steps. If a rash shows up, take it seriously. Eliminate any new foods. If the rash continues, change to a hypoallergenic soap for washing him and for washing his clothes. Eliminate wool in clothes and blankets, and feather pillows, puffs, and mattresses. If a toy is the offender, gradually introduce another. If you have forced hot air for heat in your house, cover the outlet in his room with eight layers of cheese cloth as a filter. In pollen season, shut the outlet and don't open his window at night. An air purifier helps.

As a child gets older, let him know what to do about his own disorder. Give him a chance to tell you when he needs something for his skin, his wheezes, or his runny nose. When you administer medication, remember to tell him afterward, "See, you knew what to do. And when we did it, it worked."

The most frightening, anxiety-producing aspect of an allergic disorder for a child is the feeling that no one knows what to do about it. To parents, I suggest several things. First, act preventively, as just described. Then, when a symptom occurs, call and get help early. Let the child know what you're doing and why. Later, letting him be in control of his own symptoms is the best prevention for the anxiety and feeling of helplessness that accompany and exacerbate allergic manifestations, such as asthma and eczema (see chapter 14).

Shifting Attachments A child will almost always treat each parent very differently. He will be the hardest on the parent he can count on most, usually the mother. He may treat his father more like someone special. This different treatment can stir up jealousy. Parents need to realize that this is normal and that it is an important part of testing out strong attachments.

The shifting dynamics in the family will continue in the months to come as the child, who has been everyone's center of attention, strives to become more independent. If he is still being cared for by one parent at home, that parent will often start thinking about going back to work part-time or introducing the child to a play group. It's probably no coincidence that the toddler's independence and the dependence that balances it—following the parent around—drive the parent to think that way. A small play group is excellent at this age. The toddler will learn so much from his peers in this next year. After he's gotten used to a small group of one or two his own speed, it is easier to think about what kind of day care to choose. The second year is a great time for him to start making relationships with other children.

Individual Differences The second year seems to highlight differences among toddlers. The quiet, watchful ones become even more observant and sedentary, in contrast to active, intense children who are always moving. The latter hardly sit still long enough to learn to speak or demonstrate their new cognitive skills. They are on the move. Parents are likely to label them hyperactive, for indeed they seem to have short attention spans. Movement is such a powerful drive. For the less active, the intensity goes into small motor activity and observation.

Parents can become concerned by these differences. When children are on either end of the spectrum, they need reassurance. So much time in parenting is spent comparing one's child with other children. "Why isn't my child walking yet?" "He never seems to move around like other children." Or, "He never stops moving. He can't sit still long enough to look at a book or sit in my lap. All his friends are so cuddly."

Since so many parents engage in these comparisons, I wonder what their purpose can be. Parents learn about the processes of development by observing these in others. By analyzing the differences between children, a parent can visualize a full spectrum. In my own work, it has been rewarding to see how much can be learned from the very different individualized styles of different babies. What worries me is that so much energy can be wasted in anxiety about these comparisons. Instead of accepting the baby they have, parents seem to want to press him into the mold of an "ideal" child. If I could do one thing as a pediatrician, I would hope to help parents relish the individuality of their own baby. The danger with comparisons is that they can give a child a sense of inferiority. For example, boy babies are nearly always a bit slower in motor development than girls. And, yet, parents of boys want them to be quick and active. It seems important to me that parents focus on their child and take pleasure in that child's developmental style, rather than pressing him to conform to some notion of the "average" baby.

When parents start in on comparisons, I head them off, describing how *their toddler* is learning—his particular quirks, struggles, and triumphs.

11
EIGHTEEN MONTHS

When a toddler comes into my office, she starts exploring. As she walks up to my desk or lamp or bookshelf and reaches out, then announces "No!" I get a preview of what her parents' questions will be. Nearly all of them will concern the toddler's increasing negativism. "She won't listen to me anymore! She drives me to the point of spanking her, but I really don't want to. But she'll tease me and tease me until I have to do something. When she has tantrums, she knows how to choose the most embarrassing spots." Mothers will get teary as they speak of the changes in the child. Fathers tend to raise the question of punishment. I know that my biggest job will be to help them understand this continuing surge in independence and negativism. Their questions reflect their need for control. This is a touchpoint for reiterating the importance of discipline and for discussing again that it's a long-term teaching project.

I also emphasize that "she's perfectly normal. All toddlers go through a phase like this." Parents will nod in relief. But reassurance will help them for a brief period only. Understanding that the purpose of negative behavior is to help a toddler sort out her own independence becomes important. The provocative acts that drive them to discipline her reflect a passionate search for limits. They must find effective ways to discipline in order to teach her these limits. The turmoil that leads to tantrums is also a reflection of how passionate she is about her independence. If I can help them understand her search, they may be able to admire and enjoy it.

Today, many parents of toddlers are both away all day in the work force. When they return at night, they dream of a loving reunion. They don't get it. A healthy toddler will save up all her most intense feelings for them. Parents who are at work all day come home to—or pick up at day care—a baby who has been waiting all day to break down. When she sees them, the toddler lets it all go. She lies down on the floor, screaming and kicking, and banging her head on the floor. At the day-care center, if a parent tries to gather her up to dress her to go home, she kicks and screams pitifully. One father told me he nearly dropped his toddler as she disintegrated in his arms. "What's more, I wanted to. I had rushed through work to come for her. I was so anxious to see her. What did I get but a screaming meemie who made me hate her. The worst thing was that her teacher looked at me, and said, 'She never does that with me.' Boy, did that make me feel awful."

A substitute caregiver rarely gets the same passionate disintegration that meets a parent. This teacher may have wanted to reassure him that his child wasn't unhappy at the center. But, her remark was an instance of gatekeeping. We have spoken of the unconscious, unspoken competition between two parents. This goes on as well between caregivers and parents. Unfortunately, her remark came at a time of day when this father was frazzled and vulnerable. If the caregiver had said instead, "She's been waiting so eagerly for you. This is the most passion she's demonstrated all day," her father would have read her disintegration correctly.

Negativism is one side of the coin; the other is cooperation and caring. In any passionate developmental process, opposite feelings must surface. The toddler must try out both her negative and positive feelings. Without an intensely negative period, a child could be passive and inwardly conflicted. In the second year, a child's conflicts need to come out. A parent's role is to recognize them as part of an important process and accept them, but also to help the child learn to contain them. Learning how to exercise self-control and how to live with conflict is a long-term process, and these early lessons can be stormy ones. "You seem to love negative children," said one irritated mother when I admired her toddler's negativism. I do—as long as they aren't mine.

A toddler needs to explore the limits of tolerance with her various caregivers. Her parents and another caregiver will see different sides of her. For instance, a nanny or a grandmother will say to me that while she's taking care of the toddler, she has found ways to help the toddler calm down after getting high. "If I don't, she gets higher and higher, breaks things, and has tantrums, and she seems miserable. When I give her time out by rocking her, she is so easy. When her parents arrive at the end of the day, she begins to tease them. They seem overwhelmed by her. I hate to see her get out of control, but how

Discipline

can I help them?" To answer such a question, I first reassure the caregiver that the child is learning about self-discipline from her. Second, I point out that children act differently with different adults. Finally, I would expect the child to act up at the end of the day for her parents. I recommend that the caregiver stay out of the way when the child's parents arrive. Otherwise, the situation becomes a triangle, and no one will win. Just as a child learns a different approach with each parent, so she will from the different nurturing of another caregiver.

Within the limited hours available to working parents, firm discipline can seem impossible. Parents tell me, "We are so glad to see her, but after thirty minutes of her kicking and screaming, we start wishing we could just leave her again. On the weekends, it's almost as if she wanted to see how far she can go. She tests us until we are furious and exhausted. I know she's punishing us for being away all week, but we don't have any fun together anymore." The guilt felt by parents fuels this situation. They cannot stand being disciplinarians after being away all day. But discipline is important to the child. A toddler who is testing is sending out very clear messages. She's saying that she needs help in sorting out what she can do and what she can't. Punishment is not the issue. Setting limits and teaching a toddler about them are not the same as punishing her.

If parents can see calm, consistent discipline as a necessary part of loving her, it needn't stir guilt. I tell parents, save it for important things. Then, when a cycle of provocative behavior begins, stop it early. Pick her up to contain her. If that doesn't work, have time out—in her room or her bed, or in a chair. Sit down with the child afterward. Try to help her see why you stopped her. Don't wait too long, and don't talk too long when you do. Let her know you mean it, and that you are expecting her to stop.

If a parent tells me, "She'll never let me do that when she's out of control! She's too upset and so am I," I suggest the following. Plan ahead of time for what you need to do. Then, move quickly. Tell her you love her but you can't tolerate her behavior. If you are ambivalent, she will know it. Hug her when she is behaving. Sit down and rock together. She needs to know that you aren't mad at her all the time. Discipline is part of caring and of teaching a child about limits. It takes a long time. No one method is ever magically effective. Spanking is no good, as we've said before. It says that you believe in settling things by force—and I don't believe in that.

Feeding

Issues of feeding need to be discussed at every visit. A child has to explore every technique in the books. A toddler of eighteen months will learn to use a spoon and fork, but at some point, she'll want to regress to fingers. Parents can set out food that she can eat with her fingers or spear with her fork, whichever she chooses.

Mothers who are still breast-feeding will have concerns. "I wanted to finish the first year. Now it's hard for me to give it up. She continues to come and unbutton my shirt. I find it embarrassing but hard not to go along with her." The only reason I'd urge weaning would be if it were interfering with her becoming independent. But if she is autonomous in all other domains, the closeness is all to the good. I've studied cultures where mothers breast-feed the new baby on one breast and the other children up to five years of age on the other. (They won't come after five.) The children do fine, but the mothers look haggard. "Everyone tells me I should quit, that I'm just indulging myself," breast-feeding mothers often say. Why not? A reunion at the breast is so lovely after a working day or after a day of negativism and turmoil.

With toddlers this age, mothers begin to wonder how to wean from the bottle. Many toddlers no longer use it for milk, but continue to walk around during the day with it hanging out of their mouths. That use of a bottle bothers me, for they are simply using it as a crutch—not for milk. When you divorce it from feeding and from communication, the bottle loses its significance. As we saw in chapter 9, you can gradually help the child make a transition to a blanket or doll or other lovey by tying it to the bottle. Here are the specific steps I recommend to parents. Offer her milk in her bottle in your arms only at meals. When she asks for it between meals, promise her that she can have it before naptime and bedtime, but that you want to give it to her. Make it part of a bedtime ritual. Start with a book, in a rocking chair, then the bottle. In this way, you can bring a child down into a relaxed, sleepy state. Never put her in bed alone with her bottle. She deserves a special time with you. Milk in her mouth through the night will damage her future teeth, as we said earlier. Apart from this damage, she is missing out on an important ritual and a sense of security. She needs you if she still needs a bottle.

Sleep   Nightwaking will appear with each new stress, such as a parent's absence, a grandmother's visit, a big day on the town, or a stormy play group. A firm, comforting approach is necessary. Parents are teaching her to be independent at night. They can fall back on the patterns they have used at other times—using her daytime attempts to be independent and reinforcing her when she's able to comfort herself during the day. Then, the same pattern of expecting her to be independent at night becomes more meaningful.

One nap is all parents can expect in the second year. I recommend feeding her lunch early, then putting the toddler down from 12:00 to 2:00, with no more nap after 2:00 or 2:30. Otherwise, it will be more and more difficult to get her to bed at a reasonable evening time.

Difficulty in getting to bed will increase anyway. I urge parents to redouble their rituals and their determination to *hold the line* at bedtime. The higher a child gets at bedtime, the harder it is for her to give up. Putting a toddler to bed at this age is not for the fainthearted. The ritual of a rocking chair and a bedtime story certainly helps. A lovey—a blanket or a bear—become even more critical at bedtimes. She can fall back on it during the day and at waking periods at night. Parents often feel a bit uncertain about loveys, especially when these are ratty and pathetic. They think that a child with a lovey looks neglected. Actually, the opposite is true in my experience. When we evaluate a child at the Children's Hospital in Boston without any knowledge of her background, we are happy to see a child who can comfort herself by a thumb or a lovey. This child has already demonstrated her inner strength. She shows us that she has been nurtured at home. The ability to self-comfort is enhanced by parents who nurture.

A toddler's posture frightens parents. Will she always have a potbelly? Her swayback posture, with the potbelly, will continue into the third year. Then, magically, she will straighten up, and her belly will tighten.

Motor Skills

At eighteen months to two years, the child spends all day experimenting. Climbing into everything is more and more exciting. But she cannot be relied upon to worry about heights, so parents must protect her. They need to be sure there are rugs and padding under her favorite stairs, if she's to be allowed the freedom of climbing those. Now, she will run everywhere rather than walk.

She will start to dance, to rotate, to try out all of her new motor skills—balancing, twirling, jogging. She will try to walk away from her parents whenever she gets a chance—in a store, on a street, anywhere. Parents will need to have one hand free for her; otherwise, she will take off.

In the second year, leaving a child can be at its most painful. She is able to protest violently. I have often thought that the degree of protest may be correlated with the strength of her ego. In other words, protest is a healthy way to handle separations. Why should she want to be left, when she can now conceive of keeping up with you, and when she herself wants to do the leaving?

Separation

At Children's Hospital, we did a study on the protests that small children made as their mothers left them in the morning. The children whose parents prepared them at home had already begun to adjust to the separation. They were ready by the time they needed to separate. They and their mothers left each other cleanly—no hanging around, no prolonging the protest. The children who were not prepared at home fell into two groups. Some protested loudly. The others, who withdrew into themselves to mourn, bothered us the most. They were not able to deal with their sadness and play with the other children.

To deal with separation, the first step is that of preparing her ahead of time. Then, parents should be ready to accept a healthy outburst. Third, they need to promise to return, and upon doing so, remind her that they did. This is the basis of future trust.

Learning and Play A burst in development is the parents' reward for all her stormy behavior. When parents have enough distance to see the rapid learning that accompanies a toddler's turmoil, they won't need to consider this the terrible twos. Learning from other children by imitation takes a spurt in the second year. A toddler needs peers. One or two regular playmates is enough. But it is a critical time to get the toddler out of the cocoon of mother-father-child and into the rough-and-tumble world of other children. If she has older siblings, it is less urgent, for she will have the chance to learn from them. This is the time to learn about herself and her relationship to others. She will learn more about herself from other children than she'll learn from her parents.

The most wonderful thing I know of is to watch two children of this age playing in close proximity. They play for long periods side-by-side. Their play is parallel. They never seem to look at each other. Yet they pick up large hunks of play behavior from one another. They seem to absorb play patterns through peripheral vision. Whole sequences of toy play and of communication are repeated, though they do not watch one another. The first child bonks a toy. "No! No! No!" The second child does the same. The first child makes a tower. The second child makes a tower. First child: "No!" He knocks off the blocks. Second child: "No!" and knocks off the blocks. The imperious gestures, the body postures, and the facial attitudes are all similar. Think of the amount and quality of learning that are contained in such close imitation.

Hildy Ross, a psychologist in Canada, paired a two-year-old and a one-year-old in parallel play. Their desire to communicate and to imitate drove them to exchange their individual techniques in favor of the other's. The two-year-old dropped back to about a fifteen-month-old level of play. The one-year-old stretched to a fifteen-month-old's level. They wanted so much to identify with each other. This study showed me how important peer relationships can be.

The desire to test one another can go astray. Biting, hair pulling, scratching, and hitting all surface and get imitated. Often these are aimed at one's "best friend." Horrified parents and teachers overreact and punish the biter or the hitter or hair puller. This overreaction sets the pattern rather than eliminates it. These apparently aggressive behaviors do not start out as aggressive. They occur at times when the child is overwhelmed and loses control. After they've happened, the aggressor is as horrified as the recipient. When parents intervene, guilt sets in. With the next buildup, the pattern repeats itself. Adult interference reinforces it.

Biting carries the greatest charge. All parents are frightened about this—about their child biting and about her being bitten. What seems to be the most frightening is the loss of control: "Will it go on forever?" I would try to comfort both children—the biter and the bitten. The former needs the most, for she will be frightened by her loss of control, more even than the recipient by being attacked. The caregiver needs to sit down with her and say, "No one likes to be bitten. You wouldn't either. Next time you feel that way, remember, I'll help you." This will have to be repeated over and over. One ingenious mother bought her toddler a rubber dog bone to bite on instead of attacking her friends.

In the past, I have kept lists in my office of two-year-old children so that parents could get them together. Two or three who are at similar stages of learning about themselves can learn the most from each other. Two biters or two hitters can be put together. If one gets upset, she will bite the other. The recipient will bite back. They'll look at each other as if to say, "That hurt! Why did you do it?" And they'll never do it again. I think that children at this age really do not understand that it hurts. They don't mean to hurt and are frightened afterward. Since the symptom is a result of a loss of control, it is too late to stop it at the time. But, over time, they can learn

to control it, for they want to. The give and take of relationships between toddlers is the best way for them to learn.
Adults only interfere with this learning.

Mothers of biters wonder if they should bite back. No! That
is getting down on the toddler's level and is degrading for her
and for her mother. The issue is to teach her calmly about the
unacceptability of this behavior and to try to give her an
acceptable substitute, such as a toy to bang—a way to work
it out.

Play remains a child's most powerful way of learning. She
can test out many different situations and actions to find
which one works for her. It is hard to overestimate the importance of play for a small child.

Self-Image The psychologist Michael Lewis designed an ingenious experiment to find out about the child's image of her
own body. A child is given a mirror in which to view herself.
After awhile the researcher moves the child away and dabs
rouge on her nose, without attracting her attention. When put
back in front of the mirror, the child's reaction depends on her
age. At one year, a child will watch herself carefully, recognizing the strange color on her nose. At fifteen months, the chil-

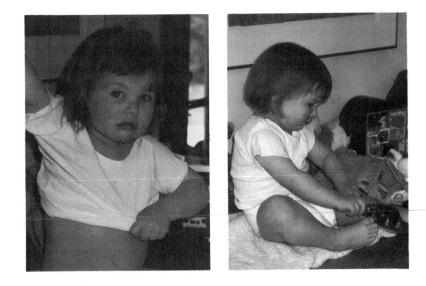

dren touch their own noses on the mirror and try to wipe off the rouge. They recognize themselves and have an idea that something is different. By eighteen months, they try to wipe the rouge off their own noses.

Self-exploration at this age becomes heightened. A toddler is intrigued with her eyes, her nose, her mouth. When she gets a chance, she is intrigued with her navel and her genitalia. Little boys at this age are excited by their penises when they are undiapered. Girls begin to poke a finger into their vaginas. This part of their body must be very special to them when it is finally exposed. It is covered and out of sight for so much of their experience. No wonder it becomes an area of heightened sensation. Parents needn't try to stop this exploration. These are parts of the children's bodies, and they need to get familiar with them.

Toilet Training I advise parents to hold off a bit longer. **Looking Ahead** Although most parents understand the reasons for waiting until a toddler has the concept of what we expect of her and is ready to do it for herself, some will get impatient. "I don't want her going to college in diapers." A very real source of pressure is the requirement of most preschools that children be toilet-trained. Many day-care centers want them trained by two and a half, at the latest. If possible, I'd look for a school that respects the child's need to decide when she wants to be trained. There's nothing magical about the age of two and a half. And it is critical to leave it to her. While few parents want to coerce children, unless they are aware of their own internal pressures to have the child clean and dry, there is a good chance that they may push her.

At this point, it may help parents to look ahead and know what to watch for.

At around two years of age, several developmental steps will begin to come together. When they do, the child will be ready. It will be time to turn the training over to her.

1. She'll be over the excitement of walking and will be ready to sit down.

2. She will be ready to understand such words and concepts as: "This is your potty seat. Mine is the big one. Someday you'll go on yours like I do on mine."
3. There is a period at about two years of age when children want to imitate. A boy walks like his father, a girl like her mother. Subtly, they are identifying with the important adults around them. They want to wear your clothes. They are even absorbing gestures like adults around them. Imitation can be used to capture toilet behavior.
4. At two years of age, most children begin to put things where they belong. They have a concept of orderliness and of where parents put things. This urge to put things away like parents do can be transferred to urine and bowel movements.
5. Negativism comes and goes at around two. Before that, it is always near the surface. To start when she's negative would mean failure, for sure.

All of these developmental mechanisms can be captured to help a child conform to society's demands that she be clean and dry all day and all night.

"What behaviors should I go by?" parents will ask. When a child grunts and pulls at her pants when she's going into her diaper, this shows that she's aware of her productions. When she reaches a relatively tranquil developmental period—not too negative or too feisty—I'd watch to see whether she is interested in your going to the bathroom. Is she getting tidy? Is she very imitative? Can she follow two or more commands? For example, if you ask her to go to the closet, find your slippers, and bring them to you, can she follow that sequence of three requests? That is a sign that she's acquiring receptive speech and can keep two or three sequential commands in her mind.

Given all the pitfalls in toilet training, some parents wonder whether doing nothing is the way to avoid making mistakes. However, a child might not understand what we expect of her that way. It is still necessary to show her the steps, although she must be allowed to refuse if she wants to. Since it is almost impossible for parents to conceive of an eighteen- or twenty-four-month-old child wanting to cooperate in any way, the best thing to do about toilet training is to put it off until she is ready.

Times to Be Firm with a Toddler In some situations, such as crossing a street, waiting for a toddler to make up her mind is not possible. When these occur, I tell parents, make clear that you are serious. While introducing a new vegetable is not the moment to have your way, there will be times when your authority must prevail. For instance, parents call me in desperation about giving medicine to a toddler. When the situation is this important, let her know it is not up for negotiation and it's different from other times like mealtimes. She *has* to do it. If necessary, you may have to put it in her mouth while she's lying down. If she chokes and spits it out, do it again and again until she accepts it. I remember my boiling frustration when, as a pediatrician, I had to do this. One of our children spit pills right back at me, each time looking me straight in the eye. Eventually, she gave in. When I hugged her afterward, I don't know who was more relieved.

Another way to give medicine is for a second adult to hold the child tilted back in his lap with a full nelson hold—arms up under hers and alongside her head. With her head tilted back so she can't spit it out, you can then pour the medicine in so she either chokes or swallows. She'll make the right choice.

All of this seems brutal, and it must be saved for a *real emergency situation* (see chapter 27). When a child knows you are serious, she will usually give up the struggle quickly.

This is the age when children start to climb out of cribs. so they need cushions or mats under their cribs. It certainly can happen that a toddler will fall out, but it doesn't happen often. When she begins to climb out, you will have to put the crib sides down. Then, the room can act as her crib, with a gate at the door. I always hope that this won't happen too early. The beauty of the crib is that it says implicitly: here is where you belong at night. Once children are in a bed or sleep on the floor, there's no real limit on their roaming. The crib is a symbol of the limits that are necessary to protect them at night. The most dangerous thing I know of is to have a child wandering around the house alone.

An eighteen-month-old toddler can be virtually fearless. On the stairs, she steps right out and could easily hurtle through space. Teach her how to climb up and down either by crawling or by stepping while you hold her hand. She'll learn fairly quickly. But a gate is still vital. All the fearless, rambunctious, insatiable energy of a toddler has to be both celebrated and contained. Gates, cribs, and firm restraining arms represent security as well as limits.

12

TWO YEARS

The longer the span between visits, the more dramatic and exciting it is for me to see the child's strides in development. For the parents, it is rewarding to demonstrate these to me—an interested audience. They will beam when I say, "Isn't he glorious?"

One of the most delightful characteristics of two-year-olds is the way they strut in, mirroring the walk of one of their parents. Gender identification will often be striking. A boy walks, gestures, and smiles like his father, a girl like her mother. Subtle identification already!

Negativism is still uppermost, but both the toddler and his parent know how to handle it better. We need to discuss it again, but there won't be the same anxiety, the same wonder about "Can it ruin our lives?" that each parent felt at the last visit. Usually, the child will be able to play in the toy corner with intense concentration while his parents and I talk. If not, if he is too clingy or too frightened to leave his parents, it is time for us to wonder why. He should be ready for more independence by now. I am pleased when parents raise questions like "How much independence should we promote?"

"How far shall we let him go?" or "What kind of discipline do we need to use? " If he is "too good" at this age, I do worry.

As the child enters my office, I look for the kind of confidence and security that shows in a child who has developed an expectation to succeed in life. After only a moment, I can say whether these are present. In that brief observation I can tell some of the following things:

1. *Self-confidence*—As the child enters my office, he must master memories from previous visits. A secure child will charge over to the play end of my office as if he owns the place. Coming in ahead of his parents, he is sure that they will follow. He demonstrates in his secure stride that he is ready to master the new situation. His curiosity about my toys tells of an inquisitive mind, ready to conquer new challenges.
2. *Competence*—A two-year-old strides firmly, legs close together, arms at his sides, with upright posture. As he zeroes in on the toys and leans over to pick them up, he uses a firm, coordinated grasp.
3. *Speech*—His "hi" or "car" or "no" is vibrant and melodious, not strident. It has an inviting musical sound.
4. *Gender identification*—A boy has already absorbed his father's behavior and a girl, her mother's. This identification is clear by two years of age and speaks to the power of imitation and early awareness of a child's own sexuality.
5. *Handedness*—A right-handed child will reach for a new toy with his right hand. He might have held his right hand out to me for a greeting. If he's a lefty, he will use that hand confidently. If he's confused and bimanual, I need to take note of it, for this could interfere with his dexterity.

Play and Development

All of this gives me important clues as I talk with his parents. I watch him play as we talk. As I watch, I learn more about his ability to master the cognitive tasks appropriate for a two-year-old. For instance, a child might make a square out of blocks, a sort of room. Into the room, he places a girl doll. "Go home," he says as he brings the boy doll up. "Knock, knock! Come in?" He pushes one block aside to let the boy doll enter the room. The two dolls embrace.

In this scene, the child demonstrates his ability to use *symbolic play*. He uses the dolls to imitate the people in his life. The big event for this particular child would be his father's return at night. Symbolic play brings out *imitation*. In his use of *sexual differences* and the doll's behavior, he demonstrates his fantasies. Often, a child's imitation of the conversation and the questions that occur in the household demonstrate his ability to take in his parents' behavior and to imitate it. He shows his ability to pick up subtle inflections. When he pushes the block aside to let the male doll in, he demonstrates a sense of *means–ends* (what needs to be done to accomplish the task) and a sense of *causality* (if you open the door, it will allow you to enter).

Even a small bit of behavior like this confirms all kinds of accomplishments. The child might bring the windup truck to the "house." Placing the dolls delicately in the truck, he will line them up flat, parallel with the floor, so as not to drop them out. He then winds the key to make the truck run. Fantasy play in a toddler reveals his ability to take in and conceptualize the behavior and the meaning of the events around him. It is evidence not only of cognitive competence but also of a kind of emotional freedom. The fantasy play of a tense, unhappy child will be thin or nonexistent.

The level of delicacy with which a child handles toys, his *fine motor competence* as he winds a key, for instance, tells me that his neuromotor system is intact and easy for him to utilize. A child with mild cerebral palsy or any neurological impairment has clumsy, shaky movements; often has difficulty centering his behavior; and overshoots his target. All of this can be identified in the observations of a brief period of play.

At the same time, I'm learning about the cost to a child to take in information from his world, to digest it, and to organize it for action. In other words, is his nervous system accepting and utilizing information efficiently? Or is he having to overcome subtle delays in information processing? A child's prolonged attention, his ability to shut out all the other toys, to choose the ones that fit into his symbolic play, is evidence of good control over incoming stimuli. When a child has a hypersensitive nervous system, every new visual or auditory signal distracts him. He darts from one toy to another. If we talk near him, he is distracted by our voices. Sometimes by two years such a child has learned ways to master any auditory distractibility. For instance, his eyes may jerk over to our voices each time we speak. When this happens, he may force his head forward toward the toys to overcome the effect of our voices on his raw nervous system. Though at the mercy of auditory signals, he has learned to master them by redoubling his attention to his task (a costly but effective adjustment). He will also master his hypersensitivity with increased motor activity, which both partially overcomes and discharges the effects of this hyperreactivity. These signs may indicate an attention deficit disorder (ADD) and should be checked. Such a child will need our attention as he enters preschool or school. Mastering the distractions of a group of other children can be hard for him.

To watch for signs of hypersensitivity, I clap repeatedly to see whether the child can shut out repeated auditory stimuli.

To identify difficulty in organizing information, I give him a simple puzzle; a child who is unable to figure out the spatial relationships will soon drop it. To spot difficulty in mastering balance and space, I watch to see whether he has to anchor himself with one hand in order to free up the other to play.

All of these observations can be made while the child is playing and I am listening to the parents' concerns. If I observe any of these problems, I examine him for minor neurological deficits and/or for processing or attentional deficits. If I am concerned, I refer him for more thorough testing. I am convinced of the value of identifying these difficulties early. Observant parents are often the first to make these observations. Many have told me that they knew quite early that the child was having more difficulty in solving simple tasks than their other children. They observed him (1) frowning as he worked to achieve a task, (2) taking twice as long as he should to achieve a task that he already knew, (3) giving up quickly to go on to a more familiar and practiced routine, and (4) using all kinds of maneuvers to divert an adult's attention if offered a puzzle to solve that he knew he couldn't tackle. All of these observations from parents have made me aware of the child's valiant and resourceful attempts to overcome difficulties in assimilating information and utilizing it. When I confirm their concerns, they are likely to be relieved as we discuss how to help him.

If the difficulties seem mild, I suggest the following things to parents. Try reducing pressure and offering extra support. First, let the child know you can understand that it's hard for him but that he *can* do it. Then, choose times when there aren't other distractions for either of you. Sit down in a quiet, uncluttered place to solve a particular task together. Talk quietly and use only one modality—voice, movement, or eyes. Without putting him under too much pressure, which would just make him turn off, demonstrate the task step by step to him. Let him try it, fail, try it, fail. Then show him each step again, slowly, one by one. When he masters one step, encourage him, but not too overwhelmingly. After each small step, encourage him to try the next. If he can achieve small steps one at a time, he can gather the self-confidence to try another. Each one will add to his sense of competence, which has already been so battered. Allow him to break away, rest, and come back.

Pacing for such a child is important. If he can learn to pace himself, he'll have learned a great step toward mastery of his nervous system's overload. The hardest job for a parent will be not to hover and overprotect him. Parents need to let him get mildly frustrated so that when he achieves a task, it will be *his*, not theirs. Pulling back and letting him try are important. It is no easy task to parent such a child. But by giving him a sense of his own capacity for achievement, parents will have fitted him for the future. Needless to say, I'd always choose things he can do well to start and end with (see chapters 18, 26, and 34).

Getting Used to the Doctor

In the doctor's office, a two-year-old should decide whose lap to sit in or whether he wants to go on the examining table. If a child will allow me to participate in his dressing or undressing, I can be sure he'll see me as a trusted friend. I don't remove the diapers, as I've found it is important to leave on some clothing as a symbol of privacy. With luck, the child will have brought a dirty, bedraggled doll or bear, whose grimy face and tattered body show me how beloved it is. If not, one might be found in my office. I ask, "Can I be Teddy's (or whoever's) doctor?" The child will usually grin. "Teddy Doctor," he might say. I take this as an assent and ask, "Why don't you put the stethoscope on his body?" I let him use the stethoscope, then the otoscope. "Can you hold Teddy so he won't be worried when I look in his ears?" Holding Teddy tight to his chest, he may turn one of its ears for me, then the other. After this, it is a snap to examine each of his. "Show Teddy how to open his mouth—*wide*. We won't need to use a throat stick if you can show him how to open it really wide." By the time we've been through all of this, he will usually let me examine Teddy's belly, then his own belly and genitalia. "Teddy's just great! And so are you." The child will glow with pride and, once released from the exam, may almost dance over to my scale for me to measure his weight and height. I hardly need to reward him at the end, so rewarded is he by mastering his own stress. When we can build a firm, respectful relationship, it is an important touchpoint between us, an achievement for him and a window into his development for me.

Speech

A two-year-old will be using sentences with verbs and is beginning to use adjectives and adverbs. "Go to store." "Pretty dress." "I *want* that. It's nice." So far he hasn't identified spatial adverbs, but he might say "up" when he wants to be picked up, "down," to be put down. If you ask him, "Go get a toy in the other room, bring it in here, and put it on the chair," he will demonstrate a clear comprehension of these three layers of receptive speech. The timetable for all this still varies widely. In a nonspeaking child, the most useful diagnostic measure, I'm told by psychologist Dr. Elizabeth Bates of San Diego, is the use of gestural speech. If he can gesture clearly and use his body to make language, he already comprehends the communicative codes and is likely to speak eventually. He isn't delayed intellectually. Gestural speech is observable in speaking children when they can't quite say what they would like. They will point and act out their wishes in an almost intelligible manner.

If a parent wants a two-year-old to say words, she can push him by saying, "I think I know what you want, but you must say it to me. Try it. Is it a truck . . . or a house . . . or a doll?" The toddler may well try to imitate the word.

Dialogue with parents is by no means the only way speech develops in a toddler. Katherine Nelson, a psychologist at the City University of New York, taped a single child's speech from the age of twenty-one months to three years. These tapes included long monologues when the little girl was alone in her crib. Dr. Nelson and her colleagues, a distinguished group including Jerome Bruner and Daniel Stern, then analyzed the tapes and wrote about their findings in a book called *Narratives from the Crib* (see the Bibliography). One most interesting theory to emerge is that such monologues are not simply practice or play but attempts to make sense of daily experi-

ence. There was evidence that this very small child was actually re-creating her world for herself. Key experiences, such as
being left at nursery school (at thirty-two months), were retold
and interpreted:

Her daddy and mommy will . . . stay the whole time . . . but my mommy and daddy don't. They just tell me what's happening and then go right to work, 'cause I don't, 'cause I don't, 'cause I don't cry.

Out of these monologues emerges a meaning to the child's experience and a developing sense of self.

Speech can be delayed for many reasons:

1. Hearing deficits should *always* be ruled out in case of any doubt.
2. A child who can comprehend and can use clear body language may be refusing to speak—evidencing negativism. Parents should ask themselves whether they are hovering and making it too easy for him, so that he may not need to speak to get what he wants.
3. A third or fourth child is not likely to speak early. The older children do everything for him. Parents should watch him for gestural speech by which he may be expressing himself to them.
4. Bilingual households tend to delay speech production for as much as a year. The child is having to use different language sounds to make words. He will do it, but later. I think it's well worth the wait, for he will eventually end up with two languages.
5. Auditory processing disorder can cause a delay. This must be identified by an expert in hearing and learning disorders. Parents need to ask the pediatrician for a referral if difficulties persist.

Parents are often concerned when a child stutters. Most two- and three-year-olds stutter and stammer when speech is coming in so rapidly. They can't keep up with it. It's like falling over their feet when they're learning to walk. Correcting or saying words for the child only adds to the pressure. Everyone should give him time and not push or let him feel pushed. Unconsciously, all of us as adults put pressure on a child who's learning to speak. Every time they say something, we say it correctly right after them. We are programmed, one might say, to lead them toward adult speech. Any more pressure right now can turn transient difficulties into chronic problems. Given time, most will disappear. If a child is really delayed in understanding and in expressing himself, he deserves a complete evaluation. A speech therapist can tell a great deal about a two-year-old's abilities.

Most parents use some baby talk. Will that hold the child back in learning to speak like an adult? I don't think so. Everyone talks baby talk to a baby. Baby talk says to a child, "Now I'm speaking to *you*, not to anyone else." At some point, I'd change. That will say, "I'm proud you are growing up and want to speak." Adult speech gives him a chance to model on yours.

Sleep   The new language developments may show up in the periods of light sleep when the child is trying to find his way back down. Not really awake, he'll start talking, saying all his new words. He can soothe himself back down to sleep on his own.

Night terrors may begin to appear now. If they do, they frighten both the child and the parents. They occur in deep sleep and are accompanied by out-of-control screaming and thrashing. When a child is tested, these show up as small seizures on an electroencephalogram. If the episodes are very bad, parents can seek out a sleep expert. Otherwise, the calm presence of a parent coming in to rouse the child may be enough. The child sees the parent, is comforted, and settles back down again. Night terrors usually appear on the nights that follow a tough or stressful day. Perhaps there have been visitors, or parents were hard on the child near bedtime. The terrors may be a way of working off the leftover steam from the day.

Parents who have gotten out of the child's sleep pattern will now enjoy hearing him talk himself to sleep at night. He'll lie in bed after the bedtime ritual, rehearsing everything he's done during the day. These "crib narratives," mentioned earlier, are sometimes addressed to a doll or stuffed animal. Parents can recognize associations from the child's experiences in the day. Monologues may last for half or three-quarters of an hour. Then, he'll drop off to sleep. All the parents' past efforts to teach a child to get himself to sleep are now really paying off.

This gift of autonomy makes possible exciting mastery. By rehearsing his day and interpreting it, he masters the leftover frustration or tension.

When I ask parent at the two-year-old visit how feeding is going, the answer is, "He's a slob." The child will drop food off his fork and get frustrated. Then he may smear it around or throw the whole dish on the floor. If he is in control of the meal, he won't let parents help him. If they comment or try to suggest anything, he falls apart. They have to ignore him. The child wants to master his utensils so much that failure is a blow. He wants desperately to do it the way his parents do.

Feeding

Allowing this independence is very difficult. It's all parents can do not to urge the child on. The more trouble taken to "fix something special," the more he may balk. He *must* establish the fact that he's in control. The parents' longing for him to eat "something special" puts him on the alert. The second the parent makes even a helpful suggestion—for instance, that peas are easier to hold on a spoon than on a fork—he falls apart: "No peas!" Parents who persist are asking for feeding problems. If they respect the child for the struggle he's having in learning to eat like an adult, to make his own choices, and accept the mess involved in learning to use utensils. Meals will eventually be a pleasure. Waiting for table manners is a must. While this may seem like forever, it will not be more than a year or so. If parents push to feed him still, they are likely to set up feeding problems that will last a lifetime.

As we've said, perhaps too many times, only a child can decide when the time for toilet training has come. Any pressure parents may feel from grandparents, nursery schools, or helpful friends had better be disregarded. It's *got* to be his achievement, not theirs.

Toilet Training

Not until all the signs of readiness spelled out in the last chapter (language, imitation, tidiness, the waning of negativism) are evident should toilet training begin. Probably this will happen sometime during the third year. When parents and I confer over this important touchpoint, the steps that I recommend are as follows:

First Get him a potty chair on the floor, so he can take it wherever he wants. Call it his and let him get used to it as his. The big one is for you, his parents. The little one is for him to learn with.

Second After a week or so, take him to sit on his toilet, *in his clothes*, while you sit on yours. Read to him or give him a cookie to keep him there momentarily. This is just to establish the daily routine of sitting on it. If you take his clothes off, it's too invasive and may frighten him.

Third The next week, ask him if it's all right to take his diapers off so he can sit on it, once a day. You sit on his potty, he sits on his. Reiterate: "This is what Mommy does every day. This is what Daddy does. This is what Grandma does. Your (doll, bear, etc.) can do it. We go to the potty when we're big like you."

Fourth The third week, take him to his pot with his dirty diaper to undo it, then drop it in the toilet seat. Meanwhile, say something along these lines: "This is where you can go someday to do your b.m. This is what Mommy and Daddy do every day. This is your pot. This is mine." Don't flush his b.m. away in your toilet while he watches. Parents tell me that their children are fascinated to see it go out of sight. This may be, but the child is also wondering where it goes as it disappears. Children may wonder for years where their b.m.'s have gone. Any child feels it's part of himself. Don't get rid of it until he loses interest and walks away.

Fifth The next step is completely at the discretion of the toddler. In fact, if at any time he resists a step, forget training for a while. You are simply showing him each step so he can take it up for himself. At this time, if he's been interested in the previous steps, you can offer to take his clothes off and let him run around with a bare bottom. If he's ready to try it by himself, offer to put the potty in his room or out in the yard with him. He can go to it himself when he wants to. Then, I'd offer to remind him every hour to try to go. If he's ready, he will be able to cooperate on the pot. If he does produce something, leave it there for him to admire. You can congratulate him, but don't overdo it. Too much praise can take away his own excitement about his achievement.

Sixth If he's really ready, you can leave his pants off for longer and longer periods. If he wets or has a b.m. on the floor, go right back to diapers. Don't make a fuss of it. Simply say, "We'll try again. There's no hurry. Someday you'll do it like Mommy and Daddy and Grandma." You are depending on his desire to imitate and identify with important persons.

Each step must be at his timing. If he gets worried or resistant, pull back quickly and forget it. Some children begin to care so much that they will have tantrums about whether to go to their pot or not. They will stand in front of the toilet, jumping up and down, saying, "I want to go." The pain in their faces and behavior shows the struggle in their resistance to cooperating. Once they're on the pot, they will hold back. If you push them to try at this time, you are putting on more pressure. The system is already overloaded. Like any other temper tantrum, if you enter into it, you reinforce and prolong it. In an area like this, where autonomy is a critical ingredient, the child himself must settle his own internal struggle and must make up his own mind. As with a tantrum, you can prolong it but you won't help. The decision is his. He must resolve it, however painfully, before he can make it his achievement. Offer him back his diapers, especially at naptime and nighttime. Try to forget training for a while. He knows now what you are expecting of him, and he must do it when he's ready.

A mother will often say to me, "He's been holding back on his b.m.'s. He stands in front of the potty, screaming as if in pain. I say, 'Johnnie, just try. You know what to do. If you'll just go to the pot, your pain will be all gone.' " This is wrong. The pain is in his head; it is the pain of tortured indecision. The mother's involvement is just fueling this indecision. She must pull out of it and put him back in diapers. If she says that "he acts as if being in diapers is a form of punishment," she may have built up getting trained as too important. She can only pull back and leave it to him to let her know when he wants to try again. She can tell him, "The diapers are really to help you go when you want." When either parent asks, "Then, will he go to school in diapers?" that question in itself shows me how uptight they are about his getting trained. They will need to reevaluate their own feelings to be able to pull out and leave it to him. Most of us were trained too early or too coercively, and it's hard not to reproduce this with our children. But, don't.

When a child begins to hold onto his bowel movement, he is demonstrating a resistance to pressure—either internal or external. For reasons that may have nothing to do with his parents, he may have caught on and may want to achieve his own training before he is ready. The danger with holding back b.m.'s is that it can quickly lead to constipation. The old myths about constipation poisoning the system are groundless. Children can have a weekly b.m. and be perfectly healthy otherwise. The large intestine will enlarge to adapt. When their pattern changes to a more normal one, the large intestine will adapt again to its normal size. So, staying out of it and leaving his resistance alone are best.

The trouble with withheld b.m.'s is that they are likely to become large and rocky hard. They hurt the anal sphincter when they are eliminated. A fissure in the anus is painful. Then, whenever the b.m. is felt, the memory of a painful one is revived by the fissure. The anal sphincter clamps down to withhold the b.m. A vicious circle ensues: withholding for psychological reasons is coupled with reflex withholding at the sphincter level. The cycle of constipation, chronic anal fissures, and even a condition called megacolon can result.

When you see this developing, you *must* eliminate any pressure. Place the child back in diapers at naptime and nighttime, at a minimum. Tell your child, "You can have your b.m. safely, and I'll see that it won't hurt you." Then, offer him petroleum jelly and place it up in the anus to protect the fissure. Also, obtain an effective bowel softener from the toddler's doctor. This may have to be used for a long time, until the child *and* the sphincter have forgotten about the painful b.m.'s. He must have soft b.m.'s that cannot repeat the injury to the sphincter. You must be prepared to say, "All this fuss about going to the pot has given you b.m.'s that hurt. Now we're going to see that they won't hurt, so you can go whenever you want. It's your choice, not ours."

Seventh In learning to urinate at the toilet, a boy should start sitting down. Any boy who learns to stand first won't want to sit down. It's too much fun to stand and spray the back of the toilet (or the wall), to make sounds with the spray, and manipulate his penis. When the child has mastered going on the pot, the father can take him in to watch.

Some fathers are not sure they can be un-self-conscious. If they can remember that the little boy will be overjoyed to share this with them, they can forget modesty. If the child doesn't want to sit down again after he's learned the excitement of standing and spraying, a father can model that for him, too. Modeling this behavior comes so naturally.

A father must be prepared for his child to want to compare penis size. He may even want to touch. The father can simply say, "Mine is bigger than yours, just as I'm bigger—my feet, my hands, all of me. Someday, you'll grow bigger like me everywhere." When the boy asks about pubic hair, the father can add, "Someday, you'll get hair on your face, your body, and around your penis, just like me." This encourages questions.

Eighth Night training shouldn't begin until he's dry at his nap, and until he gives some signal that he wants to stay dry at night. Wait until he's really ready—dry diapers or no urine for at least four to six hours a day. A child will have to be really ready to cooperate at night to make it worthwhile. Until he wants you to help him, or he does it spontaneously, I'd eliminate nighttime as a project until he's three years old or older. Most children aren't ready to stay dry until four or five.

Girls are often ready sooner than boys. We don't really know why. A child has to be really ready to wake up and to get up to go at least once or twice a night. Just holding it and controlling it in the daytime isn't enough. When the child is old enough, he will get a signal in sleep that allows him to wake up in order to empty his bladder. It doesn't help for you to do it for him by carrying him to the toilet at night. When you've shown him the steps, you've done your job. After that, stay out of it. Children vary as much as a year or more in their readiness. As a society, we are far too uptight about pushing children to be toilet trained. I don't even like the phrase "toilet training." It really should be "toilet learning."

If you have more than one child, you may never need to train any but the first. Children with older siblings may learn from them. You may, however, have to keep the older one from expecting too much. It is amazing how much a younger child learns from the older ones—and it seems to be relatively painless.

Sexuality   Toilet training will increase interest in genitals, in both sexes. Masturbation and exploration, like other touchpoints of development, are entirely normal at this age. Little boys play with their penises. Little girls find their vaginas and even insert objects into them—all as part of normal exploration. Parents ask, "How much is too much?" If the child withdraws to masturbate when there are other exciting things to do or masturbates to tease you and others when he's in public, this is a sign of tension in the child's life. If a child begins to masturbate in public, assure him that it is absolutely okay to investigate and to play with himself. But it is a private sort of thing, and you'd like him to save it for a private place. Other people don't like to watch him. Then, if he's doing a lot of it, look for reasons. Like too much thumb sucking or rocking or head banging, excessive masturbation can be a sign that the child is under too much pressure. These are all normal, healthy patterns for the end of the day or for discharging tension at peak times, but if they persist and occur a great deal, parents should lighten up on any pressure such as meal behavior, manners, toilet training, and so on. As the child gets older, he'll find other more acceptable ways of releasing tension.

Parents needn't worry when a girl first tries to insert objects into her vagina, for she won't be likely to hurt herself or rupture her hymen. If parents are offended by her explorations, they'd better learn to relax. If she seems particularly involved with masturbation, as we said before, they might look for the cause, but all little girls try to "find out where their peepee is" and why they have a vagina. All little boys explore themselves, too. Sometimes, they cause themselves to have an erection by their masturbation. Play it cool, I tell parents. If they ask you, give them an answer to this question. Try not to get too long-winded or too complicated. This will only make them wonder why you are so involved about that part of their bodies.

We all worry about heightening a child's interest in sexuality at this age. I have a doll in my office with a hole in her back. At first, I started to throw her away because it is a distortion of a toddler's expectation. Now I use the doll diagnostically. When I see a toddler looking at it quizzically, I can say, "You wonder why that is there, don't you? You and I know that all of us have holes in other places—in our belly buttons, and in our penis or vagina, and in our bottoms. She's not like us, is she?" A child will look grateful as early as eighteen months. They know already where their anuses and their vaginas are. What they are looking for is acceptance of their curiosity and a response to their questions about their belly buttons or genitals, the more obscure parts of their bodies.

Negativism and Aggression

Two-year-olds continue to have violent shifts of mood. Suddenly, they will become angry and out of control. When parents try to help, the child will be likely to bite or kick or bang her head.

Breath-holding spells can occur at such times. These scare parents to death. They wonder whether the child will ever start breathing again. Will she turn blue and damage her brain? Not likely. Once she stops breathing, she'll relax; and even if she becomes unconscious, she'll start breathing again. Circulation will recover immediately. Breath-holding spells are terrifying, but they aren't likely to hurt the child. They surely hurt parents and even make them hesitate to discipline the child. This is too bad, for she needs discipline just as much as before, and maybe even sooner, but with more firmness and comforting or holding. The most effective response is to hold her, then put her down in her room, where she's safe. Then parents should walk away, saying, "When you are through with that, I can come back. I don't like this behavior, and I can't seem to help you with it." Afterward, they can comfort her and say, "Someday, you'll learn to control this yourself."

A child who is very aggressive in a group, always taking everything away from the others and knocking them down when they try to defend themselves, may not know how to stop. Other parents won't like him or trust him. That's hard on him, for he will know that he's not liked. Parents can talk to such a child *before* he goes into a group and remind him that other children don't like to be pushed around. They should tell him that at the point where he begins to do it, they'll have to leave with him—then, follow through. When parents do leave, they need to let him know that he's got a job to do—to learn to control himself. Meanwhile, parents should find a playmate who is just as aggressive. The children will learn from each other about what their aggression means, and they can learn about controls together.

If a child has trouble sharing, I suggest discussing this with him before another child comes to visit. Parents can decide with him which toys he will share and put the others away. Learning to share is a hard job of childhood. If this is expected of him, he will learn. This is the age to begin.

Looking Ahead   **Helping around the House** When can a child learn to help with chores and housework? This year is not too early. In busy, working families, help will soon become a wonderful asset. For the child, a great boost in self-esteem comes from feeling useful and competent.

At first, of course, teaching a child to help takes *extra* effort. Parents will have to set aside times during the day to show the child how to set the table, how to rinse a plastic dish, how to pull off lettuce leaves—anything they think he can do. Then, he can be praised for doing it as a contribution to the work of the family. Every moment spent this way is an investment for the future. Boys and girls who learn how to help in this generation will be much better prepared for a world in which both parents must work. They'll be ready to share household chores and will not expect to be waited on.

Television Small children are exhausted by television. It is a demanding medium—demanding a kind of "hooked" visual and auditory attention. Watch a small child at the end of a program to which he's paid attention. He will be fractious and out of control. Most of us know the feeling of coming out into the street after a daytime movie, jangled, out of synchrony with the world.

Fortunately, most toddlers will not sit for too long in front of a set. They are too excited by their own activities. If they do want to watch all the time, I'd worry. No toddler should watch for longer than a thirty-minute period, and even then, he should be comforted afterward. When parents use television as a babysitter, they must realize that the programs are assaulting all of the child's senses, and there is a dear price.

On the other hand, healthy learning from television is certainly possible. Just as children model aggression and violence

from TV watching, they can be expected to learn from a kindly, paternal figure (e.g., Mr. Rogers) about empathy. They certainly do pick up messages from "Sesame Street." Toddlers will see an *A* in a book and start to sing the song that "Sesame Street" plays for an *A*. This potential makes it even more important that the quality as well as the amount of television watching be monitored by parents. Programs should be carefully chosen and viewed no more than one-half hour at a time, no more than twice a day. Ideally, a parent should be participating during at least one of these periods.

A New Sibling "When is the ideal time for us to have another baby?" a mother will ask. "Ideal for whom?" I generally reply. "Well, I'd like him to want the baby—and to see it as his." This is wishful thinking. No first child ever wants the invasion of a second child. Parents should decide for themselves when they feel they can handle another. Often, they worry about breaking into the close attachment with the first child. When I hear this, I'm pleased, for parents who can love a child through his second year are really in love with him! Once they feel they can handle another, the first child can handle one, too. Though it will not be easy, in the long run, giving him a sibling is giving him a gift. He will have to learn to share if he has a sibling. An only child may or may not learn to share; a sibling forces the issue.

An older child can identify with his parents and can help with the baby. He may not like the new baby, but he'll learn to accept her as a sibling, and he'll learn so much else in the process (see chapter 36).

13

THREE YEARS

Just as a child turns three, she and her parents are likely to enjoy a kind of second honeymoon. The toddler's negativism and struggles seem to resolve miraculously. A two-and-one-half- to three-year-old becomes tranquil and cooperative in ways that make the previous year and a half seem worth it. Parents can't believe this is happening. They feel carried back to the delicious love affair of the middle of the first year, when all was rosy. This tranquil period comes between the negative second year and "the beginning of the early adolescence" between four to six years. Struggles over sexual identification and aggression will stir them up between four and six, but three years can be a blessed time for peaceful readjustment.

If earlier problems persist, this is a good time to face and try to resolve them. We have a clinic at Children's Hospital in Boston for children with issues that develop over the first three years. Many parents seem to be able to face, with a three-year-old, problems that have arisen before. Such rapid learning has been going on, for both the parents and the toddler, that there hasn't been time or energy to pull back and to face lingering issues before.

Among the problems that may not have been solved is that of *sleeping* through alone. Learning to sleep for an eight- to twelve-hour period, as we said in earlier chapters, demands that a child be able to cycle through three periods of light sleep and rousing. When she wakes, she must handle the feelings of separation and the fears of night with its "monsters" and memories of conflicts left over from the daytime. There is no period free of them, including this one—even though she may appear to be tranquil.

Another problem at night may be her *fears*. A three-year-old is beginning to be aware of aggressive feelings. Fears for herself accompany the surges of aggression that will begin to surface. Fears will be acted out, and dreamt about at night. Unless nighttime patterns are already well set, dreams will begin to crop up at REM cycles. They are likely to be of aggression, and fears will accompany them. These dreams are likely to disrupt sleep in the third and fourth years. When there is stress in the child's environment, or when she must make an adjustment to a new situation, fears will surface at night. The child will need to learn to comfort herself over time, but this can take a while (see chapter 37).

Whenever parents realize that they and the child are stuck in a struggle, it's time to reevaluate what's going on. Independence is critical to the child's development of a good self-image. Control is a parental issue. Parents need to respect the child's need for autonomy. But these needn't be in conflict, unless parents are stuck with "ghosts" from their own past—unresolved conflicts from their own childhood. In order to foster a resolution, they often need to face these deeper conflicts of their own.

Meals　By three years of age, a child is ready to eat only at mealtime. Meals can now become a shared, family event. She needn't be fed in between, nor does she need junk food. She needs to look forward to the conversation and the fun of a family being together. Setting her day up so that this can occur is important. Everyone can get up earlier so breakfast is relatively relaxed and have supper together, even if the child has to have a snack to tide her over. Families can emphasize that "at our house, we eat meals together that we all prepare. We all help, and we are proud of them."

For a finicky eater, the basic minimum diet is not very elaborate: sixteen ounces of milk, two ounces of protein, some whole-grain bread or cereal, a few ounces of fruit, and a multivitamin. The latter is needed only if she is not eating well. Again, parents should watch out for the ghosts from their own childhoods, such as memories of a mother making a child sit at table for two hours, then angrily putting away what was left to be eaten later. A child's refusal to eat will remind parents of the desperation and of the humiliation they felt. By recognizing this, they can avoid repeating it. Parents also set rules for themselves, and the child that will help change old patterns.

For the Child

No in-between snacks (unless planned to allow a late dinner).

No returning to the table after leaving. The child doesn't need to stay, but once she gets down, that's it.

For the Parent

Try to set an example of table manners, but do not nag.

Don't use desserts as bribery.

Don't talk about food or plead with the child to eat.

Don't cook special things for the child alone—you'll be disappointed when she refuses them.

If food hasn't already become a battleground, a three-year-old will begin to model herself on those around her. She'll eat the things they eat. She'll even pick up a few table manners. If parents can make mealtime a family time with fun and pleasure attached, they won't have a problem. For working families, this is not easy, with different schedules, time pressures, and so on. But one or two mealtimes together become even more important when a family is stressed.

These pressures are all the more reason to get everyone to

help. Parents shouldn't do it all for the child. Setting the table, preparing simple foods, and cleaning up afterward are wonderful training for a child's future. Though involving the child may still take twice as long as parents doing everything, they shouldn't cajole or beg. Instead, they need to expect her to help, show her how to do things, encourage her, and explain that she must help every day. When she does, she deserves to be rewarded. All this time and effort will certainly pay off in the long run.

Since many of the child's friends will eat candy bars and drink pop, parents may worry about making her different by eliminating them. A parent can point out that this is the way we are; they are "different from us." Cookies and candy can be treats. If the child goes next door for junk food, parents can try to have a heart-to-heart talk with the neighbor, or other culprits, such as grandparents, explaining their own efforts to help the child develop decent, predictable feeding habits. The culprits should help. If they don't, the parents will know who their allies are—and aren't. Any substitute caregiver should also know the parents' position.

Toilet Training

By now, a three-year-old may well feel as if she had always been trained—at least in the daytime. Any mistake such as soiling or wetting will be taken very seriously by her. Any regression in training will occur at an understandable time, such as when a father or mother goes away, or around a new baby. Parents need to help her understand about any accidents. Otherwise, she may feel guilty and overwhelmed. If she can understand the reason for mistakes, she needn't get so upset that she'll keep repeating them. Repeated failures are likely to occur because of parental pressure or because she's just not ready. Parents shouldn't let her feel inadequate. Diapers need to be used not as a punishment but as a way of relieving her from the fear of making mistakes. When she begins to get control again, parents can remind her of how much she's achieved, let her know that it has been her achievement, and express their pride in her.

As soon as she realizes that she's gained control, she's ready for training pants. The beauty of them is that she can pull them down easily. Using them as "big girl pants" before she's ready can surely reverse any gain. These need to be saved until she's ready. If she wets through them onto the floor, she's not ready, and she's likely to feel like a failure. She may give up and fall back to wetting and soiling again. My advice is to always stay one step behind her. Getting ahead of her amounts to pressure in her eyes.

A genuine understanding of the child's need to follow her own timing makes toilet training a touchpoint, an opportunity to prevent problems such as bedwetting (enuresis) and constipation. A child will let parents know when she wants to be out of diapers at night. She will start by staying dry at naptime and controlling herself for the first part of the night. Parents need to wait until they are sure their child is ready. She'll demonstrate in the daytime that she can hold on to stay dry even after parents know she needs to urinate. The child's interest in being dry all night is what parents are waiting for—and she will lead the way.

At some point, children begin to realize that they want to grow up. They want to be like everyone around them. Most children begin to be aware of being dry at night by the fourth year. Three-year-olds at nursery school pressure each other: "Are you still in diapers at night? Not me. I'm dry!" The other will blush and say, "Me, too," even if she is not. Peer pressure begins early. Adding parental pressure doesn't help.

No matter how often I reassure parents about toilet training, they picture *their* child as staying in diapers forever. No parent feels certain her child will ever really achieve the next step. In such a charged area as bedwetting, unspoken parental anxiety can lead to conflict. Parents care too much. There are a certain number of boys (fewer girls, it seems) who have an immature bladder. These boys have a difficult time learning how to hold onto a bladder full throughout an eight-hour period at night. Many of them aren't ready to be dry until they are six or eight years of age and their bladders mature. Many sleep too soundly to wake up. They have immature sleep patterns, which need to be respected, too. Pressure from family and peers increases their guilt and their conflict about being able to stay dry. Parents need to be reassuring, so that they may not feel so devalued. Certain maneuvers can help them, but I'd only offer suggestions when they ask for help: "Try to hold on a little longer each time after you feel like peeing during the day." That way, they can consciously "teach" their bladders to hold on longer. But parents need to be careful—even this can be pressure and can be devaluing. It's got to be the child's achievement or the child will feel like a failure.

For parents who are helping their son, I talk with them and suggest the following steps. Once the child has expressed interest, offer to put a pot beside his bed. Even though he may be only a step away from the bathroom, it's still an effort to get out of bed and go there. A special potty can be a symbol that you want to help him. You could let him paint it with luminous paint in a design of his own choosing. Then, suggest to him that you'll come to get him up before you go to bed. If he wants to and is ready, he'll wake up when you do go to him. If he won't wake up, it's no use. Taking him to empty his bladder is useless. What you want to do is to teach him how to *rouse himself* at night. When he's ready, he'll recognize the signal of a full bladder in light REM sleep. Then, he'll get up and go. He'll rouse himself the first thing in the morning. Be sure you don't take him out of diapers at night until he's ready and can make it easily. It is likely to undermine his interest in getting dry if he fails on successive nights and wets the bed. At some point, a boy begins to care a great deal. Then, it is awful for him to fail.

Another deviation on the road to successful toilet training is that of withholding bowel movements. As I mentioned in earlier chapters, it is natural for a child to be conflicted about giving up her b.m.'s to the toilet. Why some do and others don't, I've never quite understood, but their unconscious conflict had better be respected. The pain of defecation becomes feared. The cycle of holding back—creating a large, hard b.m., which then hurts at each defecation—is quickly created. The conscious fear of pain redoubles the unconscious desire to retain the b.m. This cycle needs to be broken as soon as it is recognized. Parents should follow the suggestions offered in chapter 3 about stool softeners, a high-fiber diet, and petroleum jelly around the cracked anus. Reassuring the child that this will keep the movement from hurting is important. By

talking about what's going on, parents counteract both conscious and unconscious fears. When a bowel movement is
produced, parents should leave it in the toilet until she's lost
interest in it. She may prefer to go back into diapers to produce it safely, so parents can offer them to her at naptime and
nighttime for this purpose. Once again, boys are more likely to
get into this kind of turmoil than are girls, though we do not
know why (see chapter 42).

Fears and Phobias

The widening world of a three-year-old will bring new fears
and phobias. She may begin to worry about fire engines with
loud noises or dogs who bark. Phobias about going to strange
places and to the doctor's office surface. These may have
reality behind them, and a parent needs to try to help with
preparation and understanding, without expecting reassurances to wipe out the fears. Important issues may underlie
these fears.

As an example, a child may worry about all the babies in the
neighborhood. She won't go near the house next door because
the neighbor has a new baby. Her own baby sister is already
nine months old, so her parents are puzzled that she is getting
so upset all of a sudden. They thought she'd be "adjusted" by
now. However, an older child never completely adjusts to a
new baby. At each new stage of the baby's development, the
rivalry will surface again. As the baby gets more mobile and
more attractive, the older child will have a new surge of rivalry. Underneath her terror of new babies, this three-year-old
is likely to be working out her feelings about her own aggressive feelings. As she feels herself likely to react, she must make
more and more effort to contain herself. Her effort is costly.
Fears, phobias, and nightmares crop up at such times. They
represent the cost of controlling unwanted feelings.

Parents can talk to a child about the feelings they know she
has and prepare her for the surge of fear she'll feel when she
hears a fire engine or a barking dog. She also will need to learn
how to open up and become aggressive in safe ways. I offer
parents the following advice. One way she can learn is by
identifying with you the ways you express aggression. Take

her along when you run or play sports. Talk to her about safe ways to handle dangerous feelings. She may not entirely understand you, but she'll be comforted by sharing discussions with you. As her aggressive feelings surface, she'll be more likely to fall back on putting them into words and asking you questions.

During this period when fears and phobias are appearing, it is more important than ever to limit her television watching. Parents need to be there during potentially scary programs. An hour a day is always enough, with half of that as a shared viewing time, followed by time to talk. Discussions not only reassure her but offer her an opportunity to learn your parents' important values.

This is the age when a child's imagination begins to take fire. She will be watching everyone around her in new ways. She'll be learning about them not only by observation but also by imagining whole scenarios about them. She will assimilate this new learning in her imaginary play. Symbolic play (in which she uses toys and dolls to act out events and interactions) has already surfaced in the second year. Now she can use people around her as symbols. She will make up her own imaginary people.

Imagination and Fantasy

First children develop imaginary friends at this age. The imaginary friend can perform miracles. She can do all of the bad things and experience all of the good things of which the three-year-old dreams. A child will talk about her imaginary friend as if she were real. Parents who are used to being everything for their child may even feel jealous of this beloved companion and worried about her lapse from reality. They needn't. Any first child is likely to develop such a fantasy friend. She needs her to rely on. A second or third child rarely is allowed to develop such a friend. The older child prevents this. For the first child, the friend serves so many purposes. The friend can act out all of her imagined experiences.

Adults must respect the private nature of such a fantasy. It is precious. As soon as adults invade this privacy by asking about the friend, they anchor the child's fantasies in reality. Imaginary friends melt away when adults talk about them. After sharing them, a child may never mention them again. Either they go underground, or the magic goes out of them. Once, when I asked my grandson what his "friend" looked like, he said scornfully, "Bapa! He's *only* imaginary." As Emerson said, "Respect the child. . . . Trespass not on his solitude."

With all this bubbling imagination, two new attributes appear. A sense of humor is likely to surface, and a child's ability to show empathy for others will become apparent. When a baby cries, she may want to go to it. When another child is hurt, she will watch him carefully to see how he handles it. She may even show sympathy for his pain. These two traits are important as I assess children this age for flexibility in their own personality and for evidence of a good self-image.

Where do these new personality traits come from? They come from the many sources we've discussed—the identification with parents and others around her, and from careful observation of their reactions in such situations. They also come from her awareness of increasingly complex feelings—of aggression and a desire to transgress. The richest source of humor, empathy, and compassion is the child's imagination and all of the rich experiences that her fantasies provide for her.

Peer Relations In the third and fourth years, experiences with others the child's own age are becoming more and more important. She needs these peer experiences. Not only can she learn patterns of behavior from other children, but she can try out her own patterns in safety. All three-year-olds tease each other. They push each other to limits that they dare not test themselves. They make each other angry. They make each other cry. They can't wait to see each other. They hug each other, ferociously locking in each other's arms and legs. They learn from each other the safe ways and the dangerous ways to try out their new and complex feelings. Friendships are important, and rivalry is a critical part of friendship. A three-year-old will treat a dear and safe friend as a rival, as a baby to be mothered, as a parent, as every possible partner. Sexual exploration rapidly becomes a part of this learning. Most three-year-olds play some form of "doctor" and "nurse." This makes for a safe kind of exploration of their bodies.

This exploratory play and this experience with others lead to a surer sense of her self. I would worry about a child who doesn't begin to have secure relationships at this age. If other children don't like them, parents should take this seriously. Other children sense it when a child is in trouble, and they keep their distance. An anxious child or an angry child threatens the balance they've achieved with their own fears and aggression. If a child is isolated by her peers, there is likely to be a reason.

Sometimes parents can help with early experiences in a group. If a child hasn't ever had experience with other children her age, parents can introduce one friend first. They need to find someone who is like her in personality, make a big effort to get them together, then take them on excursions together and let them learn about each other. If a child can make it with one member of a group, she'll learn more about how to handle herself, and the other child will help her enter the group.

If sharing is her problem, parents can explain to her in advance that no one wants to have to share, and then they can help her with techniques. I'd suggest offering to let her take along one or two precious toys she needn't share and talking with her about being ready to share all the others. When she makes even a small step toward sharing, parents need to give her credit. Learning to share is one of the hardest jobs in life.

The dawning of empathy for others comes when a child voluntarily shares with another. Sure, she's been told over and over, "You must learn to share." But, she suddenly does it without pressure. "Do you want a bite of my cookie?" Then, she watches the face of her friend to see whether this newfound generosity pays off. She knows she needs and wants a friend. This is the first glimmer of a very important cognitive process called altruism.

Looking Ahead

In the next three years, parents of a three-year-old can expect a period of intense development. The kind of tumultuous learning that a child does in this period seems to me to be a preview to the turmoil of adolescence. The way a four- and five-year-old learns about sexuality and aggressive feelings will probably parallel the style in which she'll face them again in her teens. Some parents see this as a frightening prospect. "I wish you hadn't told me," they will say. Actually, this period can be fun to watch and be a part of, if you can see it as a great spurt in her development. It is a wonderful opening up of new experiences if a parent can learn not to take the testing, the turmoil, and the resistance personally.

Learning about Sexual Identity What does it mean for a child to enter such a period? She needs to learn how to handle strong feelings in a safer, more mature way than she did as a toddler. She needs to learn how to identify with each parent.

She needs to know how they work—how she can be like them and *not* like them. How will she do it? She'll swing from one parent to the other. In this period, she will focus her passion and completely absorb one parent for a period, ignoring the other. If you observe a child of this age closely, subtle but identifiable characteristics of one parent can be seen in the child's style of walking, her speech rhythms, her food preferences, and many other areas. But soon, she will turn away completely to act as if that parent no longer existed. The other parent becomes her favorite. She chooses the new favorite for everything, acting as if the former one had no credibility. She ignores one parent to pick up every gesture, every word of the new favorite. Why does she need to swing in such a preferential fashion? I think it is economical. In order to absorb each parent so thoroughly, she needs to focus. If she were distracted by attention to both of them, her absorption would be incomplete and more expensive. The episodes of attachment to the parent of the opposite sex have been termed "oedipal" by Freud. When they occur later in adolescence, they are even more intense and passionate. This first "rehearsal" prepares a child—and her parents—for the job of sorting out important sexual identifications later on.

Needless to say, these shifts in allegiance can be excruciatingly painful for the excluded parent. "She used to wait for me to come home," a father will say to me wistfully. "She was so joyful and so much fun when I arrived. Now, she turns her back on me. As silly as it is, I feel rejected." If parents know what is going on and can be patient during these passionate shifts, they will feel less hurt. Don't give up, I tell them. She'll come back. Just don't let her feel rejected by you. Adopt an attitude of not taking it too personally at the time. At a calm moment, you can say, "I want a time with you all to myself." Read to her at night—alone—or have a special time each weekend in which you and she go off alone. Don't expect too much. But it can be a time for cementing your relationship while she does the work she needs to do—of learning everything about each of you. All this behavior will last a few months, and then it will change. The parent who is then the center of attention can help the other by acknowledging earlier feelings of being turned away.

Sometimes being the favorite can be uncomfortable, too. When a little girl becomes cute and seductive, a father may feel uneasy. Once again, if this is seen as a normal way of trying out her identification with her mother, it can be enjoyed. This seductiveness may also be used on other men. In this way, a child can tease and hide her intense feelings for her father. It's the other side of the same coin.

Aggressive Feelings The more difficult and less obvious work of this period is that of learning how to handle anger and aggression. That is indeed a long process, and is likely to take many forms. Testing each parent to the point of a reaction is one way a child learns what is and isn't acceptable. A return to previous patterns of temper tantrums is another. She may become openly angry and unpredictable. Or, she may become "too good and too compliant." I worry more about the latter. I would rather see a child of this age get angry, tease, and provoke her parents. She is expressing her turmoil openly and learning more. A child who is eager to please everyone around her costs herself a lot and will have to do more testing later (see chapter 19).

Habits Many "symptoms" such as stuttering, lying, stealing, and masturbating will crop up during these next few years. I see them all as exploratory. Children go through them, try them out, then go on to other patterns of exploration. If parents have had a problem with them in their own past, they are likely to overreact. Then, these stick as habits in the child. Concerned parents may pressure the child to stop, or they may studiously ignore the symptom. The child senses and responds to the tension around her by repeating the symptom, which is then likely to become a habit.

If this seems to be happening, here's what I tell parents. I'd sit down with her to discuss the problem. Emphasize that you didn't mean to be so harsh. Let her know that *she* isn't "bad," and that she will learn how to control it as she gets older. Be sure she knows that you think she's great and that she'll handle the problem for herself. You will only help if she wants help, but stay out of the situation and support her. Any three-year-old needs to know again and again that you respect and love her just the way she is (see chapter 24).

Cognitive Development In the pressured world of families today, many parents of children aged three or younger will wonder when to begin teaching them to read and write. My response: Don't, until she demands it. It's all too easy to overdo teaching letters and numbers. To me, the timing is not as important as the child's own desire to learn. Be *sure* the idea of learning these things is coming from her. It's so easy to push early learning on a child who is compliant at this age. But it does more harm than good. We've known this for some time.

In the 1960s there was a movement toward early teaching, led by a professor at Yale, Dr. O. K. Moore. He felt that if children could be taught early to read and write, they'd be more competitive when they entered school. It was true. In order to please adults around them, three-year-olds could read and write successfully. They didn't seem to know what they were reading, but they could do it. When they reached first grade, they were ahead of other children, and they received the adult approval they needed. But other children didn't particularly like them, and many of these "precocious" children hadn't learned the skills they needed to get along with peers. They were adult oriented.

In second and third grades, they began to slip. The rote learning processes they'd used to learn earlier didn't generalize to the more complex learning they needed in later grades. They seemed stuck with more primitive learning methods. When they began to slip from the top of the class, they lost the adult approval for which they'd been performing. These unfortunate children then hit bottom. They were not the stars any longer; other children had deserted them; adults were disappointed, leaving them sad and deserted. Despite this and later evidence that such precocious early training is costly, many parents are still eager to give children a "head start." Books and programs promising ways to "teach your baby to read" continue to proliferate. Stay away from them.

A child learns best who learns for *herself*, not others. Play is her way of learning. When she learns by play, she tries different techniques, to find out what works for *her*. When she can't achieve something she is interested in doing, she gets frustrated. Frustration drives her to find out how to do it. When she finally does it, she gets a wonderful feeling: I did it *myself*! This is the most rewarding fuel for future learning that there is. Ambitious parents must learn to watch the child, to stay in the background and let her learn for herself. It's difficult, but necessary. A parent's job is to admire and approve, but not to push.

Choosing a preschool can be done with the same philosophy in mind. Play is the powerful way children learn their most important tasks at this age—how to play with other children, how to handle other adults, and how to learn about themselves as social people. The tasks of this age group are enormous: (1) experiencing socialization, (2) learning about aggression, and (3) learning how to identify with everyone around you. They are emotional tasks, not cognitive ones. I'd choose a preschool for the people who run it and who interact with the children, not for the learning program. If there's pressure to perform and to learn, there may be too little time for children to learn about themselves. Parents should go to

school and watch—see firsthand how much time the children have for undirected play and for learning about themselves as people. Learning about oneself and about one's peers is the best learning that parents can provide in these preschool years. The one thing I'd like for all children to feel about themselves at this age is, I'm important! Everyone likes me!

two
CHALLENGES TO DEVELOPMENT

14

ALLERGIES

Allergies are best treated by prevention. Treating allergies after they are established is much more difficult. In my practice, I've always made a point of working with parents to identify the potentially allergic child. The danger of looking for possible allergies is that parents might label a perfectly healthy child as vulnerable. If this can be avoided, however, there is every reason to feel that preventing allergies, or treating them from the beginning, may prevent a situation in which a child feels helpless and fragile, and a vicious circle of symptoms, depression, and psychosomatic expression of the allergy develops.

Allergies and Anxiety

Avoiding frightening outbreaks of asthma or eczema is very important to the future well-being of a child. Today, we have so many more ways of helping these patients that an all-out effort from the beginning pays off. Once an allergy is set in motion, and if a treatment that works is not found, children feel increasing anxiety and helplessness. It is at this point that the psychosomatic aspects of the disease take effect.

Although problems such as asthma can become overlaid with anxiety in this way and may well become partly psychosomatic after a few frightening episodes, I should make clear that I do not think asthma or eczema *begin* because of psychological problems in the child or underlying family difficulties. There is likely to be a genetic predisposition, reinforced by environmental allergens. It is only as the disease manifests itself that the sufferer gets frightened and involved with it.

Asthmatic children are likely to demonstrate their anxiety to their parents and are likely to "use" the symptom for all kinds of manipulative reasons—such as rebellion, fatigue, provocation, or simply attention getting. Parents will be drawn into the situation inevitably as their own anxiety mounts. If they are unable to control the child's symptoms, their guilt, anger, and concern will heighten tensions in the family and in their relationship with the child. In this way, asthma can all too easily become a psychosomatic focus for the whole family.

For children with allergic reactions, simple infections can become prolonged and complex. A cold, for example, can hang on for two or three weeks, phasing into the next cold, which in turn adds to congestion left over from the first. Likewise, a simple sore throat may be complicated by congestion, which adds a week onto the infectious period. The tissues swell and make the child snore; the adenoids enlarge and begin to block canals to the inner ear or to the sinuses. Inner-ear infections may need to be treated with antibiotics to reduce the swelling that is putting painful pressure on the eardrum.

Eczema and asthma are more severe expressions of allergic tendencies and tend to develop a self-perpetuating course. With eczema, itching leads to scratching, and scratching aggravates the problem. The need to scratch can become an automatic response to anxiety or even boredom or frustration and can become a habit all too soon in infants and young children.

With asthma, when the child wheezes and can't breathe, he rapidly becomes frightened. Wheezing makes him anxious; anxiety intensifies wheezing. He gets a feeling of helplessness, of being unable to handle the disease or his fear of it. No wonder these allergic conditions become "psychosomatic" before very many such cycles have occurred.

There is no need, though, to let eczema or asthma go this far. When I know that there has been a tendency toward allergies in other members of the family, I try to alert parents to a reassuring fact: the older a child is before he shows allergic symptoms, the less severe they are likely to be, and the more easily they can be treated. The child who might have had eczema all over his body had he developed it in his first year will, in his second year, have only a mild case in his elbow creases and the backs of the knees.

There seems to be a threshold for tolerance of allergic stimuli that gradually increases with age. This threshold is more likely to be crossed by a combination of allergens than by any one of them alone. Although a child can be quite allergic to one thing—such as cat hair or chocolate or fish—and blossom out with his symptom after just one exposure, most children build up allergies over time. It is like piling one block on top of another. He may manage to live with several small allergens, to which he is mildly sensitive, without any symptoms. But when he gets a respiratory infection, eats too many eggs, or inherits a feather pillow, then the tower of blocks may topple, and he may show an allergic symptom.

Taking Preventive Steps Prevention must start early. I urge that a new mother from an allergic family breast-feed her infant. I have never seen a baby who was allergic to mother's milk and have seen far too many who were sensitive to cow's milk—responding with a congested nose, vomiting, diarrhea and, worst of all, full-blown eczema. Eliminating cow's milk and using a soybean milk substitute will clear these symptoms dramatically, although it may be a week or more before they disappear completely. I know eczema in babies can be prevented, because over the past fifteen years, I have had only one case of generalized eczema among the several thousand infants I have treated.

Next in importance to breast-feeding for new parents from allergic families is to see that the baby's bed be free of allergenic toys and that his lovey, whether a bear or blanket, be made of synthetic materials. Pure, mild soaps must be used for his bath and for his clothes. Traces of detergents stay in clothes and can produce skin rashes in sensitive infants. Certain baby oils, powders, and lotions also contain ingredients that can bring out skin rashes. If that should happen, cornstarch and mineral oil are excellent substitutes.

The most likely reason for setting off skin rashes in an infant under a year is the introduction of a new food to which he may be sensitive. The rash usually appears about four or five days after the food has been started. In our tower-of-blocks metaphor, the new food may be that very one block too many.

In order to avoid this problem, I urge that parents wait as long as possible over the first five months to start any baby food at all. Most milk allergies will begin to show up in these months, though they may not surface until more allergens—which could be certain additives in prepared foods or grain fillers—are added. More specifically, I tell parents to take the following steps. When new foods are started, add only one at a time, waiting at least a week or ten days before adding another. Never use mixtures of foods unless you are sure that only one ingredient represents a new challenge. Using mixed cereals and mixed foods, such as fruit mixed with farina or tapioca, is a good way to get into trouble. Read the labels on food jars and buy the purest one, or, better yet, prepare food yourself. This doesn't have to be a special process before each meal. You can freeze several days' worth in an ice tray and warm up one cube or two at a time.

Eggs and wheat are the most likely food sensitizers. They are less likely to cause trouble after the baby is six months old. So, parents should wait to add them until he is older. This represents another instance of a baby's tolerance rising as his age increases. I ask parents to wait for nine months to try their baby out on wheat in bread, then wait two more weeks before challenging him with egg yolk and another two weeks before adding egg white. When an infant breaks out with a skin rash or with acute gastrointestinal symptoms from a new food, the slow introduction pays off. You can drop back immediately to a simpler diet long before the allergic symptom gets set and becomes a problem. The rash will disappear, and you will have saved the child a lot of distress and discomfort. Fortunately, foods are not likely to remain as very important allergens, and most children outgrow mild allergic tendencies in the second year.

Learning to Control Allergies

Once an allergic symptom is out in the open, it is harder to get rid of. At that point, we must eliminate not only the immediate cause but also the milder offenders. If a parent is willing and able to do this, the child may be able to tolerate the more potent stimulus from time to time. So, with a child who gets hay fever with each cold, or eczema every time he eats wheat, or asthma every time he is upset, a preventive approach will seek to eliminate *all* the allergens he lives with, even though he can live with them most of the time.

I would advise cleaning up a child's bed and bedroom first,

since he spends a major part of his day there. This is a big job: feathers, hair mattresses, kapok, wool blankets or puffs, stuffed animals, except those filled with foam rubber or synthetic materials, pets, dolls with real hair, fuzzy animals that can become dust catchers, and flowering plants all must go. If the condition persists, it will be necessary to eliminate rugs and curtains (which are dust catchers) and oil mop the floor weekly to control dust and molds. Air conditioners and air filters are expensive, but they do help protect children from polluted air and airborne allergens that cause infections.

Although all of this sounds overwhelming and depressing, it must be considered if a child is beginning to get into a vicious circle with hay fever or asthma. By the time he has had two bouts of bronchitis with mild respiratory infections or has had two colds that have ended up in his ears or caused prolonged congestion, I would urge this course of action. In addition, I would suggest that antihistamines be used; the child is more likely to be able to fight a cold successfully if his breathing isn't obstructed.

The most important aspect of a consciously preventive approach such as this one is that parents, and the child too, can begin to feel control over allergic symptoms. By not allowing the symptoms to build up to a major problem, parents may well prevent the development of the psychological component of the disease.

I learned how important this sense of control is from a little boy whom I'll call Timothy. Tim was a lively little boy, who loved to play ball and tease his friends, and joked with me when he came for a routine checkup. But Tim had asthma. When he began to wheeze, his whole appearance and outlook changed. He became beaten-looking and worried, and his eyes took on a haunted look. His face grew pale, and his eyes evaded mine when he came to be examined.

Tim sat on my table with his shoulders hunched, wheezing slightly, his chest pumping away more dramatically than his asthma seemed to warrant. "Tim," I said, "you seem worried about yourself." "You'd be, too," he replied, "if no one knew what to do about you—and everything was wrong." In these few words, Tim was telling me a great deal; he felt frightened, discouraged, and helpless. When I gave him a shot of adrenalin to relieve his wheezing, I told him what I expected to happen. When it relieved him, I said, "You see, we do know what will work. Now we have to find things that you and your parents can do that will stop your wheezing before you need me."

We discussed the medication his parents could give him, emphasizing that when the drugs worked, he would notice the difference. Then, I gave him some chores to do on his own behalf—cleaning up his room, staying away from cats, which were poisonous to him, turning on an air purifier when *he* felt he needed it, and feeling free to ask his parents for asthmatic medicine when he felt a wheeze beginning. In later checkups, when the suggestions I made had begun to help, we talked about how *he* was mastering his own wheezing.

One day, Tim came bursting into my office with a cold, wheezing slightly, but cheerily bright and teasing. "Dr. Brazelton, don't use that needle medicine on me. I've got some medicine in my pocket I'm going to take *after* you listen to me. Just hear my chest first, because then I'll show you how I can stop it *myself*!" I examined him. He then proudly swigged his own medication and asked to sit in the waiting room for a bit. I called him in thirty minutes later to listen to his clearing chest, and he looked up at me, eyes gleaming, as if to say, "We've got it now, haven't we?"

Tim outgrew his asthma in adolescence, as do many children whose allergies are well enough controlled. He taught me a great deal about the psychological effects on a child when a disease recurs and recurs, and none of the adults around know what to do, and also how, with support, a child can begin to feel in control.

The following are my guidelines for parents in controlling allergies.

1. You must handle your own panic so as not to convey it to the child. This is the first and maybe the most difficult step.
2. Eliminate common allergens—such as dust, molds, greases, pollens, animal hair or fur, toys or animals stuffed with kapok or feathers, feather pillows, wool blankets, and hair mattresses—from the baby's bed.

3. If respiratory infections last longer than a week in small children or cause wheezing or unusual congestion, ask the doctor whether allergies could be compounding them. If so, a vigorous approach to each upper-respiratory infection might prevent the more serious symptom buildup.

4. Asthmatic wheezing should be treated immediately with allergic cleanup of the child's environment and medications that work. Antibiotics may be necessary for the infection, and antiallergic medication may be needed for wheezing. After the child improves, he can be reminded that the medication worked. Assuring a child that "we know what to do" will give him a feeling of mastery and will combat the natural panic that is likely to accompany lack of breath and wheezing.

5. Consult with your doctor about the use of adrenalin or aminophylline if home medication does not work. It is easier to break the vicious circle of wheezing and panic if effective treatment is given early.

6. If home and office medications aren't working, consult an allergist. He or she can give tests to identify the allergens and plan a more refined treatment.

7. Be patient and remember that adolescence can be a real turning point. Many children become free of allergies as adolescent changes come about.

15

BEDWETTING (ENURESIS)

Bedwetting is an upsetting problem. The important question to ask is, Whose problem is it? At first, it is the parents' problem. As soon as they hear that other children of the same age are dry at night—certainly by three and four years of age—they will start to worry if their child has not achieved this. When peer pressure begins, it becomes the child's issue. In a three- and four-year-old play group, competitiveness will soon surface. "I don't ever wear diapers anymore. Do you?" "No." "Are you dry at night?" "Yes, I am." Often, adults hear this, knowing that the respondee is still bedwetting. He (it is usually a boy) feels guilty and under pressure from his peers. By the time a child is five, in our society, everyone concerned will see bedwetting as a problem.

When should parents start worrying about bedwetting? With a child-oriented approach to toilet training, leaving each step in the hands of the child, most children will achieve their own daytime success by three years of age. Is there a predictable timetable for success at night? There are many children who are not "ready" to stay dry when we expect them to. Dr. Ronald MacKeith in England was among the first to point out that many children have an immature bladder, which leads to difficult night control. There are also children whose sleep patterns are immature. Their arousal patterns in light (REM) sleep are not well developed enough to alert them to get out of bed to stay dry. These children need to develop on their own schedule, which must be respected. Peer and parental pressure can add guilt and feelings of inadequacy, but they won't change the child's developmental patterns. Parents need to be patient and to wait for such a child. Also, they need to help the child understand the reason for her "lack of success." Otherwise, it can lead her to a poor self-image—one of failure. A six-year-old boy looked at me pleadingly in my office. "Will I ever be able to do it?" "Doing it" meant staying dry at night and pleasing those around him. His eyes contained a look of defeat and hopelessness—at six!

The Child's Readiness

If children continue to wet the bed, their urine should be checked for infection. This is part of any good routine check-up and is especially important if a child is having urinary difficulties. Urinalysis can rule out kidney or bladder difficulties that might contribute to urinary incontinence in both boys and girls.

Daytime control seems easier for girls (on average, they achieve it 2.46 months earlier than boys), and they are also less likely to wet at night. Some of this may be due to anatomical differences, but it surely is also due to differences in societal expectations and in subtle sex-linked patterns of behavior, and to expectations little boys have of themselves. By the age of five, a boy is likely to try to hide his "defect." Denial will set in, and he will refuse to share any of his feelings of shame or failure. When I see a bedwetting boy in my office, he is already guarding himself. He will cross his legs when I try to examine his penis. He will blush or get more noisily active when we discuss his toileting. He has already begun to feel vulnerable and guilty. Parents who see this situation developing might want to consult their physician to rule out physical reasons. Recognizing that many children have immature bladder control and sleep patterns, the parents will first want to reassure the child that he is okay and then do all they can to lighten up on pressure. Few tests, besides a routine urinalysis, are necessary. X rays rarely turn up a defect. Generally, the job is to help the child achieve a further stage of maturity in sleep patterns.

How Parents Can Help

Above all, staying dry at night must become the child's goal, not parents' or society's. Parents must somehow relax the urgency they feel. If this seems impossible, they might consider turning to a counselor or someone who can help figure out how to defuse undue pressure on the child, as well as the parents' own involvement. The parents' task is to listen to the child's feelings and to support her own efforts to stay dry.

If there are issues of poor self-image, of psychological immaturity, or of self-devaluation, they need to be addressed. If the child is under too many pressures from those around her—from school, peers, or family—these need to be lifted as much as possible. A father should reinforce his closeness to his son. A regular weekly excursion together gives the boy a chance to identify with his father and his father a chance to understand his son's self-image. Parents shouldn't probe, but make themselves available.

When the child is ready for them, here are some other steps I recommend when talking with parents (again, especially with parents who have boys).

1. Ask your child to hold onto his urine a bit longer during the day, to help increase bladder control.
2. With the child's permission, you can wake him before you go to bed. At that point, he must take control, or it won't work. Don't carry him to the pot.
3. A special excursion to buy a "nighttime pot" for the

child's bedside, one that can be painted with luminous paint, could become a symbol of parental support. Then, you can wake him up to use it. This must be supportive and *not* pressured. No matter how close the real toilet is to his bed, this special symbol can be meaningful.

4. An alarm clock by the bed to wake the child at 2:00 A.M. could help *when* he's ready. Before that, it is unnecessary pressure that will work the wrong way.

5. Subtle efforts to reassure the child and support him about his masculinity and his success during the day can shore him up for the night. But, if overdone, they can also make him self-conscious.

6. When your child wants to talk, you can discuss his feelings, the pressures on him, and the fact that his bladder may need to grow up and that it may take a little while for him to learn to wake up in time. If this is a real dialogue, it can be reassuring to him.

7. You can help dispel the myth that there is a magical cutoff date of five or six years, after which all children become dry. Societal pressure, coupled with parents' expectations, is too much for a small child to handle.

8. If bedwetting continues past the ages of seven to eight years, or if it interferes with a child's adjustment—his own self-image, his ability to relate to his peers, or his ability to see himself as a successful male—it is time to seek a consultation with a child psychiatrist or psychologist, or a pediatrician skilled in these issues. This could strengthen him at an important time in his development.

16
CRYING

A crying child makes adults dissolve. Yet, all children cry, and at times, they seem to need to cry. When should you worry, and when should you leave it to the baby?

Before viewing crying in any individual child as a problem, it is important to understand that crying is a universal, adaptive behavior and a baby's most effective form of communication. As we saw in chapters 2, 3, and 4, there are at least six cries in the small infant: pain, hunger, colic, boredom, discomfort, and letting off steam at the end of a stressful day. A new mother can learn to distinguish between these types of crying by three weeks. Studies have shown that even after three days, a mother can tell her baby's cry from another newborn's in the neonatal nursery.

The Language of Crying

Various cries in the newborn are distinct enough to be used for diagnosis. The quality of the cry reflects the functioning of the central nervous system (CNS). A baby with mild or major CNS disturbance has a characteristic high-pitched, painful cry that reflects his inner turmoil, and it can produce anger and turmoil in those around him. Child abuse and neglect are correlated with these painful sounding cries. In the crack-cocaine epidemic we are facing now, the rapidly increasing number of babies with intrusive, high-pitched, intractable cries is a major challenge for all those who care for them. Parents or foster parents can hardly tolerate the crying of these infants. The cry of the newborn is an important signal to society and to the family; it reflects the baby's state of well-being.

An assessment of crying—its rhythm, its timbre, its latency (that is, how long it takes to start up)—and the baby's ability to self-calm and be calmed is an important part of any newborn assessment. The quality of the cry and the ability of the newborn to be soothed give the assessor two important windows into the baby's future—a window into his temperamental style and into the "work" the parents must do to comfort him. An intense, driving baby is likely to demonstrate a high activity level, a short latency to crying, and a loud, high-pitched kind of crying that may be difficult to soothe. A quiet and sensitive baby is likely to be slower to warm up and to have a lower-pitched but insistent wail. He may make repeated attempts to calm himself—by sucking his thumb, looking around, or changing positions. When he finally can't be comforted, his wailing can be insistent and disturbing. These patterns are part of each baby's temperament and style. They seem to be stable in small babies and predict their future temperament with some accuracy. (I describe these individual differences at some length in *Infants and Mothers*.) They also shape the parents' image of the child and influence the adjustment parents must make as they try to get to know him.

Meeting the demands of a newborn's cry is one of the first challenges for new parents. Is he hungry? Is he uncomfortable? Does he need to be changed? Is he tired or bored? Or, could he be in real pain? All of these are questions that mobilize adrenalin and an "alarm reaction"* in new parents, forcing them to search for a solution. Each time their efforts work,

*An alarm reaction is one that mobilizes instant alertness, increased circulation and blood pressure, and higher oxygen to the brain in the face of a perceived emergency.

they are encouraged by a successful experience. When these don't work, they are likely to try one maneuver after another, often with increasing anxiety and tension. However, I feel that parents learn more from failures than they do from successes. Hence, a failure to find an immediate solution may lead new parents to stop, pull back, and wonder what next—and, in the process, to learn to observe the infant. As they do, they learn more and more about him.

Prolonged or Fussy Crying

The irritable, fussy crying seen at the end of the day in 85 percent of infants is often called colic and is attributed to gastrointestinal disturbances or to hyperactivity. For new parents, it is a severe test of their ability to nurture this baby. In chapters 4 and 5, I discussed this touchpoint, as parents and pediatrician prepare to deal with the regular, predictable episode of crying from around three to twelve weeks. When the baby is two to three weeks old, I help the parents to anticipate and see this fussy period as a kind of "letting off steam" and as a daily reorganizer of the immature CNS. In preparing parents, I hope to give them the reasons for it from the infant's point of view. I hope to prevent the anguish and overreaction of parents who don't expect such behavior and find they can't alleviate it. At a time when he needs to be left for short periods to "cry it out," they are likely to overdo their attempts to quiet him.

When the crying period starts, parents need to decide on an approach to it. They need to be reassured that the baby's emotional and physiological systems will mature in a way that will make the crying period unnecessary by twelve or so weeks of age. Generally, cutting down on stimulation is the best solution.

If parents become conflicted and anxious about a baby's crying, they tend to reinforce it. At a time of day when the baby's nervous system is raw, parents' overanxious, hovering ministrations can overload the baby's capacity to take in and utilize his stimuli. Colic can result. The seeds for failure in their interaction are laid down. Constant handling may even interfere with the baby's own patterns of self-comforting and self-consoling.

When the time for normal irritable fussing has passed, parents may remain too eager or too withdrawn. The baby's cries no longer get an appropriate reaction. The parents either jump too fast and overstimulate her, or they are unresponsive or inappropriate in their handling. Depressed or angry parents quickly convey their feelings to a small baby. More crying and more difficult-to-interpret crying ensues. When this cycle gets locked in, the result can be a frightened, hypersensitive infant.

If the crying in this period increases and the usual maneuvers of reducing stimulation neither stop it nor soothe it, or if the crying spreads to a longer period than two hours in the evening, it is a sign that there is more diagnostic work to be done. One reason may be that the infant is hypersensitive and easily overloaded. If this is the case, soothing, low-keyed maneuvers may work. The caregiver shouldn't look *and* talk *and* rock. Doing only one low-keyed thing at a time is best. If these doesn't work, the infant could be expressing a gastrointestinal intolerance or a disturbance of an other-than-normal type—such as a hypersensitive, hyperreactive, disorganized nervous system.

Other babies may cry as a response to a nonnurturing environment. The infant's inability to be soothed may reflect parental disorganization or depression. Babies who have severe colic often have depressed parents, who need help for their inability to understand and meet the needs of an active, intense baby. A pediatrician can evaluate the baby's contribution and, if necessary, seek a counselor or a support system for the overwhelmed parents. Postpartum depression is present in a significant number of new mothers. If serious depression goes unrecognized, it can lead to problems for the mother and/or the baby (for example, self-destructive patterns, stresses on the marriage, delayed development in the baby). These are unnecessary, for, with adequate treatment, postpartum depression can be managed and treated. Our present society does not adequately nurture and protect new parents.

For a hypersensitive infant, any occasion, such as a new experience, a transition, or a stranger, can set off inconsolable crying. The baby's activity is constant and disorganized. He may show gaze avoidance, repetitive "autistic" movements or behaviors (such as head banging, head rolling, hair pulling, or picking at her body or face). He cannot be calmed by ordinary comforting measures, such as using a soothing voice, holding his arms to stop him from startling, or even swaddling, offering a pacifier, or feeding him. He seems to be crying for a deeper kind of understanding.

Such a baby and his parents need an evaluation by a trained infant observer, a child psychologist or child psychiatrist, who can assess the baby's contribution to the problem and help the parents understand their baby's and their own contribution. A few new parents have an instinctive and deep-rooted ambivalence toward the new baby they have. If they can be helped to understand the reasons from their own past (their ghosts), they can learn to reach out for the infant. Therapy of this sort is developing into a new field called infant psychiatry. As a pediatrician, I would rather not call it psychiatry, for that seems to imply a chronic mental problem. I see such troubles, instead, as eminently reparable if parents can seek help at an early stage. (See the address for the National Center for Clinical Infant Programs [NCCIP] at the end of this book.)

In later infancy, crying continues to reflect the baby's inner state and calls for attention from parents in very much the same way we have described for the newborn. Hunger, pain, boredom, fatigue, and discomfort, as well as a cry for attention, all have different cry characteristics when they are mapped on an instrument called a sound spectrograph. For example, a pain cry is absolutely characteristic: a sharp scream, followed by a brief period of apnea (no breathing), followed by repeated, anguished cries, then another sharp, penetrating cry. All other cries are different when they are plotted. A pain cry continues when you pick a baby up. Not so with the other cries.

As the infant progresses, the parents' task is to determine how much each of these different cries demands attention from them, and when and how the infant can "learn" to comfort himself. I am always happy to see a six- to nine-month-old infant who has learned ways to comfort himself—a thumb or a pacifier, a blanket or a teddy bear, or a special behavioral pattern that helps him settle down. When we see such a baby at Children's Hospital in Boston, we know that child has been loved and has developed inner resources to which he can turn when he's lonely or distressed. A baby who has been neglected or ignored will not have learned to depend on his environment or on himself for solace. Such children have a kind of empty hopelessness that comes through in their cries. They make you want to reach out and gather them up. But when you try, they withdraw, turn inward, and are almost impossible to hold because of their physical resistance. Intervention is critical for these babies' capacity to develop emotionally and to develop relationships in the future.

In the regressive periods associated with spurts of development—the touchpoints described in part 1—crying is part of the usual disorganized behavior. Such crying may also be hard for parents to understand. If they get too frantically involved, they can increase the amount and intensity of it. At some point, it becomes necessary to push a baby to learn to calm himself down. This is when a thumb or a pacifier as a self-comforting pattern can be a major help. This should be

Crying as Part of Development

"taught" during the day, when he's not too upset to learn it. Then, he can be pushed toward it at other times. Should we encourage such a "crutch"? It seems to me that the answer must be yes. We are living in a stressful time, and even babies need to learn early how to handle their own stresses and those around them.

Crying in the second year, or even in the first year, that is aimed at parents and that has no obvious cause except to demand attention from them may be seen as a red flag. An anxious, unresourceful child who exhibits this kind of crying may be labeled as spoiled. Though the demanding crying is aimed at getting a response from adults, its very quality carries the message, You can't satisfy me. A spoiled child is one who has never learned his own limits, who has lived in an overprotective, overloading environment. Because of their own ambivalence or conflicts, parents may try to do everything for such a child. Often, they rush in too soon, before the child can develop any sense of wanting to do it for himself, of feeling frustrated, and of needing to try again—and before he can enjoy the all-important sense of "I did it *myself*!" This feeling is critical to his future self-image, his sense of his own competence. Such a child is often a whiny, fussy child who cries a lot.

There are times when a parent can be too involved. Sometimes when a child has been ill or has had a difficult start in life, or the parents have lost a previous child and see him as a miracle—a "Jesus" child—they hover constantly. These children are never allowed to experience frustration, to handle their own minor injuries, to fall down and gather themselves up to get going again. We call this the vulnerable child syndrome. Sad-looking and unhappy, they cry a lot. Their crying demands constant attention, as if it were necessary to fill up the space left by their lack of self-image. They test and provoke adults around them. The reason they seem spoiled to adults is that they are searching so hard for limits and for an image of themselves as competent.

Many of these children need a secure set of boundaries, learned from parental discipline. From nine months on, and increasing in the second year, discipline becomes the second most important job of parents. As we will see in chapter 19, this means teaching, not punishment. The goal is to give the small child a chance to incorporate his own limits. A child with a sense of limits is a secure child. A "spoiled" child tests limits in a search for this security. When a child is provoking or testing or crying for attention over and over, a parent should take his behavior seriously. (See chapter 19 for suggestions on different techniques for teaching limits.)

When a child repeats crying, provocative behavior over and over with little evidence of progress, a parent must wonder: Am I reaching him? Does he have a deeper issue that we are not addressing? When possible, I'd look for the issue and help him understand it (for example, a new sibling, a parent away, a new school, a friend who has hurt him). Parents can ask him to help them find a way to stop him before he disintegrates to crying, demanding, and acting out. When he can give any solutions, parents must be sure to use them—and then, give him credit for having taken important responsibility in deciding what would work.

As time goes by, crying should become clearer in its goals from the child's point of view, and parents should understand their role in meeting it. If an older infant or child cries without meaning or satisfaction, I would worry about this as a symptom of general sadness and seek counseling. If, however, it is part of a phase that precedes a new development or a new adjustment, I'd see it as appropriate and helpful in understanding the child.

17

DEPRESSION

Depression in a child can be frightening to concerned parents. When should you worry? All children are sad now and then and go through periods of being depressed. At such times, they need extra comfort and love. If their feelings are due to the usual, inevitable disappointments of childhood, the sadness will be short-lived. Adults should respond with sensitivity.

Identifying Depression

Crying is an active, healthy response to being sad or needy. I like to see a sad child cry. A more seriously depressed child will show several of the following symptoms instead.

▶ *Withdrawal*—The child is unavailable to others, including parents, siblings, and peers.
▶ *A dull, slowed-down look*—The child's eyes do not light up, her facial behavior is reduced, and body movements are sparse.
▶ *Loss of energy*—The child is uncharacteristically tired and inert.

▶ *Feelings of hopelessness, worthlessness, and guilt*—The child makes little attempt to express these feelings.

▶ *Changes in eating, sleeping, even toileting*—All these can be affected and disrupted.

▶ *Headaches or stomachaches*—These appear before any new event, such as going to school, to a playground, or to a party.

▶ *Depressing effect on others*—People feel sad around the child. She won't let anyone get close.

▶ *Change in habits*—The child is dirty, her clothes don't match, and her hair is unkempt.

Unless these symptoms are temporary and can be understood as reactions to a known disappointment as a depressing event in the child's life, they are a cause for concern.

In trying to decide whether certain of these symptoms mean serious depression, parents can ask themselves various questions. First, when does the sadness occur? If it occurs only after criticism or unhappy events, it can be seen as appropriate. If it occurs at inappropriate times or is present all the time, I would worry. The child may be saying that her feelings need to be listened to more carefully. When sadness invades joyful experiences, too, then parents should be concerned.

Next, is there a good reason for this sadness, for example, the loss of a dog or a favorite toy, a parent's absence, a new sibling, or the loss of a friend at school? Have there been events—at school, with neighbors, or at home—that could account for feelings of sadness? Perhaps there are several events that have added to each other. If these events can be identified, and the child can be encouraged to express the feelings, she is probably not truly depressed and will soon feel better. A normally buoyant, outgoing child can have periods of sadness. Unless these last for a long period, parents can expect her to recover.

If, on the other hand, the period of sadness or withdrawal is out of proportion to the event and seems to become entrenched, parents should be concerned. Two weeks is a reasonable time to watch and wait. A child who is already quiet, shy, or withdrawn, and who becomes more acutely so, should be taken more seriously. A child with learning disabilities or attentional disorders already has serious reason to be sad and withdrawn. Her self-image has already been battered. Any new signs of distress should be paid serious attention.

Responding to Sadness and Depression

While trying to evaluate the symptoms and deciding whether to seek outside help, parents can respond in certain important ways.

1. Take the child seriously. Joking her out of it won't work, and it devalues her feelings. Often, if you can recognize a child's sadness, you can also help her understand it as well.
2. Encourage activities that the child enjoys and handles successfully. Do not pressure her, however. Help her self-esteem by recognizing small triumphs and showing that you admire her competence.
3. Make clear to the child that you understand she is feeling sad.
4. Do not press a child to unload deep-seated reasons for her sadness unless they are ones you can handle. If there are deeper feelings that you sense, and you yourself feel fearful, you need outside help.
5. Help the child feel protected and cared for. Tell her, "I

understand how you feel, and we can and will help you. We're here and we love you."

Sadness and depression are a cry for help. While feelings of loss, loneliness, inadequacy, inexpressible anger, and depression are normal and occur in all children, a parent needs to evaluate whether they are transient ones that the child can handle, or whether the child feels overwhelmed. If they persist, or if they add to an already fragile child's personality and to a previous tenuous adjustment, the child should be seen by a therapist. Both she and her parents will feel relieved to find someone who can understand her sadness and can protect her from the fears and guilt that are compounded by a sense of helplessness. Doctors or nurse practitioners can refer parents to a child psychiatrist or psychologist specializing in therapy with children. Referrals can also be obtained from clinics associated with regional medical centers and medical schools.

18

DEVELOPMENTAL DISABILITIES*

If you are worried about a delay in your child's development, and if the worry persists, don't wait. Have him evaluated first by a pediatrician and, if necessary, an appropriate developmentalist. As the front line in children's health and well-being, parents should respect their own observations and intuition. If any aspect of your child's development—whether motor, cognitive, emotional, or behavioral—troubles you, call or make an appointment with your doctor. If the pediatrician or other caregiver such as the nurse practitioner says that all is well, but the problem seems to persist, ask for a referral. (For help in obtaining a referral, see American Academy of Child and Adolescent Psychiatry and National Center for

---

*This chapter is written for parents who are worried about a delay in their child's development. It is not intended as an exhaustive description of the various conditions that can cause delay, but rather, to help parents decide when to seek an assessment.

Clinical Infant Programs in Useful Addresses at the end of this book.)

Assessing Development

Earlier chapters of this book give you a general idea of what to expect at each age. There are various maps of development used to evaluate a child's progress. In the area of general development, one of the first of these was developed by Arnold Gesell and later elaborated upon by others, such as Nancy Bayley, who developed the Bayley assessment test for the first few years of life. In the cognitive area, the work of Jean Piaget led the way, and many others, including Jerome Bruner, Jerome Kagan, and Howard Gardner, have refined our understanding of how a child's mind develops. A map of cognitive development in the first years has resulted. The map of emotional development is less well outlined, but psychoanalysts such as Selma Fraiberg, Stanley Greenspan, and others in the emerging field of infant psychiatry have attempted to set up guidelines. From all this research, many screening and diagnostic tests have been designed to evaluate a child's development.

The knowledge we have recently gained about ways the immature nervous system repairs itself makes it clear that intervention should be started as early as possible. Children can recover from many problems of motor, cognitive, or emotional development. The earlier these are identified and appropriate ways to support and compensate are found, the better the outcome. It is therefore very important to seek help when you are worried.

Identifying Developmental Disabilities

Without help, anxious parents can add to the delay in development. Without realizing it, they may either hover or push the child to "catch up." Neither approach will work, and both tend to transmit a poor self-image. If the child tries to catch up but fails, he will feel like a failure. A sense of despair and hopelessness will then compound the underlying problems. Some of the symptoms that deserve evaluation are described in the following paragraphs.

Serious Delays in Motor Development Either limp or hypertonic (overactive) muscles are of concern. If a baby doesn't use a limb, or can't lift his head or parts of his body off the bed, I would worry. Do certain muscles seem relentlessly tight? A baby who has tense muscles, but who is able to relax from time to time, is not likely to have a neurological problem. But if the tight muscles interfere with his ability to try out and learn new tasks, he should be checked. Does he overshoot as he reaches for objects? Does he have a jerky, uncertain approach as he reaches or attempts to stand? Does this jerkiness and uncertainty increase at times when he's under stress or has a fever? This can indicate a neurological impairment that he overcomes under optimal circumstances but can't manage when stress is added to his nervous system. A child with an imbalance between flexor and extensor muscles (dyskinesia) will need help in learning motor skills. Among the problems not immediately identifiable that can cause motor delays are mild cerebral palsy, movement disorders (see also chapter 24), tics, and Tourette's syndrome.

If a pediatrician feels that a problem exists, he or she will refer the parents to a neurologist, who may recommend therapy. The most effective therapies capture the child's capacity to perform and combine it with ways to motivate him by reinforcing his desire to reproduce and to improve the behavior. Effective techniques will not press a child to perform in ways of which he is not capable. Discouragement or a sense of failure can defeat the process. For this reason, it is critical that skilled professionals plan, and support parents to work with, intervention techniques.

Delays in Cognitive Development As we saw in part 1, cognitive development also follows a fairly predictable map. A sense of object permanence and of the effects of gravity shows that the child's mental capacities are growing. A baby's expectation for certain kinds of reactions from important individuals around him are signs of learning about predictability. As early as one month, a baby will have different expectations for a father and mother. He expects a playful interaction with his father, and a nurturing one from the mother. His own differentiated behavior toward the parents shows this expectancy. His bouncy, quizzical look at his father, and stern, "Let's get down to business" gaze at his mother show sophisticated learning. By five months, his searching inspection of a strange place and his startle to a strange voice tell you of his well-defined expectancies. In the next few months, imitation, memory, and a sense of causality begin to appear.

When a child is delayed in the appearance of these expectations and abilities, this can indicate a delay in the baby's comprehension due to an interference in processing information, such as a learning deficit or some other form of disorganization of his nervous system. It could also be due to inadequate experience—with toys or with persons. In a nurturing environment, and in the absence of prematurity or other such conditions, it would be difficult to account for more than a two-month delay in the appearance of any of these expectations and abilities.

It is important to recognize that a motor delay or disability is not necessarily accompanied by a cognitive delay. For example, even a baby without limbs or motor experience, without the ability to act on his environment, will still develop a sense of object permanence and causality. When I tested an eight-month-old baby who had two frail arms and stumps for legs, she would look to the ground for a dropped toy. When I used a windup toy to test her sense of causality, she watched it, fascinated. Her head followed its progress across the table. When it stopped, she looked up at me and grunted as if to say, "Make it go." She moved her head and neck forward, looking me in the eye. Her mother said, "That's what she does when she wants us to make a toy go." She had learned about causality strictly from visual observation.

In contrast, a baby of the same age who was in the hospital for failing to thrive due to environmental deprivation could not respond to either test. She had no experience with objects, nor did she expect to be able to "make one go." With nurturing attention in the hospital, she began to take an interest in toys as well as people. Within a ten-day period, she was teachable. She learned about object permanence in one day. A few days later, she understood the concept of a windup toy. She looked at me first to see whether she could trust me. Then, she handed me the toy to "make it go."

The causes of cognitive delay are too numerous to describe here. They include Down syndrome and other forms of mental retardation, attention deficit disorder (see chapter 26), fetal alcohol syndrome, and various learning disorders such as minimal brain dysfunction (MBD). If the parents and the pediatrician agree that there is delay, or if parental concern persists, referral should be made promptly to a neurologist, a child psychiatrist, or a child psychologist, depending on the nature of the problem.

Sensory disabilities undiagnosed at birth, such as vision or hearing problems, of course, can also delay cognitive development. Early intervention can help the child compensate. While some simple hearing and vision tests can be done in the pediatrician's office, more subtle problems can be diagnosed only by an ophthalmologist, an audiologist, or an otolaryngologist (for speech or hearing problems, see chapter 39).

Delays in Emotional and Social Development A number of conditions can interfere with a baby's emotional development and interpersonal skills. Prematurity or prenatal stress can produce a vulnerable newborn. Hypersensitivity to auditory, visual, tactile, kinesthetic, and oral experiences can interfere with the development of attachment. Such a baby may avert his gaze when a parent attempts to communicate. He may shudder or stiffen when cuddled. When he is picked up to be held, he may either resist or slide through your arms like a sack of meal. If a baby spits up feedings, pushes them away, or has difficulty swallowing, the caregiver will feel rejected. A sense of failure and anger in a caring adult will discourage warm nurturing and play. This, in turn, will add to any problems of development in the baby.

Some of these problems can be short-lived if parents are patient and understand the cause. Medication given to the mother during childbirth, lack of oxygen, or intrauterine deprivation can make a newborn hard to reach, as we saw in chapter 2. After such insults, these newborns may be limp and unresponsive when they are fed. They suck poorly, choke, and tend to spit up. If they respond to social cues at all, it is in a low-keyed manner. They cannot bring their hands to their mouths. When pulled to sit, their heads lag. No responses are generated that can satisfy an eager, concerned parent. If the reasons for this behavior are not explained, parents can be frightened and fear permanent damage. It is important for a doctor or nurse to explain that, over time, most of these babies will improve as their nutrition improves, as the medication wears off, and as their nervous system has the opportunity to achieve a new regulatory balance. If this does not occur, a neurologist should be consulted. If neurological damage is ruled out, a specialist in behavioral pediatrics or infant psychiatry can be of help.

In assessing a baby who has had a difficult start, we look for certain things that are evidence of an intact nervous system. Interpersonal skills should continue to develop in the early months. In the first few weeks, babies learn to pay attention to social cues and to prolong that attention. Smiles and other facial expressions, vocalizations, and body movements toward the caregiver are not only signals of the baby's capacity to interact appropriately, but they are needed to fuel the parent–infant interaction. A baby in this age group who does not alert to his mother's voice or who does not show bodily excitement to his father's appearance should be evaluated. Gaze averting, frowning, and a turning away from social cues can be due to a hypersensitive nervous system. They can also be due to an environment that either overloads the baby or reacts inappropriately to him, creating an expectation for failure in communication.

If a baby seems indifferent to both toys and familiar people, if his emotions seem flat, this is cause for concern. If he also begins to develop repetitive habits—head rocking, eyes floating up in his head, body rocking, hair twirling, hands up over face or over ears—this is a reason for evaluation (see chapter 24). A nonsmiling, nonrelating infant who responds with repetitive, meaningless behavior and with a glazed, flat look in response to social cues could be showing signs of neurological damage or a developmental disorder called autism (described later in this chapter).

If there is such a problem, these symptoms will increase, rather than improve, in the following months. A depressed or withdrawn child will have a flat expression and a limp body. He will not reach for a parent's face to explore it. When you lean over him to elicit a smile or a vocalization, he will turn away with a saddened look. He resists being held or rocked. He may resist feedings and begin to lose weight. If this continues, it may result in a condition known as failure to thrive. It is seen in babies with neurological and psychological problems, and also in neglected babies. Dr. George Engel in Rochester, New York, demonstrated that if you feed a baby in a nonpleasurable environment with no interaction, he will not digest properly. If, on the other hand, a baby is held, spoken to, played with while he is being fed, his necessary digestive juices will be secreted so that he can absorb nutrients. From this, we have learned that responses from the people around a baby are as critical as food. These responses need to be geared to the baby's ability to utilize them.

A careful evaluation of a baby's behavior and sensitive interviews with parents are needed to help determine any developmental problem in the baby that may be causing the emotional delays. During such an evaluation, parents can be helped to fit their responses to the capacities of the baby.

In a child of about eight to sixteen months, delay in interest and play with toys, as well as interest in people, is a reason to worry. If a child has a flat, apathetic reaction when a toy is offered or a repetitive, meaningless approach to the toy, and little interest when he loses it, his affective (emotional) development may be impaired. In this age group, signs of depression and turning inward—with or without repetitive, meaningless motor behaviors, no differentiation between parents and strangers, and a lack of resistance or negativism—are signs of emotional problems for which parents must seek help.

The signs we have just been describing—flat emotional tone, repetitive movements, and lack of interest in people— can be symptoms of *autism*. In addition, an autistic child will avoid physical contact, may have difficulty forming attachments, is likely to be delayed in language development, and can have erratic reactions to sensory stimuli. Certain sights or sounds may make such a child frantic, while others may not even be noticed.

Diagnosis of autism is not easy, and the causes are not yet understood. A sensory impairment, such as deafness, needs to be ruled out. A pediatrician, especially one trained in developmental disorders, should see the child first. Psychiatrists, neurologists, otolaryngologists, and speech pathologists may all be needed for diagnosis or treatment.

Later Developmental Issues for Concern Children who develop normally in the motor, cognitive, and emotional areas in the early months can experience emotional troubles at a later time. In the second and third years, I would worry about a child who is "too good." One who does not develop expected negativism and tantrums may be burying his drive toward autonomy. A child who stays alone or who cowers in the face of other toddlers may be demonstrating a sense of isolation and passivity that needs attention. If other children shun him, that can be a particularly significant sign. A child with underlying emotional problems may sit in a chair in front of television sucking his thumb, twirling his hair, or fingering his nose or face. He may withdraw from any demanding situation, such as grandparents, strangers, and other children. He may show poor muscle tone and poor color, and may eat poorly. A troubled child may have a flat and unresponsive spirit, indifferent to the excitements of his world.

At the other end of the spectrum, toddlers who show extreme emotions, who blow hot and cold, out of proportion to the situation, can be of concern. If they move from crying to laughing to looking vacant, if they treat toys and people essentially the same way, they need help. A troubled child may wind up quickly and not respond to gentle, caring ministrations. He seems out of contact with people around him. Giggling, hysterical laughter, weeping, or crying reactions may lead to temper tantrums, alternating with periods of depressed behavior not related to the stimuli that set them off.

If a child seems stuck in such behavior, parents may be frightened and not know where to turn. If they consult friends or a psychologically unsophisticated medical professional, they may be told, "Don't worry. He'll outgrow it." If these symptoms appear to persist, they should trust their own judgment and seek referral to a child psychiatrist. With a proper evaluation, underlying emotional problems can be understood, and therapy can be started before the problems become more severe.

19

DISCIPLINE

Next to love, a sense of discipline is a parent's second most important gift to a child. Yet it raises much more difficult questions. At what age should discipline start? What is "too strict"? What is appropriate punishment? These are common concerns, in my experience. While most parents realize how critical it is to set limits, doing it in a consistent, effective way is one of the most difficult jobs for parents. We all want "well-behaved" children but worry about curbing a child's spirit or overwhelming her with too many limits.

In the past ten years, it seems to me that parents have become even more conflicted about limits and discipline. When both parents are away at work all day, they hate to be disciplinarians in their limited time at home. But children will save their provocative behavior all day to try it out in a safe, loving environment. Their need to learn limits is even more important when their parents have been away.

Some parents are conflicted because they remember having been disciplined too severely themselves. They don't want to repeat painful memories. If they have experienced abuse in their own childhood, they fear the loss of control that led their parents to abuse them. These parents may need help to face their "ghosts" consciously, so that they can meet the child's need for discipline.

Promoting Self-discipline

Discipline means "teaching," not punishment. What you do about any single incident is not as important as what you teach on *each* occasion. Punishment may need to be part of discipline on certain occasions, but it should follow promptly on the misbehavior, be short, and respect the feelings of the child. After any punishment is over (such as a time-out or withdrawal of a treat), you should sit down with your punished child and assure her: "I love you, but I can't let you do this. Someday you'll learn to stop yourself, and then I won't need to stop you."

Children sense that they need discipline and will go to great lengths to compel their parents to set limits. At some point toward the end of the second year, the child will make this need known by obvious testing. Whether it is touching television buttons, dumping food on the floor, or biting, the child will begin exploring what is and is not allowed, with a heady

sense of excitement and fear as she ventures forth. Once she is mobile, the outer edge of danger is always at hand.

Without discipline, children in the second year begin to act "spoiled." They become anxious, straining to provoke limits from their parents, knowing they can't set limits for themselves. From watching such driven children, I have learned the importance of establishing limits, firmly and understandingly. Consistent discipline, saved for important matters, is not a threat to a child's personality. Quite the contrary, it is part of the child's job of learning about herself.

Self-discipline, the goal of discipline, comes in three stages: (1) trying out the limits by exploration, (2) teasing to evoke from others a clear sense of what is okay and what isn't, and (3) internalizing these previously unknown boundaries. For example, when one of our children began to crawl, the stove, of course, became a desirable destination. Each time she made a beeline for it, we reacted in a dramatic, and to her, satisfactory manner. Knowing already that we'd react, she would look around to be sure we were watching before she'd reach forward to touch it. If we weren't paying attention, she'd either move away, or she'd make a noise to catch our attention. Until we said the expected "Don't touch," she was in a state of turmoil. If we were tentative at all, she'd begin to reach for the stove to get a reaction from us. If we reacted violently, as we did if we were weary at the end of a long day, she'd dissolve in tears. But, as she sobbed, her eyes scanned our faces, and we could imagine that we saw a kind of relief in those eyes. After a few months, toddling rather than crawling, she'd charge up to the same stove, stop in front of it, say "no" loudly to herself, and teeter away to other exciting ventures. She'd incorporated our limits for herself. In retrospect, we could see that our uncertainty left her uncertain. When we were clear, as we were about serious things, such as the hot stove, she knew it and accepted our limits for her own.

Most issues are not as clear as this, though. Most of the time, children seem to tease about things that really don't matter much to their parents. Parents are caught in indecision—is this one worth it? If we ignore this one, will she go on to another? Should I be firm now so that she'll pay attention to me when it's really important? Because a child senses any indecision, she tends to repeat her behavior or even to accelerate it. It is a certainty that you can spend all day saying no to a toddler, and she will spend all her day provoking you.

As I tell parents, if you save your discipline for the important issues—for things that really matter—you will be able to be firm and decided; the child will know it, and your discipline will work. Discipline works when you mean it wholeheartedly and when she senses that it is important for her to respect your decision. Her intrinsic wish for limits will then be met by yours when she exposes herself or others to pain or danger.

Discipline and Stages of Development

At each stage of development, there are kinds of behavior that seem too aggressive and out of control, but that are actually normal. If you overreact to them in this exploratory phase, you may end up by reinforcing them. Children must try out all sorts of aggressive behavior. At certain ages, they bite, pinch, lie, steal, or use unacceptable language, just as they try smoking, sex, and staying out too late at others. These "probes" may not have bad intentions attached to them when they first show up. When people react vehemently, a child will wonder why. So she'll test the behavior again, as if she needs to see why she got such a reaction the first time. As she tries it out over and over, her anxiety may build up and an unconscious compulsion may get built into it. The behavior that was unimportant at first becomes driven and charged with excitement. Over time, the child no longer has control. The behavior calls up so much anger around her that the cycle for repetition is set. The child and her parent get into a rut. If this begins to happen, parents must try to see the behavior as a way of expressing anxiety about something the child can't really understand. She is likely to be at the mercy of it and to react compulsively.

To avoid or defuse this situation, there are useful ways of reacting when the exploratory behavior first appears. The following are examples, directed to parents, of normal "misbehavior" and ways to teach limits without reinforcing the problem.

Four to Five Months Biting the nipple during breast-feeding is common in a baby this age whose teeth have just emerged and must be tried out. A mother can make clear that she doesn't like it by pulling the baby away from the nipple. Every time the baby bites you, pull her firmly away, but without too much overreaction. Let the baby bite on your finger instead.

Eight to Ten Months Babies will pull on your hair, scratch you in the eye, or poke you in the face, all without intent to hurt. They are fascinated by hair, eyes, and faces. As you react, the reaction adds to the excitement. Let the child know firmly and unexcitedly that it hurts. Let her know you like the exploration, but not the hurting part. If she continues, hold her hands firmly until she learns to stop herself. Each time, say, "I don't like it, and I'll hold your hand until you learn not to pull or scratch or poke too hard." She'll begin to understand. If necessary, put her down until she's not so excited, then pick her up again to love her and explain your actions to her.

Twelve to Fourteen Months By biting or pinching your face or shoulder, a child can explore the experience of biting, a person's reaction, and how to get a reaction. This can be handled in the same way. After putting her down, say that you'll pick her up to hug, but not to be bitten.

Sixteen to Twenty-four Months Now the child may try out biting, hair pulling, or scratching on other children. She is trying to learn about other children and how to get their attention. Often this is an overreaction to the stress of not knowing the other child or how to handle her own eager desire to get to know him. It usually occurs in a new or a heightened situation. If you or the other parent overreacts, which is easy to do—most new mothers are horrified—this will frighten both children. The one who is bitten needs to be comforted, of course, but he may also need to understand that this is just the other child's way of trying to learn about him. The biter will need the most comfort, for she will be frightened both by her act and by the bitten child's reaction. Pick her up to comfort her and explain that it hurts and the other child didn't like it. Soothe her until she's in control, and then try to give her other ways to approach the child. She will need more experience with other children. It is also important to let her know you will take her out of such a situation if she can't control herself. The less adult involvement, however, the better. If this behavior continues, find another biter or hairpuller her own age and size. Put the two of them together and let them learn from each other. Each one will probably bite or scratch the other. After one child bites, the other child will bite back, both children will look astonished that it hurt, and they'll think before they try it again.

Eighteen to Thirty Months Temper tantrums and violently negative behavior begin to appear at this age. A natural and critical surge of independence comes in the second and third years. The child is trying to separate from you to learn to make her own decisions. Often she is caught in her own indecision at times when it really doesn't matter, *except to her.*

It's not possible to avoid tantrums, so don't try. *Don't* get down on the floor to have one with your child. *Don't* dash her with cold water or try to shock her out of them. The more involved you are, the longer they will last. It's often wisest simply to make sure she can't hurt herself, then walk out of the room. Soon after you leave, the tantrum or violent behavior is likely to subside. In a while, go back to her, pick her up to contain and love her, and sit down in a rocking chair to soothe her. When she's able to listen, try to let her know that you understand how hard it is to be two or three and to be unable to make up one's own mind. But let her know that she *will* learn how and that, meanwhile, it's okay to lose control.

Three to Six Years Some children this age will throw or smash things in a fit of anger. At the end of the day, or at another time when she is falling apart, the child may lose control. The joy of such an aggressive act is coupled with the anxiety that occurs when she realizes what she's done.

First, let her know she can't do this—that you won't let her if you can help her in time. Hold her so tight that she must subside and regain control. Sit down with her in your lap until she's available to hear you. Then, discuss why you think she needed to do it, why she can't do it, and how badly you know she feels for this kind of destructive, out-of-control behavior.

Assure her that you'll try to help her before she loses control. Ask her to let you know what could stop her. If her suggestion works, give her lots of credit. This begins to restore the control to her.

When disciplining a child, thoughtful parents will wonder, Will I kill her spirit if I'm too rigid or too punitive? Loving parents don't want a passive child. If you ask mothers or fathers whether they want to have an aggressive child or not, most parents will answer, "Not too aggressive, but I want her to stand up for herself, too." Obviously, there is a connection between aggression and punishment. The job, then, is not to stamp out the child's self-defense and aggressive impulses but to help her learn to channel them into acceptable behavior.

Finding Appropriate Discipline

When parents ask how to know if they are being too strict, I suggest that they watch for the following:

▶ A child who is too good or too quiet, or who doesn't dare express negative feelings
▶ A child who is too sensitive to even mild criticism
▶ A child who doesn't test you in age-appropriate ways
▶ A child without a sense of humor and joy in life
▶ A child who is irritable or anxious most of the time
▶ A child who shows symptoms of pressure in other areas—feeding, sleeping, or toileting—and who may regress to an earlier kind of behavior, acting like a baby or a much smaller child

Any of these symptoms is a signal to parents to let up and confine discipline to important matters.

When asked for specific positive discipline guidelines, I give parents the following advice.

▶ *Respect a child's stage of development*—in particular, the kinds of learning she is exploring at each stage.
▶ *Fit the discipline to the child's state of development.* For an infant or toddler, try at first to divert her to another activity. If this doesn't work—and it won't very often—you may need to remove her bodily. For a child over two, discipline should always include an explanation

for her reasons for "acting out"; try to figure what triggered the child's aggressive behavior, and give her a chance to understand it herself.

▶ *Discipline must fit the child.* Make use of what you know about your child's temperament and sensitivities. A sensitive child will be devastated by punishment that may be appropriate to an active, wound-up child.

▶ *When your child is with other children, try not to hover.* When you get into a situation, you change it from a simple interchange between children to a complicated one, in which at least half of your child's behavior is aimed at you.

▶ *Model behaviors for the child.* Help her learn controls or ways to deal with a situation by giving her examples. Often the way you help her settle a conflict is more instructive than many, many words. A direct, firm, but loving approach can be the best kind of modeling.

▸ *After the discipline is over,* help her explain what it's all about. At the time, your own tension will just add to hers. But after the episode is over, if you or she can come to understand it, her face will brighten and you'll recognize that you've made a breakthrough in her understanding of herself and of her aggressive feelings.

▸ *Use a time-out,* but for a brief period only. After it's over, hug her and explain why it was necessary.

▸ *Ask the child's advice about what might help next time.* Then try it. If it works, give her credit.

▸ *Physical punishment has very real disadvantages.* Remember what it means to a child to see you lose control and act physically aggressive. It means you believe in power and physical aggression.

▸ *Watch out for mixed messages.* As you say, "Don't hit" or, "Don't do that," if you are secretly not sure, it may just add to the child's lack of self-control.

▸ *Stop and reevaluate whenever discipline doesn't work.* Are you are reacting too constantly, too ineffectively? Is the child acting out to tell you that she is anxious or out of control, or needs more affection?

▸ *Pick the child up to love her afterward.* This is hard to do, but critical. As you rock her and hold her, tell her that you're sorry that it's so *hard* to learn self-control. She must know that you care for her and respect her in this struggle to learn about herself. "I love you, but I can't let you behave this way. When you learn to stop yourself, I won't have to anymore."

Remember to reinforce the child when she isn't teasing you. "Look at you. You really are trying to control yourself, aren't you? I'm so proud of you."

20
DIVORCE

No one wins in a divorce. Children are bound to suffer. Judith Wallerstein's longitudinal studies on children of divorced parents show that children can still be longing for the reconstitution of the original family for as long as fourteen and fifteen years afterward. The original family may have been stressed and stressful, but the child dreams of having his two parents to himself again. When parents reach an impasse, they should think about what effect the divorce will have on the children, and how they propose to handle this. Often, parents will ask me, "Isn't it better for the child if we split than if we stay together and fight?" Not knowing the whole situation, I cannot answer that. An objective family therapist can help if consulted before a break. Split families are not easy for children. Remarried (blended) families are not easy—for children or for adults. Adults who must break up a family have a major obligation to protect the children involved as much as they can.

The most serious misuse of children is to place them in the middle of parents' animosity—to use them as a football. They all too easily work out competitive feelings and anger by using the child. That is sure to hurt the child. His capacity to make solid relationships with other adults in the future is likely to be impaired by this insensitivity on the part of divorcing parents. Treating a child this way can make it more likely that divorce will be passed on from one generation to the next. A child who is embroiled in his own parents' strife grows up expecting to become an angry, insecure, warring adult. The job of each divorcing parent is to work against this.

Parental Responsibility

Children will continue to wish for the "old family." They will feel deserted by the nonresident parent and will fear desertion by the resident parent. "If one can leave me, why won't the other?" Short-term separations become magnified in the child's mind. Every time a parent leaves, the child must wonder, Will she be gone for good? Why does she leave me? Am I bad, and no one will want me? Will she remember to come back? Who will take care of me? Before every separation, the parent must prepare a child as carefully as possible. After she returns, she must say, "I missed you. Did you miss me? Remember I told you I'd be back at (such and such a time), and here I am. You worry, don't you?" Then, the parent needs to be ready for the child's feelings about being deserted. Every time the child has a chance to air them, the adult has a chance to demonstrate that desertion is not in the nature of all relationships.

The absent parent has a parallel responsibility. Visitation should be clear, dependable, and on time. Even a fifteen-minute wait is an eternity for a small child. A visit from the absent parent becomes a symbol to make up for what he fears most—desertion. If you are the nonresident parent and must be late, call the child. When you arrive, say how sorry you are to be late. Speak to the child before you speak to your ex-spouse.

A child will fear that the reason the absent parent has gone is because she doesn't love him, because he's bad. A child takes everything personally. No matter how often he is told that a separation or a divorce is not his fault, he will continue to blame himself. Years later, children can dare to put their fears into words: "I knew if I'd been a better kid, they'd never have split up." "The timing of their divorce is my fault. I went away to school and left them." "They decided to get a divorce when they caught me smoking." Small children are less able to express it, but they feel responsible for the split. Both parents must be ready to reiterate over and over and over: "We love you and we never wanted to leave you. We grown-ups couldn't live together, but we both want to be with you. Nothing you ever do could change that for us."

A divorced parent must remember that demonstrating any animosity to your ex-spouse will frighten the child. He will take it personally. "If Dad and Mom can fight with each other, they can hate me, too. I must be a perfect child, or I'll be in for it." Any mistake or any deviation in his behavior raises the image of himself as expendable. Parents can help reassure a child that he needn't try to be perfect. The fact that he needn't press himself to change should be a constant reassurance, for he is likely to regress with the trauma of the divorce. Most children regress in the area of the last achievement. If he has just become dry at night, he will begin to wet all over again. If he has been talking well before, he may begin to stutter. His behavior may be either too good or too provocative. A sensitive parent will accept this and discuss it with the child, so he too understands it as normal and expectable.

:lping the Child to Adjust

After a painful separation, sleep problems are likely to surface. The child may well wish to sleep with the resident parent. The lonely parent is likely to "need" the child. If you're in this situation, don't do it. The space between two lonely people is a critical kind of protection. The child needs to value and develop his independence. The parent needs to work out her own issues. A child who must fill the needs of a deserted, lonely parent can be hampered in his ability to develop his own identity. The relationships with a parent of the opposite sex can become too intense without the protective presence of the third member of the triangle. A child who lives with one parent is likely to have more difficulty in sorting out his important need to identify with each parent. He can feel the closeness as dangerous in a way that he might not have felt when both parents were present.

Not only are behavior problems likely during a divorce, but the child's physical immunity is likely to reflect his inner tensions. Colds, otitis media, and other illnesses are likely to surface at such a time, adding stress to an already stressed family. They will pass eventually as the family adjusts.

At the time of a divorce, extended families become even more critical to the child. Siblings can protect each other from the fear of separation. Sibling relationships can become close. Although rivalry will surface, it needs to be seen as the corollary of needy caring for each other. Taking it too seriously can make it appear to be further evidence of the fragility of relationships in the broken family. Parents must stay out of the siblings' rivalry and allow them to work it out. It is all too easy for the older sibling to be pushed into the role of the absent parent. This is too much to ask. It is not a time for putting such a burden on a child. He will want to live up to such a role and is likely to push himself. He may well try to play a protective role for the younger children, but this isn't fair. He needs time to heal and recover. He may need to regress, to be nurtured himself.

Grandparents, aunts, uncles, and cousins can become important supports for children during and after a divorce. Not only can they give a child help in understanding the split-up, but they fill his need for reliable, caring people who remain constant in his life. They protect him from the inevitable fear of being deserted. The grandparents and family of the absent parent remain important. Resident parents need to reconcile their own feelings about their in-laws in order to respect the child's need for family.

During a divorce, grandparents are likely to "spoil" the children in the family. They may let down all discipline. The resident parent will feel threatened by the lack of rules at Grandma's. The child will use this: "Grandma gives me what I want. You're mean and you don't realize what I'm going through." For parents in this situation, I point out some common problems and offer the following advice. Since you are feeling pretty raw and deprived yourself, this criticism hits below the belt. You bristle. If these are your in-laws, you will feel even angrier at this undermining of your household rules. If you can, discuss this with your in-laws. Ask them to back you up in your effort to support the child with firm rules and discipline. Discipline becomes even more critical—and even more difficult to carry out—when families break up. Lack of discipline leaves the child in limbo—he must find his own limits at a time when he feels that his house is tumbling down. Respectful discipline ("I'm sorry, but this is *still* the way it is here") becomes a source of security.

Be careful about introducing new people of the opposite sex. Wait until you are pretty sure the child can rely on the relationship. A child of divorce will make new relationships with adults the sex of the missing parent all too easily. He will be deeply disappointed if it doesn't work. When you do form a lasting relationship, point out that "friends" and stepparents are different from parents, but having one of each is great. Talk about the child's fears of your death or your desertion of him. Tell him that you aren't going to leave him under *any* circumstance.

Find books about divorced families, or introduce them to

other families "like yours." These days, children of divorce are not a small minority, but it still helps to know other children who are adjusting to divorce.

Finally, try not to overprotect the child. Let him make his own adjustment, and from time to time, point out how well he is doing. When a child can master the stress and change, this will reinforce his self-image. Your continued love, respect, and discipline can be shown without hovering.

Joint Custody

Judges in divorce cases often do not have enough time or information to decide which parent is more appropriate for the major role in the child's custody. In an attempt to be fair to the parents, a judge may divide up the child's week. I have witnessed this too often. It is very difficult for a child of any age to move from one household to another on a half-weekly basis. This deprives him of any permanent territory of his own. I remember a four-year-old who spent half the week with each parent. She stood at the door of her room, guarding it like a watchdog. She had been my friend, and we cared about each other. Because she trusted me, I felt she was secure in saying to me, "You can't come in here. No one can. It's *my* room." I recognized that territory was at a real premium for this child, who was having to share two households. Parents who intend to share custody should consider moving in and out of the house themselves, leaving the children in their own stable territory.

If you are a divorced parent and this arrangement is too difficult, at least be sure the child's room in each house is never changed without his permission. If he has to share it, be sure he has his own territory within it. A sign on the door, like "Johnny's Room," can help. If the child moves back and forth, special toys can go with him. You and your ex-spouse may have to watch to see that these are not left behind.

Share the same routines and rules in each household as much as possible. While two parents can't really treat a child alike, shared expectations help him to sort himself out. Keep siblings together in whatever routine is planned. They need each other. An occasional time alone with a parent, however, is also a comfort. The schedule should be regular and clearly spelled out. A calendar marked with red and green for days in each house can help a child plan his week.

Save negotiation and arguments with the ex-spouse for times the child is not present. Every switch between households is a wrench for the child. Allow for temporary regressions right after each switch. Talk about them, but don't let up on rules and discipline.

Try not to keep the child from identifying with the other parent, no matter how angry you may be. When you do that, you are undermining the child's self-image. He needs that other parent. If the absent parent is indeed absent and unreliable, you may even have to portray him or her in a more favorable light for the child's sake. "He wishes he could see you more often." "She's far away, but she loves you." This is very difficult to do, but worth it for the child's future.

Stepfamilies

Blending families is not easy. No stepparents should expect their stepchildren to accept them easily or to be grateful to them. They are much more likely to feel that a stepparent is an invader and is taking the resident parent away from them. The needier the child may be, the more he will resent the new parent. The Cinderella story of the wicked stepparent is based on long experience. But these conflicts can be aired and dealt with. Crises around discipline, sleep, feeding, and virtually all developmental areas are likely to arise. A smart stepparent will step back to leave it to the resident parent to decide when and where to act.

When it comes to a showdown, stepchildren will make it clear that they do not have to obey, and do not intend to obey, a stepparent. Parent and stepparent must plan a unanimous front before showdowns arise. At one time or another, a stepparent is bound to feel that the spouse, the natural parent, does not offer backing. If the stepparent feels that the natural parent is overprotecting his or her own children, this will make discipline even harder. For all these reasons, couples often notice that they get along better in the few moments they have without the children. This time alone is very important.

Mark Rosen, in his book *Stepfathering* (see the Bibliography), offers some excellent guidelines for stepparents, some of which I have adapted in the following list.

1. Inborn temperament, which produces individual differences even in small babies (as we saw in part 1), means that contrasts between step and biological children are not all the result of differences in parenting.
2. Every adult reacts differently to every child. The differences between step and biological children are only one source of this difference.
3. The behavior of stepchildren continues to evolve, especially after you are married and they are more secure.
4. The feelings between you and your spouse will directly influence your relationship with your stepchildren. If your partner doesn't support you and disagrees about your role in his or her children's life, the chance of a good relationship with them is diminished significantly.
5. The other biological parent will always be a presence in the life of a stepfamily. The better the relationship between the ex-spouses, the less stress on the child.
6. Expect times of transition—such as visitation with the other parent—to be difficult. Talk them out beforehand and afterward. Other changes, such as the birth of a new baby, will require even more preparation and patience.

Children who have been loved and supported throughout a divorce and who have been encouraged to make their own adjustments to a newly composed family may develop special strengths. Divorced families have no monopoly on stress and crises. All children need to develop the sense of security, the flexibility, and the independence required in a world full of rapid, constant change.

21

EMOTIONAL MANIPULATION

"You don't love me! If you did, you'd let me stay up and watch TV. Everyone else's mother and father does. They love them and you don't love me!"

This blatant attempt at manipulation will be familiar to parents. It will be accompanied by a wretched, oppressed expression. The lack of subtlety of such a request indicates that the child knows she hasn't a chance. But it will still hit home, and many parents will react angrily.

Emotional manipulation is usually thought of as an attempt to control another person by artful, unfair, or insidious means. But within the parent–child relationship, it is quite normal, and unless parents overreact, not all that insidious. Children are trying out their wings. They attempt to manipulate in order to learn the parents' limits.

In thinking about emotional manipulation, parents should first remember that they, too, manipulate their children "for their own good." They often try to influence their children's behavior—with rewards, praise, bribes, and threats. Children soon learn to model themselves on their parents. Even a toddler soon learns that bringing her favorite book over to her parents is more likely to distract them from their conversation than simply asking for attention. Looking sad or nestling next to a parent on the couch is effective, too. No one would attribute an artful or insidious purpose to this behavior.

When visits to the supermarket are marred by temper tantrums, quieted by promises of a "reward" by the parent if the child will be good for "fifteen minutes only," who is manipulating whom? Does either expect to win? I doubt it. I see this as a kind of language between them. At least it makes the supermarket visit a lot more exciting than it might otherwise be. If there's always the threat of a tantrum, and if the parent is constantly trying out tempting new rewards, the humdrum chores become quite lively. And in the process, each explores the other's limits.

How Manipulation Begins

How early can manipulation begin in a baby's life? During the research at a day-care center, which was described in chapter 6, we observed four-month-old babies and noticed that these babies never became very invested in the caregivers or in play. They smiled and vocalized politely to the caregiver when she talked to them, but they rarely wiggled as they talked. We realized that they were conserving their emotional energy. However, when the mothers (or, in some cases, the fathers) came to get their babies at the end of the work day, each baby looked at her parent hungrily for the first few seconds and immediately started wailing. She would sob uncontrollably until her mother picked her up. When she got into her mother's arms, she'd squirm as if she were uncomfortable and turn her head away when her mother tried to kiss her. Each mother said the same thing: "She's angry that I left her all day." Sensitive and sophisticated caregivers point out to mothers that their babies have saved up their strong feelings all day. Now that they feel safe and loved, they can dare to let these feelings out. They cry and fall apart because they feel secure. During our study, one mother said, "You mean, he's manipulating me by this crying! But he's only four months old. How does he know it bothers me so much?'' She looked down at him to chuck him under his chin, saying lovingly, "You bad boy! You're glad to see me!"

This is but one example of the value to a small child of the chance to feel her own power. When these babies disintegrated

in their parents' arms, they could feel the strong emotions they were generating. Babies and small children need to explore the limits of their power: Can I get away with this—or not? How far can I go? Look how red in the face she gets when I tell her I don't want to wash my hands. Will Daddy get angry *every* time I leave my shoes in the front hall when he comes home? How far can I go? Teasing and manipulation are a way of testing the strength and the importance of each parental expectation. If a behavior doesn't get a reaction, it's hardly worth repeating. Often, a manipulative child is keeping an all-too-busy parent involved by such maneuvers. The behavior will be reinforced if the alternative is overworked parents, rushing to the kitchen at the end of their working day. A child who has been at day care or preschool all day is loaded with exciting events she wants to share and will work hard to do so.

Children also manipulate parents into struggles with each other. It's their way of testing who's boss and where to go for indulgence. "Mummy said I could. Now you're telling me I can't. Why is she so nice and you're so mean?" If the result of this test is an argument between the parents and the stricter one is not backed up, a lesson has been learned. The child has discovered that her parents would rather fight with each other than back each other's decisions. She realizes that she can often get her own way if she ignites a disagreement. This gives her a sense of dangerous power—heady but frightening. It makes for an anxious, insecure child.

Manipulation is involved in almost every part of a child's day. At mealtime, it takes the form of throwing food on the floor to see whether a parent will pick it up. An older child might say, "I won't eat this hamburger, but if I can have a hot dog, I'll eat it." A parent will say, "You can't have dessert until you've eaten everything on your plate." At bedtime, the glass of water or "I've got to go to the bathroom again" routines are not very subtle, but they serve the purpose of prolonging bedtime. Parents do their share when they say, "I'll let you watch a half hour more of TV if you'll go right to bed this time."

What is accomplished by all these maneuvers? They represent a power struggle, a necessary exploration on the part of both parent and child about the limits of each other's ability.

When I ask parents why they don't put a stop to the endless bedtime dramas, some will admit that they hate to end the day, to give up the child to sleep. "If I cut her off too soon, she'll go to bed feeling unloved and deserted." I'm not convinced that a child feels unloved or deserted when there are definite, firm limits to the bedtime routine, but I see how the struggle can be a way of softening the separation for both parent and child. Unconsciously, each is dodging the pain of separation, fearful of the future when even greater separations will be necessary. It seems so long ago that my own children called for one more glass of water. I miss it even now.

"You are always nicer to him than you are to me. You let him get away with it, but you always get mad at me." These invidious comparisons are a common form of manipulation. What does it accomplish? Since the accused parent is never quite sure of his or her past behavior, it has a slight ring of truth. Each of us knows that we aren't entirely equal in our behavior to our children. An accusation of unfairness strikes a chord. With this edge, the child can present her case to a slightly guilty parent. The odds that she'll get her way improve. If she's artful, she'll save it for rare but important occasions.

Responding to Manipulation

Should you, as a parent, allow yourself to be manipulated on such occasions? It certainly depends on the circumstances and on the importance of the event. There is no reason why you can't enter into the game of being manipulated and share your child's pride when she sees how cleverly she has maneuvered. The ability to manipulate subtly and artfully is an asset for every child's future. However, you also want to set the record straight: First, you don't need to treat each child or each event alike, and her effort to manipulate you makes you a bit angry. At the same time, you admire her cleverness and want to acknowledge it. You may still not let her do what she wants, but you see her side of it. In this way, you let her see the pros and cons of her attempt, and you demonstrate your respect for her.

As we said, a parent's praise can be seen as a way to "teach" the child. When she tries to tie her own shoelaces, any parent will reinforce her attempt. "That's just great, Susie. Now let me show you how to make a knot!" With the reinforcement, you are attempting to maintain her interest to get her to model on your behavior. When it works, it is a powerful way to channel her learning. However, it is easy to forget that the best motivation is *a child's own pleasure* in mastering a task. Too much hovering praise can rob the child of her own triumphs. Bribes, in particular, are likely to be demeaning, for they don't credit the child with the capacity to make a helpful choice. They imply that she can only be bribed—not reasoned with.

The parent in the supermarket, mentioned at the beginning of the chapter, could have prepared his child for the long trek, and kept her interested with opportunities to participate. Before waiting for her to fall apart, the parent could have sat down with his child at a counter for a brief "tea party" as a reward for her help and prolonged attention. Manipulation can be sensitive and respectful, or clumsy and demeaning.

In order to encourage cooperation and cut down on a child's attempts at manipulation, the following suggestions may help.

1. Before problems arise, discuss the issues. Openly present the choices and the way you'd like the child to behave. Use times when the child is in control to discuss issues—not when she's in the midst of a struggle.
2. Respect her for her capacity to make the choices you offer. Gear them to her age and ability to maintain control and to remember the choice she's made.
3. Remember that provocative behavior is the child's way to test herself and her own limits.
4. Examine your own tolerance for the child's misbehavior. Perhaps certain activities make you overreact.
5. Join her in what you want her to do. This not only gives her a model but also gives you both a sense of communicating with each other.
6. Recognize that escalation of pressure and of manipulations results in escalation of defiance; offer alternatives.

7. If you definitely want a child to do something, never ask, "Will you?" Instead, say, "Now it's time."

8. Praise her after cooperation is achieved.

When we as parents use manipulation, we risk undermining trust, detracting from the child's ability to live up to the situation. When parents are direct and honest in their expectations for a child, she has the experience of being entrusted and empowered. Honest communication is the most powerful system a parents can establish. A child can then make her own choice, can realize "this is my choice," and can feel the reward of achievement when she can live up to it. At the same time, parents are modeling for the child an alternative to emotional manipulation.

22

FEARS

All children go through periods of fear. Fears are normal, and they help children solve developmental issues. They also call parents' attention to the child's struggle. They generate support from parents at a time when children need it.

Fear of falling is built into each new baby in the form of a complicated clasping motion called the Moro reflex, as described in chapter 2. When the baby is uncovered or startled, or when he is dropped suddenly, his arms shoot out sideways and then come together as if to clutch anything or anyone close by. A monkey baby uses this reflex to help him cling to his mother as he is carried around. The startled cry that goes with this reflex attracts a parent's attention. Thus, even at birth, a baby is equipped to seek help with his instinctive fear of dropping or being unsupported.

Since most of childhood is beset with periods of fearfulness, parents need to understand these fears. Otherwise, parents may get caught up in them and increase the hold of these fears

Universal Fears

on the child. Fearfulness occurs at predictable times throughout childhood. Being afraid produces a surge of adrenalin and a kind of rapid learning about how to control the fear. But if the child is overwhelmed by his fearful reaction, this constructive learning will not occur. Parents cannot eradicate a child's fears, but they can help him to take them less seriously and to learn from them.

This is difficult, partly because fears in a child may call up unresolved fears in his parents. All parents recognize the scariness of witches, ghosts, or monsters. When a child first awakens screaming, with his tale of the "monster in my room," his parents remember their own fear of monsters. They are likely to overdo the comfort they give him. He senses their anxiety and it adds to his. On the following nights, the "monster" begins to take a more and more realistic shape. As the child's description becomes more vivid, he captures his parents' imagination and they, too, become increasingly mired in his fear. By their overreaction, they lend the fear a kind of credibility and make it less likely that he can handle the fear for himself. If parents can see that they are overreacting and can recognize that the fears are part of a learning process, they are in a better position to help the child.

Fears inevitably crop up at periods of new and rapid learning. The child's new independence and abilities throw him off balance. Fears call up the energy needed to readjust. As a child handles his fearfulness, he learns how to contain himself and to handle the new spurt in learning. Afterward, he may even sense that he has reached a milestone in development. Children say, "I used to be afraid of that. I'm not anymore." When a child has held himself together after mastering a painful shot in my office, I always say to him: "Look what you did! It hurt and you cried out. But then you got yourself together, and you're not crying anymore. You've grown up!" He looks up at me with a real pride in having done it and says, "I'm not even afraid of shots anymore!" He may well be whistling in the dark until the next time, but he feels proud of his achievement. We all do—his parents and I—and he deserves our recognition.

Recently, the psychologist Jerome Kagan and others have shown that shyness and timidity about new situations are likely to be inborn. In such a case, shy and sensitive parents can have shy and sensitive children. Parents who see these tendencies in their children can avoid compounding them with their own fears. By supporting the child and showing him how they themselves have coped with new and frightening situations, they can do a lot to enhance that child's inner resources.

Fear of strangers is one of the first clearly recognizable signs of fear in infancy. The ability to distinguish the differences between strangers and parents is recognizable in a baby's behavior as early as four to six weeks of age, as mentioned in earlier chapters. We have filmed small babies from one to six months of age as they react with playful adults. Even at one month, we can see differences in the behavior and the attitudes of babies toward their mother, their father, and strangers. They already know their parents' faces, voices, and attitudes, and the babies demonstrate this with clear differences in their own responses. The stranger anxiety they demonstrate at five months, at eight months, and again at a year is not a sudden awareness of the difference between strangers and their parents; rather, it represents an increase in awareness of the actions of others and their own ability to react. As we saw in chapter 6, a five-month-old baby must keep his mother directly in sight if he is not to fall apart screaming in the doctor's office. He is watching and listening to the people and objects in his environment with a new level of involvement. A doting grandparent or baby-sitter of a baby this age would be wise not to rush up to grab him or to look directly in his face without an initial period of "getting acquainted." A wise mother or father will stay well in view in any strange situation at this age.

Stranger Anxiety

The next spurt in stranger awareness comes somewhere around eight months. This time it is more all-consuming. The baby will disintegrate unexpectedly in strange places or even when a stranger passing by looks him in the face. Even if he's safe in his mother's arms, he sees this as an invasion. He is becoming more aware of new places and of new people. This is not a time to leave him with strangers without the chance to learn about them on his own terms. A parent must hold him close at first, until he's ready to be on his own. After this period of about a month is over, he will still be sensitive to new experiences, but he will have learned how to handle them. Children who are already in day care or in substitute care may have learned to handle certain strangers and strange situations. But at some point, they may get increasingly upset when their parents leave. Because of new awareness, they may start to need extra preparation and comforting when being left in substitute care.

At twelve months, this same awareness of the importance of a baby's "own" familiars and of his personal space crops up again. All through the second year, as he learns about the new, widening world that has opened up with learning to walk, he will both value and fear his new independence. At the time he's learning to run away from his parents, his dependence will also be heightened. In my office, he'll cling to his parents, noticing what a strange and frightening place it is. When I move up to examine him, he must be seated in a parent's lap. I look just past him, never into his face. With my stethoscope, I listen to a beloved doll or teddy, then to a parent's chest. As we saw in chapter 9, the process can take some time. But the benefit is that in the second year, he develops a trust in me that will last him a lifetime. With children this age, adults who respect their need to be fearful of overwhelming new experiences help the child to overcome these fears and learn to cope with new ones.

In the second and third years, children need to learn how to handle themselves in peer groups. Of course, they will be fearful as they walk into a new group of noisy children. For parents with a two- or three-year-old, I suggest the following steps. First, expect your child to cling to your skirt or trousers. Prepare him ahead of time for what and whom he will meet. Tell him honestly whether you'll stay with him. Tell him how long he can cling to you and how you'll help him get used to the new situation.

If you are taking him to play with other children his own age, let him cling to you until he can begin to identify with one of them. Then he'll slowly sidle up, if that one seems accepting. Try to get him into play with at least one other child before you pull away. After he's made it, get out as soon as you can and leave it to him. If he gets into a battle, stay out of it and let the two children handle it. He'll learn more about himself if he's on his own than if you continue to advise or protect him. Toddlers are ready to learn from each other about handling themselves. Small peer groups help children learn how to handle overwhelming situations—one step at a time. A regular play group of two or three children is one of the best insurances against growing up too shy and fearful of other children. If a child is overwhelmed by too many aggressive children, he'll probably continue to be fearful and shy.

Between the ages of three and six years, children are bound to experience fears. As a child learns about his own aggressive feelings, he will become fearful of aggression in other people and situations. As he learns about his burgeoning feelings of independence, he will need fears to help him master them. This period is comparable in its struggles to adolescence.

Types of Fears in the Young Child

Fear of Dogs and Other Biting Animals As a child learns how to handle his own instincts, one of which has been to bite when he was stressed, he may become afraid of anything that he thinks might bite. Anything new and unusual can make him afraid of being bitten. Just as an unknown dog or animal might "bite," so might a new child or an unusual person. For example, a two-year-old riding the streetcar with her mother saw some nuns dressed in long black habits. She'd never seen a nun before. She looked at her mother inquiringly and asked, "Bite baby?"

Fear of Loud Noises Fire engines, ambulances, and doors slamming suddenly call up violent, frightening reactions in a child. He may be reminded of his own sudden loss of control and feel somehow implicated when these sounds are repeated. For the same reason, aggression on television, or even in older children, raises the specter of his own powerfully aggressive feelings. He is frightened by seeing it in others.

Fear of the Dark—of Monsters, Witches, Ghosts Fears always surface at night. Dreamed-of predators become fearful

images projected into the darkness. These occur at a time when the child is going through rapid growth toward independence. The child is becoming aware of and conflicted by his dependence on his parents.

Fear of Heights Fear of jumping off of furniture or out of windows (the Peter Pan fantasies of flying) can arise at this age and linger on. Even adults remain frightened of heights and of the feeling they might throw themselves off. These fears come when a child becomes more aware of the danger of falling from heights and realizes that he is independent enough to have to protect himself.

Fear of Parent's Death Fears about a parent's death play into school phobias, or into a fear of leaving home to go to parties or on a visit. In part, they are due to shyness and the natural fear of being overwhelmed. They are also related to so-called oedipal wishes. Unconsciously but deeply attached to each parent, the child is fearful of his own wish to get the other parent out of the way. A child's fear of his own death can arise around five years or so. It can be due to fear of retaliation for his "bad" wishes. Although these feelings are too deep-seated to bring to a child's awareness, realizing that they are normal ones may help his parents. They may then avoid overreacting to his sudden fear of death—either for himself or for a parent. This is a time when parents can assure a child that they are there to protect him and that they will neither allow him to be endangered nor disappear themselves.

When death comes to someone in the family or to a beloved pet, parents should respect the feelings and fear that will arise. These are times for parents to discuss their own ways of handling their fears (see chapter 29).

Fear of Strangers and of Being Molested The fear of strangers doing harm is on parents' minds so much today that the problem may be as much to protect a child from undue fear as it is to prevent the child from being molested. A small child should not be put in the position of having to decide whom to trust. It is the parents' job to protect small children as best they can.

While parents must start to teach a five- or six-year-old how to protect himself from strangers, it's all too easy to overdo it. I worry that this generation of children will never dare to make any relationships with new people if we frighten them too successfully about "new," strange people. Children this young should not be placed in a dangerous situation. When giving the child advice about not letting anyone he does not know touch his body, a parent must carefully balance this with making him overly sensitive about his body. He certainly needs to be wary of strangers at school or on playgrounds who make him uncomfortable, but that needs to be balanced with a sense that there are people whom he can love and trust wholeheartedly. Perhaps a child's best protection from being overly burdened is the knowledge that he can communicate *any* fears or worries immediately to his parents, knowing that they will listen and respond.

Fears of Aggressive Children As a child gets older, peer relationships become increasingly important, and they are increasingly complex. The child needs to learn to relate to others from the second year on if he is not to be a lonely, isolated child in the later school years. As mentioned earlier, I suggest several things to parents. Try to let him learn through one or two children how to make it into a group. If he is shy, let him take his time. Find him a child who is like him, and help them become friends. Then help your child learn a specialty. If he can perfect himself in one sport or in music or in any area, other children will respect him. When he comes home, decimated by having been teased, remind him that everyone needs to learn to be teased. "Children always try to tease their friends." Let him know that if he can stand up to the teasing, it's not likely to recur too often.

Fear of Failure All children are afraid of failure. It's a natural state for all of us. It can be used to drive us on to success and toward perfection. But it also can be destructive. If a child seems to be overwhelmed by fears of failure, perhaps he needs more basic self-confidence. Let him know you appreciate him the way he is. Commend him for small successes, and don't push him to succeed. Perhaps he needs less pressure to perform and more spoken rewards when he does succeed. He may need chances to succeed in small ways. I would suggest low-keyed experiences with children with whom he can compete and learning experiences he can easily and successfully master. If this can be done without increasing pressures on him, encourage his particular talents and skills so that he will stand out in his group. If he sees himself as successful and as special to his parents, he will begin to gain the necessary self-confidence—slowly and step-by-step.

Fears of War and Nuclear Disaster Children sense their parents' feelings of helplessness about our country's arms escalation. From the media, they've learned about military aggression and the destruction that can result. Small children have no sense of perspective in which to put these fears. The fear of annihilation that we all harbor fits into fears of their own aggression and of the retaliation that they fear they deserve for their aggressive wishes. So, they worry, and when adults around them are worried, too, their fantasies get out of control. As adults, we must give small children a sense of the limits on the world's aggression. As parents we need to convey hopefulness for our society as well as a deep-seated responsibility toward others that can gradually counteract the violence around us.

Ways to Help a Child Deal with F

The following advice applies not only to parents but also to all other caring adults who want to help a child handle his fears. First, listen carefully and respect whatever the child tells you about his fear. Help him see that it is natural to be afraid and worry about things. Only then reassure him that what now seems scary and overwhelming can be handled and that as he gets older, he will learn to overcome his fear. You can certainly look under the bed or in the closet for witches and monsters with the child, but don't get too agitated or involved. Let him know you both know they aren't there, but that every child worries about them.

Support the child as he struggles to find ways to handle his fears. Let him regress. Let him be dependent, and let him cuddle his "lovey" and be a baby at such a time. He won't want to be a baby for long. Even as you hold him, you'll feel him try to squirm away. Then you can reinforce him for his bravery and for being so "grown up."

Help the child understand the reasons behind his fears— such as the fact that he's trying to learn about new and rather scary situations. Talk about how he's trying to venture out, to stand up for himself, and to get away from you, and how all this is scary. Use his own terms. Don't get too intellectual or beyond him. It won't help.

Reassure the child that all children have fears at his age. Suggest that he ask his friends how they handle their fears. Talk about your own fears at his age and how you learned to overcome them. "I always used to feel funny before going to a party. Even now I stand at the door until I see someone I know or have met and then go talk to them. You'll learn how to do that, too. I know just how you feel."

Meanwhile, for parents especially, take the child out alone with you each week to do things together. This will open up the possibility of his confiding in you but, even more important, it will give him a chance to identify with you. If he's learning about aggression, he can learn how to be safely aggressive—in the ways that you are. You may not even need to talk about these ways; he can see them for himself.

When he finally conquers his fears, point this out to him so he can learn from his success. Commenting on his achievement will not only take it out of the realm of fear and put it in the realm of conquest, but it will mark a pattern for him and for you. You can refer back to it when other, new fears arise.

If a child's fears, or fearfulness in general begins to invade his lifestyle, or if the fears last over a long (six-month) period, or if they affect his capacity to make friends, I would seek professional advice. These fears may be the child's way of crying out to you for advice. Ask your doctor or nurse for help in finding a therapist. A clinic connected with the nearest large teaching hospital can give you a referral to a child psychiatrist or psychologist.

23
FEEDING PROBLEMS

From the very moment that a mother first clasps a newborn to her breast, she instinctively knows that the loving messages that go with feeding are as important as the food itself to her baby's well-being. She is right. Without these messages, food won't be enough to foster a child's emotional, or even physical, growth.

As mentioned in chapter 5, there is a syndrome called failure to thrive in which we see wizened, eight-month-old babies who still weigh the same as they did at birth. They may have been given enough food, but loving communication has been lacking. By the time they are admitted to a hospital, their faces are hopelessly unresponsive, their eyes are dull, they look past caregivers, and they can't communicate. They withdraw from any human contact as if it were painful. Because of the lack of nurturing care, the food they are given passes through their intestines without being digested. As soon as a caring person can show these infants that they dare to look at a loving

The Feeding Experience

adult's face, or can allow themselves to be sung to, rocked, or hugged at the time of feeding, they cease arching away or averting their gaze. At this point, they begin to gain weight and to thrive. They can then become happy, confident little people. These babies represent extreme cases that make clear that loving messages must accompany a feeding in order for it to meet a baby's needs. While food is critical to survival, the quality of a baby's future life also depends on the nurturing that parents offer along with a feeding.

While all parents would like their babies to enjoy feeding, parents are likely to have their own hangups. Feeding experiences have been imprinted from our own childhoods. We have all had experiences that dominate our behavior at an important time like feeding. Our reactions are not consciously thought out, but are based on old patterns: "You'll sit right there until you eat your vegetables. You'll never grow up unless you drink your milk." That statement *may* have had some truth fifty years ago, but it certainly is not true today. With adequate vitamin supplements, no single vegetable is crucial to a child's health. The spinach that made Popeye powerful is only one of the dustier myths left over; many more dominate our behavior. We create unnecessary problems because we feel our responsibility so strongly. *Of course* we are likely to overreact to the responsibility of getting our children fed. A "good mother's" job, we have always believed, is to get food into her baby.

Parents face their own "ghosts" when they run into any feeding problem with their child. They need to recognize that it is part of wanting to be a good parent. If they can remember their own experiences with feeding, they needn't perpetuate them. Pushing a child to eat is the surest way to create a problem. In order for feeding to be a pleasure for a child, *she* must be in control—of choices, of refusals, and of when she can stop eating.

By its very nature, feeding is an arena in which parents and baby work out the continuing struggle between dependence (being fed) and independence (feeding oneself). No other area of development is as likely to be caught up in this struggle. Independence must win. The way feeding is handled can even influence whether a child grows up with a decent image of herself as a competent, complete person. Her need to express herself in feeding becomes every bit as critical to her development as the number of calories she consumes. But this is hard for a caring parent to see. The job is that of making each feeding a deeply satisfying experience, so that as she grows older, the child can learn that feeding herself reproduces that same pleasure.

The question of whether to breast-feed can be viewed in this light. Breast-feeding can be a close, warm, intimate experience for mother and baby. Since breast milk is also adapted to the human infant—nutritionally, digestively, allergenically, and as a natural protection against infections—every mother should consider it as the first choice. However, if, for whatever reasons, breast-feeding does not feel right to the mother, or if it becomes an unpleasant experience for her or the baby, this should be taken seriously. Her feelings are conveyed to the baby and will affect whether they get off to a good start. A baby held closely and lovingly while bottle-fed (*never* with the bottle propped) will do very well indeed, as mentioned in earlier chapters.

Feeding Patterns and Stages of Development

At first, the baby needs to set the schedule. When you, her parents, are trying to understand her, it's better to follow her demands and to learn *gradually* which cries mean she's hungry and which ones mean that she's bored or tired. In the beginning and at later times of crisis, it's always good to fall back on demand feeding. However, once you have a feeling for her needs, it is possible to begin to push her toward a predictable schedule. Everyone in the family will be relieved to count on set times for feeding, sleeping, and playing. By six weeks of age, a full-term baby should be getting predictable, and feedings should be at roughly four-hour intervals. By twelve weeks, she should be down to five feedings a day at predictable times. At twenty weeks, most babies need only four feedings, at 7:00 A.M., noon, 5:00 P.M., and 10:00 P.M.; by six or seven months, feedings (with solids) at 7:00 A.M., noon, and 5:00 P.M. and milk at 7:00 P.M., then, down for the night!

From a nutritional standpoint, babies don't need solid food

until six months of age. They don't actually learn to swallow solids until after three months. Before that time, they suck them down, but they don't swallow actively. However, by four or five months, many babies need solid foods to help them sleep through the night or to stretch out from one feeding to another during the day. If a baby has reached a four-hour schedule and has been stretching to eight hours at night, and then changes to shorter intervals, I would try solid foods. Milk alone may no longer be adequate to satisfy her needs.

By eight months, a baby will be ready to use her new and exciting pincer grasp—thumb and forefinger. If you give her two or three soft bits of table food when you sit her down—to finger, to pick up, to smear, and finally to put into her mouth—you'll find she is absolutely enthralled. She will work to master these few bits for as much as an hour at a time, so rewarded is she by this sense of mastery over feeding herself. She will even let you feed her mushy foods while she works to master her newfound achievement. In fact, if you don't let her start feeding herself by the last of the first year, you are likely to create a feeding problem in the second year. At a year, she will be shaking her head, clamping her mouth shut, and throwing food at you—telling you in no uncertain terms, "I want to become independent in feeding myself."

By a year, the baby should be able to be on her own with finger foods. Soft table bits that she can gum up will go down easily. If they're too lumpy or tough, she could choke on them, so be sure they're appropriately soft. By a year, she will begin to refuse certain foods—vegetables one month, meat another, eggs another. Once again, she is showing you she needs to feel in control, to be able to decide what she wants to eat. If you can let her *choose and refuse* throughout the second year, you are not likely to have a feeding problem. But it means *you cannot be in control*. She must feed herself. She won't master a fork or spoon until sixteen months, so she needs to be free to choose from bits of table food. Feed her just what you eat, unless it's tough. If she doesn't want it and teases you for something else, just say, "Next meal you can have it," and don't push what she doesn't want.

A toddler's meals are full of refusals, of negativism, of teasing to find out the limits. In the feeding area, *of course* she'll always want what you haven't got ready. Don't let it get to you—the kind of food isn't important; it's the game that matters. If you want to tease back and forth, play her game. It will be easier, though, if you set firm limits. You can just say, "This is what we have at this meal. If you want peanut butter, I'll give it to you at the next meal." She won't want it when you give it to her, anyway.

Parents find it much easier to relax about these erratic meals if they realize how simple a child's nutritional needs are at this age. As mentioned in chapter 9, there are only four requirements:

1. One pint of milk or its equivalent (four ounces of cheese, or a pint of yogurt, ice cream, etc.)
2. Two ounces of meat or one egg—if she won't eat either of these, you can beat up an egg in her milk or give her an iron supplement to cover her need for iron
3. One ounce of orange juice or a piece of fresh fruit, for vitamin C
4. A multivitamin preparation, which will cover anything she needs from vegetables through this negative period

Many babies don't like vegetables in the second year. Your mother or mother-in-law may hint that you are a bad parent if your child doesn't eat a "rounded diet" of green and yellow vegetables. I have seen very few toddlers who will—and I've seen thousands who won't but who have thrived in spite of a diet of *no vegetables* for a year or so. Perhaps a generation of toddlers who are not forced to eat them will end up asking for them at meals!

By four or five, *if* you haven't made food an exciting battleground, a child will begin to try new foods, to eat the famous "well-rounded diet." But it still doesn't matter nutritionally—the four basics I just mentioned will cover her through early childhood.

As for manners, forget them until the third or fourth year. She'll learn them from modeling on you. She won't learn them by being told "Do this. Do that." However, I'd set firm limits on how much food she can throw or smear around. When a toddler is particularly negative, I'd give her only two bits at a time. When she begins to rub them into the table or to throw them around, stop the feeding. Put her down until the next meal. Don't feed her snacks between meals if you want her to learn about limits. Snacks are for four- and five-year-olds who have already mastered the three-meal-a-day routine.

Parents who pride themselves on their cooking—and those who have postponed childbearing into their thirties—often find it harder when their tasty efforts are rejected. If you can realize, first, that it is an injury to you personally and that of course you'll overreact, the situation can be defused. Unless your child is missing the very few essential foods just mentioned, tell her she'll have to wait for another meal. Make clear that she can always refuse what you are offering, but she can't pick and choose what she wants to have substituted. Then remind her that you and she both know perfectly well the game she's playing.

Feeding and Independence

Some small children will appear to go on binges—peanut butter for two weeks, for instance. This won't hurt a well-nourished child. But going on binges may represent other issues—being negative, being like her friends, or testing you to see whether she can manipulate the family at mealtimes. All of these are familiar, normal reasons for such fads. Let her have her way, and if possible, help her to understand *why* she's going on binges. Then let her get tired of the binge food. Don't jump to make up a substitute. If you do, she'll decide she wants something else from you.

Binges, pickiness, refusals of certain foods, and many other variations in feeding are entirely normal phases in a child's development. She needs to establish independence about feeding. She needs to find her identity in the family, to make her own choices, and to test out the limits of your tolerance. Meals will be a lot more enjoyable if you can recognize and respect this. If you can't, and if (like so many of us) you are a parent who gets hung up or uptight about how little your child has eaten, you can expect fireworks at mealtime. Your clever inducements, tasty alternatives, bribes, and diversions may get the meals eaten for awhile. The trouble is, they won't work in the long run and you'll have unnecessary feeding problems.

Feeding herself is a precious and exciting activity for a child, and it must be an area for autonomy. Otherwise, feeding will become a battleground, and *the child will win*—one way or another.

On the other hand, if your child refuses over a consistent period of months even the necessary requirements I've outlined, this may be a time to seek help. If she is not gaining weight and is falling below the standard weight chart, it is time to seek outside advice. Your doctor can advise you about where you can find appropriate help from a child psychiatrist or psychologist. Since any physical disorder will affect feeding, the doctor will first want to rule this out. If there is no medical problem, a therapist can evaluate the child and help both of you with your side of feeding issues. Don't despair and don't wait too long.

24

HABITS

As they grow, children explore a wide variety of behaviors. A number of repetitive actions, such as head banging, sucking, and rocking are tried out as ways to ease tension or as self-comforting maneuvers. If these are not fixed as patterns, either by parental attention or because the child has a particular need for self-comforting behavior, the child will abandon them and try out other behavior. In this way, a child explores a whole range of habit patterns. Fixation is likely to occur only when too much is made of the particular pattern of behavior.

The importance to a child of self-comforting measures, such as sucking a thumb or clutching a beloved doll or blanket, was made clear in part 1. These are the child's safety valves in a stressful world and should not be seen as problems. Other habits, which can begin as normal exploration but can become problems if parents overreact or the child is under too much stress, include masturbation, nail biting, and tics.

All infants begin to explore themselves by the second year, whenever their diapers are removed. A boy can produce an erection by manipulating himself. He looks amazed, then pleased with himself, experiencing a new sensation. A girl inserts her fingers into her vagina, her eyes looking glazed, her body rocking, as she finds out that this part of her body has special feelings. Since this part of the body has been covered up by diapers throughout the first two years, the toddler can become fascinated with the new sensations. He may hide in a corner to explore himself. When he senses parental disapproval, his desire to find out more about this exciting experience is heightened.

Masturbation

Even when parents can tolerate this behavior in the child in private, they worry about whether it will become all-consuming and appear in public. Since such normal behavior was often shrouded in shame and mystery in the parents' own childhoods, they find it hard not to worry.

I remember some solemn-faced parents who consulted me in a state of deep concern. Their fifteen-month-old girl would lie down on the floor to rock, using a pillow or her fingers to stimulate herself. Her faraway look and the flush that came over her face as she rocked frightened her parents. They thought she was having a seizure. When I observed her "spells," I realized that they were a normal kind of masturbation activity.

This little girl lived in a busy, exciting household. There were three older children and six adults. All of them played with her constantly, teasing her and pressing her to respond. As a balance to this, she retreated into her own world, using masturbatory activity as a technique for withdrawal. I told them that it was normal, but I suggested that they reduce the excitement around her and that they put her in her room alone twice a day for rest periods. "Won't she just masturbate in her room?" the parents asked. I replied that she might, but that she needed the opportunity to calm herself in some way and to get out from under all the pressure. The parents of course also wondered what to do when the child began rocking like this in public. I suggested that they see this as a sign that she needed to withdraw from too much stimulation. They should pick her up, hug her, and take her off into a quiet atmosphere. The parents tried these measures, and the symptom "disappeared" within a week.

When parents worry about a child masturbating, the first advice I offer is: Don't emphasize the behavior. Don't show disapproval or try to inhibit it. If it is frequent, look for underlying reasons. Is the child very tense? Is he overstimulated? Has he other ways of self-comforting?

If your child is tense, comfort him by holding him quietly, rocking and soothing him. If the child masturbates in public, take him out of the overstimulating place. Put him in his room or another quiet place. Don't worry about what he does in his room; in fact, point out that masturbating in private is okay.

Find out if others around the child are paying too much attention to this habit. Other children or adults in the house may be overreacting and telling the child that it's taboo. Instead of helping him, this serves to fix masturbation as a pattern.

If the masturbation is excessive and if the child withdraws from participating in interesting activities, I would worry, particularly if he uses such a pattern a great deal. Is it a constant pattern for handling stress and overload? Maybe he should be evaluated for hypersensitivity or some form of autism. Have you had his urine tested? Does a girl have vaginitis? Occasionally, both girls and boys have a physical reason for excessive masturbation.

Nail Biting   All children go through periods of nail biting. They sit in front of television, or in their beds at naptime and nighttime, biting furiously on one fingernail or another. Parents who watch them find their adrenalin rising. They cannot refrain from pushing the finger out of the toddler's mouth. Or they say, "Aren't you hurting yourself?" The child nods silently but continues to search for a free splinter of nail. Parents try valiantly but cannot refrain from the next comment: "Remember how you made your finger bleed last time?" The toddler continues to nod silently. By now, he's rocking himself gently, and his eyes are glazed, looking off into the distance. Parents feel shut out, even jealous. They may try again—in vain—not to comment. Finally, in a last effort to stop the behavior and regain contact with the child, the parent will blurt out, "Just stop it then."

The child's eyes come alive. He stops the behavior and looks directly at his parent, as if to ask, "What's the problem?" Automatically, the wet finger starts toward his mouth again. This time he strains to hold himself back. He pushes his hand reluctantly under himself, sitting on it. He is impatient for the episode to end. When his mother leaves the room, he is relieved. He resumes his search for a ragged edge of fingernail.

By their protests, parents have reinforced his behavior, bringing it from an unconscious regulatory status (used to comfort, soothe, or control himself) to a conscious one, which the child now uses as rebellion against the parent's unwelcome and poorly understood intrusion.

Most habits get set in this way. Most of us have experienced this same form of intrusion from our own parents. When we see this withdrawal behavior in a child, it is difficult indeed not to wish to break through it and make contact. Parents, as well as others around a child, see such behavior as a sign that the child is somehow "deprived." They are likely to feel that only a poorly nurtured, lonely child would keep on in this way. This is not true. Thumb sucking, nail biting, rocking, and so on are intensely private self-comforting patterns, necessary to most children and many adults at certain times. During predictable stages of a child's development, they tend to reappear. They tend to become entrenched habits when the outside world resents them and tries to intrude.

Tics

A tic is a sudden jerk of a part of the body—the face, the neck, or the shoulders—that occurs unconsciously and repeatedly. In a child, tics often appear when he is concentrating or is under tension. Most often, the child is not aware of the tic. If you, his parents, call attention to it, the pattern increases. You then worry. Often parents associate the sudden jerks with a seizure. This response transmits a sense of anxiety to the child, which exacerbates the problem. If tics can be ignored, they fade away after awhile. They occur in the fourth or fifth years and recede by six or seven. They may recur when the child is going through a stressful time, such as an adjustment to a new school or a new baby. Since they recur at a time when parents are feeling stressed, too, parents are even more likely to reinforce them in some way—by calling attention to them or by worrying openly about them.

Unless tics are associated with other unusual symptoms, they should be ignored. If they continue, look for the underlying tension and try to address that. If the child is going through a period of adjustment, be sure he has plenty of support and affection. But expect him to handle the stress and to learn from it.

25
HOSPITALIZATION

While hospitalization is frightening both to children and to
their parents, it can also be a positive experience. With the
nurturing atmosphere that pervades most children's hospitals
these days, a child can grow in self-esteem and maturity by
learning to conquer the fears and anxiety of a stay in the
hospital. At Children's Hospital in Boston, we have learned to
help children gain a sense of mastery from their hospital experience. Studies that we have conducted have shown that such
efforts are successful. The experience of being away from
home, of being sick or hurt, and of being taken care of by
adults who are not her parents will always be a traumatic
challenge for a child. A parent's role, then, is to support the
child in ways that will help her learn from and master such an
experience.

I draw on my experience and observations when I offer parents the following advice. First, prepare *yourself*. Before you
can help your child, you must handle your own anxiety about

**Preparing a Child
the Hospital**

the separation and the coming event. Ask your doctor or ask at the hospital about the procedures to which she'll be exposed. Arrange to be with her at critical times, such as the day of admission, the day of an operation, or at the time of any painful procedures. Plan to spend at least the first night or so, until she adjusts to being there. Even if you have to fight with the hospital to arrange this, I would advise it. No hospital should expect a child to be without a parent for the initial adjustment and for any of the painful, frightening events she may have to endure. The presence of a parent is vital if a child has to face separation from home and painful procedures. Prepare the child in advance as much as you can. Then repeat your words as you and she go through it all.

We know from experience that the best way to prepare a child is to be as honest and as complete in the description of what will happen as possible. Depending on the child's age, you can say, "You'll be in a ward where other kids are sick, and where they have bandages and tubes running into the veins in their arms. You may be frightened, but I'll be with you. After an operation, you'll have tubes in your arm, too, because that's the way nurses and doctors feed you while you are getting better, and while you don't feel like drinking or eating. You'll have to have needle sticks—some in your finger and some in your arm. They hurt, but not for long. You can get the nurse or doctor to show you what they do with your blood. That's the way they tell how sick you are and how to make you better. It doesn't feel good to be pricked in the finger. I'll hold your other hand if they'll let me, and if you squeeze me so tight that it hurts *me*, maybe it won't hurt you so much. See if you can squeeze me that hard! And cry when you want to! It's okay to cry!"

If your child must have anesthesia, ask the anesthesiologist what method will be used. Warn the child about the face mask, the smell of the ether or gas, or the needle stick, and tell her that you will try to be with her as they give it to her. Again, fight for that. Assure her that you'll be there as she wakes up and that you'll help her through the day or two of feeling sick after the operation is over. When she feels better, she can have ice cream and so on. Knowing that you are near and will protect her as much as you can is critical to her sense of security. Most hospitals for children now have nurses and child-activities specialists who know about children's reactions to pain and to hospital procedures. Ask them to help you.

To prevent problems, many children's hospitals today offer prepared tours for the parents and the children who come in for elective admission. These tours are wonderful. Staff members take the child through the admissions office, up to the floor where she will be and then show her, in the safety of her parents' company, the operating room, the treatment room, her bed, and finally, the playroom. They give her and her parents an overview of what will happen when she comes to be admitted. In the studies I mentioned earlier of children's recovery after surgery, we have found that there is a significant difference in how well and how quickly they recover physically if they are prepared for the procedures they will have to endure. The symptoms that we used to see after the child went home—such as bedwetting, fears, night terrors, and regression to babyish behaviors—are short-lived when a child has been well prepared for the hospitalization. These same studies showed us that children were most willing to listen to the explanations and preparation *if* the parents were present. A child needs to know that her parents understand and approve of what will happen to her. Then, she can trust that the medical procedures are not so dangerous.

What helps when children cannot be prepared in advance? Over half of the hospitalizations are emergency admissions. Our Children's Museum in Boston has a special display for children to see what goes on in a hospital. There are stethoscopes, doctors' and nurses' gowns, an operating room all set up, a hospital bed that cranks up and down, and even a laboratory with a microscope to examine the blood that is taken by a needle prick on admission. We think that this is valuable preparation for children who may have to be admitted in an emergency. I would recommend that parents introduce children to such a display when they are well.

No one, of course, can predict the events that surround an emergency. This is a time when the child needs a parent the most. If you are there, you can explain every procedure as it comes and support her through it.

A national organization called the Association for the Care of Children's Health can give you information and alert you to booklets for preparation of the child (see Useful Addresses at the end of this book). They can also support your fight to be present with your child, if you need help.

In the Hospital   The parent who is present with the child can explain the necessity for medication, needles, or intravenous feedings or injections; what they will consist of; how painful they will be; and how short-lived the pain may be. Give her a reason for the procedures and explain how they will help. When each procedure is over and she's made it, congratulate her. Point out how tough going through the procedure was, but that she's conquered it!

The fears of mutilation that occur in a child's mind whenever she is ill are important for a parent to consider and to talk about. Also, illnesses, for a child, seem endless. In the midst of feeling sick, she has no sense of ever having felt differently. She will feel that this illness is permanent. The sense of helplessness that goes with an illness is both overwhelming and alarming. A child will inevitably feel that this is a retaliation due her for something she has done. When a parent says, "If only you'd worn your boots," she hears it all too well. Her mother's statement serves to confirm what she already believes—that sick children are really bad children.

This sense of responsibility and the inability to be in control reinforce the underlying feeling that she'll never be well again. A kind of fearful resignation can set in affect a child's ability to fight the illness and to recover. She'll refuse to take her medicines. She'll act out in negative, willful ways that deserve punishment. She'll almost demonstrate relief when she is punished or reprimanded. If you see this pattern developing, you must sit down with your child to talk it out. Let her know that she is not responsible for her illness. Let her talk about her feelings. Reassure her that you and her physician know how to treat her, and that she will get better. As she begins to cooperate, remind her that she is helping herself. When she does recover, give her a chance to realize that you and she did

know what to do, and that now she is all better. Most of all, let the child feel a sense of conquest after an illness or hospitalization is over. Giving her a sense of mastery over illness can be a base for conquering future difficulties.

As mentioned, most children's hospitals have a playroom and a child activities specialist. Such a specialist is trained in child development and in therapeutic play techniques. Ask that person what kind of play would be appropriate to help your child work out her feelings. These playrooms are usually equipped with dolls who have bandages and splints, and even with intravenous equipment. In the playroom, a child can feel safe and can meet other children who are going through similar ordeals. There, they can learn about themselves and their illness and can get a sense of conquering it themselves.

Whenever possible, give the child a sense of being in some control over her world and her own destiny. Even a child swathed in bandages and immobilized in splints can blow at a mobile or spit at a tin can. Let a child smear finger paints or knock down blocks or do whatever activity she can. If she can feel in control at all, she is no longer completely at the mercy of the painful world of illness.

As we said before, stay overnight the first night, at least. Even if you have to sit in a chair through the night, it is worth it to the child. In the daytime, you can have another family member come in so that you can go home to sleep, but you will have supported the child through that first frightening night. If she's in for a long time, you'd better pace yourself. Plan to leave for certain periods of the day. A break in the day can be a godsend for you, and it can push the child to learn to rely on the nurses, the doctors, and the play specialist. She'll feel more secure when you can feel confidence in them, too.

When you leave, prepare the child for your leaving. Never lie or try to slip out. She must be able to trust you. Tell her when you will return and try to be on time. Before leaving, help her relate to a special nurse or playroom person. Help her to know her doctor and her nurses as people who care about her. Then, while you are gone, she can feel that you approve of your substitute. When you return, remind her of your promise. A child's fear of being deserted is intensified while she is separated from home and in such a strange, threatening place. Each time you return as predicted, she'll feel safer.

Whenever possible, have other members of the family come in to visit. Many hospitals allow sibling visiting. Nothing can cheer up a sick child as much as seeing a brother or sister.

When Your Child Comes Home

After the child goes home, expect a reaction. Most children regress to an earlier stage of development. They usually give up the last developmental achievements they have just made. For instance, a toddler who has been toilet trained for months may start wetting her pants and bed again. Or, a four-year-old who has given up fears and nightmares will start seeing monsters in her room at night. She will wake up several times screaming. These reactions are normal and even healthy. Not only must you expect them, but you should help your child understand that they are all right and perfectly normal after a stay in the hospital. Helping her understand her reaction is like opening a door for her toward understanding herself. Then, she needn't feel so guilty for this regressive behavior.

Also, helping the child talk out or play out her reactions to the painful experiences and the separation from home is therapeutic. You might set up a doll-sized hospital where her doll or teddy bear can relive the experiences she has had. That allows her to express her fears and anxiety in the safety of home. The terror, the pain, and the fear of a repetition can all surface. She can be reassured, and assure herself, that she has managed it all successfully. She will have gained a sense of mastery from what might otherwise have been a traumatic experience.

26

HYPERSENSITIVITY AND HYPERACTIVITY

While all children may seem "hyperactive" to their parents at some time or other (especially after meals!), hyperactivity is not just overflowing energy. A truly hyperactive child has a short attention span and is driven by frenetic activity, uncontrollable impulsiveness, and emotional volatility. These problems interfere with the child's life at home, in school, and with other adults and children.

Identifying Hyperactivity and Hypersensitivity

Hyperactive children are much more likely to be boys. Few girls are truly hyperactive. Hyperactivity is probably due to a "raw," hypersensitive nervous system at the mercy of every incoming stimulus. The child is not able to shut out unimportant stimuli and thus cannot focus on the more useful, comprehensible ones. There is evidence that the problem begins in the brain, involving what are called neurotransmitters. Every

incoming signal is transmitted without being screened. The discharges of the nervous system into activity are just as uncontrollable. The brain does not have the capacity to shut down at any level. In much simplified terms, this neurological problem can arise when one or more small areas in the brain are injured, perhaps by prenatal exposure to drugs or poisons such as lead, or at birth. We do not always know the reasons. The process of repair may set up hypersensitive fields around the injured areas. This hypersensitivity then spreads to the entire central nervous system.

The hyperactivity, which is often not diagnosed until a child begins school or preschool, must be distinguished from hypersensitivity in infants resulting from undernourishment in the uterus. This latter condition can be gradually diminished with appropriate care. Infants who have been stressed in the uterus for one reason or another show extreme hypersensitivity. Such easily overloaded infants, long and skinny at birth, are called small for dates. The placentas that nurtured them are small and inadequate, for completely unaccountable reasons.

At Children's Hospital in Boston, we have studied many such small-for-dates babies. Although malnutrition, accidents, alcohol, smoking, drugs, and infections can interfere with placental function in a similar way, the mothers we studied had not suffered from any of these conditions. The infants had not stored adequate fat before delivery. Their skin was dry and peeling, their hair was sparse, and their faces were tired, old-looking, and worried. Every stimulus made them startle. Their ability to shut out repeated stimuli was significantly reduced. (See the discussion of habituation in chapter 2.) They could not sleep deeply or pay prolonged attention to interesting stimuli because they were so distractible in either state. They literally shot from an alert or a sleep state into an unreachable crying state, as if crying were the only way they could control their environments. This rapid change in state allowed their parents no time to reach them with touch, voice, or visual stimuli. This, in turn, created anxiety in the parents, whose reaction was to increase their efforts. The result was that the hypersensitive, hyperreactive condition persisted throughout infancy.

In our research, we looked for ways to interrupt the vicious cycle of hyperreactivity and overanxious parental efforts. When we handled these babies very gently, we were able to help them organize. We learned that we must reduce stimulation to reach them. If we played with them or fed them in a darkened, quiet room, they became available. In a noisy, distracting environment, they averted their gaze and refused to accept any of our attention. If attention was offered during a feeding, they spit up the feeding. They were extremely fussy infants in the three- to twelve-week period. Unreachable, crying for long periods, they seemed to be using crying as a defense against overstimulation.

When the crying periods ended, these babies remained highly sensitive and distractible. At five and again at nine months, they were still at the mercy of every sight and sound. Activity began to replace crying as a way of discharging the pent-up inner turmoil that resulted from too much stimulation.

Helping Hypersensitive and Hyperactive Children

At each of these and later ages, an understanding of the underlying hypersensitivity helps parents and caregivers working with hyperreactive children. By using one low-keyed stimulus at a time and slowing down at the first frown, or when the baby's quick reaction or state changes, you can gradually calm such a baby and communicate with him. You can pick up such a baby slowly and gently and hold him cuddled until he finally relaxes. Only then can you look down at his face. He may stiffen again, but he'll finally relax. Then, you can croon slowly to him. Again, he may stiffen before relaxing again. Finally, you can rock and sing and look at him. At this point, he has "learned" to organize several stimuli at once. In our studies, we demonstrate this tedious process to parents. Because of their concern, they usually overdo each attempt to reach these sensitive babies. A sense of failure on both parents' and babies' parts is the result. After we demonstrate the necessity for one stimulus at a time, many parents are able to change their approach. Feeding and other important activities, such as diapering, playing, rocking, and getting the baby to bed, are best done in a protected, quiet, nondistracting environment. Handled carefully, each slowed-down activity gives the baby an opportunity to learn how to manage his raw nervous system.

The challenge for parents is to overcome their natural over-concern. This is compounded by the guilt parents feel about "why" their baby is so sensitive. We usually don't have answers. But we do know that, over time, many of these hypersensitive infants can learn to manage better and better, *if* their environment can be protective. The ultimate goal is a child who expects and is determined to succeed, in spite of his difficulties.

When the cause of the hypersensitivity and hyperactivity is organic—that is, a physical impairment in the brain—the treatment will have to continue over many years. As we said before, true hyperactivity sometimes is not recognized until the child gets to school. A watchful parent or pediatrician will see the signs and symptoms much earlier, however. The child (usually a boy) will be at the mercy of every impinging stimulus. In my office, if I clap as such a child plays with toys, he will startle. As I keep clapping, his startles may diminish, but they will continue. A normal child will shut out my clapping by the third or fourth clap. An anxious child may need five or six. A truly hyperactive child will blink for ten to fifteen claps. He may startle for the first five or six, but then he'll find ways to diminish the impact of my clapping. He may start to sing, turn his back, become active in other ways as he attempts to shut out these repetitive noises. After I stop, he will invariably become noisy and active, as if he were trying to discharge the stored-up overload.

Hyperactivity is likely to include a kind of heedlessness. The child may trip easily or run into furniture. He may not appear to notice when he hits himself or when he fails at a task. He has become familiar with failure. An indication of this expectation to fail is a child's attempt to cover up or to distract the observer from his failure. He will try to lead your attention into other areas. He may try to divert you to another task. As he fails, he will not be able to stop himself, and he propels himself into a kind of emotional lability. Crying, laughing, and running around the room are all attempts to handle his impulsive recklessness. He cannot control himself.

Hyperactivity is often associated with attention problems. Because the child cannot shut out unimportant stimuli, his attention span is short. He will start and stop an activity, then become excitable or restless. If attention problems are severe and seem to involve a defect in the screening mechanisms of the brain, the condition is called *attention deficit disorder* (ADD), as mentioned in chapter 12. Although hyperactivity often accompanies ADD, some children with ADD are not hyperactive.

All this can only be sorted out by professionals who have had long experience with these problems. If parents notice that their child is distractible and at the mercy of stimuli, if he is emotionally labile and can't manage himself, if his frantic activity seems to be the result of an overloaded nervous system, I'd recommend an early evaluation.

A multidisciplinary evaluation is best and should include a pediatrician, a psychologist, and other specialists. An evaluation that just produces a label is not enough. The goal should be to single out the child's strengths as well as weaknesses and build a treatment plan on these.

Treatment may consist of family counseling to help organize a supportive environment, special education, psychotherapy, or in some instances, medication such as Ritalin. Medication should always be prescribed and monitored by a physician. If it is to be given, the child needs to be included in the decision. Parents should let him know that the medication is to help him achieve what he's trying so hard for: the ability to stop his activity and to pay attention. If it helps, he can take part of the credit.

In addition to providing a calm, nonstimulating environment, the parents' role will be to reward each bit of progress. Even the simplest positive behavior, such as sitting still for a brief meal or finishing an easy task, should be praised. Parents need to let the child know how proud they are when he can manage to control his disorganization. Because bringing up a hypersensitive or hyperactive child is a long, taxing job, each parent must have some time to relax and recharge. Parents who believe in their child's strengths, and who cooperate in treatment programs with optimism rather than anxiety, will convey this to the child and contribute greatly to his growing self-control.

The most serious potential complication of this disorder can develop from the child's recognition of his own inability to control it. He grows up with an expectation to fail that dogs all his other efforts to learn and to conform. This sense of failure and the poor self-image can be more serious than the disorder. For, as his brain matures, he will outgrow the hyperactivity; but if he expects to fail, he will have already learned patterns that set him up for failure.

I have been suggesting to parents of these children at three and four years of age that they make a chart of (1) how he behaves as he builds up to a peak of discharge, (2) how he behaves at the peak, and (3) afterward. I follow up with some questions: Can he then calm down to pay attention? By introducing a crutch (a lovey) or a behavioral pattern on which he can rely, can you help him cut off the peaks by learning to anticipate them? Can you remind him that, as he builds up, he can fall back on his thumb or on his lovey or on rocking in his seat? If he can cut off the peak of activity, maybe then he can

pay attention and quiet himself. When he can achieve this kind of mastery, he deserves the reward of knowing that he has worked hard to overcome a very disturbing disorder. If he can achieve such a pattern by five or six years, he may be able to master school and the prolonged periods of attention that it will require. This can be a long and demanding conquest for him. He needs a lot of patient encouragement. He also needs a sense of himself as a success!

27
ILLNESS*

Children get sick so fast—nearly always in the evening, after doctors' office hours. One moment they are playing energetically; the next moment they're cranky and disorganized. Suddenly, they stagger or lie down. Their eyes glaze over and their color changes to either a fierce red or a chalk white. Their breathing rate doubles, and they seem to be gasping for breath. Small children whimper inconsolably or won't cry at all. They can't tell you what's wrong. They obviously feel awful. Their collapse is all the more sudden in that while they are playing, they resist giving up. When they finally do, they are so pitiful. All but the most experienced parents will feel a painful surge of anxiety.

---

*This chapter is not a guide to the care of sick children, but in keeping with the subject of the book, offers simple first steps to relieve the anxiety normal in parents and sick children. In all cases check with your own doctor.

Recognizing and Handling Emergencies

What should you do? I always remind parents that there are only a few emergencies in which waiting and watching won't tell you whether they're serious or not. Three important exceptions are unconsciousness, obstructed breathing, and convulsions. For those situations I recommend taking the following steps.

If the child is unconscious and there has not been an injury, take her to the nearest medical facility immediately. If there has been, or could have been, a head or spinal injury, *do not move* the child. Call for emergency medical assistance immediately.

If a small child is choking, hang her upside down and clap on her back so that she will gag the obstruction out. I do not recommend the Heimlich maneuver for children, because they can be hurt too easily.

Except for convulsions (see later in this chapter), further first aid is beyond the scope of this book. All parents should make the following advance preparations:

1. Have the phone number of the doctor, the emergency room of the hospital, and the poison control center by every phone in the house.
2. Make everyone who takes care of the child aware of these numbers.
3. Buy a reliable guide to emergencies, such as *The American Red Cross First Aid Book* or the *New Child Health Encyclopedia* and read the advice on preparing for emergencies (see the Bibliography at the end of this book).

Preparations such as these enable a parent to be calmer and more effective in an emergency. Anxiety will be powerful and is normal. It provides the adrenalin needed to rise to the emergency.

Fever

Fever is not an illness but an indication of the body's effort to fight an infection. Children aged three and under are likely to have high fevers because their bodies' temperature-regulating mechanisms are still immature. Fever is a healthy response of the immune system to infection, both viral and bacterial. Ninety-five percent of fevers will not need antibiotics or other medical treatment. Giving your child a chance to build up her immunity by fighting most diseases on her own is the best thing you can do. If a feverish child is brought to me too soon, I can't always tell where her infection will localize, and I won't know whether she can handle it herself or whether she will need help. Unless she's too ill, I'd rather see the child after she's fought her own battle for at least twenty-four hours. At that point, I can make a proper diagnosis and determine whether treatment is necessary.

Taking the Child's Temperature Until a child is five or six and can cooperate, oral thermometers are too dangerous. Plastic skin strips are on the market but are not always reliable. If you can, hold the child against you with her arm tightly against her chest and enclose the thermometer in her armpit for two to three minutes. This may be hard to do with a wriggler. If you take her temperature rectally, lay her across your lap on her belly. Insert the tip of the thermometer, greased with petroleum jelly, only one inch into her rectum and hold it tight. Use your thumb and forefinger. The rest of your hand should rest on her buttocks, so that your hand and fingers holding the thermometer bounce with her as she wriggles on your lap. In that way, you won't lose the thermometer or break it or hurt her with it.

Taking a small child's temperature is not easy! Nor is it always necessary. To tell whether a fever is dangerous, don't go by degree of temperature alone. That is not the most critical factor. A child with a high fever who looks alert and responsive is much less worrisome than a child with a low fever who is limp and unresponsive. In other words, the way she reacts is the most important symptom.

When a fever climbs suddenly, most children change dramatically. They shiver as their systems try to bring up body heat; they often seem drowsy and unreachable at first. If this happens to your child, check for three things:

I. Is her neck stiff? Can you bend it forward onto her
   chest? A child with meningitis cannot be bent forward,

whereas a child with aches from the flu won't like bending forward but will be able to do it. A really stiff neck needs attention.
2. Is there interference with her air passage? All children with a fever breathe faster than normal, but if there's a wheezing or a crackle with each intake of breath, she may need medical help.
3. Does she pull on her ears as if they were painful? Ear infections accompanied by high fever will require medication, so she'll need to be checked soon.

If your feverish child has any of these symptoms, call your physician or nurse practitioner. If not, you can afford to try your own remedies at home first. You can see whether she'll improve on her own for at least twenty-four hours.

The first step with a sick child is to pick her up, comfort her, and assure her that you are going to help her feel better. Illness is a time both children and parents reach out for each other, and children will remember for the rest of their lives the way their parents took care of them when they were sick. Working parents will need to find a way to stay home with a sick child.

Dehydration The first concern with a fever is dehydration. Get some clear fluids into the child as soon as possible. Dehydration is one of the main reasons children with a fever look so terrible. It must be combated constantly in order to help them fight the infection behind the temperature. With infants, dehydration can even be life-threatening. Feed clear fluids in little sips at a time, for a fever is often accompanied by an upset stomach. If the child is nauseated and vomiting, it is even more critical to start to counteract the dehydration. One teaspoon of liquid—*not* milk or water, but a sweetened fluid with a bit of salt, such as ginger ale, weak sweetened tea, or a formula of one pint of water, one tablespoon of sugar, and one-half teaspoon of salt—can be spooned in or drunk every five minutes for the first hour. A tablespoon every five minutes the second hour and an ounce every few minutes the third and fourth hours will counteract both an upset stomach and dehydration. A quart of liquid a day is a goal in fighting dehydration accompanied by a fever.

If a child continues to feel miserable, an aspirin substitute (aspirin in certain rare instances has been associated with a condition called Reye's syndrome) can be given according to the instructions on the package or the advice of your doctor. If the child still looks sick after twenty-four hours, no matter what her temperature, it is time to call your doctor. If you have been able to bring the child's temperature down by aspirin substitutes or by a lukewarm tub, she will feel and act better. If she doesn't, she is telling you that she needs attention from a physician.

Convulsions In a small child, a high fever (above 103 degrees) can sometimes cause a convulsion (febrile seizure). Convulsions are likely to occur in children under three or in slightly older children who have a low threshold for them. Seizures are frightening. The child stiffens out, arches, and seems to stop breathing; then, as her breathing begins again, her limbs will jerk spasmodically in repeated jerks. She will have lost consciousness in the process. Be sure to position her on her side or with her head lowered, so that you can keep her airway clear. Contrary to old wives' tales, a child will not swallow her tongue.

In the case of a febrile seizure, unlike the other emergencies mentioned thus far, there is something parents can and should do. To bring the child's temperature down quickly, lower her gently into a lukewarm tub of water. If she recovers in the tub, you can wait to talk to the doctor. If not, get a neighbor to call an ambulance or the fire department, and call your doctor to tell him or her to prepare for you at the hospital. In all likelihood, the seizure will be over before you can get there, but if it's a first seizure, it's critical to have the child checked out.

Sometimes rushing off to the hospital before you bring the fever down may actually prolong the seizure. Once the child is alert and conscious, give her clear fluids and an aspirin substitute. Be sure to read and follow the directions on the label.

If a child has a fever and has had a seizure once before, I'd recommend starting her on an aspirin substitute every four hours. Every time she gets sick, you can do this to prevent a sudden rise in fever, which brings on seizures. In any case, you will want to discuss with your doctor ways to handle and prevent seizures. Many doctors give phenobarbital in regular doses to children who are likely to convulse. Incidentally, a child who has had a high fever without a seizure is much less likely to have one with the next high fever.

Refusal to Drink When my daughter was two, I faced just that problem. I knew she was getting dehydrated because she hadn't urinated in eighteen hours, her lips were dry, and her eyes looked sunken. If she would not drink, we were faced with hospitalization to rehydrate her.

I'd told the parents of my patients that if they were determined, the child would know it and would cooperate, but I hadn't had a two-year-old of my own then. I knew that if I didn't make my daughter drink fluids at home, someone at the hospital would. So, I warned her that if she wouldn't drink the warm, flat ginger ale, I would hold her nose and pour it down her throat. She refused again, and so I used a turkey baster to drop it into her mouth as I held her in my lap. She vomited it, looking me straight in the eye. I then held her nose and poured it in a second time. (Don't worry about the child choking, as long as she's alert.) Again, she started to spit it out, but I assured her firmly that I'd simply pour it in again. She finally began to drink and was soon rehydrated and cheerful. She didn't seemed to bear me a grudge for my brutish behavior. But it certainly did bother my conscience for a long time, even if it did keep her out of the hospital!

Colds The common cold is likely to last for a week in older children, two weeks in toddlers and babies. These are trying times for families, especially when small children begin day care or pre-school and the illnesses are bound to be more frequent. In order to make the child comfortable, encourage plenty of fluids, use an aspirin substitute every four hours, and use a vaporizer to help her breathe. For many children, I'd stop food for this period, so that they will drink more. A vaporizer makes a child much more comfortable, as it liquifies secretions so they can run out. I do not like nasal suction unless it is absolutely necessary, as the suctioning device is intrusive and causes as much nasal membrane irritation as it relieves.

Propping your child up in bed so that her head is slightly higher than her feet will help reduce nasal congestion. Administer diluted saltwater nosedrops (one-half teaspoon salt per eight ounces of boiled water), or use a nasal spray half diluted with water before meals, so that the child can drink and eat even though her nose is full. But, as we said, when a child has a cold, eating is not a priority; fluids are all she really needs.

It may be necessary to repeat the diluted nosedrops every four hours at night to help the child breathe. If the cold isn't visibly better within two or three days of administering home remedies, consult your doctor. Common colds do serve one positive purpose: they help raise the child's immunity. But that's small comfort if she gets complications with each of them—and many do.

Croup

Croup is a particularly frightening ailment to parents and children. It is caused by swelling and obstruction of the airway and is often a complication of a cold. The child can't pull air into her lungs without a harsh croaking cough. It has been compared to the bark of a seal. When the child tries to speak, she is hoarse. Not being able to get enough air is alarming to the child. As she panics, her airway goes into a greater spasm, making breathing even more difficult.

When parents become frightened, too, this aggravates the problem. If you have encountered croup without being prepared for it, you will remember the episode as one of the most frightening of your child-raising years. Knowing what to do can defuse much of this anxiety. The following steps help in the majority of children.

1. Put a chair in the bathroom, a rocking chair if possible.
2. Turn on the hot shower full blast to steam up the bathroom quickly.
3. Sit down near it with your child in your arms, rocking and singing to soothe her.
4. Give your child a lollipop to suck on. It will soothe her throat and help her relax.

After an hour, the croup should get better. If it doesn't, you need help. Call your physician immediately.

If you must take your child to the hospital in this croupy condition, try to keep her as calm as possible. Being handled by strangers in a strange place will add to her anxiety, so stay close to her. If she is put into an oxygen tent, get in with her—it won't be so frightening.

If the condition improves at home, set up a "croup tent" around the child's bed or crib. Secure a sheet to the top and two sides of the crib, or to the bedposts, leaving two sides open for air to circulate. Run the steam from a vaporizer in under the sheet. Prop the child on pillows and sit beside her to comfort her; unnecessary crying can make her airway tighten up again. Stay near her through the night. If you can get her through the night with these techniques, she'll be dramatically better by morning. She may worsen again every night, but she won't get as sick or as frightened the second or third nights. Most croups (95 percent) can be handled at home, without medications, but if the child gets worse and runs a temperature, it's time to see the doctor.

Diarrhea   Dehydration is the primary danger for a child with diarrhea. Up to four loose stools a day won't be likely to dehydrate her, but if there are more than six a day or if she stops urinating, she is getting dehydrated. Push her to drink clear fluids (as described earlier), but don't give her milk or solid foods. Her digestive system needs to rest, so give her only foods that can be absorbed easily. Clear liquids—broth, sweet tea, flat ginger ale, or diluted clear juices like apple juice—are best.

A child who has recently been toilet trained may need to return to diapers. Just offer them; don't make a fuss.

Blood and mucus in the stool are danger signs. If you spot any or if severe diarrhea persists for more than twenty-four hours, call your doctor.

Earaches

Most of us remember the misery of earaches in childhood. They are very common. Very young children can't tell you what's wrong but will finger their ears and cry. The most usual reason for ear pain *without fever* is swimmer's ear. This is caused by wax in the ear canal that traps water behind it. If there's no fever accompanying an earache, I'd treat for swimmer's ear, as follows: Put four to five drops of hydrogen peroxide in each ear with an eyedropper, four or five times a day, to bubble out the wax and fluid. If that doesn't work but it does help a bit, warmed-up rubbing alcohol used as eardrops may finish the job. There are antibiotic eardrops available for more severe cases, but they must be prescribed by a physician. Never insert anything into the ear. Call the doctor if the pain persists.

The next most likely cause of ear pain is when the ear is blocked from inside the throat. This kind of earache will accompany a cold or nasal congestion. The tissues in the throat swell, blocking the opening of the internal ear canal, which is directly inside the ear. If you can shrink these tissues, the pressure can be relieved. Two maneuvers may help: (1) An antihistamine or decongestant may shrink the throat tissues, and (2) diluted nosedrops aimed directly at the internal opening of the ear may unblock it. To do this, have the child lie on her back. Put nosedrops (half water and half decongestant nosedrops) into each nostril, then quickly turn her head onto the blocked ear. Keep the child there a few minutes until the decongestant nosedrops can work. Repeat every three to four hours.

If the earache persists for more than twelve hours, your

child may have an abscessed ear (otitis media) and should be treated by a doctor.

When ear infections keep recurring, you need the advice of an ear, nose, and throat specialist (an otorhinolaryngologist). Medical treatments may include mild antibiotics or, in most severe cases, removal of adenoids if they are blocking the ears. Tubes can be placed in the eardrums—a method of treatment that really helps with chronic ear infections.

Nosebleeds

Nosebleeds are also frightening and always seem twice as bad as they are. First, try to stop the bleeding yourself by pinching the nose to put pressure on the vessels inside the nose. Place ice on the bridge of the nose and at the base of the neck. Have the child lie down on her back. Wad a bit of toilet paper into a half-inch square and push it firmly up under the upper lip so it presses up on the septum (the dividing wall) of the nose. Once you've stopped the nosebleed, tell your child to try not to blow her nose too soon, or it certainly will start bleeding again. If the bleeding lasts for more than an hour, the nose may need packing by an expert.

As a preventive for recurring nosebleeds, apply petroleum jelly morning and night inside the nose, along the middle septum. This works when the air, indoors or out, is hot and dry, or when your child is suffering from a cold or allergy. If nosebleeds keep recurring anyway, consult your doctor.

When to See the Doctor

Parents today are often well informed about medical care and are concerned about overtreatment of illness, side effects of medications, and the problems of unnecessary tests. The possibility of nonessential tests being ordered has been compounded by the rise in malpractice suits and the resulting climate in which physicians must work.

When you are trying to decide when to take your child to a physician or to a hospital, these concerns will necessarily come to mind. Using judgment about when to start with home remedies rather than rushing to a doctor's office or hospital can not only save a child from the added anxiety but also give her that extra security of feeling that, you, her parents, know what to do.

In any emergency, or with any unexplained change in a child's health, of course, such concerns are irrelevant, and you should call a physician right away. In the more common childhood illnesses, too, there are good reasons to seek medical care. These include treating any persistent infection, forestalling complications after a child has fought the infection long enough, preventing recurrences, and making a child more comfortable when you've tried all you know.

A physician or nurse practitioner can tell whether the child is sick enough to need treatment or further investigation. He or she will assume responsibility and offer a more objective opinion than you can muster. Finally, a physician's very authority can relieve you and the child of feeling responsible for the illness. A small child feels that an illness is her own fault and that she's been "bad" and deserves it. Sometimes this perception is hard for a parent, the voice of discipline, to counter. Parents, too, have normal guilt feelings that surface when a child falls ill. Through calm explanation, a doctor can exorcise this guilt and offer comfort, as well as medical treatment, to the family.

28

IMAGINARY
FRIENDS

Nearly all three- and four-year-olds develop imaginary friends. I'm always delighted when they do, for these are signs of a child's developing imagination, as I've mentioned earlier. The need for privacy that they represent is a reminder that children do not want to be invaded.

The Importance of Imaginary Friends

At first, this excursion into fantasy is too vulnerable to share with parents. A child's own private language and private friends are precious and must be respected by adults around them. Older siblings, unfortunately, are likely to get wind of these imaginary beings. When they do, they may make fun of them and destroy the freedom to explore fantasy that they offer. A first child has the opportunity to explore and revel in his newly developing imagination. A second or third child is never left alone and is likely to be shoved into reality by older siblings.

Parents, too, resent imaginary friends. Why is this? I think most parents feel left out and are jealous. Giving up a child is one of the most difficult tasks of parenting. The more intensely he protects his private language and his private friends, the more shut out and jealous his parents are likely to feel. Also, a four-year-old's creative exploration is so new that it frightens first-time parents. They are likely to wonder whether a child really "knows" the difference between reality and the fantasies he is constructing. Will he get lost in unreality? Will he use a "bad" friend to lie his way out of difficulty? Will he prefer this fantasy life and begin to shut out playmates? These are common concerns of parents at this age.

Imaginary friends are to be welcomed, as I suggested in chapter 13. From a cognitive standpoint, imagination is a very important sign of complex thinking at this age. The child is trying to get away from the concrete thinking that dominates his world most of the time. As imagination surfaces in the third year, a child's ability to keep reality and wishful thinking apart is not yet well developed. The capacity to make up an imaginary world, to construct imaginary people, to bring a beloved doll to life, is a sign of a child's rapidly developing ability to test the limits of his world. It becomes a way to cast out the devils that besiege him—hate, envy, lying, selfishness, and uncleanliness. All these can now be ascribed to someone else—an imaginary friend. Or else, he may insist that he is the imaginary friend, as he tries to shed his misdeeds. We can see this as a child's first effort to conform to what everyone expects of him, to search for right and wrong. This search is only a beginning, it is fragile. The child wants to accomplish it independently. A child must be able to engage in these explorations apart from his parents. Their intrusion diminishes his ability to find out about the world on his own.

From an emotional standpoint, imaginary friends can serve a very important purpose. They give a child a safe way to find out who he wants to be. He can dominate these friends, can control them, can be bad or good safely because of them. Through them, he can identify with children who are overwhelming to him. He can safely "become" another child. He can also identify with each of his parents in the safe guise of these imaginary friends. He can try out being a male or a female. He can try out all sides of his personality. This is one of the ways a four- or five-year-old gradually finds his identity.

Concern about a child's retiring into loneliness is valid. He should be learning to socialize with peers his own age. But he still needs time to himself. If a child could not give up his imaginary friends for real ones, I would be worried, too. If he withdrew from active participation in school or in play, the imaginary friends could represent a symptom of too much isolation and of a lonely child. But if a child can leave his private world to play with other children, I wouldn't worry.

What effect does TV have on this important process? Undoubtedly, it cuts down on the time a child might devote to exploring his own fantasies. If he is allowed to watch television for too much of the day, he will not have the necessary time or energy to explore the world on his own. Television forces a child into a kind of overwhelmed passivity. Bruno Bettelheim pointed out that storytelling and bedtime stories stimulate the self-exploration of aggression and the identity seeking that a child needs at this age. Television, except in small doses, has the opposite effect, imposing an artificial world of violence and unreachable good and evil, and numbing the child's own imaginative adventures.

Responding to Imaginary Friends

What about a child who uses an imaginary friend to "lie" his way out of a bad situation? This is an extremely common event at these ages. A parent may well wonder whether the child knows the difference between the wish and the reality, for lying at this age so obviously represents wishful thinking. Without confronting him the parent can point out the child's need to wish for a different outcome. By accepting the wishful thinking but bringing the child back to reality, the parent is helping him learn about his limits within the real world. The message a child needs to hear is, "You don't need to lie. I can love you, even if I don't like what you've done." It also lets a child safely explore an unreal world, because he knows his parent will bring him back to reality.

Should parents get actively involved with the child's fantasies? Should they set the table for the friends, or should they deny their existence? I would follow the child's requests. Many children ask their parents to stay out of the imaginary friend's world. If parents do not ridicule him and show respect for his friends, he may want them to accept his friends at the table. Then I would certainly do it. Playing his game with him will not prevent him from knowing the difference between imaginary and "real" friends. Imaginary friends can be a kind of rehearsal for future friendships.

If parents feel they need to cut short the child's imaginary play because he is too involved or too isolated from other children, I would recommend the following steps.

1. Discuss the issue with him, and suggest that you want him to have more playmates. Let him know that you value his imaginary friends and you respect his wonderful fantasies, but you'd like to see that he has "real" friends, too. His real friends will have their own imaginary friends, and maybe they can share them.
2. Set him up with one or two regular playmates who are his speed—not too overwhelming or too aggressive. Don't push him but do give him regular opportunities to get to know them. Help him understand his shyness and reasons why he can't enter a group right away. Many inexperienced children at this age need to be backed up as they learn to socialize. Pushing them makes them feel inadequate and guilty for not pleasing you. When your child does make it, let him know that you recognize how hard it's been and that you're proud of him.
3. When he hides behind his imaginary friends, don't confront him. He will then use them as a way of withdrawing more actively. Explain that you understand why he needs them. You love him and his imaginary friends, but you want him to feel safe enough to play with other children. You will help him.

In short, a child's life is enhanced by imaginary friends. These are a sign of healthy emotional and cognitive development among three- to six-year olds. Parents need not be concerned unless a child remains isolated. However, they must deal with their own feelings of being left out of their child's world. If they understand the important developmental processes that these wonderful friends are serving, they will be better able to handle their own natural jealousy.

29

LOSS AND GRIEF

Learning about grief and loss can be an important experience for a child. It can also be an opportunity for the whole family to share the feelings, the belief systems, and the defenses that are necessary for handling grief.

When the *Challenger* space shuttle exploded in 1986, I was asked by the media to suggest to parents how they might shield their children from the anguish of that tragedy. The death of the teacher and mother who accompanied the astronauts was a personal loss for all the children who had watched the launch on television. Like many other adults, I was sure that all American children would identify with her children and with her pupils who were watching as the rocket exploded.

"Why did that mommy get lost? Where is she now?"

"Why did she leave her children? Were they bad?"

"Why did our president let that mommy get killed?"

Underneath these questions are the universal fears of children in the face of death: Will my mommy leave me? If she does, will it be because I'm bad? If I let myself get angry with Daddy, will he go away, too? The children watching television wondered if their parents would die like that. They wondered if they themselves would die that way and why a figure of authority, like a mother or a father or a president, would allow something like that to happen. Where does the body go? What is death anyhow? A child's nightmares about dying can be triggered by such events.

That night, I urged that every family sit down together to share with each other the sense of tragedy. Children needed to hear that their parents would not leave them. They needed to hear from their parents that the death was not a child's responsibility, that it did not result from a child's bad deeds or wishes. It was necessary for families to share the grief of the children who had lost their mother and their teacher. We cannot and should not try to protect our children from a deep, caring identification with others who suffer great loss or from their own grief. Grief is a vital and inevitable part of life. Longing for someone who is temporarily or permanently lost adds an important dimension to a child's ability to care about others.

We have few opportunities in this country to share with our children this kind of personal grief. At such times, we can put into words the beliefs that enable us to face loss and death. We are given the chance to explain our own feelings about death, as well as our convictions about religion, about an afterlife, and about the memories that keep others alive after death. When a close member of the family dies, parents can be so overwhelmed by their own grief that they may not be able to face grieving in their children. A national tragedy like the *Challenger* explosion or the death of someone in the community can be a kind of preparation for tragedies when they occur close to home.

Loss in the Family   If a parent or grandparent or aunt or uncle dies, it is important for adults to share their feelings with their children. Trying to shield them from the parents' own feelings of loss or depression can be disastrous. Children know all too well when a parent is depressed or is in a crisis. Attempts to hide the event or the feelings it engenders amount to a desertion for the child. Parents often say to me: "Isn't she too young to learn about death?" I can assure them that it is better for a child to learn about a death from her own grieving parents than it is to experience a parent's withdrawal without having been given a reason for it. A child's sense of death is more primitive than an adult's. She will tend to equate it with being left alone or deserted. If parents withdraw without sharing the experience they are having, it is confirmation of the child's worst fears: Grandma has died. Now mother is so sad that maybe she will die, too.

When parents can convey their grief, their own questions about mortality, memory, and the meaning of suffering, the child has an opportunity to experience *in safety* the kind of questions that plague all of us. She can share the intense emotions of grief and of sadness with her parents. The parents themselves experience the wonderful thing that happens when there is a child around—a child in a bereaved family gives the rest of the family a sense of future and of purpose. When she makes her weeping mother smile, the child can experience a rare sense of power in changing her mother's mood to a positive one, if only briefly. I am constantly struck with the observation that a small child will attempt to comfort a grieving parent.

I remember once making rounds in our hospital and meeting a young mother who told me about the loss of her new baby and began to sob silently. Her two-year-old was playing quietly in a corner of the room. When he saw his mother's tears, he toddled over to her lap. As he crawled up, he reached to pat her cheek clumsily and to wipe away her tears. His mother looked down at him to smile and to draw him close. He had reminded his mother that he was there to balance her grief.

Explanations about death can be tailored to the age of the child. I would tell a child as much as you think that she can understand. It need not be too frightening. You must prepare her for conversations that she will overhear. You might say, for instance, "Grandpa was getting so old that he wasn't able to do all the things he wanted to do. When you get old, you get pretty tired. Now he can rest." A child may ask, "But why did he leave us? Couldn't we help him rest at our house? I miss him, and I want to play the games we used to play." You can answer honestly: "None of us knows why someone we love has to die and go away. The body just gives out. We all feel terribly sad and lonely. We all worry about where he has gone, whether he's happier and more comfortable now. We want him to be peaceful, but just like you, we hate to have to give him up. What I plan to do is to remember all I can about him. I'd like to talk about all the things we can remember about him, so we can keep him with us that way. Can you remember some things about him to tell me now?"

In talking about death to a child, a parent can listen for indications of fear that her thoughts or deeds have brought about the loss. Magical thinking is a part of being three, four, five, or six. At these ages a child will need repeated reassurances that being bad doesn't bring retaliation and that angry thoughts don't make people die.

Sooner or later, a child will begin to wonder about her own death: When will I die? What does dying feel like? Where will I go? Will I be all alone? All of these questions will present opportunities for observant parents to answer what can be answered to allay some fears, and to share their own similar feelings about death and loss. If you have religious feelings about death or an afterlife, this is the time to share them. If you find solace in nature, in myth, or in memory, try to convey this to your children. Children love stories from the past. Talk about what it was like when you were a child and your parents were young and taking care of you. Make your own life as a child come alive for your children. They'll get the point, and it will be a balance to the grief.

The Death of a Pet

This should be taken as seriously as the loss of a person. Never lie about it to a child. You will lose her trust. Tell her what you can about the animal's life and the animal's death. Encourage the child to unload her grief and her anger at losing a beloved friend. Allow her a period of mourning before you introduce another pet into the family. It is important for the child to realize the loss and to experience the sense of caring that goes

with losing a beloved pet. Again, expect her to feel personally responsible for having caused the loss, and explain whether it was an accident or a natural death.

When another child is sick or dying, children will be vulnerable to deep fears. They will identify with the sick or dying child: Will I be next? Will the same thing happen to me? Why do her parents let her die? Was it because she was bad and deserved it? I wish I hadn't ever been bad to her. Maybe I made her die.

Although many of these questions may seem irrational and are not based in reality, any adult who has experienced a serious loss will recognize that the fears they represent are

The Death of Another Child

universal ones. When someone is very sick and suffering, we all feel responsible. We all feel as if we deserve retaliation for our misdeeds or our inadequate caring. In explaining the reality of the other child's illness or death, parents can also make clear that they have the same feelings. Trying to deny or hide the reality of the illness or the grief and fears of adults would be a great mistake.

Schools can do a lot to help children deal with their fears about illness and death. One of my patients told me about the way a local school handled the situation of a six-year-old who had an inoperable brain tumor. He had been experiencing frequent headaches and had had to miss school because of them. When he came back to his class one day, he had a convulsion in the schoolroom, which all his schoolmates witnessed. After that, he was too ill to return to school. The teacher realized that witnessing this convulsion and the inevitable deterioration of the ill child had been devastating to her class. She talked to them about the boy's illness and tried to explain it as well as she could. But the sense of loss still invaded the mood of the classroom and left some children inhibited and scared. The teacher called all the parents together to tell them about the sick boy and urged them to share their children's grieving. She warned them about the likelihood of certain feelings and fears: feelings of guilt, of identification with the dying boy, and of sharing the responsibility for his illness. As she talked with the parents, she realized that the children needed a chance to say goodbye. She got up her courage and went to see the boy's parents to request that she bring the children by to see him. The parents were touched and knew what it could mean to their son. They chose a day when he was at his best. All of his schoolmates came to see him. Each one had made a special little present. Each one sat by him, touched him, and gave him a sign of how much they cared about him. He was exhausted but exhilarated after their visit. He went downhill rapidly afterward but talked constantly to his parents about "my friends." The children in his class now felt as if they could talk about him, could remember him as "theirs." They had said goodbye and had shared a bit in his illness.

At the Children's Hospital in Boston, we have instituted

family visits. All family members can come in to visit with a sick child. Parents, of course, are urged to stay as much as they can (see chapter 25). When we first asked the hospital personnel to allow siblings to visit, they resisted. They brought up the dangers of other children who might bring in more infection. The activity of normal, noisy children might upset the sick child, they said. We asked for a chance to try out such visits.

There was a terminally ill two-year-old, whom we will call Willie, who was dying of cancer. He'd lost all his hair from the X rays and the chemotherapy. He was terribly thin, virtually skin and bones. But he had a charming, winning smile. He was a favorite of all the nurses and doctors. His parents were wonderfully attentive, and one day they asked whether they might bring in Willie's two older brothers, four and six. They, and we, were afraid that Willie might not get to go home again, and they told us how devastated the two older boys were. We used this as a test case.

Willie was sitting in a playpen in the middle of the nurse's station when his parents arrived. His wispy face brightened a bit when his mother came over to pat him on his bald head. His father touched Willie's hands when the tiny boy held them out to him. We could tell that his father was almost afraid to pick him up because he looked so fragile and weak. His mother said, "Will, we have a surprise for you!" Willie's eyes lit up a bit, and his cocked head seemed to be asking what it was. At that moment, the two older brothers came off the elevator and rushed over to this little skeleton of a boy. When Willie saw them, tears began to stream down his cheeks, he pulled himself up to stand at the side of the playpen and hung over it, both arms extended toward his brothers. He kept repeating, "Oh! Oh! Oh!" as if he couldn't believe they were really there. The four-year-old reached out to Willie to rub his head and his face. He touched and touched and touched his little brother. Willie fawned and squirmed with each touch, as if he couldn't get enough of this touching. He looked adoringly up at his brother, as if he hadn't seen him for far too long. This older brother pulled a chair over to the playpen to sit down beside Willie. He asked his parents whether he could hold him in his arms. By this time, there were tears in the eyes of every one of us who was watching. The head nurse nodded to the parents. The father picked his son up gently to put him in his brother's lap. The six-year-old began to rock and to croon to Willie as if he were a baby. Willie cuddled up into his brother. He reached up to feel his brother's face with his all-too-delicate hands. He explored his brother's eyes, his hair, his mouth. Eventually, exhausted, he laid his head back on his brother's shoulder.

Since that episode, we have had unlimited visiting for siblings. All of us could see what his brothers meant to this child and what he meant to them. We could see how critical it was to any dying child and to the other children in a family to have a chance to reunite and to say goodbye.

At the hospital, we have a wonderful program called "Good Grief." This program not only helps parents and children to face and share their grief, but it also addresses the grief of hospital and school personnel who must deal with the loss of a child or of a parent. This program institutes the open sharing of feelings—on the wards, at home, and in the schools. (See Useful Addresses and also Grollman, LeShan, and Viorst in the Bibliography at the end of this book.)

30

LYING, STEALING, AND CHEATING

In any period of rapid learning, a child's imagination serves a vital function. In his fantasy life, he can explore the ideas he is developing. In fantasy is safety. He won't need to act them out if he can dream them out. Imagination and the use of magical thinking help a child explore his new world without the dangers of going overboard. He can be a powerful, frightening wolf in his dreams at night. He can roar like a fire engine. He can learn about witches and robbers as he revels in his fears. An active imagination gives him a chance to be a monster, an aggressive animal, and an adored parent—all in one dream or fantasy. The cognitive process of symbolic function—that of letting a toy animal or a truck or a doll stand for something else—comes within the child's reach in the fourth and fifth years.

Play and imagination are necessary in learning boundaries and in realizing oneself as a person. Secure sexual differentiation and self-control over aggressive impulses are the goals of this tumultuous period. One of the arenas that a child must explore to achieve these goals is the meaning of lying, stealing, and cheating. These are normal behaviors in four- and five-year-olds and can be opportunities for parents to teach a child about responsibility to others. That lesson is a lifetime project for all of us.

The main difficulty parents have when these kinds of behaviors first appear is to control their own overreaction based on their memories. They may have been caught at such acts, and shamed and punished. They may have been told of children who get into serious trouble. The painful, unresolved fears of parents make them react with horror at the first signs of lying, cheating, or stealing. If they can think back to their own past, it becomes easier to understand the child's side.

Lying   All four-year-olds lie. An active imagination is a sign of emotional health at around ages four and five—*even* if it leads to untruths. And it will.

Take a child, whom we will call Alex, who watches his father play with a new personal computer every night. Totally absorbed, the father smiles, frowns, and even laughs out loud as his computer comes up with unexpected results. One morning, when his father leaves for work, Alex steals into the workroom to inspect his father's computer. Imitating his father, he begins to play with the buttons and keys. All of a sudden, the computer whirs, rings bells, hums, and continues to hum until Alex's parents return that evening. Frightened by the noises that he can't control, Alex hides. His father, horrified at the state of his computer, storms into dinner, accusing each member of the family in turn. When he comes to Alex, the frightened little boy blurts out that the sitter went in there and smashed the "puter." By now, Alex wants so much to believe his story that he begins to add details to make it more credible. By the time the sitter arrives to deny her involvement, Alex's father is horrified at the complexity of the lies that Alex has constructed. He punishes Alex harshly. By this time, Alex's wishful thinking has made him believe that his story is true. He feels betrayed and undeserving of his father's anger.

As a result, there is little chance that he will learn anything positive from this experience. He has lied in order to protect himself from his father's initial accusation, making a creative attempt to please his father and to erase the damage he has done in trying to identify with his father's devoted attachment to his computer. The angrier his father gets, the further Alex is pushed into his fabrications.

Parents of four- and five-year-olds need to be prepared for such lies. As a child's magical thinking surfaces, a parent can enjoy, if possible, the fanciful results. Overreacting is likely to set them as a pattern.

What to Do When a Child Lies First, try to understand the circumstances that led to the episode. Trust the child to mean well, and try to understand his reasons—his fantasies and wishful thinking. Help him understand them, too.

Next, don't corner the child or overreact violently. Conscience at this age is just emerging; guilt comes *after* the act and in response to the recognition of disapproval. The long-term goal is to help the child incorporate a conscience—as psychoanalyst Selma Fraiberg said, "to bring the policeman from the outside to the inside." Requirements that are too rigid, or punishment that is too severe, may end up with one of three results: (1) a conscience that is too rigid and relentless, (2) fierce rebellion that makes a child seem amoral, or (3) compulsive repetition of lying.

When you have overdone your criticism or punishment, or when you are wrong in your accusations, admit it to the child. Use this as an opportunity to discuss how anxious his lying makes you. But assure him that you understand his side of it. Remember that a child's love for his parents is greater than his love for himself. You can all too easily undermine his sense of competence.

You will know that you are making progress when you and your child can discuss each episode and when you can help him understand his own reasons for lying. When he can begin to acknowledge the truth, you can be certain you are on the right track. At a later stage, a child will begin to respect others' feelings and rights.

If, on the other hand, lying is repeated again and again,

becoming more and more insidious and less related to reality or understandable, you are probably putting too much pressure on the child. Other indications that a child does not feel safe to develop his fantasy world at his own pace are a child who punishes himself and begins to withdraw, to become unavailable, who shows signs of generalized anxiety and self-depreciation, with increasing fears and night terrors. In such a situation, you must lay off harsh punishments and reevaluate your own reactions. Also evaluate the child's life circumstances and the pressures on him. Let up on any unimportant issues. Admit to the child that you've been reacting too harshly. Sometimes it helps to use dolls or stories to talk and play the issues out with the child.

If you're really worried, have a professional evaluation. Remember that consistent lying is just a symptom of underlying anxiety or fearfulness. It needs to be addressed, not suppressed.

Stealing

Small children engage in stealing for at least two reasons. First, everything "belongs" to a three- or four-year-old until someone tells him differently. Hence, if he sees a toy in a toy store or is wheeled by a bag of cookies in a grocery store, the things he sees are his—until he learns that such things belong to others. Learning this takes time. As with lying, a traumatic punishment will only drive the behavior underground. Gentle explanations of how to respect possessions, coupled with firm limits, are much more effective.

A more subtle reason for stealing is the desire to identify with others. As the intense desire of a preschool child to identify with his parents, his siblings, or his schoolmates increases, he may take important things from them. In his own concrete way of thinking, he will believe that having a possession of the other person's amounts to being like the other person. He does not yet have a conscience. Guilt feelings emerge later, because of the disappointment of others.

Stealing first appears at the ages of four and five in most children. It is exploratory and acquisitive rather than a sign of being bad. If you explode, you are likely to engender fear and repetitious acting out in the child. Of course, it frightens a parent when a small child steals from another, and particularly if he seems to understand what he's done by lying about it. But, if you can understand the universality and the motives behind a preschooler's stealing, you can avoid overreacting and causing the fixation of this behavior as a future pattern. A parent's goal, for stealing as for lying, is to use each episode as an opportunity for teaching. Helping a child understand his reasons for taking others' possessions without feeling overwhelming guilt leaves him available to hear you when you discuss other's rights. Learning to respect others' possessions and territory is a long-term goal. Handled with sensitivity, each episode of stealing can lead in that direction.

How to Prevent Stealing First, don't make a huge scene. This will only frighten the child. Try not to label him as a thief as you talk to him, and try not to harp on the incident afterward. It is wise not to confront the child by asking him whether he stole; this may just force him into a lie. Simply make clear that you know where the object came from, asking your child to produce it if necessary, and saying, "I'm sorry you took something that isn't yours."

Then help the child return the object to its owner and apologize, even if it means going to the grocery store and suffering the embarrassment of returning the object or paying for it. Let the child work off the cost by doing chores. Be consistent about all this each time.

Preventing stealing involves a lot of calm teaching. Show the child how to ask for what he wants. Have simple rules about sharing with others, such as "You don't take another child's toy without asking her and offering her one of yours." Explain the concept of borrowing and returning a toy: "You may ask whether you can play with it. If they say no, that's it. If they say yes, you must offer to return it." "If we are in a store and you want some cookies, ask me whether you can have them. If I say yes, wait to take them until I've paid for them." In this way, you are teaching the child respect for others' things, demonstrating the manners he needs for asking, and helping him learn to delay his gratification.

It is also important to explain why such rules are necessary—"in order to protect others' toys the way you want to protect yours." When a child does steal, use a time-out as a disciplinary measure, but soon afterward sit down to discuss it with him. Your goal is not to punish but to teach him about others' possessions and about curbing his own wishes for those possessions. Try to understand why he did it, and help him understand himself. Help him see your point of view: you can't allow him to take other's possessions. Make clear that you're trying to understand his side of it. Then ask him how he plans to handle it, and give part of the responsibility of limits to him. Finally, and most important, when he succeeds, be sure to let him know you are proud of him.

If stealing continues, look for possible underlying reasons. Is the child guilty and frightened and reacting by a sort of repetition-compulsion? Is he so insecure that he needs others' possessions to make him feel like a whole person? Do others already disapprove of him and label him? If he repeats his acts of stealing, he may be asking you for therapy. Don't wait until he feels like a failure and the labels stick. Seek outside help—a referral from your doctor or the child psychiatry department at a teaching hospital.

In order to understand that other people do not like a child who cheats, a child must be mature enough to understand rules, in games or at school. He must have matured beyond the provocative behavioral state of a three-year-old. By five to six, a child can learn the concept of open bargaining rather than subversive cheating. Maturity brings with it more logical thinking, and the egocentrism of the three-year-old gives way to an awareness of others. A social conscience is now in the making.

Cheating

A parent's job is to further this awareness. Punishment that is inappropriate or too strong will just stunt these developmental processes. A better technique to stop cheating is to handle it gently and openly. You can explain the consequences of cheating in a nonjudgmental way:

"It isn't really fair to her, and she won't like you."

"Would you want him to cheat on you?"

"What is fair for you is fair for everyone else."

"If you win by cheating, she might never want to play with you, or else she'll learn to cheat you back. Do you want that?"

"Are you trying to make your teachers angry—or me? I'm just disappointed, for I know you know better."

"Can you give me any ideas about how to help you with this?"

Dramatic play can be a powerful way of introducing respect for others. It can also give you a chance to teach a child ways to bargain that are acceptable. Let the child show you, in a made-up situation, how he would like to be disciplined in order to help him learn responsibility for himself.

A child's social conscience is modeled on yours and the rest of the family's. Be sure you are giving him a chance to understand your own social values—in his own terms.

31

MANNERS

In most cultures, teaching a child manners is an important part of early training. The respectful bow of a Japanese child, the hearty greeting of an African child, and the curtsy of a European child are marks of respect and acceptance of the other person.

Manners represent our values, our social styles. We need them throughout life in order to enter and fit into a group. The manners that we use reflect our social structure, the framework of any social situation. They signal our respect for other people and are essential to gaining the acceptance of others.

Their importance begins early. Two-year-old children playing on a slide will stand in line, respecting each other's turn. If an aggressive child crowds in, the "line" will decide as a group whether to allow this or to shove her out. By the age of two, a child is already expected by her peers to respect the rules of the game. Rules, like manners, define the behavior that others expect from us. A child who is either too aggressive or too retiring to follow the rules is labeled undesirable by the other children.

We cannot escape rules and manners, but we can decide

which ones matter and which ones don't. Our children will model themselves on our decisions.

Children begin learning about rules and manners in infancy, though most parents aren't even conscious that they are teaching these lessons. For example, when a baby bites her mother's nipple, the breast-feeding mother is shocked and reacts with both pain and surprise at her five-month-old's aggressiveness. She pulls back, takes the baby off the breast, and reprimands, "No, you can't do that!" She has just taught her baby the rules of nursing. The baby is already learning respect for the other person while learning these breast-feeding rules.

Learning about Manners

Not until a child begins to tease and test limits in the second year do parents recognize their role in "teaching" manners. One of the first real battlegrounds of manners is feeding time, as mentioned in earlier chapters. While learning the rules, a two-year-old must try out all possibilities. She must drop food over the side of her tray, pour out the contents of her cup, mash food into her hair, and refuse one food after another, testing each rule in a search for limits.

During the second year, the opportunity to explore limits and her own autonomy is more important to a child's development than is learning the manners we will expect later on. By age four or five, after she has mastered the basic mealtime skills, she'll begin to identify with the adults around her and pick up the manners she sees practiced by her parents and older siblings. On her own, she'll use a napkin to wipe her face, handle a fork and spoon, and ask if she may be excused from the table. At this age, children have a strong desire to imitate the actions of those around them. On the other hand, if directed to "do this" or "don't do that," any vital four-year-old will rebel. Learning how to do things herself has become too important and exciting for her to acquiesce to parental direction. That's why your best chance of teaching acceptable behavior is simply to model it for your child. If you have a three- or four-year-old I urge you set an example but not to comment too strongly on your child's progress in learning manners.

Social Rules   Once a child begins to learn the basic rules of mealtime, bedtime, and bathtime behavior at around four years old, she is
ready to be introduced to some of the social rules.

Going to see grandparents can be an excellent opportunity
for learning. You can prepare your child with a little story
about what will happen when she visits her grandparents'
house and what will be expected of her. As you talk to her,
help her rehearse the desired behavior. For example:
"Grandma and Grandpa will be so glad to see you. Will you
be ready to hug them and to let them kiss you? Or will you
want to run and hide? Lots of kids your age are shy, but
grandparents have waited so long to see you that they can't
help wanting to hug and kiss you."

When other people will be present, prepare your child to
greet them, as well. "Do you remember Mr. Green, who lives
next door to Grandma and Grandpa? Well, he's going to be
there, too, and I'll bet he holds out his hand for you to shake,
like this. This is called shaking hands. Daddy will shake hands
with Mr. Green, so you can see how grownups do it. Then
maybe you can do it, too."

If and when your child does practice these mannerly
behaviors, comment favorably, but don't overdo your praise.
You are setting up an expectation, not making a big event of
it. If she is unable to live up to your requests, don't nag.
Simply let her know that you'd still like her to learn these
formalities, and you hope that next time, she can do what
"everyone else does." The result of both too much pressure
and too much praise is to convey that manners are negotia-
ble. Instead, manners, like mealtime and bedtime routines,
should become part of a well-established pattern, rather than
an issue for negotiation.

When it's time to say goodbye, again let your child know
what you expect of her. "You can thank Grandma and
Grandpa for the neat dinner and give them a hug goodbye.
Grandma and Grandpa told me they'd noticed how grownup
you are!"

If either grandparent has a disability or uses a cane or
crutches, you'll have an opportunity to prepare your child to

be sensitive to others. You might tell her, "Grandpa has to use crutches now because his legs hurt, but he's a little bit ashamed that he needs the crutches. Sometimes even adults are ashamed to be different from everyone else. So the best thing that we can do is to be sympathetic and helpful, but not talk too much about Grandpa's crutches. You might ask him how he's feeling and try to notice the times when he needs help. For example, if his crutches fall, you could pick them up and give them to him."

At four and five, a child's awareness of differences is at a peak. She is likely either to be embarrassed or to overreact. For instance, if she sees a blind person on the street, she might announce loudly, "Look, Mom, she has a cane!" All such situations offer opportunities to teach consideration for others. "Yes," you might say, "she uses a cane because she can't see, and the cane helps her feel the curb and the walls she might run into. Shut your eyes and see how hard it would be to get around by yourself. It's wonderful that she can do it alone, don't you think?" Helping your child find ways to handle her feelings actually comes as a big relief to her. When you model appropriate behavior, you help her to reduce her feelings of anxiety.

Conveying the Pleasure of Man

Manners make life easier and more pleasant. If you can explain this, instead of presenting them as a chore, you'll get better results. For instance, if you say "excuse me" in the supermarket when you accidentally jostle someone, your child will imitate your behavior. Most people will smile back at this welcome behavior. Children can learn to understand that manners not only make relationships easier but also help them cope with unusual, stressful situations. For manners not only offer a framework for responding to everyday situations; they also help children deal with the unexpected. A child who feels comfortable with routines for the usual events is likely to handle the unusual ones more successfully. When your child does rise to an occasion, be sure to recognize her for it. Saying something like, "Everyone admired the way you helped that little boy get up when he tripped and skinned his knee," will make your child feel good about herself.

When a child learns good manners without pressure from parents, she is proud of the skills she has mastered. Rather than an artificial structure imposed on her by adults, her manners spring from within. She has control over them and they are hers. Most of all, she will feel secure in her sense that manners—and the help they give her in winning the esteem and affection of others—will always be available to her.

Rudeness One common reaction to excess pressure to learn good manners comes out as conscious rudeness. When a child is aware of what is expected, she may act out with overtly rude behavior. This indicates that the child knows what she should do, but she feels more pressure than she can handle, and reacts with behavior and language that are sure to get a response.

If your child reaches this point, you might say: "Of course,

I'm disappointed. You and I know you know better. Maybe you're feeling like I expected a lot from you. But I do. I want other people to respect and like you. I know how great you are, and I want them to know it. I'm sorry you felt this way, and I hope you can be more sensitive to other people next time." At the first sign of resistance, you should avoid adding pressure. The child may not be able to hear your comments, and this little lecture can be saved for a later time.

If a child is rude all the time, I would worry about her. There is no reason to put up with constant insensitivity to others by the age of four or five. This is a sign of inner turmoil, and if it continues, you might seek psychological help for her. If it persists and invades all of a child's reactions, a consultation with a child psychologist or psychiatrist might be wise. Rudeness shuts out the world and compounds the child's anxieties.

Swearing

Four- and five-year-old children go through a period of using the most devastating words they know. Their ability to choose the word that can best offend an adult or older sibling is uncanny. It is exciting to them to see the reaction. A public setting is best of all. Conversation stops. Parents look at each other in horror. They dare not look at mortified grandparents or at the other snickering adults who may be present. The child knows she's created a stir. She repeats it until someone recovers enough to reprimand her. After a few such occasions, swear words become a set part of her vocabulary. She is likely to try them out on any occasion.

Swearing or trying out "dirty" words is a sign of rebellious and provocative behavior and is normal and inevitable in four- to six-year-olds. It persists solely because parents or other adults overreact. Negative reinforcement is the best approach—no response at all. Enlist the cooperation of others so that no one reacts to the teasing behavior. At another time, you can speak to the child about the fact that you don't like it and others don't either. You understand that she needs to try out her new vocabulary, but some words are to be used only in private. Give her permission to try them out at home. If you pay little attention, this testing should die out.

If it continues, you may have to work out a way of reminding and disciplining the child. Talk it out before you go anywhere. Decide with her what you and she will do if it happens, then do it. Tell her you'll try to help her control herself. If she can, congratulate her.

Boys seem to swear more than girls. Perhaps it is because we expect more social control from girls and, unconsciously, reinforce boys for "naughty" behavior. Boys are likely to use swear words as part of their macho behavior at five and six—and later.

Parents worry whether swearing is likely to go on—to become part of the child's personality. If the child gets enough rewarding reinforcement from it, it will. It may also occur as a symptom of a child's insecurity and/or unhappiness. If the child is using swear words in an unnecessarily provocative way and in inappropriate places, I'd see it as a call for help. Have her evaluated for an underlying depression or a poor self-image.

As we said at the beginning of the chapter, manners reflect the agreements underlying our social behavior. They are less important in themselves than as keys to the larger social realm. A welcoming set of manners is like a passport, allowing freedom and access to people beyond the family. A child who is sensitive to people's feelings and has "nice manners" will find more smiles and new friends than frowns and wary resistance as she sets out to explore the world.

32
PREMATURITY

The birth of a premature baby is a shock. All the work of
pregnancy as preparation for labor and for the new baby's
arrival is cut short. Both a premature baby and his parents
face many adjustments.

A mother automatically wonders about her own role in pre- **Parents' Anxieties**
mature birth. Why was I unable to carry him? Was there
something defective about me—or him? Did I do too much?
Was I eating wrong? What did I do to this baby? Automatically, grieving sets in. The mother blames herself and feels
helpless, even angry—at herself, but also at the world. She
is likely to project her anger onto her husband and onto
the caregivers of her baby. "Why aren't they doing more
for him?" is a thinly veiled coverup for her own feeling of
inadequacy.

Once they learn that the baby will survive, both parents
begin to worry about whether he'll be "normal." The inevitable comparisons to a normal full-term baby begin—and may

last the rest of his life. Any parent who has been through the trauma of delivering a fragile infant will automatically classify that infant as vulnerable for years to come. The danger of hovering and of creating a "vulnerable child syndrome" is great. Parents need help in focusing on the infant's developing capabilities instead of on "what he might have been." This will take time. When parents can concentrate on the baby they have, instead of the one he might have been, all their energy can go into reinforcing his potential growth and development.

If, on the other hand, parents are constantly comparing him to their friend's babies, they are bound to find him lacking in some area. This drives them to try to help him compensate. They will watch his every move, lest he fail. Before he can build up the desire to try out a task, to fail initially, and to generate enough energy to try again, to become frustrated until he succeeds, they rush to help him. Each success will be theirs, not his. His self-image will gradually become that of a helpless, inadequate ex-preemie—a truly vulnerable child.

The high-tech, alarming surroundings of the neonatal intensive care nursery (NICU) reinforce parents' image of their baby as fragile. Only when they see the strengths of the baby will parents begin to escape these anxieties. Over the years, those of us who have worked in these nurseries have fought for parent involvement and also for less overwhelming, overlit, noisy environments for the infants themselves. Concerned parents can be incorporated into the care of a premature baby early on. They can watch his recovery, and their own recovery can parallel his. With very small, very sick infants, denial has to be a major defense mechanism. As he recovers, this need for denial can diminish. If a nurse or pediatrician takes time to include them in evaluations, they can see their baby organize himself and demonstrate the behaviors seen in the neonatal period in full-term babies (see chapter 2).

Recovery and Growth

In the quieter atmosphere of a modern NICU, with less bright light and other stimuli, the fragile nervous system of a premature baby can organize more quickly and more effectively. He can gradually learn to shut down and to alert to the world around him. A premature baby who is not overloaded cycles through the six states observed in all newborns. He will slowly learn to pay attention to positive interpersonal stimuli as he recovers from his early delivery.

Any stressed infant is likely to be hypersensitive. (See chapters 2 and 26.) The more attractive is the stimulus (such as the human voice and face), the more the baby will overreact. As we said earlier, in order to reach such a baby with information that he can utilize for learning about himself and his world, each stimulus must be reduced in intensity, in rhythm, and in duration. We have found that a premature or stressed infant can take in and respond to only one modality at a time—either touch or voice or face or being picked up—and with very careful adjustment to the baby's responses. When he breathes fast and hard, when his color changes, he is saying, "I've had enough."

Deep sleep can be a defense for a premature baby. Fussing and crying can be a way of shutting out the world, though one that drains energy. An alert state is vital to his learning, but it may overload him, too. Caregivers must respect this low threshold. As they interact with him, they must watch for cues of exhaustion.

The infant's motor behavior is another way he can signal exhaustion; his movements become limp or jerky, changing from their previous tone and quality. These changes are observable and are part of the premature baby's language of communication.

As the infant recovers, he will become more and more able to accept a parent's handling, talking to him, and looking him in the face. When he can accept all these at once, he is already recovered and well-organized.

Parents are encouraged to visit the NICU daily and participate in feeding, changing, and cuddling their baby. They gradually overcome their natural fear of handling him. As they see him recover, they learn to identify his strengths and capacities for progress. Little details such as the tiny knit hats seen in some NICUs, names and pictures on the incubators, and toys brought by the parents personalize the tiny being and help parents see an individual child.

We have learned so much in the past few years. Even impaired infants can profit by the new techniques for early intervention. There is increasing evidence for resilience in the nervous system of a premature baby. The pathways in the immature baby's nervous system are what we call redundant. In other words, even if there are damaged areas, other areas can take over the functions of the damaged ones if early intervention is started in time. Of course, we cannot help an infant to regenerate damaged nerve cells. But just as a blind baby learns to utilize touch and hearing with an increased sensitivity, there are ways now to help an infant make up for neurological impairment. These techniques must be started as early as possible. For this reason, all premature infants should be assessed before discharge to judge the need for early intervention. Parents deserve to know how to reach such an infant and help him build on his own strengths. A baby at risk can either learn to fail or to succeed as he matures. We can see that he succeeds as effectively as possible if we start early.

The premature baby is likely to develop at a slower rate, because of the cost of organizing such a fragile nervous system. If parents expect this, their anxiety will be lessened. To arrive at an age for expectable development, the number of months of prematurity, plus the weeks or months during which a baby has been in intensive care, should all be subtracted from his age. There is evidence from electroencephalographic research that, while an infant is acutely ill or on intensive support systems, such as a respirator, his brain goes on hold and does not mature. All of his energy goes into his physical recovery. After he's well, his brain will begin to make progress and "catch-up" can begin. If parents expect a definite delay in his development, they may be spared the anxiety of wondering when he will ever catch up to his age group. They can help him where he is and see his real progress.

While the majority of premature babies grow up with normal abilities, the incidence of learning disabilities and attentional disorders or hyperactivity is higher in premature babies than it is in full-term ones. These conditions can be watched for. If parents suspect one, they should have an assessment by a qualified infant observer. If they can be guided to understand the challenges the baby is coping with, they can help him master his difficulties. As we said, children can learn to compensate for these problems. Early recognition of them can help the child progress toward his own potential rather than become set in a pattern of frustration (see chapters 18 and 26).

33

SCHOOL READINESS

Several issues need to be addressed in considering preschool for a child. Is this the right school? Is she ready? Can she separate from home? Can she begin to learn at this level? Will she be able to make it with other children? Will behavior problems interfere?

All of these questions need to be faced as a child starts preschool, and they will come up again before first grade. Although the adjustments at preschool and again at kindergarten levels make an enormous difference to a child's ability to face later challenges, the same kinds of adjustment issues are likely to recur at each transition.

If there is a choice of schools, you should visit each one. Look for a balance between cognitive and social learning. Too much emphasis on cognitive learning at this age may mean that the child's need to grow as a social being is neglected. The physical layout and the amount of adaptation of rhythms of activity, teaching, and relaxation to individual children reflect

the approach of each school. Watch the very active or the very quiet children to see how they are helped to fit in. Above all, assess the teacher's capacity for warmth, patience, and ability to encourage the individuality of each child. Will she be able to like your child? Your own reaction to the teacher may be the most sensitive way to predict this. Her personality may be more critical than her teaching ability in reinforcing in your child a good self-image at this critical juncture. For now, I would urge you to place more value on your child's stage of emotional development than on her cognitive potential. A bright child will always learn if she feels good about herself.

Readiness

Parents today are often haunted by the feeling that children must be prepared to compete early, to succeed from the start. Few can resist the urge to prepare their children by teaching them the skills they'll need in school—reading, writing, and arithmetic. The pressure on children to perform early seems to me to be cheating the child of opportunities for self-exploration, for play, and for the learning that comes from experimentation. Failure, followed by frustration or boredom, can set the stage for an eagerness on the child's part to learn when the appropriate chance comes along. The age at which a child starts to develop academic skills is not the point. Too many "precocious" learners burn out later. Most important is the child's own eagerness to learn and her self-concept. She must feel that she herself is in control of her learning.

School requires many things of a child. She must be able to concentrate and pay attention. She must have the physical stamina and patience to sit for long periods, as well as the capacity to fit into the rhythms of rest and activity of the school. A child must have the capacity to understand, remember, follow two- and three-part directions, do assigned tasks, manage personal possessions, and handle her own clothing.

Fine motor capacities such as cutting, drawing, and writing demand a considerable neurological and emotional maturity. It would be a fallacy to think all children are ready at the same time. "Late bloomers" deserve to be identified and have their pace respected. The way a child is accepted at this time may shape her image of herself for the future. Giving a child who needs it an extra year in which to mature may be much more critical than timing preschool so that a child arrives in first grade when he is six. The goal should be to build an interest in learning in the child herself. Too many children are pushed because they are bright enough, but not enough attention is paid to their maturity and readiness.

As decisions about preschool, kindergarten, and first grade arise, the following reasons to give children extra time should be considered:

► Family patterns of slow development—"late bloomers"
► Prematurity or physical problems in early life
► Delay in physical size or development
► Immature motor development—awkwardness, poor motor skills, such as in catching or throwing a ball, drawing, or cutting
► Easy distractibility and short attention span
► Difficulty with right–left hand or eye–hand coordination, such as in copying a circle or a diamond
► Lagging social development—difficulty taking turns,

sharing, or playing. If the child is shunned by children her own age, take it seriously.

Each of these might be a reason to allow a child to mature another year before starting preschool, or to stay in preschool or kindergarten a year longer. However, if any such delays or disabilities continue to interfere with the child's progress, arrange for a careful assessment—neurological and psychological—to identify the underlying problem. While the child may well outgrow the problem, it is important to understand the reasons for the delay and also identify her strengths. There are many programs for children with attention disorders, motor delays, and learning disabilities. (See Useful Addresses at the end of this book and in chapter 18). Find one that fits your child's difficulty, and be sure it's a positive and exciting one— not one that pushes such a child to "grow up" or to "be good" or to "pay attention." Such programs can be punitive, and they fail to reinforce the child positively for her successes. Instilling a sense of failure will surely lead to more failure. Find a program that bolsters the child's confidence and also one that focuses on helping you understand your child better.

Preparing a Child

Parents' readiness to separate from a child is as important to a child's school adjustment as being ready herself. Every parent worries, What will they think of her? Will they see how smart and wonderful she is, or just focus on her difficulties? Will the teacher be kind and encouraging, or will he kill her spirit? All of these concerns reflect a natural anxiety on parents' part about sharing their child. These questions cover up the fears of separation and the inevitable competition between parents and teachers. Parents see the child's entry into school (or day care, if this has occurred earlier) as the beginning of the end of their intimacy with her. "Next, she'll be a teenager! Before we know it, she'll be gone." Parents must face their own issues about separation before they can help the child with hers.

Preparing a child in advance for separation and the demands of preschool will make a big difference. Tell her whatever you know about what to expect. Take her to meet her teacher and to see her room beforehand. Be sure she knows one or two of her classmates. If necessary, woo them ahead of time, by taking them together to a museum or zoo (see chapter 45). Maybe you and the friend's mother can introduce them to school together the first day. Let the child take something special from home. When you get to school, introduce her to her teacher, to the cubbyhole for her belongings, to some other children, and to the play area. Demonstrate your confidence in the teacher by a complimentary statement such as, "I see you've planned an exciting day. We feel very lucky that Georgia can join this class."

Tell the child when you are leaving. This is very important. Kiss her goodbye, and don't prolong it. Tell her when you will be back, and *be there on time*! Once you have said goodbye, leave and don't turn around. Compliment the child afterward on how well she has handled it. She's made a big step! Listen to the account of her day. Don't send a child by bus the first few days—until she feels equal to it.

Many children adjust nicely at first but then show signs of regression at home. Symptoms, in apparently unrelated areas such as sleep, feeding, or temper tantrums, which have long since been handled, may recur. To me, these regressions demonstrate the kind of energy a child is mustering to meet the challenge. When a child has to handle a new situation, she is likely to regress temporarily, as if she were gathering energy for the important adjustment. By regressing, she can return to an earlier stage of development, collect whatever parental backup she needs, and reorganize herself. Regression often frightens parents, but it needn't unless it lasts too long. The learning that occurs during this period of reorganization is well worth the recurrence of old symptom patterns. Each child is likely to fall back on the developmental issues that she has last conquered. If she's just conquered fears at night, she'll begin to see monsters again. If she has just stopped biting her nails, she is likely to start again. Your role will be to support her in understanding the reason for her symptoms and to help her understand herself as she strives to cope with the new challenges at school. As she begins to succeed, let her know how proud you are.

Some children will begin to have stomachaches or head-aches in the morning before they must leave for school (see chapter 40). They may beg to be allowed to stay home. If these problems continue, or if the episodes of regression increase, they may be signs of too much pressure. The first step is to talk to the teacher. Find out whether there are stresses at school that you can alleviate. Is the child making it with her peers? Is she learning? Does she show signs of feeling inadequate?

Don't set yourself against the teacher. Even though a child may complain that she (or he) is too strict, that "She's so mean to me," you won't help by agreeing. Let your child know that you and the teacher will both be trying to make life become easier at school.

Talk to the child about her symptoms. Let her know that you understand about them, and you'll try to help. Explain that staying home won't really help and that you expect her to keep going. Assure her that all children go through periods like this when school is new and scary. It doesn't mean that she's bad or lazy, but that she's facing a new, demanding life and also leaving the safety of home. If you feel that the child is afraid of leaving home, try to understand the underlying issues. Ask the child, "Are you afraid that something will happen to me? It won't, for I won't let it." "Do you wonder whether I'm playing with your little brother (sister) and forget-ting about you? I never could. I'm so proud of my big girl. I think of you all the time, but I *expect* you to grow up and be ready to leave home. Your brother will have to learn this, too, and you'll be able to help him."

Since a child's ability to cope with the stress of leaving each morning could well be tied to her physiological status, be sure you know that she's not rundown or anemic. Many children wake up with low blood sugar levels at this time. Low blood sugar can contribute to headaches or stomachaches. Anxiety pushes the blood sugar level down even farther. I recommend that parents leave a glass of ginger ale or orange juice by the child's bedside. She should drink it as soon as she wakes, before she gets out of bed to move around. If she feels better, she will eat a better breakfast and will then be able to handle the stress of school and separation from home.

The period of adjusting at school can be stormy. Parents

worry that the child's bad behavior will label her in her teacher's mind. They may press her at home to "pay attention and be good in school." This won't help. Instead, remember that each child adjusts at her own rate. Try to make home a welcoming oasis of safety and warmth. Let the child blow off steam at home to balance the school pressure. Don't pressure her to perform in all areas at once—give her space. Back up her self-esteem: the basis for that is laid at home.

Going off to preschool or kindergarten is a child's first and most important opportunity to learn about adjusting to the outside world. She will be able to learn to participate as part of a group, to read social clues, to conform to grown-up expectancies and rules, to learn about social mores of children her own age, and to develop her own style for making and keeping friends. Specific skills and academic achievements will come in time. What the child learns about handling herself in a group and about embracing new situations will last her forever. (See also chapter 35.)

34

SELF-ESTEEM

The excitement of mastering a task can be seen in young babies as they roll over, grasp a cracker, and stack blocks. These experiences ultimately provide a base for a feeling of oneself, of self-esteem. When parents encourage a baby who has just learned a task by himself, they reinforce or encourage a good future self-image. As the child struggles and finally triumphs, the light in his eyes begins to glow. Parents' expectations and past experiences will influence whether they can afford to let a child experiment, get frustrated, and then make it on his own. Without this combination of freedom and encouragement, a child can develop an expectation of passive compliance or of failure.

How can you, as a parent, convey both freedom and support to a baby? What can you do to encourage a child's positive self-image? Being warm and loving is certainly the first step. But you also need to transmit ways of thinking, as well as ways

Encouraging a Positive Self-Image

of solving problems. These are usually picked up by a baby as he identifies with his parents. In addition to identification, there is the child's self-image. For example, take a baby who is playing with a simple puzzle. It is essential to be able to sit back and watch the baby as he tries to fit in the pieces, turning them one way then another, dropping them in his frustration. As he picks up the pieces up to try again, he mouths them, watching the puzzle as if it were an adversary. Finally, he takes the chance. He places the piece on the puzzle board. He turns it and it fits! He looks around triumphantly. At this point, your best move is to say softly, "You just did it—yourself!" You will be reinforcing him as he recognizes his own achievement. Had you stepped in earlier—to show him, or even to encourage him to keep trying—you would have cut his triumph in half. *He* persisted and *he* did it. It is very difficult for a parent to sit back and allow a child his own frustration and time to fail before succeeding. But it may be a critical part of his recognition of success when he does succeed. Frustration can be a positive force for a child's learning—about himself— as long as it doesn't overwhelm the child in the process.

How can parents find this fine line between the challenge of frustration and overwhelming obstacles? This is possible only by watching the child and observing whether he shows curiosity, persistence, and the ability to succeed at a problem, or a look of defeat and inertia. Both too much encouragement and too much pressure defeat a child's own incentive.

Balancing Praise and Criticism

The pressure on a small child to learn to read, to write, and to perform tasks that may not be appropriate for his age and stage of development is a danger when parents overwhelm the child's own sense of competence. It is quite possible to teach a child to read, to write, or to play an instrument at a surprisingly early age. He gathers in rewards from everyone around him as he performs. But precocity carries a price. His performance may be motivated by a desire to please others, rather than by any inner curiosity of his own. Failure in play and exploration of ways to succeed are necessary to a child's learning for himself. If he learns just to please others, he may not get the same sense of having achieved for his own reasons.

A certain amount of positive reward, such as praise and flattery, reinforces a child's awareness of his own success. As mentioned before, too much praise or flattery can overwhelm this sense and can become pressure rather than encouragement. Criticism can induce passivity rather than energy to solve problems. How do you know when to criticize and when to praise? Once again, watch the child. If he's becoming irritable, he's probably under too much pressure. If he's not sure of himself, he may need constructive encouragement and less criticism.

An increasing number of studies are showing how strongly children identify with our patterns of behavior. If we are critical, the child will learn to be critical and will see it as an acceptable way of life. If we are too assertive, he is likely to lose his curiosity and creativity, and he may become stubbornly inert as an attempt to cover up his feelings of inadequacy. If, on the other hand, our expectations of ourselves or a child are meager, he may lose his initial excitement in learning and exploration.

While we cannot change our own styles and outlook just to influence our children, we can learn ways to nurture a child's initiative and boost his self-esteem. In any new task, encourage the child, but don't shape it for him or press him. Praise him gently when he succeeds. Let him try out several different ways of doing the same thing, and let him fail until he finds one that works. If he gets in a jam or follows a dead-end course, don't rush to help him. Let him discover his predicament, and praise him when he tries again. Let him try every new task in his own bumbling, exploratory fashion. Let him tangle his laces, spill his milk (don't give him much at a time!), mash the banana, knock over the stack of blocks, or break the crayon. All this, of course, must be within the bounds of safety and respect for others. But never forget the enormous power of frustration to fuel a small child as he searches for mastery and a sense of his own competence.

Boosting Self-Esteem at All Ages

The following is a brief outline of the many opportunities to boost a child's self-esteem through play, feeding, and encounters with other children:

Early Play

1–4 months: Lean over the baby to elicit his smiles and vocalizations. As he smiles, you smile. But wait then for his next smile or vocalization. When he produces his, then reinforce it with a *gentle* imitation. As he repeats it over and over, watch his face for recognition of his achievements in producing these behaviors. Don't overwhelm him.

4–6 months: As you lean over him, vocalize gently. Wait for him to try to imitate you. When he does repeat it, let your face express your realization of what he's done.

6–8 months: Peekaboo in a way that will elicit his imitation of your play. Then follow his behavior, don't lead.

8–10 months: Using a cloth to play peekaboo, put it on his face, and then let him take over.

Feeding

5–8 months: Let him hold a spoon or cup when you feed him.

8 months: Let him begin to pick up two or three small bits of food to feed himself. Don't worry if he drops them.

10–12 months: Let him imitate you with a few sips in a cup and with a spoon. Let him choose his own finger foods, giving him only a few bits at a time.

12 months: Let him continue to feed himself finger food, hold his own bottle, and imitate with a cup.

16 months: Let him use a fork to spear his food. Let him decide whether he wants to eat or not, but don't try out a hundred things to try to please him.

Other Children

1–2 years: Give him occasions for parallel play with peers. Prepare him ahead of time. Don't leave him until he's ready, but encourage him eventually to stay in a play group without you. Don't interfere in toddlers' play. Even biting, scratching, and hair pulling can be learning opportunities if you stay out of it. However, don't leave a child over and over again with an overwhelmingly aggressive or passive playmate. He will not learn as much as he will from more equal relationships. Don't push him to share his toys. Let other children teach him.

3–5 years: Encourage him to play independently with siblings or peers. Stay out of their crises. Reward him for his successes in learning about others. Encourage one or two regular buddies, playmates who come regularly, so that he can get to know them well, to understand and rely on them. They'll give him a feeling of being competent with other people, and they'll teach him to share and to be considerate of others' feelings.

35

SEPARATION

Day Care   "Leaving my baby for someone else to take care of is the hardest thing I've ever had to do. When I look back at her in another woman's arms, I can hardly bear it. It is as if I'm leaving part of myself. I'm not sure I can do it day after day."

This mother is putting into words what so many mothers feel when they put their baby in day care to go back to work. The way this mother expresses her feelings makes clear that the pain of separation is *hers*. Given good care, babies adapt more quickly than parents.

Both parents must grieve when they leave a small child in someone else's care. The passionate attachment that has swept over them in the first months of the baby's life is intense. The surge of nurturing feelings that have been uncovered drive new parents to say, "I've never been in love like this before." Learning to become a nurturer is both the most exhilarating and the most demanding task any young adult will experience. Attachment to a new baby can be both rewarding and painful.

Underlying any intense attachment is a deep fear of loss. As a parent gives himself to deep caring feelings, the other side of the coin must surface. What if I lose my child? Will she care

as much as I do? If I share her, will she love someone else
more? The first real separation is bound to bring a grief reaction. When parents turn a baby over to another caregiver, they
will feel loneliness, guilt, helplessness, and even anger: Why
must I do this? Certain defenses against the intensity of these
feelings are common:

1. *Denial*—saying that the separation doesn't matter, either
   to the baby or yourself
2. *Projection*—assigning the role of competent caregiver to
   the other person and the bad one to yourself, or vice
   versa; both admiring and resenting the "other" and
   suspecting her of endangering your baby
3. *Detachment*—attempting to dilute your intense feelings
   to soften the pain of leaving your baby

Mothers and fathers are likely to face such reactions after a
passionate start with a baby. These reactions are usually unconscious, but they demand energy and result in depression.

I urge parents to recognize these feelings and to allow them
to surface. An awareness of the anguish that separations will
bring frees a parent to confront this reaction and to master it.
Burying such feelings, on the other hand, can become debili-
tating and destructive. Work can suffer, and home life can
become tense as both parents try to suppress their feelings.
Separation and reunion with the baby each day become extremely charged events. "Why does she always turn away
when I come to get her? Is she angry with me? Have I lost our
closeness? Am I damaging her future?"

Expressing these normal, universal feelings defuses them.
Learning to understand the grief of separation and the defenses against it can lead to ways of mastering them without
diluting the intensity of the relationship. When working mothers tell me how guilty they feel at having to leave their baby,
I reassure them. Guilt is a powerful, motivating force. It drives
people to find solutions for coping with separation. The baby
will make it if the parents do. Babies have plenty of love to go
around, but they need to know that parents are there for them
at the end of every day.

The baby, in turn, will learn her own ways of coping if she
is in the care of a nurturing person. Her protest when you

leave is necessary and healthy. She will turn to the other person. It is important for her to develop a caring relationship with that person. (See chapters 6–9.) Together with colleagues, I have observed babies in day care as they learn to cope with separation from their parents. They seem to cut down on the intensity of their interactions during the day, as described in chapter 6. They play, but not as vigorously as they would with parents. They nap but don't sleep as deeply. They store up their powerful reactions for the reunion at the end of the day. When the parent looms into sight, the baby often pointedly turns away, as if to master the intensity of her feelings at the waited-for reunion with this all-important person. Then, she is likely to blow. She has saved up her protest, her intense feelings, all day for the one she can trust. No wonder caregivers will say, "She never does that for me, dear." Parents need to realize that these intense reactions are necessary to a passionate reunion.

When you understand that the pain of separation is, first, a parental issue, you can learn to handle it. Part of the challenge is learning to compartmentalize yourself. As we have seen, the baby can do it. So can you. Once you have searched for the best possible care and can feel assured that your child is safe and in the hands of someone who can love and nurture her, you will need to trust that person. It's difficult, for your natural competition will surface at each separation and reunion.

Certain steps can help a great deal.

▶ Get up early enough to have a few minutes of cuddling and relaxed play with the baby before you leave for day care.
▶ Let her refuse food. Let her tease you about getting dressed. A few moments of this will give her a sense of being in control of her day. At day care, she may not dare to express negativism.
▶ As soon as she's old enough, develop a routine of talking to her about leaving, but always add, "I'll be back." This is for you as much as it is for her. You are preparing yourself, and her, for separation.
▶ At day care, work with the caregiver to develop a separation routine. Take off the child's outer clothing

yourself, hug her, turn her over to the caregiver, then say, "Goodbye, I'll see you this afternoon. Ms. ———— will love you while I'm gone." Then, go. Don't prolong the parting. It makes it much harder. Be prepared for protest. By leaving, you give her a chance to protest but also to turn toward the activities of the day. Children are remarkably resilient in an environment that respects and cares about them.

From the child's standpoint, a first separation from home is never easy at any age. But as they grow older, children need peers and play opportunities that you as a parent can no longer provide, as mentioned in chapter 13. Even if a child is in a family with other siblings, she needs peers her own age. The opportunities to learn about herself in a social situation are great. The pain of this initial separation will therefore be balanced by her and *your* awareness that she needs to separate. The attraction of other children, games, and group activities balances the pain of leaving the safe coziness of home. Again, there are ways you can ease the transition:

Nursery and Preschool

- ▶ Prepare yourself first so that you can face her feelings.
- ▶ Read to her about separation and about the exciting aspects of play with other children.
- ▶ Introduce her to at least one other child in the nursery school or play group. Invite them somewhere together.
- ▶ Introduce her to the caregiver or teacher beforehand and see to it that she knows you like that person. Stay with her for the first week or so—until she's adjusted.
- ▶ Allow her to regress—dress her in the morning, don't put pressure on her at meals.
- ▶ Let her take a "lovey" or a reminder from home each day—even a picture of you.
- ▶ When you get to the nursery school, take off her outdoor gear. Be sure the caregiver or teacher says hello to her.
- ▶ Hug her and be sure she has a chance to turn to someone else—a child or adult.
- ▶ Remind her when you'll return.

- Leave—don't linger.
- When you pick her up, hug her and allow her to blow up at you. Hug her until it's over. Then say, "Now we can go home and be a family again. I missed you and I know you missed me. But we'll always have each other at the end of the day."

A child is likely to have a delayed reaction to her first separation from home. Her renewed dependence will probably surprise you. Long after she's made the initial adjustment, she'll regress to a clinging protest about leaving home all over again. Regressive symptoms may well reappear, such as soiling, wetting, crying more, increasing thumb sucking, becoming more dependent on a bottle or a lovey, or by having sleep difficulties, night fears, and bad dreams. All of these are evidence of the stress of learning to handle new feelings. See this regression as normal. Reassure her that she'll be able to give it up when she's in control again. Meanwhile, you'll help her.

When this delayed reaction occurs, you may have to repeat all of the steps in separation. Talk it over with her caregiver or teacher and ask whether you should stay again for a few days to soften separations. Talk it over with your child so that she understands herself.

You and your spouse should now institute a special time with the child each day and a saved-up special time for the weekend. At such a time, each of you can be with her alone—with a bedtime ritual or some other special time. Ask her about her life at nursery school. This special time will allow her to identify with each of you more intensely. On the weekend, you should each save at least an hour alone with her. In that hour, you do what *she* wants. Use it as an opportunity to get close to her. Talk about it all week, as "our time together again."

Each year, the first few days of school will be difficult. The rigid routines and the expectations of school close in on the child. Each new school year is a rite of passage, a reminder to a child that she is growing up and must become independent. The hardest thing about these days is likely to be leaving home and the old routines. If she has younger siblings at home, she'll wonder, What will they be doing while I'm gone? Will my parents miss me? Leaving home can be a thrilling step into the world, but it brings a sense of loss. This sense of loss is bittersweet, carrying with it all the warm security of home that the child is giving up as she makes each step into the world (see also chapter 33).

Moving

Losing friends and an old neighborhood can surely be a setback for a child. When it is necessary to move, a child should be prepared in advance. She should have a chance to make a new friend in the new neighborhood as soon as possible. But she mustn't be expected to give up her old ones. I'd have a going-away party before you leave. Then, if possible after the move is made, take her back to see her old friends and the old house. Even if you have to travel to get back there, I'd do it. If the old friends are not too far away, try to have them come over at least once or twice to visit. It won't be long before the new friends will take over. Find one or two that you think might be likely. Take them out together once a week until they feel close to each other. A new child can enter an already closed group only through another child. Encourage her to talk about the old neighborhood and the old friends. Pull out pictures of them to remind her. Telephone them. Write them for a while. Giving up close relationships in childhood can be painful. But it can also be a time to learn how important friendships are. (See also chapter 45.)

36

SIBLING RIVALRY

Rivalry between siblings is normal and inevitable. Children learn about each other and about themselves in rivalry. At the same time, they learn to care about one another. Despite this, parents find it almost impossible to stay out of their children's fights. Why? The renowned psychoanalyst Erik Erikson pointed out to me that no parent feels entirely adequate to more than one child. When children get into a struggle, an underlying guilt makes parents feel that they must protect one or the other. They quickly make any situation into a triangle. The children's rivalry is fueled by the goal of getting parents involved.

A parent's feeling of not being capable of loving two children begins when a mother is pregnant with a second child. In my office when a mother proudly announces her second pregnancy, I sometimes sense this worry. I ask, "How does your older one feel?" The mother will flush and look sad. Some may start to weep. It is so difficult to anticipate bringing home an invader of the love affair that one has created with the first

Accepting Rivalry

child. Sibling rivalry is fueled by these feelings. At first, the older child will aim his anger at his parents for desertion. Then, as the baby begins to be mobile and to get into his toys, he will find ways of torturing the baby in order to involve a parent in his rivalry. He will manage somehow. As the baby gets more and more attractive to outsiders (most second children learn early how to win an audience away from the first child), the older child's face will sag, and his whole body will droop. He may withdraw to sit in his parent's lap, thumb in mouth, watching visitors play gaily with the charming baby.

Learning to live with others in a family is one of the most important learning opportunities that anyone can have. Learning to share is not a task that is taught very often these days. We as parents may worry too much about protecting a child from his feelings of rivalry. The ideal is to teach a child how to feel responsible for his sibling and for the whole family's well-being. Learning responsibility for others may be the most important thing you can teach him. That comes from learning to share with a sibling.

Here are some suggestions if you have more than one young

child. Depending on the first child's age, give him tasks to do for the baby: feeding the baby, bringing diapers, helping to hold her and to cuddle her when she's upset. Let him choose the baby's clothes, help get the baby dressed by lying down to talk to her while she's changed, hold the baby for part of the feeding, and help push the carriage.

When you are taking them out together, prepare the older child: "Nearly all strangers love babies. It's not that they don't like you. Come and sit with me when you are feeling lonely, neglected, and jealous." Then, gather him up when everyone fawns over the baby.

If you're at home with the children all day, you will have a special set of worries. How you adjust to different personalities and different age levels? Perhaps the most demanding aspect of being an at-home parent is to spend all day with individuals of different ages and temperaments. Also, if you're at home, you feel you should be making it pay for the children, since that is the reason you're at home. Rivalry makes you feel you're unsuccessful. When the children fight for you, as they will, you feel completely unrewarded.

If you work outside the home, it is critical to plan for your reentry each day. Expect the children to fall apart as you walk in the door and to set up an intensely rivalrous situation. Calmly but firmly, sit down with one on each side to ask about their day. After you've talked with them both, you can start the end-of-the-day chores. Be sure they help. Let them choose which chores they'll do, and reward them for their choices. Be sure you have some time with each one at the end of the day.

Each parent should plan a special time *alone* with each child at the end of the week. Talk about it all week as the time when "we'll have a special time together." Be sure you keep it to make it reliably special. This is a time to get close to each child as an individual.

Parents often wonder how to treat each child equally. The answer is simple: You can't. Each child is a different personality and needs a different approach. However, it can be exhausting to try to shift gears for each one. It makes a real

Valuing Individualit

difference to talk openly but nonjudgmentally about their differences. For instance, you might say to one, "You need me to speak softly." To another, "You always need me to speak angrily." This eventually gives them insight into themselves.

When they torture you with "You're always nicer to him than you are to me," you can say, "You are very different people, which is great. I need to treat you differently. When I speak loudly to you, it's to make you listen, but I am speaking just as lovingly even if it's louder." If you don't get caught up in feeling guilty about the different feelings you have for each one, they needn't feel it either. Children from large families, or those who are raised with other children nearby, seem to have an easier time in respecting each other's differences.

Children who are supported by parents, though in different ways, have the best chance themselves. By valuing each child's individuality yourself and then conveying your awareness of his or her individual strengths, you'll support each one. As you make these strengths explicit, the child will be able to understand and value them. Even if you yourself have preferences for certain traits, based on your own experiences, you don't need to pass on negative labels for other traits. If you can understand the basis for your own preferences, you will be less likely to pass them on in any pejorative way.

When parents can stop feeling guilty about shortchanging one child or the other, they will find it easier to stay out of sibling fights. As long as you are involved, there's a triangle that allows each of them to manipulate you. They never get a chance to work things out with each other. Leave their fights to them, saying, "You know, I don't know who's right and who's wrong. You'll have to make the decision yourself." Then leave the room. You'll find that they fight a lot less if you aren't there to reward them. I have never heard of siblings really hurting one another when a parent wasn't present or very nearby.

Sex Differences Although many parents feel sex differences strongly, no one wants to stereotype boys and girls. Such differences are indeed complex.

Despite the desire of modern parents to treat children of either sex in the same way, the child of the opposite sex will have a particular appeal to each parent. You will inevitably treat children differently because of their sex. What you must not do is to devaluate either one. Just as every little girl needs an admiring father, every boy needs a mother who believes that he's *the* greatest boy of all.

Tattling and Teasing When tattling occurs, which it will, try never to reward it. Remind the tattler that he would be very upset if someone told on him and that you really don't want to be involved that way. Since parents need to stay in touch with children's play for safety reasons, staying out of fights and not responding to each wail are difficult. Keep an ear out for unusual sounds (or an ominous lack of noise), but try to leave children to play alone as much as possible.

If siblings continue to tease each other endlessly, resist taking sides. If necessary, separate them for a time-out period. Consider inviting friends for each one. A playmate of each age helps enormously. Reward a child when he has been positive in his reactions to his sibling. Stay out of it when he's not. Your involvement becomes a powerful incentive for continued rivalry.

Age and Birth Order A child's age and place in the family will necessarily influence how that child is treated. The oldest child will always be a special child to his parents. This will be a mixed blessing. While he gets all the pressure and can suffer from new parents' mistakes, he also gets a very special relationship. He is likely to be given responsibility for a certain amount of baby-sitting, of caregiving, and of housework. This kind of responsibility can give him a sense of competence and importance to his parents that will last into adulthood.

A second child may complain that no one loves him, that he is always "second," on and on. This will be compounded if he is a middle child. If parents can avoid feeling guilty, the child won't feel rewarded by his complaints and will eventually see that he gets his share, too. Most second children become competitive and make up for being second by being successful at competing with the first.

Subsequent children will feel lower on the totem pole, of course. Their reward will be that they have many "parents."

They will learn so much from their older siblings. No parent need feel guilty about what they themselves can't give to younger ones. In a tightly knit family, third and fourth children have a rich variety of mentors.

If the last child is treated as "the baby," he is likely to be indulged, and it will be necessary to be sure to expect as much of him as of the others. If he is too indulged and stands out in the family for it, he will devalue himself as "spoiled." As much as possible, it is wise to point out that learning to share and learning to participate equally is very much to his advantage.

When older children continue to fight with each other and you feel exasperated, you can try to sit down with them at a tranquil time. Ask them to advise you about what you should do. Should you intervene, or should you leave it to them? In this way, you can give them a feeling of being responsible for their own behavior.

Left alone, children will learn to respect and care for each other. The ultimate reward for sibling rivalry will come when they begin to be "pals." I remember hearing ours plot together against us. That seemed like progress! When squabbling gives way to a united front against "the ogres," siblings are on their way.

37

SLEEP PROBLEMS

When parents call me in desperation to ask how to get their child to go to sleep at night, I can anticipate the story they will tell. By the time my advice is sought, there has usually been a long history of nighttime turmoil: of parents waking up to hear the child crying at 2:00 or 3:00 A.M., dragging themselves to the child, and then rocking, singing, and cajoling to try to get the child back to bed. Parents also report that once they arrive in the child's room, she becomes winning, delightful, and full of charm; she has had her sleep and is ready for several hours of play. When her charm begins to fail in the face of her parent's desperation, she may fall back on whimpering or wailing as if in real pain. Or, she may stare accusingly at the parent with a look that seems to say, "How can you leave me alone when you can see how much I want you to stay?" At any level, the urgent message she conveys is that she has needs that have not yet been met, and her lament reaches across any self-protective barrier the sleepy parent may attempt to set up.

Parents tell me they "try everything." They even try letting the child "cry it out," but they give up this approach after a few nights when the crying goes on for one or two hours and

380

shows no signs of stopping. They try giving the child a bottle and a night light, neither of which works. The only thing that works, they tell me, is to take her into their bed. She can sit there and play for an hour or two, and they at least can sleep.

However, since there is an unwritten taboo in our culture against allowing a child into her parents' bed, many mothers and fathers work very hard not to do this. They have found that going to the child before she is upset saves a longer period of calming down afterward. They often tell me that they go to the child every two hours after 2:00 A.M., quieting her, giving her milk, rocking her for a period, and successfully keeping her in her room. They can time their intervention so well that they have to remain only thirty minutes out of every two hours, whereas if they wait until she is upset and wailing, the visit takes an hour!

What is going on here? Why don't all children make such demands? Why is it that in one family all but one child learns to sleep through the night? Is it a sign of insecurity on the child's part, and is it a reminder to the parents that she has not had enough love or attention during the day? Why is it that certain children who go to sleep at 6:00 P.M. continue to awaken and make demands on their parents at about 10:00 P.M. and again at 2:00 and 6:00 A.M.?

Understanding Sleep

As described earlier, every infant has characteristic cycles of light and deep sleep. These cycles are already entrenched at birth and have been established in synchrony with the pregnant woman's own daily cycles. They are usually not parallel to the maternal cycle, since the fetus sleeps while the mother is active and wakes when she lies down. But the mother's activity period leads to the baby's in the following period. Thus, the newborn infant already has a sleep–wake rhythm. After birth, the environment tends to press the new baby to more and more wakefulness in the daytime and to longer and longer sleep cycles in the night.

By the age of four months or earlier, the periods begin to get set into a pattern—usually a cycle lasting three or four hours. In the middle of the cycle is an hour to an hour and a half of deep sleep in which the baby moves very little and is difficult to rouse with any stimulation. For an hour on each side, there is a lighter, dreaming state in which activity comes and goes. And at the end of each four-hour cycle, the baby comes up to a semialert state in which she is very close to consciousness and awakens easily. At these times, each baby has her own activity pattern—she may suck her fingers, cry out, rock herself, or bang her head rhythmically. Older babies may move around the bed, try out new tricks like standing or walking, or fuss or talk to themselves.

All of these behaviors seem to be in the service of discharging energy stored up from daytime activities and of getting the child back down into the next cycle of sleep. When these intervals of semiconsciousness can be managed by the baby herself, the sleep cycles become stabilized, and the child begins to stretch them into longer cycles so that she finally manages to stay asleep for eight and even twelve hours at a time.

Research has shown that the prolongation of these cycles depends on a kind of conditioning. If the infant is in an environment that reinforces each alert period with a response or by a feeding, she is not likely to prolong the cycle by propelling herself back to sleep. But if there is no response, she will be pressed to find her own patterns for discharging activity and comforting herself back down into the next cycle.

In the first year, as mentioned in earlier chapters, there are predictable times when a baby is likely to start waking at night, even though she may have been sleeping through before. At eight to nine months and again at a year, there are rapid increases in cognitive awareness (of strangers or strange situations, of new places, of changes in the daily routine) that coincide with spurts in motor development (such as crawling and sitting at eight months, or standing, walking, and climbing at twelve to fourteen months). With this increased activity comes a new capacity for getting away from the safe base of mother and father. The excitement and fears generated by this new capacity may temporarily interrupt the child's sleep patterns.

According to research on the normal sleeping pattern of babies, 70 percent of American children go eight hours a night by three months, and 83 percent are likely to be doing this by six months. By one year, only 10 percent do not sleep through the night.

Most children sleep through because of a combination of influences: parents' slower response at night, the lack of other stimulation, and the child's own need to stretch out in some part of the twenty-four-hour cycle.

Patterns of Night Waking

About 17 percent of babies, then, are not stretching out at night by six months, and 10 percent still aren't sleeping at one year. Again, a combination of factors is probably involved. Prematurity and limits on the infant's ability to nurse may play a role. There may also be parental factors such as a reluctance to encourage independence in the child and let her work her way back to sleep. These parents have often had issues in their own childhood that make them vulnerable to the pain of separation at night. A mother might remember feeling deserted by one or both of her parents in childhood. A father might remember night terrors when no one came to him. Some working mothers and fathers who are away all day need the closeness of the baby at night. A single parent who feels the loneliness of having to face the daily adjustments of parenting by herself might not want to give up any night feedings.

Issues of autonomy and independence are thus often at the root of sleep problems. Although there are many forces in our society that press a parent to feel guilty about holding a child too close or too long, most parents are not quite ready to push a baby of five or six months who cries out at night into self-comforting patterns. It is natural to want to cling and be clung to. Most parents secretly long for the lovely, warm comfort of a sleeping baby next to them. All this makes it hard for parents of babies who do not slip easily into sleeping through the night. They may need the guidelines that follow at the end of this chapter.

There are babies of three different temperamental types that seem prone to night waking. One kind is very active and intensely driving, with such excitement for learning that she is literally unable to stop herself when she is learning a new task. At night, the frustration of not being able to accomplish the task she's got in mind—usually a motor achievement—seems to drive her with the same intensity that drives her during the day. For example, shortly before she begins to walk, when she comes to a state of semiconsciousness, she may get up on her hands and knees to rock in frustration or may pull up on her crib endlessly—and then she will awaken. Waking at night is a normal part of the intensity that marks every new developmental milestone.

This pattern may not subside after walking is achieved unless the parents begin to intervene by pressing her to master her nighttime sleep pattern, for the child may be just as frustrated about other tasks and other steps toward mastery in the second, third, and later years. If her sleep has become an outlet for frustration in the first year, it may continue to serve this purpose.

If parents rush to these children in order to comfort them, they must realize that they will prolong the night waking. Light sleep cycles occur frequently during the night and are self-limited *as long as* the child can quiet herself and then bring herself down into deeper sleep again. If she is stimulated by her parents' presence or if she uses their presence to wake up and start playing, she may indeed turn night into day, and a vicious circle may easily get set in motion. The child rouses; the parents become tense as they try to quiet her, inevitably adding their stimulation to the child's own, thereby waking her; the child senses her parents' hostile feelings and stays awake to tease or play or try to establish a bond with them.

Another group of infants who may wake at night and need to be comforted could be classified as "low motor expenders" during the day. They are the quiet, alert, watchful children who take everything in and think deeply about things, and they may not be very active. As they don't invest a lot of activity in their daylight hours, they don't tire themselves enough to sleep as deeply at night. Their sensitive thinking processes may be patterned to increase wakefulness at night, and when light sleep cycles occur, they may come easily to a full awake state. If they cry out or fuss in each of these cycles, they may bring parents to their side. As long as both they and the parents profit from this kind of closeness, it may seem to serve them all. But as their independence in the second year

surfaces, it will be a time to consider pushing them to be more independent at night.

The third kind of baby who may find it difficult to settle down at night into a reliably prolonged sleep pattern is likely to be a sensitive, easily upset child. Her sensitivity to new or strange situations makes her rather clinging, and her parents may play into this unknowingly. Around each new demanding situation—either a new developmental step or a demanding social situation—she is likely to regress in her behavior during the day as well as at night. Since the parents of such a child want to help her, they may protect her from new and demanding situations. They are likely to hasten to comfort her when she is overwhelmed, often before she has had the chance to try out her own efforts at coping.

At night, this pattern of overprotection is likely to affect the behavior of both parents and child. The child demands their presence and comfort long after she may really need it, and the parents in turn find it difficult not to give in to her overly sensitive demands. They may take her into their bed or allow her to ask for and receive four or five nighttime visits from them. As they get exhausted and angry—with themselves and with her—her sensitivity to their ambivalence increases her misery, and this very ambivalence drives her parents to meet all her demands.

Learning Independence

In our society, at least, to be able to sleep alone in childhood is part of being an independent person. Whether or not that is right can certainly be questioned, but it is difficult for a child or a parent to reject the general consensus of society without the danger of lowered self-esteem and a feeling of being inadequate to the job of establishing autonomy.

When sleep problems occur, it is likely that parents and child alike are having difficulties believing that the child can make it alone. Parents who work away from home during the day often feel torn between putting a child to bed alone or keeping her close. When a naturally stressful event comes along that produces a period of waking in the child, the issue of separation at night is likely to arise all over again.

I would urge parents to examine their feelings about independence and autonomy *before* trying to establish a routine for the child at night. Pressing her to sleep through will require real purpose on the part of everyone in the household. Parents will have to be sure that they are ready to back each other up. They will also have to be sure that they believe it is an important, even a necessary, step for the child to take.

In my private pediatric practice and in my hospital work, I have seen the problems that can be stirred up in whole families when a child is awake and demanding during the night. I knew these families needed help, and I knew it would help their relationship with their child if I could give them a base for understanding the underlying issues. What I didn't realize was that certain parents do *not* believe in helping a child learn to sleep alone at night.

Such parents feel that sleeping alone is a custom our society unreasonably demands of its small children and that it isn't *necessarily* to the children's advantage. When a child needs them at night, they feel it more important to be with her than to worry about conforming to our cultural expectations. They say that they and she really like being together as a family at night, and that the child will outgrow the habit of sleeping with her parents—without psychological scars.

I have learned a great deal by listening to this point of view. I agree with the concern that sleep problems may indicate that the child is going through a time of stress and should not feel deserted at such a time. I also worry about whether our culture isn't demanding a great deal of small children in many ways, one of which is to require that she learn to sleep in a room all alone. But I also believe that the needs of the parents at night have to be considered, as well as most parents' ultimate goal for the child—the ability to become self-reliant.

In considering whether to keep the child in their bed, parents would do well to consider some of the potential problems. Will the child be more dependent during the day if her parents keep her close at night? I'm not sure she needs to be—but that could be a pitfall, and one I'd urge parents to watch for. If a child is developing independence during the day, perhaps my argument for leaving her alone at night need not be taken as seriously.

Will sharing her parents' bed as an infant and young child make it difficult to separate from them later on? Certainly, the lore based on psychoanalytic theory has it that a child may not want to separate from her mother and father and may continue to cling to their bed, and as she gets older and more conscious of her oedipal feelings, she may feel that she can and does come between them.

To offset this tendency on the child's part, I would urge parents who want to continue the practice of sharing their bed to be sure that they agree that it is comforting *to them* as well as to the child. Her presence can certainly come between them if she's allowed to continue to sleep there; and if it does, the child will suffer more than she might from being weaned to her own room. Hence, if parents are not comfortable and do not agree upon this practice and if it is allowed to cause friction in a family, I'm sure it will be destructive to a child's future development. For this reason, I would urge parents to discuss the arrangement openly and reasonably at regular intervals. A good relationship between her parents is probably more critical to a child's development than her sleeping arrangements.

Parents must also watch the child for any signs of tension about sleeping with them. Eventually, she will begin to show that she no longer needs their comfort at night and will express a need for independence. If we can extrapolate from other cultures (India and Mexico, for example, where this is a common practice), it would seem that the third or fourth years would be the time to watch for signs of the child's readiness to sleep alone, even if she hasn't been able to do this before. It will probably be up to the parents to give a necessary shove— talking to the child as she goes to bed, providing her with a beloved toy for company, giving her a night light, and helping her make the transition. I would worry about an older child's image of herself if she still needs to be close to her parents at night. She may well have a more difficult separation later in childhood.

Since I believe that achieving independence of thought and action is a critical goal of childhood, I would urge that parents consider sleep as one of the major areas in which to achieve that independence. In the end, whether a child sleeps alone or with her parents may not be as critical as whether she is learning how to cope with her own needs and managing to get herself back to sleep when she comes to awakening periods during the night.

When night waking continues to be a problem, the following suggestions might help a child learn to get back to sleep by herself. Bear in mind that they are dependent on the individual situation and particularly on the child herself. Each of these steps should be taken singly and slowly over time.

Guidelines

1. Be sure you both agree on the program. If you, her parents, disagree, the child will sense your ambivalence.
2. Have a look at the child's day. Does she sleep too long and/or too late in the afternoon? For babies older than a year, naptimes should be started early (by 1:00 P.M.) and last only one to two hours at most. If the child is over two, the nap can be given up completely. Any rest or nap after 3:00 P.M. will certainly break up the cycle of activity and diminish the need for continuous and deep sleep during the night.
3. Be sure you have instituted a relaxing, nurturing routine at bedtime. If the child is old enough, talk to her at this time about the steps you are about to take toward helping her sleep alone and through the night. Roughhousing and play should be followed by a calming, quiet ritual time. A bedtime story is a wonderful routine. Television is not.
4. Let the child learn to get to sleep when you put her down at night. Don't put her to sleep in your arms or at the breast. Get her quiet but then put her in and sit by her to help her learn her own pattern. Give her a lovey or her fingers. Pat her down soothingly. If she protests, assure her that "you can do it yourself."
5. Wake the child at night before your bedtime. At that time, you can repeat the bedtime routine—talking to her, hugging her, giving her a bottle or a feeding if that has been part of the routine. In this way, you will ease your own conscience and not lie awake wondering, Is she okay? Is she hungry? Have I done enough?

6. Reinforce a particular lovey—a blanket, an animal, or a doll—as part of her self-comforting routine. (But, as mentioned in earlier chapters, do not allow a child to sleep with a bottle of milk in her mouth; this contributes to serious tooth decay.) Many toys in bed are in no way as good as a single beloved one. They dilute its value and its meaning.

7. Expect a child to rouse and cry out every three to four hours at 10:00 P.M., 2:00 A.M., and 6:00 A.M. After you have prepared her for the program and are really ready to start it, greet her waking with as little stimulating intervention as you can. If you have been taking her out of bed to rock her, don't; soothe and stroke her with your hand, but leave her *in bed*. She won't like it, but she'll understand. Stand by her crib and tell her that she can and must learn to get herself back to sleep.

8. After a period of going to her each time, begin to stay out of her room and call to her. Tell her that you are there and that you care about her, but that you are *not* coming, and remind her of her lovey. It amazes me that a child can begin to accept one's voice for one's presence.

9. Finally, let her try all of her own resources. Wait at least fifteen minutes before you go in for the first time or for a subsequent time. Then, deal with her perfunctorily, repeating the unexciting regime just outlined and again pressing the lovey on her.

After forty years in the practice of pediatrics, I am convinced that while a child's independence may not be easy for parents to accept, it is an exciting and rewarding goal for the child. Being able to manage alone at night helps a child develop a positive self-image and gives her a real feeling of strength. You can further encourage this feeling of achievement by shoring the child up emotionally during the day. Once she becomes independent at night, she deserves all of the credit and loving praise that you can give her.

38
SPACING CHILDREN

In the course of routine office visits, I find I can expect a question about when to have a second child at certain times in the first child's development. These times are related to the first child's spurts in independence. After the initial adjustment to the baby, and when the first few months of sleepless nights and erratic schedules are over, new parents begin to experience the pure euphoria of being in love. Every time they look at their four-month-old, he smiles back at them adoringly. A vocalization from the parent produces a sigh or an "ooh" in response. The baby wriggles all over as he attempts to communicate with his devoted, hovering parent. Few moments in life are as delicious as these minutes of reciprocal communication with a communicative, vocalizing infant. A parent feels competent and in control of the world. But it is hard to be head over heels in love without the nagging fear that sooner or later it must come to an end. In our Calvinistic society, we are steeped in the foreknowledge that sooner or later we must pay for our blessings.

Considering a Second Child

As if on cue, the mother of a five-month-old baby will say, "Now that Johnny is growing up, when should I start another baby?" The reluctance to give up Johnny is couched in the word *should,* as if it were some sort of duty or penance—payment for caring so deliciously. The timing of this question seems incongruous if one looks at Johnny. He is round, soft, and dimpled. As he lies on the examining table, he looks carefully around the room, his face serious as he surveys each new object. Every minute or so, he glances back at his mother or his father, who both lean on the table near him, talking to me. As he looks at them, they look back reassuringly. His face crinkles, his eyes soften, and he smiles gratefully up at them, his legs and arms wriggling as he thanks them with his whole body. This lasts only a few seconds. He returns to his job of processing the information about the strange place. They return to their job of communicating with me.

In that moment, I have witnessed an example of the depth of their attachment to each other. Each of them has felt a surge of loving feeling, and each has felt deeply the importance of the other's presence. The baby has said with his eyes, "You are my anchor, and I can afford to be here in such a strange, exciting new place because I can look back at you and you'll be there!" The parents have had a chance to feel the depth of their own importance to this new individual. Doesn't it seem amazing that, at that point, one of the parents asks, "What do you think about having another baby?" Or, a breast-feeding mother may ask, "When should I wean him?" If I pursue either of these questions with the parents, it will become apparent that they don't want another baby yet, nor does the mother want to wean this one. But the questions guard them against caring too much and help to balance the overwhelming attachment.

As we saw in chapter 6, the four- or five-month-old baby is showing a first ripple of independence. He interrupts a feeding over and over—to look around, to listen to a door close in the next room, to stop to gurgle up at his mother, to smile brightly across the room at his father. For a mother, these are signals that the baby doesn't need her as much anymore. For the baby, these represent a burst in his awareness of things and people around him. For enraptured parents, they seem to be a reminder of the future when the child will indeed become independent of them.

For breast-feeding mothers, this can also be a physically vulnerable time for conceiving the next pregnancy. I have seen many instances of unexpected second pregnancies that were started in this period, the mother thinking she was protected by lactation and unsuccessfully predicting when she was ovulating because her periods had not returned. If a new mother is not using adequate contraception, she may start the second baby before she is ready to give up the first one.

Having two children as close together as fourteen to eighteen months is comparable to having unequal-aged twins. Raising them successfully certainly can be done, and it can even be fun at times, but it is hard work while they are little. Having two highly dependent individuals of different ages is demanding both physically and emotionally. The danger for the babies is that a physically exhausted mother is likely to lump them together. Her tendency will be either to treat them as if they were babies who were the same age, or to press the slightly older toddler to grow up too quickly. As the toddler resists by acting just like the baby, a mother unconsciously resents the demands on her and presses the older one to take more responsibility than he is ready for.

In planning for a second child, parents should try to keep in mind their own energies and tolerance. Their reasons for hurrying or delaying in spacing children may be the best guidelines they can follow. A mother who wants to have her family quickly so that she can get back to work may resent being kept at home for too many years and indirectly take it out on her family. Parents who feel they need time between each child to get in a better position financially may also be feeling that they can assimilate only one child and one responsibility at a time. The problem for most families is that they can't anticipate their own reserves and their own tolerance.

Guidelines for Planning There are a few guidelines from my own experience over the years that may be helpful to young families who are trying to plan intelligently.

First, assume that it will be hard to give up the intense, reciprocally rewarding relationships with your first child. It's hard for a baby and it's hard for you, his parents. If you have the time to begin feeling that you've really done all you can for him, it becomes easier. In other words, if you can feel that you've really belonged completely to your first baby and he is solidly independent, it becomes easier to share him with the next baby. Inevitably, the new baby will demand time and emotional energy. Almost as inevitably, a mother will push the older child to grow up quickly when the new baby arrives. In

traditional cultures, there is usually a ritual associated with weaning the older child when the mother is expecting a new baby. She will openly push the responsibility for the older child onto another member of the family—a grandmother, an aunt, or an older sibling. Through this symbolic act, she will be saying, "Now I must turn my back on you so I can devote myself to the new one." Although this is often done in a harsh way, I have seen the anguish that the mother hides as she gives up her child. But given her heavy responsibilities, she knows she must force herself to "turn her back," or she won't have the energy available to nurture a new baby.

Also important as you plan for a second child is the normal but passionate burst of independence and negativism in the toddler. As a toddler hits the second year, he needs time to sort out his choices. Does he really want to be independent? Does he mean no when he says it so forcefully, or did he really mean "yes?" After a flaming tantrum, which leaves him exhausted, who besides his parents can help him sort out the reason for the tantrum, the limits on himself that he must learn? Who else can refuel him to go on searching for the boundaries and the strengths that will help him become an independent person?

If parents cannot be available to a toddler and cannot see this struggle for independence as critical and exciting, both they and their baby will feel stressed and frustrated throughout the second year. Instead of seeing this year as a rich period of learning and of testing, they may lose their sense of humor, which they sorely need to give them some perspective. Ideally, then, parents might plan for the second child to arrive after some of this second-year turmoil has had a chance to become resolved.

Parents who are considering this kind of two-and-one-half- to three-year spacing between their children wonder whether the children will be too far apart to be friends as they get older. My own experience has led me to the feeling that, if the parents can enjoy the spacing of the children, the children will be better friends for it. If parents are stressed by too many children who are too close in age, the children will spend most of their childhood in competitive rivalry. For, as we saw in chapter 36, these squabbles are aimed at parents. Children are inevitably rivalrous, and they will sort out their competitive feelings by themselves if parents are not involved. When parents feel that they may not have been adequate parents to each child, they get involved, and the feelings of rivalry are reinforced. In other words, children had better not be planned to please each other, but to suit the parents' requirements for available energy.

Helping Your Child Adjust to a Sibling

By the age of two or two and a half, most toddlers are basically independent. Their mobility is established, their play is rich and can be independent, they should have established autonomous eating and sleeping habits, and many of them are beginning to want to be toilet trained. In addition, by two years of age, children are ready for group play with others their own age. A peer group can be the highlight of a toddler's week. The learning that occurs from each other and the discharge of tensions and sorting out of negativism that can take place in a small play group demonstrate the marvelous availability of children of this age to each other. This means that parents can set up regular play groups with other parents, or they can feel comfortable about placing their toddler in a day care or group setting. This is both for the toddler's *own sake* and for the parents' sake, for they can be available to a new infant. Spacing children two or three years apart can be made to benefit each person in the family.

By the age of four or five, a child is ready to participate in the care of a new baby. An older child can feel the baby belongs to him. He can learn to feed, hold, rock, diaper, comfort, and play with the new baby. Once he recovers from the initial disappointment that the new baby isn't his own age and an equal in the games he's planned, he can begin to participate with his parents in the game of learning about the new baby and in watching the baby acquire each new developmental step.

I remember a five-year-old boy who came bursting into my office saying, "Dr. B., you should see my baby walking! He doesn't fall down anymore!" With that, he rushed over to his eleven-month-old sibling and held out his hands. His brother grinned all over at this attention from his hero. He gratefully and greedily grasped the older boy's hands to pull up to stand. Barely balancing, he held tightly to his brother's outstretched arms to teeter across the room. As the older boy backed up to lead his brother on, he chortled with delight, "Look, look at that!" As I watched this elegant example of an older child not only teaching the baby to walk but passing on to him the excitement of learning, I thought to myself, Isn't a younger child fortunate to have such an opportunity for learning about the thrill of living? These brothers are not only acquiring learning skills from each other, but they are learning what it means to be deeply dependent on each other.

At four and five, a child is naturally ready to care for and teach a smaller individual. Margaret Mead, the eminent anthropologist, said to me once that one of the most serious deprivations in our culture is that children ages four to seven so rarely have the opportunity to care for smaller children. She pointed out that in most cultures around the world, older siblings are expected to be responsible for younger ones. In this way, they learned the skills of nurturing and are more prepared when their time for parenting comes.

A space of several years between children automatically provides this kind of experience for the older child. And, for the younger, the opportunity to learn from an older sibling is a real privilege. Our last child has acquired most of his skills and has learned most of his values from the careful, patient teaching of his older sisters. A child's hunger to learn from an older sibling is founded in a kind of blind adoration. This is quite different from the more charged situation when we as parents try to teach the same tasks. I have always been struck with the eager, longing looks with which a baby or toddler watches an older child. And I am amazed at the speed of the imitative learning that goes on when an older sibling stops briefly to teach a small child a new skill.

When you are expecting a new baby, prepare the older child for the separation and for the invasion of your relationship. Let him learn to participate with you and identify with you as a caregiver for the new baby. Instead of pushing him away "to protect the new baby," let him learn how to be tender and gentle, how to hold and rock and feed the baby.

After the new baby is at home and too many things demand

your time and energy, be sure you save a special time for the older child *alone* and without the new baby nearby. Each older child deserves a small segment of protected time with each parent. The amount of time is less important than making the time reliable and one to one. An hour a week per child per parent can be like pure gold in maintaining your relationships. It must be for that child *alone*, and should be his to use in any way he wants. And it should be talked about all the rest of the week—"Even though I don't have time to stop feeding the baby right now, remember that we *will* have our time together later. And it's my time with you (and without the baby) because you are my first baby and I still care about you."

Affirming Individuality

Another issue that may trouble you, if you have more than one child, is your awareness of not feeling the same about each child. Parents will automatically feel like protecting the baby and pushing the older child to grow up. They may wish to push a daughter to be responsible and a son to be adventurous. They may have different dreams for each. These feelings cause guilt and resentment. It is my belief that a parent does not need to feel equally about each child, as I've said before. Each one is bound to affect you differently, based on unconscious, past experiences. "She looks like my brilliant sister" or "He's a powerhouse like my brother" are valid reactions. If you face these responses honestly, the child can benefit. If you try to hide them, any deviation from these images will disappoint you and undermine the child. However close in age or far apart, and however different from one another, children deserve to be seen as competent and loved individuals.

39

SPEECH AND HEARING PROBLEMS

Lack of hearing is a vital insult to a baby's development. Profoundly deaf babies are slowed down in all spheres. They are likely to appear depressed and unreactive—slow to develop motorically and to react to parents' attempts to elicit an interaction. They may lie in their cribs passively, or they may develop autisms—such as head rolling or other repetitive behaviors, as if to fill up empty space. At the same time, the other modalities, such as sight and touch, become heightened. This can make a baby hypersensitive and easily overwhelmed.

The hearing of a new baby can best be tested when she is asleep or as she is just rousing. I use a soft rattle and a bell, in a quiet room. After several startles, a baby with normal hearing will shut out or habituate to either of these sounds (see chapter 2). If I test a baby in a noisy environment, she may have already shut out auditory input. Then she can appear to be deaf, even though she's not. The reason for the two stimuli is to test the range of her hearing. Another test would be to give the baby a chance to respond to my voice when she's awake and looking at the ceiling. If she quiets and slowly turns to my voice, I know that she hears me. If her mother and I compete on either side of her, she should choose the higher-pitched female voice.

If there is concern about a baby's hearing, the primary physician usually refers the child to an otolaryngologist (ear and throat specialist), who can examine the ears and upper respiratory tract. If the cause is a temporary condition, the otolaryngologist will provide treatment. If the hearing loss seems permanent, the child may be referred to an audiologist who can perform further tests. Tests, such as auditory evoked responses (AER), detect gross hearing impairment in babies. As a baby gets a bit older, by one to three months, she can be tested by so-called paired techniques, which offer her a different sound on each side.

Otolaryngologists and audiologists can detect hearing loss in infancy and before it interferes seriously with the child's development. If there is any indication that a baby is not hearing or hears in certain ranges but not in all, I'd suggest a complete evaluation. In the second year, this may become more obvious, as she garbles words in a regular fashion. I would always be aware of hearing impairment as a possibility in a child who is not developing properly, particularly in areas of communication.

Otitis media (infection of the middle ear) can threaten a child's hearing. Many infants develop a tendency to chronic otitis media. After an acute earache, the pressure and the discharge seem to linger despite antibiotics. Otitis media is sometimes called glue ear—as if the ear contained glue that was hard to mobilize. Chronic infection of the middle ear can cause hearing impairment. Infants in group care or infants with older siblings in school who are exposed to many different infections are particularly vulnerable. Ear infections may follow colds as often as every two weeks. Each ear infection becomes more difficult to treat. Parents and physicians get discouraged. The baby's general condition is often affected; she seems to become rundown and vulnerable to everything. At this point, an ear and throat specialist should be consulted. It may be necessary to use tubes in the child's eardrums. They allow drainage, reduce pressure in the inner ear, and prevent hearing loss.

Following the development of speech and other forms of communication is the most important way of determining whether there is hearing loss. With an older child, if you are concerned about hearing, try whispering in one ear or the other. Be sure to whisper something to which you know the child will want to respond. There are many periods in a child's development when "selective attention" can be operating. Whisper a welcome question, such as, "Do you want to go to town with me?" or "Do you want a cookie?" Inattention peaks at four, five, and six. I would never expect to determine a child's ability to hear by testing her with a parental command!

In my office, I put my finger in one of the child's ears and whisper in the other, "Do you want a lollipop?" This is almost sure to get a response. If there are no responses and/or speech is developing inappropriately, I refer the child for evaluation by an otolaryngologist or testing by an audiologist.

While speech problems will rarely be evident until well into the third year of life, the foundations of communication are laid in early infancy. In the first weeks, a baby is learning to differentiate between important and unimportant sounds, as described in chapter 2. To an intrusive or unimportant sound that is repeated, she will habituate and shut down her responses. To an important or interesting one, even a newborn will alert, quiet any motor activity in order to pay attention, and turn toward it with an alert, inquisitive look. By seven days of age, she will choose her mother's voice from another female voice in a paired situation. By two weeks, she will choose her father's voice in preference to another male voice. By six weeks of age, she will demonstrate predictable behavioral patterns for each of these important persons. She will, by her behavior, show them that she recognizes them. In an experimental situation we have set up, with the baby in a baby chair, the parent leaning over her to communicate, we have shown that by three months, a baby will have learned an

Communication ar
Speech Problems

attention–inattention rhythm four times a minute. In the periodic attention, she will alert, vocalize, and smile. When parents fit into this rhythm, she learns to imitate their vocalizations, facial movements, and movements of their heads and bodies almost precisely.

As adults fit into this pattern, they too will imitate the baby almost precisely. They will match her rhythms, inflection, and motor behavior, as well as the attention–inattention rhythm. In the process, they are reinforcing her attempts at speech, as well as the rhythms that underlie later communication. As adults match the baby's behavior, they add a little extra onto it. The baby tries to live up to the slight added difference—to match it and to imitate them. Parents pitch their voice differently to babies—not only with baby talk but with slowed rhythms and simpler words. This baby talk has the significance of saying, "Now I'm talking to you." At all other times, adults are speaking over the baby's head. So, the baby talk takes on a special connotation. The baby tries to respond—with a smile, a vocalization, or an arching forward with a wriggle of the whole body.

The following are signs of speech development for which parents can watch.

1. By three months, a small baby will be making vowel sounds like "ooh-agoo." These are likely to be responsive at playtimes or feeding times, but they also occur at diapering and while she is lying in her crib talking to herself.
2. At six to eight months, inflections and speech rhythms begin to be richer. A baby will continue to test vocalization and has a few consonants, including "mamama" and "dadada." These are not yet attached to the appropriate person.
3. At one year, a baby will talk a stream of gibberish but will usually attach "mama" and "dada" to the right person. She can respond to one-step commands, such as "Give it to me."
4. At fifteen months, a baby will continue to emit completely unintelligible gibberish, but with more actual words immersed in it. Words for giving and taking are

important. Her receptive speech will be richer, that is, she can understand more commands. A baby of this age may have ten or more words, but there is immense variation in this.

5. At eighteen months, a toddler will probably be able to say "ball," "doggie," names of special people, and action words such as "bye bye." "Yes" and "no" are very important. Both nouns and verbs will be represented in her speech, and she will use complex gestures for communication. Many toddlers can handle two commands ("Go in the other room and get me my slippers"), which shows their increasing level of receptive speech.

6. At two years, a child can start combining words. She may put nouns and verbs together: "Daddy home," "Mommy go." Her receptive speech—understanding suggestions, questions, and warnings—shows that development is progressing. Even if children are not combining words, rich and appropriate gestural speech means that actual speech is likely to follow.

If these signposts are delayed, a child should be evaluated for auditory impairment.

At the same time, parents can evaluate how well they are encouraging speech. Here are some questions I explore:

▶ Do you speak to the child, or do you talk over her?
▶ Does everyone in the family rush to the child before she needs to verbalize?
▶ Do you read to her?
▶ Do you enlarge slightly on her speech? This leads her on.
▶ Do you offer encouragement, responding to her words with your words and with your gestures?

Other ways to encourage speech include speaking directly to the child, waiting until the child has a chance to speak back, and assuring the child that she has plenty of time. You can also ask her siblings to help; she may learn more easily from them by imitation than from adults. If the child is stuttering or stammering, don't push her; encourage her by waiting patiently.

In bilingual households, speech may come more slowly. By about age three, a child will be speaking both languages. Before that, she will understand which language goes to which person.

Many normal children are "late bloomers" as far as speech goes. Patience and the encouragement just mentioned will usually be rewarded. However, there are certain signs that call for early evaluation:

- No intelligible speech by two years
- High-pitched or nasal quality to utterances
- Dull look as the child tries to speak
- No rhythm of communication, or turn taking
- Evident overload or inattention when the child is spoken to or looked at

▶ Incessant repetition of adult speech, without variations or combinations on the child's part

Apart from hearing impairment, there are several kinds of problems that can interfere with speech development. The *fluency* of speech can be disrupted, as in stuttering. Stuttering is normal and inevitable as children begin to speak. Only when it continues or is combined with other speech problems should parents seek help. A child can have problems in *articulation*, that is, in producing sounds correctly. A nasal quality to the voice can mean a problem with *resonance*, and there can also be difficulties with *pitch* or *loudness* or the *quality* of the voice, as in hoarseness or shrillness.

If you notice these problems, or if a doctor does, the child can be referred to a speech and language pathologist. If the doctor feels that the cause has to do with structural defects (as in cleft palate), he or she will refer the child to a plastic surgeon or other specialist. The earlier that repair of a defect or speech therapy is started, the better this will be for the child's overall development.

40

STOMACHACHES AND HEADACHES

All of us have certain organs that reflect tension and unusual pressures. This is true even in children. Some have a flare-up of asthma when they are tired or upset (see chapter 14). Others get stomachaches or headaches. Parents need to be aware that these can be symptoms of stress. They can look for pressures that may be unnecessary and overwhelming to the child. They can also begin to point out to the child the reasons for this psychosomatic response. In this way, the cycle of uncontrollable symptoms can be broken, and the child can eventually learn to be more in control.

Stomachaches   Stomachaches often occur in four- and six-year-olds, as pressures from school and peers increase. This is also a stage when the child is beginning to be aware of aggressive feelings. Stomachaches are a sure way to get the attention that a stressed child needs.

When a child complains of stomach pain, you should first consult the child's doctor to rule out other serious causes. Before doing so, you can check for an acutely painful area. Distract the child, then place your hand on his belly, to press gently throughout. An acute abdomen is boardlike, and you cannot press over the inflamed area. If this is the case, the child should see a doctor right away. An inflamed appendix or an intussusception (an intestine that has telescoped in onto itself) must be ruled out. A physician can feel for an acutely tender area and can use a stethoscope to listen for bowel sounds. An "acute abdomen" (such as an inflamed appendix or a blockage) will have a silent area around the inflamed, blocked organ. High-pitched bowel sounds will be heard in other parts of the abdomen. If it is not acutely tender, you will be successful in pressing all through the child's abdomen without finding a tender spot—*as long as* you distract him. Get his attention on something else and press all through his belly. If an area is painful, he is bound to guard it.

No bowel movement in twenty-four hours or more can be a common symptom of obstruction. If there has been one, the doctor will ask whether you have checked for blood, usually blackened blood. Has the child been constipated? Many children this age forget to have b.m.'s. They get chronically constipated. Then, they produce a liquid stool from around the hard stool. No one thinks they are constipated. The hard b.m. hurts the anal sphincter, so it tends to hold back the b.m., and the constipation worsens. A stool softener, or a suppository to help the child produce the hard stool, may become necessary as a last resort, but only if the doctor recommends it. To prevent chronic constipation, include plenty of fruit and fiber in the child's diet.

If the stomachache does not seem acute, you can try an aspirin substitute. This will not affect an obstructed or inflamed intestine. Wait an hour to see whether the pain diminishes. If it does not, call the doctor.

If the pain goes away, or a doctor finds no problem, you can reassure the child. Your anxiety and the child's can be allayed. That is always an important first step.

If stomachaches are not acute and recur over and over, check to see whether they are related to any special foods.

Keep a diary of foods eaten from day to day. Many children are mildly sensitive to milk and milk products. At times of tension or fatigue, this sensitivity may surface. Under normal conditions, it won't. Eliminating milk for a period can determine this. A diary of the foods the child eats at the time of stomachaches can turn up such a common denominator.

If the stomachaches are related to mealtime, check with the doctor. Ulcers or colitis flare up at regular times close to meals. If there is urinary frequency or burning, there could be a urinary infection. The doctor will want a urine sample to be tested.

As with asthma or other recurrent problems that have a psychological component, a stomachache can be brought on by several mild triggers, such as certain foods, food additives, and milk. These can act alone or together to produce a bellyache when a child is upset. Eliminating these triggers will allow him to get tired or stressed without the recurrence of pain.

Does this stomachache occur on school days—not on weekends? Does it occur when the child is stressed by any particular event? If it occurs each morning before school, try to rule out contributing factors. At breakfast, feed the child light foods that he can digest easily. Try not to rush. Then, he may be able to face the stress of school more easily.

At each episode, reassure the child and offer an explanation of why stress brings the symptom out. When the stomachache goes away, remind him that you and he knew what to do about it. Learning to live with stomachaches may be necessary, but they will improve if the child's anxiety can be diminished.

Headaches Rarely does a toddler or preschool child complain of a headache. If he does, I would certainly have him checked out by a doctor. Eye exams, including looking in the pupils with an ophthalmoscope, will be part of the check. A urine exam can rule out certain conditions that lead to headache, such as kidney disease. Blood pressure could also be a factor. A neurological exam can reassure you and the child's doctor that the headaches are not a sign of a more serious problem.

Migraine headaches have a genetic component, usually occurring in families in which other members have experienced them. There are likely to be many triggers for migraine. Certain foods, food additives, inhalants (mothballs, cleaning fluids, and so on), stress, fatigue—even flashing lights—can be triggers for them. As with other symptoms, any one trigger alone may not contribute to a migraine. Two or three together will. If you can't be sure, keep a diary of all the foods, events, and stresses that occur around the time of the headache. Migraine sufferers soon build up a dread of the headache, which adds to it.

If headaches are associated with difficult vision, nausea and vomiting, fatigue, or sleepiness, consult a physician. There are specific medications that may prevent a migraine headache if they are taken early. The child should know about them. If headaches occur in spite of the preventive medication, the physician can prescribe more potent medicines. There is also a form of acute stomachache that is associated with migraine. An electroencephalogram may be indicated to help with the diagnosis, although migraine does not always show up on an EEG.

Headaches that are not serious are likely to occur at special times—in the morning when the child's blood sugar is low and in the evening before supper when fatigue and low blood sugar couple to bring on such a symptom. These can be treated by raising the child's blood sugar with a sugary drink before he gets up or a snack in the afternoon before he begins to feel cranky or upset.

If the headaches are mild and are not due to any of the physical reasons just outlined, I would follow the same guidelines indicated for stomachaches. Respect the child's need for loving attention; let him rest while you talk to him soothingly to reduce stress. Reassure him that the doctor did not find anything wrong, and help him try to understand what is behind the headaches. Gradually, explain whatever you have observed about his symptoms and when and why they occur. Help the child learn to live with his headaches. Like all problems with a psychosomatic component, they are likely to improve when the child feels more in control and less anxious about a recurrence.

41

TELEVISION

Other than a child's family, there is no force today which influences behavior as powerfully as does television. The average child spends more time in front of a TV set than she does studying in school or attending to parental instruction. In other words, children learn more about the world and values from television experience than from family or community. This places enormous responsibility on the media and on concerned parents.

Action for Children's Television, the organization founded by Peggy Charren (see Useful Addresses at the end of this book), has had more influence than any other in raising the national consciousness of families, government, and the media in regard to children's programs. Among its accomplishments is the hard-fought-for bill that reduces the amount of time spent on commercials *per hour* in children's programming from 14 down to 10 ½ minutes on weekends and to 12 minutes during the week. In other words, commercials will be beamed at children over one-sixth of their TV time instead of one-quarter of it on weekends. This seems like a small victory, but it's a vital one!

My cable television show, "What Every Baby Knows," has linked me to more families than my books and articles could ever have done. The intimacy that viewers feel is very precious, and I respect it. But it also frightens me, for it represents the power of that medium. Adults are affected at all levels by viewed experiences on television. When these are positive, they are grateful. When the experience is negative, they can be passionately angry. It is clear that television has the power to invade our personal feelings. Adults are able to express those reactions and to defend their inner core from this invasion. Can children do the same?

Eyes glued to the screen, a small child sits in front of the television set. Her face and her body are immobilized. Any sudden loud noise on the program makes her startle, showing how deep is her concentration. Noises in the room around her don't penetrate her isolation. If parents want her attention and touch her on the shoulder, a startle, then a weeping protest may greet this interruption of her mesmerized attention. At the end of even a half-hour's viewing, a child who is pressed into another activity is likely to dissolve in tears or in hysterical screaming. After this tantrum allows release of the tension she has built up, she can be docile or sullen. But at least she can be reached.

Stresses of TV Viewing

I worry about the cost of such intensity. A child's entire physical and mental capacity is involved in watching television. Her body is passive but tense. Her cardiovascular system is working at its peak. Muscle tension reflects a stressed, not relaxed, child. This combination of inactivity and tension is physiologically demanding. Psychologically, the cost to her is reflected in the way she disintegrates afterward, or in the other ways she may demonstrate the price of her concentration. In small children, aged one to four, this price needs to be questioned. Preschool children have a limited capacity for heightened experience. Television watching is one of the peak experiences of their day. Parents of a child of this age should weigh this against the other influences in their child's development. When they do, few parents continue to use it as an automatic baby-sitter.

Children between four and six years concentrate on important adults, imitating their speech, their movements, and their ideas. Of course, they will identify with a television star. Children in my office speak softly and tenderly, imitating Mr. Rogers. Three- and four-year-olds chant the songs of "Sesame Street" that accompany the *A*s and *E*s as they read my eye chart. But the hosts and actors on children's shows are not the only models. Commercials have a powerful impact on small viewers. Parents need to be aware of this. Do you want to reinforce this impact? Do you really want to buy a particular cereal just because it is being promoted with a clever commercial? With preschool children, you still have a choice.

Many researchers, including psychologist Albert Bandura of the University of California, have demonstrated that five- and six-year-olds model themselves on the activity they have viewed on the screen. If it is violent, they are more likely to engage in violent behavior in the period immediately following a program. If the program contains sexually explicit language, children will test it out afterward. By the same token, a gentle, nurturing program can lead a child to model herself on the nurturing behavior she has viewed.

TV Messages and Peer Pressures

As they get older, children need to conform to their peer groups. They "need" to be hooked on Ninja Turtles. They "need" to wear the same clothes that their friends are wearing. During this time, television commercials are at their most powerful. A parent can have a balancing influence, but not without taking into account the importance of the child's need to be part of her group. With an open discussion of current fads, you can work out where to draw the line. If you can't afford to buy all of the accessories that are promoted, you can make that very clear. This is an important message: "I can't afford them. If you really must have them, are you ready to work to pay for them? If you are, I'll try to help you. Then, you can decide whether to use the money you have in this way. You know I don't feel that this stuff is necessary, but if you earn the money, it's your choice. Let's work on it together."

In the middle years and in adolescence, the power of television as a shaper of children's thoughts and beliefs continues to

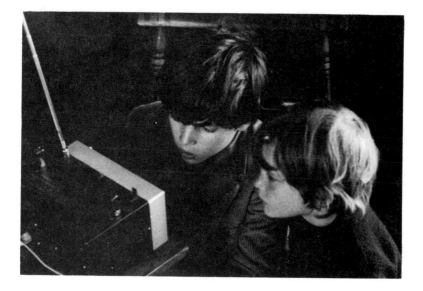

grow. Children learn behavior, language, and thought processes from television actors or celebrities. Most parents will
want to balance these influences with their own. How do you
do that? Again, you must respect the child's need to establish
her own territory and identity, often based on her peer group's
standards. The values you believe in most can be presented as
those that are important in our own family. By respecting the
balance between your child's needs and your own standards,
you can put your values into words.

Limits on Viewing Time

As to hours of television viewing, I firmly believe that there
need to be limits. The physical and psychological demands on
a child of any age help determine what those limits might be.
For example, a child with a short attention span needs time
out after a very short period. In general, I would urge parents
to have a cap on the amount of time that children of all ages
are allowed to watch. One hour a day during the week and not
more than two hours on weekend days seems a reasonable
goal.

Half of this viewing time should be "family time" in which

the adult members watch, too. After it is over, there is an opportunity to exchange ideas and to discuss the issues or the sports or the cartoons. In this way, television becomes a shared experience. The child can be allowed to help to decide which programs she will choose to watch. Choosing them each week can be a time when parents participate in choice making, not to dominate, but to help the child sort out values. There are many good programs that deserve to be watched. They can be used as special family events.

Children will haunt you with: "Other parents love their children more than you do. They want them to know what's going on in the world. They want them to know about sports and rock singers so they can be part of the crowd. They want them to be 'with it.' Your rules keep me from knowing what my friends are even talking about." These statements will shake your conviction. Then, you must remind yourself that the demands of this medium on the child's physiological and psychological capacities are enormous. Think of the other ways she can relate to children of her age, such as sports, hobbies, excursions, or camping. Can you invest extra time and energy in them?

You will need to have your answers worked out with conviction. "I realize that many of your friends can watch television for several hours a day. I'm afraid I don't believe in that, for you miss too many other experiences. In our house, an hour's television on weekdays is it. Two hours a day on the weekends, and you and I can choose them. If there is a great special, we can always make an exception. But these are our family's rules. I want you to understand why we have them and why they are important. But whether you do or not, they are the rules of this house."

However eloquent this little speech, nothing will undermine, or reinforce, your position more than your own viewing habits. In families where parents are enthusiastically involved with their children, in cooking, playing games, exploring the outdoors, or relaxing and chatting, the lure of the screen will be reduced. Parents who turn on the TV only to watch chosen, unusual programs, and who otherwise are available to their children (or plead for a peaceful moment with a book), will find that their views on television watching carry more weight.

42
TOILET TRAINING

In chapter 12, I outlined the steps parents can take once a child has shown that he is ready and wants to begin using the toilet. Parents who are able to be patient until the child shows the signs of readiness that I have spelled out in that chapter— usually between two and four years of age—are unlikely to run into serious problems.

Problems in toilet training nearly always arise because of an asymmetry in the parent–child relationship. When parents are unable to wait, and they impose toilet training as their idea, the child will feel this as an invasion.

All parents, of course, want their child to grow up and prove that he can maintain control over his bladder and intestinal tract. Also, pressure on parents to get the child to conform comes from many sources. Their own wish to see him as advanced makes them want to compete with other families. Preschools often insist that a child be "trained" before he comes to school. Other parents offer advice and condescend-

**The Danger of To
Much Pressure**

414

ing comfort when their children are already trained. Grandparents imply that toilet-training success is a measure of successful parenting and of a child's competence. The entire second year may be felt by some families as preparation for success in this area.

Parents' own experiences play an enormous role in their attitudes toward toilet training. If they have memories of early and strict toilet training, they will find it difficult to conform to the relaxed child-oriented program that I have suggested. They may try to understand my point of view, but memories will keep haunting them. "My mother had me all trained at a year. She told me how hard I tried to avoid mistakes. Why can't my child try that hard?" Memories of punishments that parents or their siblings received may seem terrible when considered intellectually, but they can undermine a parent's conviction that it's all right to let a three-year-old make his own decisions. The experiences of two parents may have been similar or quite different. Unless both parents want to leave it to the child, the one who wants to start training may raise doubts in the other. Should they be pushing or at least reminding the child to try?

A toddler for whom independence is a passionate issue anyway will have his own struggles. He may stand in front of a potty, screaming with indecision. Or, he may crawl into a corner to hide as he performs a bowel movement, watching his parents out of the corner of his eye. It is a rare parent who will not feel that such a child needs help to get his priorities straight. When a parent steps in to sort out the guilt and confusion, the child's struggle for autonomy becomes a power struggle between them. Then the scene is set for failure.

Most of these power struggles will simply make the period of training stormy and unpleasant and much longer. However, when parents really lock into the struggle, serious problems can result. A child can withhold stools, causing chronic constipation, leading to an enlarged colon (megacolon). As mentioned in earlier chapters, soiling occurs when a child inadvertently but regularly leaks into his pants around a retained, hard stool. The soiling may seem like diarrhea, when the basic problem is constipation. This is confusing to the parent and to the child, who is unaware of the reason. Control issues mount and increase the depth of the problem. A bowel softener to soften the stool so it won't hurt needs to be coupled with a letup on pressure—both within the child and from without, before he can want to get trained again.

Some children may leak urine, especially under stress. Parents complain to the pediatrician, who then feels the necessity to test whether the bladder and urinary sphincter are intact. X rays, catheters, and invasion of the genitals result. The child is frightened. If his anxiety becomes fixated on this area, the child can become more vulnerable to chronic incontinence.

Tension in the environment, not necessarily about toilet training, may be reflected in abdominal pains, cramps, and loose bowel movements. If the child then has difficulty in maintaining control, the tension will mount. Toilet training then becomes highly charged and adds to the stress on the child. He becomes more conscious of this part of his body. Eventually, GI (gastrointestinal) X rays, enemas, and manipulations are used for diagnosis. The result is that the child's lower GI tract becomes the target area for all tension.

Because of societal pressures, bedwetting (enuresis) becomes a problem for many children, especially boys, by the ages of four and five (see chapter 15). If it continues, the child cannot visit others. He dares not admit to himself or to anyone else that he's so inadequate at night. Parents become desperate about such a failure, which they see as their own. Whether hushed up or treated as a reason for punishment, bedwetting can make the child feel hopeless and helpless. He will say he doesn't care and will develop all kinds of strategies for hiding his failure each morning. Tinged with guilt over his developing sexuality at these ages, four to six, the night wetting can affect his future self-image. Excessive masturbation and enuresis are often tied together.

In bedwetting, as in all the problems mentioned, a child's need to become independent at his own speed is at stake. Though the reasons may be physiological, such as an immature bladder that empties frequently, or too-deep sleep (the result of an immature signaling system), the issue of who will control the solution is there. As parents and physicians begin to investigate reasons and institute measures (such as alarms, punishments, or signal devices that go off when he wets), the child's autonomy and need for control become lost. He sees himself as a failure—immature, guilty, and hopeless. The damage of this self-image to his future will be greater than that of the symptoms themselves.

Why do parents get so concerned about toilet training that they invade the child's privacy and even his body in their quest for "solutions"? Given that this is a developmental process that the child will ultimately master at his own speed, why do parents feel they must control it? Attempts at control are almost certainly doomed to failure and will set the child's sense of inadequacy and failure. The danger of future GI tract difficulties is increased by parental pressure at these ages.

My experience has led me to the conclusion that parents have a very hard time in being objective about toilet training, as I've said before. Our culture and the individual experiences in most adults in this culture demand that they feel responsible for the child's success. Any failure is felt as a reflection on their poor parenting. The child becomes a pawn—to be "trained." It will take us another generation before we can see toilet training as the child's own learning process—to be achieved by him in accord with the maturation—of his own GI tract and central nervous system.

When Problems Exist

The steps that I outlined in chapter 12 are preventive steps, ways of leaving the job of training to the child and avoiding future problems. If a problem has already arisen, I ask parents to try the following.

- Discuss the problem openly. Admit you've been too controlling.
- Remember your own struggles, and let the child see that there is hope ahead.
- State clearly that toilet training is up to the child. "We'll stay out of it. You're just great, and you'll do it when you're ready."
- Let the child know that *many* children are late in gaining control, for good reasons. If he wants to hear the reasons, explain them.

▸ Keep the child in diapers or protective clothing, not as a
  punishment, but to take away the fuss and anxiety.
▸ Let him alone. Don't mention it again.
▸ Don't have the child tested. Have urinalysis done, but no
  manipulation or invasions—enemas, catheters, X rays,
  and so on. Only if the pediatrician sees clear signs of a
  physical problem should you allow testing.
▸ Keep the child's bowel movements soft. Use fruit and
  fiber in the diet and stool softeners so that you can
  reassure the child that they will stay that way.
▸ Make clear to the child that when he achieves control, it
  will be his own success and not yours.

Parents who feel they are too involved might seriously consider counseling for themselves in order to relive and understand their reasons for being so concerned and so intrusive.
They need to agree with each other about their handling of
toilet training so that their conflict does not affect the child at
a level that carries a serious cost for his future—his self-image.
Controlling these areas to conform to an uptight society is not
worth the price a child must pay.

If the child continues to have problems that bother him or
interfere with him adjustment at school or with his peers, I
would seek advice and help.

three
ALLIES IN DEVELOPMENT

43
FATHERS AND MOTHERS

Since so much emphasis, in this book and in society, is given to mothers and their roles, it seems only fitting to wonder what the modern father contributes that makes him so special both for the baby and for the family's cement. For he is. In a few decades, the roles of fathers have undergone tremendous changes. Most fathers of a generation ago saw themselves as supplements to mothers. They participated when mothers told them to. The participation was almost always in sports or other "masculine" activities. They were also disciplinarians, called in when a mother was not being obeyed. Many people of earlier generations hardly knew their fathers as they were growing up. I felt that my own father allowed his role to be designated by my mother, rather than following his own inclination to be really involved in his children's activities. We ended up as rather uncomfortable pals in my adolescence, trying to talk "man to man." Neither of us knew enough about the other to make this work, and I longed to know him better.

Although these stereotypes of male behavior have begun to break down, it may take several generations before they are really gone. I have had primary caregiving fathers in my practice. They are pioneers who must work things out for themselves. I remember one full-time father who would bring his daughter to all her checkups. I marveled at his skillful participation and was also impressed by his wife's ability to step back to let him take over. When I saw them together, I noticed that she did not tell him how he might have done something better or hesitate before she handed the baby to him. However, I also found myself worrying about her own attachment to the baby. Later, I realized that this reaction came from my stereotyped expectation of what mothers should do.

Once, when I asked this same father how things were going, he replied, "Okay." "Just okay?" I asked. "That doesn't sound so great. What keeps you from feeling better?" "My daughter calls me Mama when I give her the bottle and Daddy when she wants to play." Clearly, his daughter had learned to express her desires effectively! I congratulated him for being able to play both roles for her. He went on to explain how embarrassing it was when his daughter clung to him in front of his male friends. His remark made me realize how deeply our past affects all of us, including these male friends. I also wondered whether these friends might be jealous, seeing the lovely close relationship he had with his daughter.

Even fathers who do not assume full responsibility for a child, and whose wives take off some time from work, have an increasingly vital role to play. When a new baby is coming and when the baby arrives, new parents are faced with the enormous responsibility of wanting to provide the best environment they can. In an extended family, the cushion of an experienced older generation acts as a buffer—even if you decide that you certainly won't do it their way. A new mother is likely to be immersed in indecision and anxiety as a natural reaction to her caring so much. If she has no one else, she will need another adult to give her direction and support. A father becomes an important counterpart to his wife—not as a sec-

Toward Shared Parenting

ondary "mother," but as a balance, a sounding board, even a compass. Even when parents disagree, he is serving a major purpose in this balance. The mother is not isolated in the inevitable doubts and uncertainties of raising a child. At times, he can give the mother perspective in her fierce new attachment to a baby. His role can be both fluid and vital to all members.

All of the studies that measure the increasing involvement of fathers in their babies' caretaking point to the gains in the babies' development. Not only do school-aged children demonstrate significant gains in their IQ in families where the father was involved with them as infants, but they show more sense of humor, longer attention spans, and more eagerness for learning. These studies show that fathers who are available to their children enrich the child's self-image, and they also suggest that his involvement contributes to more stable family support for the child. A recent study demonstrates that father involvement gives the adolescent a surer sense of her inner "locus of control"—the ability to resist peer pressure because she is sure of her own values.

The change in attitudes is reflected in the fact that it's no longer a mother's job to "tell" her husband when to be available. Husbands are expected to participate. The problem is now more likely to be one of competition between parents and perhaps gatekeeping by the mother. These are universal feelings that exist in every adult who cares about children. The more you care, the more you want that child for yourself. This natural feeling of possessiveness makes parents unconsciously competitive with each other. Each one can see the mistakes the other makes as he or she fumbles to learn the new role of parenting. Since learning to parent is learning from mistakes, not from successes, when each parent is ready to identify with and to back the other up, the job ends with multiplied benefits for the child.

Babies don't need parents to agree. They learn very early to expect different things from each parent. What they do need is a sense of commitment from each parent and a lack of tension around them. Competition for the baby is a sign of intense caring, not a sign of disagreement. Rather than allowing these competitive feelings to cause anger with each other, parents need to use them to sort out the jobs to be done. There are plenty. Competition can be a strong source of motivation for each parent to do his or her best with the baby.

Competition between Parents

A father can learn his role from the very beginning. He can play a vital instructive and supportive role for his wife during childbirth and enhance the outcome for his baby. Meanwhile, he shares in the euphoria of having produced that baby! As mentioned in chapter 3, new studies by Drs. John Kennell and Marshall Klaus have shown that during labor a supportive figure called a *doula* not only reduces the mother's need for medication, the length of her labor, and the number of cesarean sections that are done, but also helps a father become comfortable with his new role.

Fathers report that they feel a surge of euphoria when they see the new baby in the delivery room—akin to that reported

Fathers and Newborns

by mothers who have been awake and actively participating in the delivery process. When the delivery team hands the father the baby to hold right away, he gets a chance to see that this is really a baby—intact after all the fears. This kind of experience, shared with the mother, brings to a peak all of the waiting, the wondering, and the self-questioning about whether a man can really become a father.

At Children's Hospital in Boston, we have studied the effect on fathers when we showed them their babies' behavior in the newborn period (see chapter 3). Several such studies combined show that new fathers are eager to get to know their new babies and become significantly more sensitive to their baby's cries. They respond more quickly to the behavior of the baby. They soon know when to burp her, to talk to her, and to change her. In other words, the behavioral cues of the newborn shared in this first exciting period reinforce a new father's feeling important to his baby, and he demonstrates it by learning his baby's "language." The belief that men don't understand babies gains no support from these studies. They each show that what he needs is permission to learn his new job. A very interesting aspect of the research is that when fathers are shown their newborns, they are significantly more involved in supporting their wives. I would like to see all newborn nurseries try to include every father in the demonstration of their new baby's care and in a shared demonstration of all the wonderful things a newborn can do—such as turning to her father's voice, following his face with eyes and head, cuddling into the corner of his neck, and so on. A father, in turn, should ask to be present when the baby is being examined before discharge. Fathers need to demonstrate that they *want* to be present for checkups. Then the pediatrician or nurse will see to it that they are included in the discussions. Don't wait to be asked!

One question often raised by new parents who want to share equally in the baby's care is, How can a father share when his wife is breast-feeding? I suggest that as soon as she is home and the milk supply is established, they start a supplementary bottle for him to feed the baby. If it is given at the end of the day or in the middle of the night, it will offer the mother a needed rest. And the chance to get to know the baby all alone at the time of a feeding is such a delicious opportunity. It more than compensates for the misery of getting up in the middle of the night. Shared roles in caregiving not only allow a father a better chance to know his baby from the first, but also give him a chance to begin to understand himself and how he can unfold as a person who cares for a helpless, dependent new being.

By the time a baby is two weeks old, she will have learned her father's voice and be able to distinguish his from another male's voice. By four weeks of age, as we have seen, a baby will have expectable and predictable behavior that is different for each of her parents and for a stranger. We can watch a baby without knowing to whom she's reacting and be able to predict successfully, by the way she behaves, whether she's interacting with her mother, her father, or a stranger. With a father, the baby's shoulders hunch, and her whole face gets a look of eager anticipation, of wanting to play—her eyebrows pop up, her mouth opens, her eyes flash brightly. Even when she hears her father's voice in the distance, she has this eager look. By four weeks of age, she will have learned to expect her father to talk to her in more excited tones. The baby's special body behavior says, "There you are! Let's go!" when a father looms into sight.

The Value of Two Models

A father can also temper the intensity of the mother–infant relationship when the child needs to become independent. In every area—learning to sleep alone at night, to feed oneself, to become independent in the second year—it helps when a father can say, "Aren't you going to let her go? Let her make a mess and learn to feed herself." This role isn't necessarily popular. No mother likes to think of herself as hovering. And to be reminded that she is will inevitably set up her defenses. But she may examine her own behavior. Single mothers often have difficulty in allowing a baby to separate and to develop independence. Of course, if a father is uptight about messes or too bothered by fussing at night, his involvement will have a negative effect.

Fathers, like mothers, treat boy and girl babies differently.

A father is much more likely to be active physically with a boy and to tease him to learn new motor developmental steps. With girls, fathers are likely to be gentle, slowed down, even protective. They may cuddle and carry them more. Although a father may be unable to tell you that he feels differently, he becomes the conveyor of defined sex roles for his baby.

Both mothers and fathers are bound to have a different expectation and a different relationship from the first with sons and daughters. Rather than being ashamed of this, parents can see that, in this way, each child learns about himself or herself as a unique individual. If both parents can be open and honestly involved with each child, each sex will have models to follow. A boy will pretend to shave and to wear a tie or a hat "like Daddy" in the second year. He'll even begin to walk like him. In the fourth and fifth year, he'll begin to tease Mommy "like Daddy does." He'll also compete with him for Mommy's attention at critically important times. A girl will see how her mother behaves when her father is around. She may imitate her mother in order to capture him at the end of the day. She can successfully ignore Mommy's orders to "get to bed and leave us in peace" after a long day of teasing negativeness at the age of four or five. When Daddy says, "Okay, let *me* take you to bed," she suddenly becomes acquiescent and delightful. What more could any father need to show how critical his role is as a balance for the family? He need no longer be told that he's a good substitute for mother. He knows he's more important than that!

Few people, men or women, start out with a knowledge of how to be a good parent. They must learn by trial and error. For parents who have learned to be perfectionists in the workplace and who have learned not to make mistakes, parenting can be a frighteningly uncharted role. It may be extra hard for fathers to live up to the conviction that quality of life is more important than just being successful in the workplace, but today both parents will need to keep that in mind.

44
GRANDPARENTS

Most of my practice today is made up of "grandchildren," one of whose parents was my patient as a child. I know these former patients very well, and I know the kind of child rearing they experienced. When they come to me for a prenatal visit, I offer to share some of my memories with the new spouse. Often, we do share a few, but in general, both my patients and their spouses would prefer not to relive their childhoods at that critical time. It is as if they want to enter parenthood free of any baggage from the past. They will often say, "I don't want to be like my parents," or even, "Help me to be a different kind of parent." These statements seem to focus on the memories of failure or of painful experiences. During these months of pregnancy, none of the good times are remembered.

Why is this necessary? In order to find an identity as a parent, it is necessary to try to dissociate yourself from the past—your own past. The effort to be different and independent, the urge for a fresh start, is an important one. But it can work only partially. For the "ghosts" from your own past, the memories from your own nursery, are too vivid. They have been deeply influential in shaping you. The painful remembered part of a childhood episode is only a part of your past.

428

Learning and adaptation to stress are also a major part of your experience. That is not necessarily remembered, but it is part of the deep-seated behavior patterns with which you are bound to react when something your child does makes you recall your own experience.

When I follow these "new" families, they, like all families, are likely to have times of crisis or problems in their child rearing. I can then look back at their parents' record, and often I will find the same difficult times or the same issues of parenting. This is confirmation to me of the power of past experience.

It is fascinating to me to see how much about parenting new parents have learned at their own parents' knees. Patterns of behavior that mimic their parents' responses are universal and are to be expected. The times when the new parents will experience difficulty can sometimes be predicted in their own records. It is rather eerie, and when I see potential trouble ahead, I wish I could help families avoid it. On the other hand, there is a kind of intergenerational strength in learning from past crises and early experience that is marvelous. When I see one of "my" children parent their own offspring with skills and approaches familiar from their parents' behavior, I am awed and thrilled. This is the way parenting is handed on from one generation to another.

The power of the past is what makes grandparents' wisdom and memories both painful and supportive. Their criticism can be powerfully undermining because it strikes at the effort to escape old ghosts. Grandparents who want to be truly helpful will do well to keep their mouths shut and their opinions to themselves until these are requested. At that point, if their ideas can be discussed—not as formed opinions but as suggestions to be taken or disregarded—they can be helpful. For grandparents, such times are opportunities for reliving their own struggles and motives in child rearing. If they can honestly relive their frustrations as well as their longed-for goals, this will be far more helpful to new young parents than their advice.

Young parents who are struggling with issues of separation from their parents will naturally find it hard to turn to them at the time of a new baby or a crisis with their children. Grandparents will be wise to see their children's resistance to consulting them as part of a necessary struggle for independence. But that is not easy, either, at a time when grandparents want so much to be of help and to be part of the small child's life.

The vacuum that is created around a nuclear family without contact with grandparents can be lonely and sad. Grandparents and the extended family offer a sense of continuity to new parents. When they say, "We always did it this way," they are offering a solution from the past, adaptive patterns that have been tried and found to work. Such experience in grandparents, and in extended families, can give us some of the answers we all need. These can be specific and appropriate to a particular culture. Family and cultural traditions can be an important base for a child's self-image. I would urge new parents to treasure traditional ways. The value systems that strong families pass on are important to individuals as well as to our society. Traditions from the various European, Latin American, African, and Asian cultures that have enriched this country are strengthening as well. Grandparents are the vital link in the continuity. Our culture in the United States has lost far too much of this continuity, and we are paying a terrible price for it. Our lack of values has left us with war, aggression, power, and money as the values our nation stands for. Is this the legacy we want to hand on to our children?

Grandparents can convey family lore and expectations to their grandchildren. Whenever they tell a story from the past, they are giving the child the sense of a whole new dimension. Our culture and our values are often more easily handed on by grandparents than by parents, whose role is so charged as day-to-day disciplinarians. Children are readier to listen and to conform to grandparents. Continuity with their own heritage is linked into all the stories only grandparents can tell. In offering this continuity, grandparents would do well to remember that grandchildren learn more from modeling than they do from advice.

Competition

A natural competition for the child can invade parent–grandparent relationships. (We have seen this already in the last chapter.) If this is understood and aired, it needn't be a problem. Mothers and daughters may need to watch for this especially. With in-laws, it is easier to anticipate it, due to the mythology surrounding relationships with in-laws. In some way, the better the grandparent was as a parent, the greater the perceived threat to children as parents. As children pass in and out of stranger anxiety, accepting, rejecting, and then accepting grandparents again, these competitive feelings may be rekindled.

Grandparents can all too easily challenge young, vulnerable parents. In their intensity, they can undermine the very values they want to perpetuate. Softly expressed, firm convictions that are given when they're asked for are the most helpful. Critical statements are bound to be rejected. They challenge a parent's efforts at many levels. Parents can be deeply hurt if they feel that grandparents don't see them as caring enough about the child. Learning to parent is made up of learning from mistakes, not success. Parents must make them for themselves. No grandparent or parent can prevent painful mistakes. A grandparent who wants to be helpful can be ready to listen and especially to provide parents with a safe haven to sort out their mistakes. It is hard to sit by and watch problems develop. It's all too easy to remember how you made it work and to rub in your own success. If you want your children to learn their parenting roles, sympathetic support will do a lot more than advice or criticism. The best thing about being a grandparent is the change in relationship between parents and children. Once they both are parents, they are equals.

The Gift of Grandparents

Families need families. Parents need to be parented. Grandparents, aunts, and uncles are back in fashion because they are necessary. Stresses on many families are out of proportion to anything two parents can handle. With both working, the responsibilities for providing child care and for maintaining family values can be overwhelming. The situations of the increasing number of single parents and of blended, remarried families add new burdens for those who are trying to find stable values for their children. Grandparents and extended families offer a cushion for some of these stresses. "If only I had someone to turn to" is a common complaint in my office.

Grandparents are too often far away. If they are nearby, they may be "too busy" to stand in on short notice. Unspoken, the differences in opinion and the generation gap may easily create resistance on the parents' part to turn to their own parents for advice or help. The fear of intrusion and rejection may make grandparents wary. Maybe it's time for each generation to share concerns with each other. Children who have the luxury of relationships with grandparents, aunts, uncles, and cousins win out in all studies of child development. The opportunity for experiencing many models for learning about life adds to the child's potential. Parents offer a child a firm base, but grandparents and aunts and uncles offer options. Their presence implies an important past, and their beliefs can become a part of the family's belief systems. All of us today are hungry for values. Religious beliefs and ethnic values have been undermined in our melting pot society. Strong values are at risk for too many families. Who else but grandparents can keep them alive?

At the time of birth or of a child's illness, or when a mother first goes back to work, grandparents can cushion the stress if

they have been incorporated into the nuclear family. When both parents must work, they will be fortunate indeed if they can have grandparents nearby to back them up in emergencies and to offer support when problems arise. Since most grandparents are working, too, there are limits on such help these days, but emotional support is as important as ever. Grandparents who are available can provide the parents with an opportunity to be with each other. They can give parents a safe night out or a weekend away together.

Grandparents can also help in the stormy times when a child is fighting for autonomy and parents are trying to maintain control. This help does not consist of grandparents taking sides. If they do, neither parent nor child will have the same opportunity to work out the conflict. A grandparent can help in *only one way*: by listening to both sides and clarifying the reasons for the struggle. For example, they can help to sort out the parent's own reasons for control. As we mentioned, these often go back to ghosts in the parent's past. The present conflict may have become entrenched because it echoes an earlier struggle. A chance to share the memory of such an event with grandparents or relatives who were also involved might be a rare opportunity to defuse the old, forgotten con-

flicts. A judgmental grandparent, on the other hand, will only compound the issues. While grandparents may bring the wisdom of experience and a more objective view of the child's issues, they still must respect the parents' concerns first. Being a grandparent involves a great deal of diplomacy that is acquired on the job. In my own case, I gradually learned that to be of any real help, I had to be more aware of my daughter's concerns and not focus entirely on my grandchild's.

The most important gift a grandparent can bring is unconditional, undemanding love. A grandparent can enjoy a baby without having to worry how he behaves or when to be firm. After years of parenting, grandparents are relieved just to be loving caregivers, not disciplinarians. They also offer a continuity of behaviors, of rhythms, of ways of behaving that are familiar to the child. As opposed to a caregiver outside the family, grandparents are like an extension of the parent. Grandparents show children the mountaintops; they pass on the dreams and goals of a family. Parents must show the children how to get there. My own grandmother gave me the inspiration to become a doctor for babies. She always said, "Berry's so good with babies." I wanted to please her more than anyone else in the world, so I learned how to be good with babies. Now, I hear her voice whenever I receive that compliment. Of course, my mother was jealous of my grandmother's influence on me. But she needn't have been. I needed them both—for different things.

Guidelines for Grandparents

▸ Remember that you are not a parent; be a loving, delighted listener and hold back on advice.
▸ Don't rush up to small children unless you want them to withdraw. Never look a baby in the face; look just past him until he elicits your attention. Don't ever grab him away from his parent. Wait until he makes a reaching-out gesture toward you. I watch a small child's behavior. At the point where his face softens and he begins to play with his toys, he is ready for you to join in.
▸ Make a ritual out of your meetings with grandchildren.

Take them a toy or a small present. Tell them stories about the "old days" when their parents were little.

▸ Don't try to treat each child alike, but try to make each one special. Have separate times for each—alone with you. Acknowledge that you will feel differently about stepgrandchildren, but make a big effort to get to know them as people and as individuals. If you can, take each child out individually to get to know him or her.

▸ Agree ahead of time with your children about treats and indulgences so that they and you know where to stop. Consider consulting your children about presents for the holidays. You can overload small children and put too much attention on material things.

▸ Offer to sit when you are not working and when they need you.

▸ Provide the focus for regular family reunions and for holiday events. Even if it seems like a huge effort and the event is fraught with charged emotion, the ritual and excitement of it will linger in children's memories. Include old friends from the parents' past.

▸ When you help financially or emotionally, be sensitive to how difficult it will be for your adult children to accept this help—particularly for a son- or daughter-in-law.

▸ Respect your children's efforts at discipline. They need your help. Don't undermine them. Don't tell your own children what to do, especially in front of grandchildren, or criticize your children in sensitive areas. Of course, you will want your grandchildren to be raised perfectly, but your criticisms of your children's parenting can do as much harm as good—or more—for you will undermine their self-confidence.

▸ Listen and advise them only when they ask for your advice. Don't try to be a teacher for either grandchildren or children. You can offer much more valuable things—comfort, love, experience, hugs, and a sense of strength and stability. Be ready to offer it to both generations.

▸ When you are far away, stay in touch with postcards and letters, using drawings and large printing the grandchildren can read. Photos of parents when they were little are especially welcome, as are birthday cards and presents that fit the grandchild's stage of development and his interests.

▶ Use the telephone to say hello and congratulate your grandchildren for small triumphs. Videotapes are a great way to bridge the distance.

▶ Regular visits for short periods are best. A three-day visit is likely to be enough. Help with housework and babysitting. Try to take everyone out on an excursion while you are there.

▶ Tell your children when they are parenting well. Give them a pat on the back.

The best thing that has happened to me as a grandparent has been the chance for my daughter and me to have a whole new relationship. We are two adults, both parents, on an equal footing now. She can see my pleasure in the way she parents. She needs me from time to time, and I revel in it. A grandchild is a miracle, but a renewed relationship with your own children is even a greater one.

45

FRIENDS

Parents, siblings, and the extended family provide the basic structure on which a child's personality can develop. With friends, a child can explore different facets of her personality. She can use these friendships as a safe haven in which to try out sides of herself and also as a mirror. She can try out different styles and new adventures through the encouraging eyes of a friend. In the process, she is learning about herself. She is also learning how to attract and hold onto a friend. The necessary give-and-take of a friendship provides a child with opportunities for equal relationships that parents and siblings do not provide. A child without friends is a poor child indeed.

First Friends When should parents start introducing a child to other children outside the family? In the second year, it becomes important for toddlers to learn how to cope with other two-year-olds. In a large family or in a busy neighborhood, she may already have learned about having to share, about rivalry, about teasing, and about coping with older children or a new baby. But the kind of relationships a child can make with children who are not her age are different from those she will make with her own age group, as mentioned in earlier chapters. Older children tend to protect, to tease, or to overpower younger ones. In healthy peer relationships among toddlers, children first learn the give and take of equality. They learn the rhythms of reciprocity—when to dominate and when to submit. This is basic to important relationships in the future. A child learns which signals mean that she must give in and which ones mean that she can take the lead. As she learns these important signals, she learns how to relate to others. If she doesn't, she finds herself isolated. At this age, children are both demanding of others and sensitive to their needs. It is wonderful to watch two-year-olds at play. If parents set up regular play groups of two or three toddlers, they will all learn safely about each other.

At this age, learning occurs by imitation. In so-called parallel play, two toddlers putter alongside each other without ever appearing to look at each other (see chapter 11). And yet, each child imitates the other with entire hunks of behavior. This ability to pick up and imitate whole sequences of a peer's behavior is unique to this age. As one toddler stacks a row of blocks to make a bridge, the other will stack the same number of blocks in a bridge—using similar gestures as she does so. I have seen two-year-old children absorb whole new behaviors from other two-year-olds and perform tasks to which they have never been exposed.

Aggression

What if toddlers are not able to get along? What if one is too aggressive and overpowers the other? Is it healthy for either of them? Not really. First, the parents of these unequally matched children will inevitably leap in to take sides and will reinforce each child's unbalanced behavior. The parent of the more aggressive child will either try to stop the child or will resent the anger that she causes in the other parent. The child will sense this and will pick up her parent's overreaction. It will increase her aggressiveness. The parent of the cowering, passive child will angrily push her to fight back at a time when she cannot possibly do so, or will try to protect her. Meanwhile, the parent's anger and embarrassment will compound the overpowered child's sense of inadequacy. Every time parents of toddlers get into their children's play, they change it entirely to an adult-oriented occasion. The opportunity for the children to learn about each other is diminished.

If the children cannot right the imbalance on their own, it is wise to find another child who is more your child's speed. If possible, find a child as a playmate who is suited to your child in temperament. For instance, if your toddler is a quiet, thoughtful, rather sensitive child, try to find one like her. She'll learn a lot more from a peer who is learning to handle a temperament like hers than she will from your pushing her to be more aggressive or gregarious. When you urge a child to fight back or to act differently, it means to her that you don't approve of her. Her self-image becomes even poorer.

If your child is aggressive and impulsive, look for another like her. They'll be able to build up to peaks of frantic activity and to find ways of subsiding—all in parallel. They will learn about limiting themselves as well as about overreacting to their impulses. After playing together regularly two or three times a week, such children will become bosom buddies and will be learning more about themselves than you, as a parent, can ever teach them in any other way.

Teasing What about teasing in older children? Why do children work out their anger on others? Some are trying to resolve their own sibling rivalry. Some are insecure about their ability to make a lasting relationship. I would try to help a child see that other children don't like to be teased. They will reject the teaser and leave her alone. Although she may think this is a way to reach out, other children won't like it. You might try letting her play with just one other child and learning about friendship that way. Also you can help her by talking about her unresolved feelings.

Bullies A bully is an insecure child. She may not know how to deal with her aggressive feelings. All children run away from a bully. As she gets more and more isolated, she becomes even more insecure. Her bullying becomes an unsuccessful attempt to hide how vulnerable she feels. I would try to bolster her self-image and talk about more acceptable ways of relating to her peers. When children are cruel, it is inevitably when they are uncomfortable. When one child touches a vulnerable point in another, that child lashes out. "You're stupid," "You're a sissy," or "You walk like an elephant" comes from a child who is struggling with her own competence. Back up the bully's *feelings* with understanding and support, but let her know that her *behavior* is not acceptable.

To help the child who is being bullied or teased, you can reassure her that everyone gets teased, and it is a matter of learning how to take it. That's not so easy to put over with a small child. "Everyone has something she has to live with—maybe a birthmark, a limp, straight hair or curly hair, black skin or white skin. Everyone needs to learn how to live with the way she was born. Other children tease when they are trying to understand you. They are trying to get to know you. If you can take it without getting upset, they will respect you. And you'll end up being friends."

Parents should rarely interfere in peer relationships. The less adult involvement, the more children will learn about each other—and about themselves. If a relationship continues to be out of balance and the pain of it becomes too destructive, parents can advise a child to find other children. But the child may not follow that advice. Often the relationship is too important, even when it's out of balance.

Children relate to other children differently at each age, and they work out different sorts of issues.

Evolving Relationships

Two- and Three-Year-Olds As we have mentioned, this is a time for enjoying parallel play, for learning limits, and for learning about language from each other.

Three- to Six-Year-Olds This is a time for trying out aggression. Little boys tend toward horseplay, locking onto each other to wrestle and roll around on the floor. They threaten each other with fists, though each one knows who is the

stronger. Meanwhile, they are learning about their own aggression. Little girls tend to tease each other. They learn about provocative behaviors from each other. They giggle and often are incredibly silly. At these ages, a parent's role is to be sure there are opportunities for close playmates, chances for a child to learn how to make friends, to play and relate to others. If a child is isolated at this time, a parent should take it seriously and try to help her. This is the time to learn how to give and take with others. A spoiled or over-protected child won't make it.

Six- to Nine-Year-Olds Children form close friendships and are devastated when a friend deserts them for another. Boys form small gangs and have one or two close friends with whom they must be all the time. Girls also need their small groups. Within these groups, children exclude, they woo, they bully. A parent's role is to respect these close friendships. Even though you may not approve of the bathroom language, the provocative play, and the bullying and teasing that go into the making of these relationships, it is a critical time for every child to learn about herself. She will learn how to live up to the demands of closeness, how to test that closeness and form deep friendships.

The quality of a child's friendships is a good indicator to parents of a child's healthy development. Children are the most sensitive indicators of disturbance in a child. When I cannot be sure from the child's behavior or from the parents' report about the seriousness of a child's problems, I watch her with her peers or I ask her teachers about how other children accept her. A child who is isolated in playgroups or is shunned in school is transmitting subtle messages to other children—of anxiety, self-doubt, or turmoil to which adults may not be sensitive. Children will not accept these struggles in other children. They are too threatening. When other children shun a child, parents should take this as a warning that their child is unhappy. If she is acutely upset, other children may be sympathetic, understanding, and even protective, as long as the child retains the basic abilities for making friendships underneath the turmoil. When she cannot reach other children, it may represent basic insecurity that needs parental attention. Children can distinguish between a child who has suffered a loss or who is temporarily upset and one who is withdrawn because of deep-seated problems. Parents will want to take these signs seriously, both to get help for the child and to give her access to the world of experience other children can offer.

46
CAREGIVERS

Leaving a baby or small child in another's care is never easy. If the caregiver can be the other parent, a grandparent, or cousin, it may be easier, for they have reason to care particularly about this baby. But it is still complicated. Caring parents will grieve about sharing their baby with another person. In several earlier chapters we discussed gatekeeping and the natural competition that evolves. This competitive feeling for the child is a normal, inevitable part of caring deeply. "Will he remember me? When will I lose part of his love—especially if the other person is good with him?" Of course, parents will feel jealous. They will mourn the loss. This mourning is accompanied by three defenses: denial, projection of their feelings onto others, and detachment from the baby's care. These defenses can interfere with the parents' relationship to the other caregivers, as well as to the baby. If they are understood as normal defenses—necessary for protecting vulnerability—parents can have some perspective and avoid becoming hostile with the very person upon whom they will depend.

How do parents who must share a small child protect themselves and the child they must share? We are all aware of how critical a nurturing environment can be to a small child, and that separation from a parent is traumatic in itself. When is it best done? Can the separation be softened? Can a small child adjust to more than one caregiver and not give up the primary attachment to his parents?

As far as we can tell, the answer to the last question is yes. Even a small infant will "remember" his parents' critical cues and will develop a set of expectations that will last and serve as "memory" for the parents' return. These expectations clearly develop in the first three or four months. When mothers and fathers have been consistently involved over the first few months, they will be remembered. In order to keep the relationship strong, they do need to be fully available when

**Seeking a Nurtur
Environment**

they return from work each day, to revive the important cues on which the baby depends.

As I mentioned in chapters 6 and 35, at Children's Hospital in Boston we observed four-month-old babies in day care situations for as long as eight hours. They cycled at a low-grade level between waking and sleep states, never being very passionately involved with their caregivers. When a parent came at the end of the eight-hour stretch, the baby seemed to fall apart, crying and complaining. Someone on the staff always said, "He never does that to us." Of course not. He saved up his important feelings for his parents.

In evaluating day care or substitute caregivers in the home, you will want to watch for the consistency of caregiving behavior, the emotional investment from the caregiver, and the ability of each caregiver to respect the individuality of the baby. Hence, the qualities of warmth and empathy become the most critical things in any supplementary caregiver. Does she respect each baby in her care? Watch her when she holds the baby to see if she observes and adjusts her rhythms to the baby's. Is she sensitive to each child's varying needs for food, a diaper change, sleep, and playful interactions?

Next, I'd want to know whether the caregiver can also respect and nurture you as an involved parents. Can she allow you time to tell her what your baby has been like at home the evening before? Will she sit down to tell you about your baby's day when you come to pick him up? This is hard to tell ahead of time. But if a caregiver seems judgmental about your leaving your baby all day, I would look for a person who can understand your anguish and can accept your reasons for going back to work. The sort of person you want would say, "You know, I think he's about to start to walk," instead of, "He just walked for me today."

If you find a warm, caring person, you need to be aware of your competitive feelings and to talk them out from time to time. Give her your backing. If she does things slightly differently from you, don't worry. A child can adjust to several different styles and can learn to be flexible in the process. If you respect her ways of caregiving, the child will too, as she gets older.

A person who can remain nurturing is likely to be one who

is well trained in child development and who is not overloaded by too many other responsibilities and too many children to care for. To expect this of her, she needs to be adequately paid. Quality child care is not cheap, nor should it be. Early experiences shape your child's future. Giving him the best care and environment becomes an investment.

Child Care at Home If you can afford it for the child in the first year, at-home child care might be optimal. Your child will be in familiar surroundings. The separation from you and the accompanying bustle in morning and evening can be somewhat less abrupt and hectic. This demands that you find a special person, indeed. She must offer your baby an environment you would be proud of. This person must respect you and your household. She must have enough training and experience to understand babies, must be patient and respectful, and, above all, adjustable. She should be ready to respond to and prevent emergencies. She shouldn't be passive or depressed or in too much of a hurry. She should be full of ideas about what she can do with the baby all day and be ready to share them with you.

A nanny or mother's helper must be reliable and be able to make the baby her top priority. She mustn't have young children or a sick husband at home who needs her. Even in the best of circumstances, backup in emergencies had better be identified unless your job is very flexible.

Home Day Care Another form of care is offered by women in their own homes, to a small group of children from infants through three or four years. By the second or third year, toddlers need other children to identify with, and play with. They can profit by care with other children, especially those of their own age. Given an optimal situation, even younger children will as well. Hubert Montagner, a leading French researcher on infant behavior, has beautiful films of seven- to nine-month-old infants together who learn amazing things from each other about themselves and about the world. They obviously form deep attachments to each other. Home day

Kinds of Care

care or other group care *can* benefit infants in the first year. But it must be extremely skillful and caring.

Home day care is entirely dependent on the quality of the caregiver and her ability to relate to each child. A ratio of more than three or four babies to one caregiver is expecting too much. More than four toddlers per adult is hopelessly chaotic. The children are either "on their own" or are parked in front of a TV. The child-to-adult ratio and the personality and character of the caregiver are the first considerations, but there are many others to be taken into account as you choose a home for care. Since such home care rarely is closely monitored and supervised, you must be alert to your child's reactions if you choose home care.

As with the single person in your own home, when there is only one caregiver in a home day-care situation, you will want to know about her backup. If she or her family is ill, what will happen?

Home day care can be good for infants and toddlers, or it can have many problems. It is up to you to monitor it, before and during the time you leave your child. Drop in at unannounced times to observe. Offer to help from time to time and then observe the caregiver's techniques, rhythms, and sensitivity. And, above all, watch your child for signs of neglect or depression.

Day-Care Centers Most day-care centers are now under supervision for accreditation. The National Association for the Education of Young Children (NAEYC) is a large organization of early childhood teachers who are trained and supervised. They developed a set of important criteria for Head Start, and they are now applying these to day-care centers. These standards can protect you and your child. Check to see if the center you are considering is accredited or seeking accreditation.

Teachers at day-care centers should be trained, supervised, caring, and well paid. The child-to-adult ratio should not exceed 3 or 4 for infants, 4 to 1 for toddlers, and 6 or 8 to 1 for three-year-olds. Teachers should be backed up for illness and other absences by trained substitute caregivers.

The atmosphere of a center is critical. A center in which the teachers are happy, in which they work as a team and enjoy each other, is ideal. Test the atmosphere yourself. If they all congregate at one end of the room and leave the children to themselves, watch out! A ratio of three or four infants per teacher is no good if three teachers leave twelve infants alone. Look for teachers who seem to like children and who want to play with them. Watch to see whether they get down on the floor to play. Do they engage in playful interaction while diapering a baby? If every bid from the baby is treated as a chore rather than an opportunity, watch out. A baby lover reacts to each cry or diaper change as a reason for interaction. Babies need this kind of responsive environment. If a caregiver is too overwhelmed or too distracted, the infant will recognize it and withdraw or become depressed.

Monitoring Care

Having found a warm caregiver or a well-run day-care situation, you will still want to watch how your child is responding. The child is the best guide to the atmosphere in which he is receiving care. If he looks happy and is thriving physically, you can be pretty sure he is in good hands. Of course, he will and should protest your leaving and, as we said, save complaints for your return. An older child will be likely to "tell tales" when he wants to retaliate against his caregivers. You can't always go by what he says. But you can by how he behaves. I would observe him in the center. Watch him at critical times, such as mealtimes, transitions from the playground, and sleep. Drop in unexpectedly.

You can learn a lot by watching a caregiver and child together. Does one imitate the other? Do they adjust to each other's bodily positions, to the sensory modalities (visual, auditory, motor) that the other likes? When a baby lids his eyes, does the caregiver lid hers back? Do *you* feel good about their interaction as you watch them?

A small child will usually show signs of a truly depriving environment. But his behavior may not adequately reflect an abusive experience. He may become sensitive to your raised voice, or to your raised hand, but he may not. If you ask him whether he ever gets spanked or "touched," he will answer you in the way he thinks you want him to. You aren't likely to be able to tell by his behavior. But if his behavior changes and he regresses to an earlier stage of development, you will want to learn why. And if he becomes depressed or withdrawn, I'd certainly take it seriously. Sadness, lack of responsiveness, and delays in responding to positive or negative stimuli can be warning signs. If he winces when you change his diapers or covers himself when you change his clothes, your index of suspicion might go up.

Evaluate such signs calmly and carefully. It's all too easy to overreact these days. If a child regresses to earlier behavioral patterns—losing toilet training, waking at night to cry out, or beginning to use babyish behaviors—watch to see if these are transient. If so, they may be due to the transition from your care to substitute care, or to a temporary upset. If they are more permanent, they can be a cause for concern. You should talk over his adjustment at the center and see whether the caregivers are concerned or whether they are defensive.

If a child is depressed *and* fails to thrive—losing weight, appearing sad, or refusing food—I would worry more. Then, I'd have an assessment by his physician. Include your assessment of the center in your history to the physician.

If you have specific reasons to suspect abuse, every city has a child abuse referral center that should be contacted. But be as sure of your accusations as you can. It is easy for a parent to feel guilty and project these feelings on caregivers, accusing them unnecessarily.

The following is a checklist of other things to look for in choosing or monitoring day care.

▸ Are the staff members attentive to the children's safety?
▸ Are emergencies planned for and handled well?
▸ Is good nutrition promoted?
▸ Is the atmosphere bright, pleasant, and fun or tense and glum?
▸ What are the rhythms of feeding, sleeping, and diapering? Do these seem based on the children's needs or on a rigid schedule?
▸ How does a teacher leave three to attend to one?
▸ Are there signs of individual attention for each child?

- ▸ Would *you* want to stay there?
- ▸ How does the staff or home day-care provider recommend that you separate? Can you stay for the first week?
- ▸ Can you visit at any time without being announced?
- ▸ Can you explain the child's needs in the morning and get a report at the end of the day?
- ▸ What about sick children? How long before they let a child with a fever return? (This should be three days.)
- ▸ Is there an emphasis on early teaching? I feel that a center that respects the child's stage of emotional development and is ready to encourage it seems preferable to one that has a heavy curriculum.

No matter how fortunate you may be in your choice of care, we should all realize that today in this country, 50 percent of working parents of young children are having to leave their children in care you or I wouldn't trust—*nor do they*. There is not enough affordable quality care available now. Think what it must mean to a parent to leave a baby or small child with someone callous or sloppy or who they fear might abuse, neglect, or molest him. What does that do to the grief a mother feels anyway in entrusting a child to another person? We need national, state, and local funds to improve and assure quality child care for children all over the United States. Otherwise, we risk watching half a generation grow up without nurturing care, and a whole generation suffer the consequences.

47

YOUR CHILD'S DOCTOR

"How do I get my pediatrician to listen to my questions? He's a wonderful person, and I know he's good at diagnosing diseases in my children. But he hardly seems to know I'm alive, and when I ask him questions about my child's development, he acts as if I were a moron." "My pediatrician either ignores my questions or reassures me about being too worried. I'm worried, but what mother isn't? Shouldn't I expect him to help me raise my child?"

This is the kind of question I hear quite often from desperate mothers. The brave ones who express these concerns have a better chance of finding help. Many parents today are desperately seeking support in raising their children and don't know where to turn. In a period where grandparents work and other extended family are often far away, anxious parents are at a loss for other sources of advice and support. One place they are likely to turn is to the pediatrician, family physician, or nurse practitioner who has shown an interest in their child's physical health. They hope for a similar concern about the child's mental health.

Physicians are trained with a purely medical model—of disease and technology. The four years of medical school are crammed with knowledge of basic science, of disease and its treatments. Pediatric training is crammed with technology and still more disease. In most pediatric training, little attention is paid to child development or to parents' concerns. Few pediatricians are taught about forming relationships with parents and with children. Some family physicians, who take care of all members of a family, will be more attuned to the importance of these relationships. Because most pediatricians went into the field because they like children, they may experience the participation of parents as an intrusion. Many unconsciously blame parents for everything that is wrong with a child. This blame may be the result of their concern about the child and their inability to solve all the problems. Training in developmental issues of the kind I described in the introduction helps them understand the experiences of parents better. Those who have such training find that the rewards of making a valuable relationship with parents make pediatrics five times as rewarding.

Since, at the present time, few pediatricians get such training, they often feel uncomfortable when parents ask questions about behavior and emotions. They may fall back on their own past experiences: "My wife (or my husband) and I found this," or "My children got over this when they were three years old. Wait it out and don't worry." Or, they might put you off with "Don't worry. She'll outgrow it." Although these answers are ways of saying, "I really don't know," they are also usually expressions of caring on the doctor's part, ways of trying to help.

Pediatric Training

1. First of all, check the physician's credentials. Is he or she well trained, with access to a good hospital? Is he available when you need him? Does he have coverage? Most physicians practice in a group, so that one member is available at all times. While you may have preferences among the doctors, it certainly is critical to have someone on call. Few doctors are willing to be at the

Choosing a Doctor for Your Child

mercy of night calls day after day. If your pediatrician is well trained and available, you are halfway there.

2. Have you thought about whether a pediatrician or a family physician trained to provide primary care to adults as well as children is more suited to the needs of your family?

3. Have you asked others about the doctor's personality? One of the best ways to find out about whether you and a doctor will "fit" is to resort to scuttlebutt. Do friends whom you respect seem to like him or her? You might call the doctor's office and ask if she would be willing to meet with you for an interview. Many doctors don't like to be "looked over," but some do. I've always preferred to have prospective patients know about me and come to me with their eyes open. This gives me the chance to be sure I can work with them, too. A parent–doctor relationship is a mutual one. Each party should respect the other and be ready to work things out when the relationship becomes stressed.

4. As we said before, an increasing number of pediatricians have been trained in child development. These usually teach in a medical center and conduct a clinic for assessment and for early intervention when there are problems, physical or psychological. If you have concerns not being answered by your physician, you might consider using one of these child development clinics or set up a referral through your doctor to gather advice at certain intervals. This could supplement what your doctor does for you in the way of medical advice.

5. Many group practices now have the advantage of a nurse practitioner or of a child psychologist who can help you with behavioral "problems." If so, make a special arrangement to see them periodically—to have an assessment of the child and to get an answer to your stored-up questions. The opportunity to get to know and observe your child will enable them to help you in any decision making. If your group doesn't have one, suggest that they might profit by hiring a pediatric nurse practitioner who could answer routine questions, advise you on your child's development, and be a source of easily available support.

Having a primary physician keeps you from having to rely on a relatively less well-trained member of a nearby emergency room, who won't know you or your child. Regular checkups with a primary physician means that he or she will know you and your child when something goes wrong, and in a crisis, can benefit from prior knowledge of you and your child.

When It's Time for a Change

What if the relationship with your physician is deteriorating? I can recognize this when parents begin to be late for each visit or miss several appointments. When I see this happening, I ask them to come in specifically to discuss our mismatch, or I suggest that they might be happier elsewhere. It's a painful way to part, but it's better for the child than maintaining an ambivalent relationship in which neither of us is comfortable. The child's welfare is really the goal of a pediatric relationship, and sooner or later, a poor match is not in the child's best interest.

If, however, you want to try to work things out, ask for a special time for a consultation. When you do go in, remember that the doctor may be on the defensive and will be sensitive to the fact that you are dissatisfied. Let the doctor know that you respect and admire him or her. Perhaps you might try to meet the doctor halfway by apologizing for needing more than the doctor may have realized. Then, do your best to outline your needs. You are trying to get to know the doctor better and to let him or her know you better, to help you with your child. You both have the child's best interests as a common goal. A mutual understanding will achieve that, or it is time to change doctors. One question always worth asking yourself is, Have you done your share to make the relationship work? If you have and it is not possible, then it is better to get into another physician's hands, before the child suffers.

Building a Good Relationship

There are many ways to make a good working relationship. One of the most important ones is for both of you, the parents-to-be, to go in to meet the physician during pregnancy. You can discuss your wishes and goals *before* the baby arrives. I find a prenatal visit is a wonderful opportunity for us to get to know each other. Then, we can start with the baby together as old friends.

It is important for both parents to come for checkups whenever possible. Even though some husbands may feel uncomfortable and practically say nothing, they still can feel a part of the teamwork. The physician will be pleased to have both parents present. The chance to know both of you is "money in the bank."

Try to find out when the physician is most available, when the call hour is. If the practice has a nurse who answers minor questions, use her as much as you can. But when the nurse doesn't satisfy your needs, I'd make this clear. Ask the nurse to have the doctor call you. Explain that you are more anxious than usual for an explainable or an unexplainable reason, and you need to talk to the doctor directly. If the nurse doesn't understand, I would wonder why and continue to insist, politely.

Most physicians basically like dependency and do not mind responding to reasonable requests for help and advice. If you call at a convenient time or allow the physician to choose the time, it needn't be an intrusion. But save night calls for real emergencies. I have a call hour each morning, when I expect to be available for all degrees of questions, unimportant as well as important. This takes the pressure off for me. If parents can save minor stress until that hour, I respect them and know that they respect me. We develop a basic trust that will help in more stressful times.

Your child's doctor should be available for explanations of every problem or treatment, and I'd let him or her know that you want to be told as much as possible. Doctors withhold information because (1) they are afraid you'll misuse it, (2) they want to protect you, or (3) they aren't sure of the diagnosis. In a warm, sharing relationship, a doctor can be honest with you in each case.

Parents can try to press a physician into an anticipatory role. "How can I treat this when she first starts to wheeze?" "How long should I wait?" "Is there anything I can do to prevent these recurrent earaches? I hate treating them after they're already full-blown."

Questions about guidance must be geared to the physician's

expertise and availability to discuss them with you. Developmentally trained pediatricians often enjoy this kind of relationship. They can be gold mines for support and anticipatory guidance. Other physicians may be excellent in the physical sphere but may flounder and defend themselves in the area of child development. In this case, as we said, use other sources, and don't be angry for what the pediatrician isn't equipped to do. You'll endanger your chances of getting the best medical care possible.

Most important of all is that the child feels that "this is my doctor." I find that the most rewarding experience in pediatrics is for a *child* to want to see me and to trust me to help her with her illness. My day is made when a child calls me herself or when a mother calls to say that "Emily wanted me to call to find out what to do about her problem." Any disease has a psychosomatic aspect to it. A child is naturally frightened when something is wrong with her. If she can feel that "her doctor" will know what to do, she will feel a sense of trust and of belief in her own ability to handle the disease. Whenever I am prescribing medication or making suggestions for a child who is four years old or more, I am sure to include them in my instructions. For I want them to know what we are doing and why. After they are recovered, I try to say to them, "See, we (you, your mommy, your daddy, and I) knew what to do, and now you're better!" This implies that the child has had a part in mastering the disease, and it will reduce anxiety for the next time.

The Doctor–Child Relationship

Routine visits are opportunities for me to make a relationship with the child—as well as to enhance it with the child's parents. As indicated I never expect a baby to leave her mother's lap from nine months to three years for an examination. By respecting the child's need to be close to a parent, she knows I respect her. I never look her directly in the face or ask for her to accept me. In this period, I gradually approach her, using a doll or teddy and her parent to show them what I am about to do—stethoscope, otoscope, exam of the throat, or abdomen, and so on. By the time I examine her, she's seen the maneuver. I have watched her face and body for permission. When she relaxes, it means she has accepted me and is ready. Weighing her in her mother's arms is another sign of respect. It is easy to subtract the mother's weight, thereby determining the baby's full weight.

I make a big effort, described earlier, to get a child to want to come into my office—loading it with toys, a fish tank, a climbing gym, a rock collection, and lollipops for rewards. Children see all of these as my attempt to be an ally. When they can leave their parents in my office to play freely, I know the children have accepted me.

I am always looking for ways to make a special relationship with a small child. As she comes into my office, I watch to see how comfortable she is. If she is frightened about me, I respect that. I never look a worried child in the face. I wait until she is willing to leave her parent's lap. As she eyes my toys, I shove one of the trucks in her direction, carefully. But I never let her catch me looking at her. As she begins to play with the truck, I push another close by. If she looks up at me, I can look back toward her, but still not daring to look her in the face. All of this time, I am talking to her parents, so I am actually not spending much extra time in this attempt to solidify our relationship.

By the time I must examine her, we have begun to push trucks back and forth between us. If she is ready, we can exchange comments on the trucks. As I examine her *in her parent's lap*, I urge her to listen to my chest and to examine me. We are sharing the experience and she knows it. She also knows that I respect her privacy and her natural anxiety about being examined. We are setting the stage now for a long future relationship.

With her in the room, I comment on her temperament and mode of play. She knows I understand her. She listens. Anything her parents and I need to discuss is talked about in front of her, and I try to put it in her terms. I want her to understand what we are talking about. No secrets! I prepare her for a shot and urge her to cry and to protect herself. After it's over, I congratulate her on her success.

As a child gets older, at four, five, and six, I urge her to ask her own questions and to call me on the phone. She won't yet.

But by six or seven, she will. We can discuss her illness between us. As she gets older, and when she'll let me see her alone, we can share confidences without it being a triangle. If she still needs her parent, that should be respected. But, even if her parent is present, I talk to *her*.

At four, five, and six, I never ask a child to remove her underpants. I can briefly pull them down to inspect the genital area, but I know how intrusive it is to be examined carefully at that time. By the same token, I do not use a vaginal speculum for adolescent girls.

Examining the throat with a throat stick is another intrusive manipulation. I can see the nasopharynx well if the child imitates my "Ahh" and can use a spoon or a less symbolic instrument to check the sides of the mouth.

When children are preadolescent, I would rather see them alone. I am listening and watching for cues about deeper concerns. They may not be willing to share them, but I know such concerns are there. Preadolescents today must face the choices of drugs and sex at a time when these aren't understood. If they can talk with me, I can give them some idea of the reality of these issues and can offer to support them when peer pressure begins to make choices more difficult.

Often, after a question or a bid for a confidence, the shy child will shake her head to say no. I then can say, "Your head says no, but your eyes say yes. Can you tell me which I am to believe?" Then, I try to shut up to listen. Waiting to get an answer from a preteen or a teenager takes enormous patience and many abortive tries. But they know I'm on their side. As they get older, they show me how much they've appreciated this caring approach.

As indicated in chapter 14, I believe in sharing all I know about each illness with the children themselves. My goal is to help them take an active role in conquering their own diseases. If they can call or talk to me, and receive and carry out my advice, this lesson will stay with them. When they recover, I can congratulate them: "Look how you knew what to do—and it worked!"

During a school-aged child's visit, I always attempt to ask her about her school. For example:

"What is your teacher's name?" No answer.

"Is she a girl or a boy?"

"A girl, silly."

"Does she ask you questions?"

"Of course."

"Do you know the answers?"

"Sometimes."

"Are you ever scared?"

"Uh huh."

"What do you do?"

"I cry." That tells me a lot.

"Do you have a best friend?" No answer.

"Is it a boy or a girl?"

"A girl, silly."

"Is her name Andrea?"

"No, it's Susie."

"Does Susie like to go to her doctor?"

"No!"

"I'll bet Susie won't talk to her doctor either." Laughter.

Then we can start to communicate, not with words, but with play and with gestures.

When she starts to undress, I like to be able to help. If she will allow me to remove her shoes and socks, it is a gesture of closeness. Whenever a child allows me to help with her clothes, she will probably remain my friend afterward.

At each visit, I look for an entry into my patients' lives. I try to talk about their siblings, their teachers, their close friends, their school. As they get to the age of sports or music, we talk about these interests. I am not exploring for information, and I try to make that clear by my interested but nonintrusive questions. I am concerned with making a relationship and letting them know that I care about them as people. I make a note on my chart about any area with which they are concerned. If I can use that as an opener on the next visit, it can ease the way to our relationship.

These visits are touchpoints of their own. When I can make each one a step toward closeness, a child will begin to see me as "his" or "hers." That is my goal.

I want to be able to see a child of eight or nine by herself for at least part of the visit. I want her to trust me enough to talk to me about her school, her headaches, her stomachaches, her fears, and her friendships.

By eleven or twelve, I want the kind of relationship that will allow me to talk about her budding sexuality. Does she know about it? Can I answer any questions she may have after she and her parents have talked?

Do they talk about drugs at her school? Does she know about them? Can we discuss any questions she has? I find that the issues that bothered adolescents fifteen years ago are the concerns of preadolescents today. Headaches, stomachaches, and school absences are coverups for these concerns. If a young person can trust me, I might hear some remark such as, "I know I will have to face drugs and sex soon, and I don't even know what they are!" I want to hear her concern. I want to be someone she can share it with. I won't have answers for her, but we can discuss ways to cope with the stress she feels.

These early talks will put me in a position to offer her a safe place for questions in adolescence: about drug experimentation, the risk of AIDS, and the peer pressure that is so heavy on adolescents today. The earlier touchpoints in our relationship have prepared us to share this stressful period and have made up for all the earlier efforts we have made together.

The other day, I had a visit with a fourteen-year-old patient whose early school life had been a pretty tortured one. She has severe learning disabilities and had had to attend special classes all along. As is frequently the case, she has finally learned to manage her disabilities, and special tutoring is no longer necessary.

"Lilly, I am so proud of you. You've struggled so hard, and you've finally overcome those learning problems you've been plagued with!"

Her eyes filled with tears: "Dr. B., do you really understand?" This communication was worth all of the work we'd put into our relationship.

When children must go to the hospital, it becomes even more critical that a physician explain the reasons and the procedures in front of the child. We have found that preparation for acute or chronic hospitalization mitigates the anxiety in the hospital (see chapter 25). Preparation shortens the child's recovery and reduces the reaction and symptoms of anxiety afterward. Most parents dread the separation and trauma so much that they need a physician's help to face it in preparing the child. Of course, I feel pediatricians should fight to see that parents accompany and stay with the child in the hospital as much as possible. Even though the child will be under the care of various specialists, I always go to visit them and to interpret her treatments and illness.

In my office practice, the best reward for me at the end of a busy day comes when I hear a child's chortle of delight as she rushes in to see me and my familiar toys. Then, I know we are off to a good start.

Sharing Responsibilities

I would urge you to seek to establish this kind of trusting, respectful relationship between your child and her doctor. You must do your part, as well. It is no help to enter the office saying, "He's going to cry," or, "She hates coming to see the doctor." That is sure to undermine both the child and the doctor as they struggle to make it with each other. Instead, prepare the child ahead with reassurance about what is likely to happen. Remind her that you will be there, that it's her own doctor who wants to be her friend. The doctor knows how to help her when she's well and when she's not. It is surprising to me how much it helps a child's self-esteem to learn to trust her physician.

Working with a pediatrician is a mutual job of learning what you can—and cannot—get from each other. You must demonstrate respect, and you deserve respect in return. Both of you have the same goal—a healthy, competent, confident child!

bibliography

Abrams, Richard S. *Will It Hurt the Baby? The Safe Use of Medications during Pregnancy and Breastfeeding.* Reading, Mass.: Addison-Wesley, 1990.

Alexander, Terry Pink. *Make Room for Twins.* New York: Bantam Books, 1987.

Ames, Louise Bates, et al. *The Gesell Institute's Child from One to Six.* New York: Harper and Row, 1979.

Ames, Louise Bates, and Juan Chase. *Don't Push Your Preschooler.* New York: Harper and Row, 1981.

Bowlby, John. *Attachment and Loss.* 3 vols. New York: Basic Books, 1969–1980.

Baron, Naomi. *Growing Up with Language.* Reading, Mass.: Addison-Wesley, 1992.

Boston Children's Hospital. *The New Child Health Encyclopedia: The Complete Guide for Parents.* New York: Delacorte Press/Lawrence, 1987.

Brazelton, T. Berry. *Infants and Mothers.* New York: Delacorte Press/Lawrence, 1983.

———. *Neonatal Behavioral Assessment Scale.* 2d ed. Philadelphia: Lippincott, 1984.

————. *On Becoming a Family.* rev. ed. New York: Delacorte Press/Lawrence, 1992.

————. *Toddlers and Parents.* rev. ed. New York: Delacorte Press/Lawrence, 1989.

————. *To Listen to a Child.* Reading, Mass.: Addison-Wesley/Lawrence, 1984.

————. *Working and Caring.* Reading, Mass.: Addison-Wesley/Lawrence, 1985.

Brazelton, T. Berry, and Bertrand G. Cramer. *The Earliest Relationship.* Reading, Mass.: Addison-Wesley/Lawrence, 1990.

Brooks, Joae Graham, and members of the staff of the Boston Children's Hospital. *No More Diapers!* rev. ed. New York: Delta/Lawrence, 1991.

Brown, Roger. *A First Language.* Cambridge, Mass.: Harvard University Press, 1973.

Bruner, Jerome. *Child's Talk: Learning to Use Language.* New York: Norton, 1985.

Bruner, Jerome, A. Jolly, and K. Sylva. *Play: Its Role in Development.* New York: Penguin, 1946.

Chess, Stella, and Alexander Thomas. *Know Your Child.* New York: Basic Books, 1987.

Cramer, Bertrand G. *The Importance of Being Baby.* Reading, Mass.: Addison-Wesley/Lawrence, 1992.

Dixon, Suzanne, and Martin Stein, eds. *Encounters with Children.* St. Louis: Mosby–Year Book, 1987.

Dunn, Judy, and Robert Plonim. *Separate Lives: Why Siblings Are So Different.* New York: Basic Books, 1990.

Erikson, Erik. *Childhood and Society.* New York: Norton, 1950.

Featherstone, Helen. *A Difference in the Family: Life with a Disabled Child.* New York: Basic Books, 1980.

Feinbloom, Richard I. *Pregnancy, Birth and the Early Months.* 2d ed. Reading, Mass.: Addison-Wesley/Lawrence, 1992.

Ferber, Richard. *Solve Your Child's Sleep Problem.* New York: Simon & Schuster, 1986.

Fraiberg, Selma M. *The Magic Years.* New York: Scribner's, 1959.

Galinsky, Ellen. *The Six Stages of Parenthood.* Reading, Mass.: Addison-Wesley/Lawrence, 1987.

Gilman, Lois. *The Adoption Resource Book*. rev. ed. New York: Harper and Row, 1987.

Goodman, Joan. *When Slow Is Fast Enough*. Foreword by Robert Coles. New York: Guilford Press, 1992.

Greenspan, Stanley, and Nancy Thorndike Greenspan. *First Feelings*. New York: Viking, 1985.

Grollman, Earl. *Explaining Death to Children*. Boston: Beacon Press, 1964.

Holt, John. *Learning All the Time*. Reading, Mass.: Addison-Wesley/Lawrence, 1989.

Hopson, Darlene P., and Derek S. Hopson. *Different and Wonderful: Raising Black Children in a Race-Conscious Society*. Foreword by Alvin F. Poussaint. New York: Simon & Schuster, 1992.

Huggins, Kathleen. *The Nursing Mother's Companion*. rev. ed. Boston: Harvard Common Press, 1990.

Kagan, Jerome. *The Nature of the Child*. New York: Basic Books, 1984.

Klaus, Marshall H., and John Kennell. *Parent–Infant Bonding*. St. Louis: Mosby, 1982.

Klaus, Marshall H., and Phyllis H. Klaus. *The Amazing Newborn*. Reading, Mass.: Addison-Wesley/Lawrence, 1985.

Klaus, Marshall H., John Kennell, and Phyllis H. Klaus. *Mothering the Mother: How a Doula Can Help You Have a Shorter, Easier and Healthier Birth*. Reading, Mass.: Addison-Wesley/Lawrence, 1993.

Konner, Melvin. *Childhood*. Boston: Little, Brown, 1991.

Leach, Penelope. *Babyhood*. New York: Knopf, 1976.

LeShan, Eda. *Learning to Say Goodbye: When a Parent Dies*. Boston: Atlantic Monthly Press, 1986.

Mahler, Margaret, Fred Pine, and Anni Bergman. *The Psychological Birth of the Human Infant*. New York: Basic Books, 1975.

Manginello, Frank, and Theresa Digeronimo. *Your Premature Baby*. New York: Wiley & Sons, 1991.

Nelson, Katherine, ed. *Narratives from the Crib*. Cambridge, Mass.: Harvard University Press, 1989.

Nilsson, Lennart. *A Child Is Born*. Text by Lars Hamberger. New York: Delacorte Press/Lawrence, 1990.

Plaut, Thomas H. *Children with Asthma.* 2d ed. Amherst, Mass.: Pedipress, 1989.

Rosen, M. *Stepfathering.* New York: Ballantine Books, 1987.

Sammons, W., and J. Lewis. *Premature Babies: A Different Beginning.* St. Louis: Mosby, 1986.

Schorr, Lisbeth, and Daniel Schorr. *Within Our Reach: Breaking the Cycle of Disadvantage.* New York: Doubleday, 1989.

Spock, Benjamin, and Michael B. Rothenberg. *Dr. Spock's Baby and Child Care.* New York: Pocket Books, 1985.

Stallibrass, Alison. *The Self-Respecting Child.* Introduction by John Holt. Reading, Mass.: Addison-Wesley/Lawrence, 1989.

Stern, Daniel. *The First Relationship.* Cambridge, Mass.: Harvard University Press, 1977.

Treyber, Edward. *Helping Your Child with Divorce.* New York: Pocket Books, 1985.

Turecki, Stanley. *The Difficult Child.* New York: Bantam Books, 1985.

Viorst, Judith. *Necessary Losses.* New York: Simon & Schuster, 1986.

Wallerstein, Judith, and Sandra Blakeslee. *Second Chances: Men, Women, and Children a Decade after Divorce.* New York: Ticknor & Fields, 1990.

Whiting, Beatrice, and Carolyn Pope Edwards. *Children of Different Worlds: The Formation of Social Behavior.* Cambridge, Mass.: Harvard University Press, 1988.

Winnicott, D. W. *Babies and Their Mothers.* Introduction by Benjamin Spock. Reading, Mass.: Addison-Wesley/Lawrence, 1988.

————. *The Child, the Family and the Outside World.* Introduction by Marshall H. Klaus. Reading, Mass.: Addison-Wesley/Lawrence, 1987.

————. *Talking to Parents.* Introduction by T. Berry Brazelton. Reading, Mass.: Addison-Wesley/Lawrence, 1993.

Zigler, Edward, and Mary Lang. *Child Care Choices.* New York: Free Press, 1991.

useful addresses

Action for Children's Television (ACT)
20 University Road
Cambridge, MA 02138
(617) 876-6620

American Academy of Child and Adolescent Psychiatry
3615 Wisconsin Ave. N.W.
Washington, DC 20016

American Academy of Pediatrics
P. O. Box 297
Elkgrove Village, IL 60007
(write for list of publications)

American Speech-Language-Hearing Association
10801 Rockville Pike
Rockville, MD 20852
(301) 897-5700

Association for the Care of Children's Health
7910 Woodmont Ave., Suite 300
Bethesda, MD 20814
(301) 654-6549

Birth and Life Bookstore
7001 Alonzo Ave. N.W.
Seattle, WA 98107-0625
(206) 789-4444
(800) 736-0631 (orders only)

Exceptional Parent
1170 Commonwealth Ave.
Boston, MA 02134-9942
(800) 562-1973

Good Grief Program
Judge Baker Guidance Center
295 Longwood Ave.
Boston, MA 02115
(617) 232-8390

ICEA Bookstore
P. O. Box 20048
Minneapolis, MN 55420
(617) 854-8660
(800) 624-4934 (orders only)

La Leche League International
9616 Minneapolis Ave.
Franklin Park, IL 60131
(312) 455-7730

National Association for the Education of Young Children
1834 Connecticut Ave. N.W.
Washington, DC 20009
(202) 232-8777

NCCIP (National Center for Clinical Infant Programs)
2000 14th St. #38C
Arlington, VA 22201
(703) 528-4300

Parent Action
2 Hopkins Plaza
Baltimore, MD 21201
(410) 752-1790

Touchpoint Videos
P. O. Box 2284
Burlington, VT 05407
(800) 437-2625

...omen, acute, 406

...se

...ar of being molested, 282

...onitoring caregivers for signs of, 448–50

...on for Children's Television, 409

...ression

  ...ages

  two years, 196–97

  beyond three years, 212–15

...ting, hitting, and scratching, 149–50, 174–75

...ar of aggressive children, 283

...iends and, 438–40

...m reactions in parents, 232

...hol, pregnancy and, 14, 27

...rgies, 219–26

...ildren's anxiety and, 219–21

...eyond fifteen months, 162–63

...arning to control, 223–26

...ilk, 70, 221

...eventing, 98–99, 221–23

...lid food and, 87–88, 98–99, 222–23

American Red Cross First Aid Book, 313

Anderson quintuplets, 156

Anesthesia, 299

Animal bites, fear of, 280

Anorexia nervosa, 158

Anxiety in children. See Fears in children

Anxiety in parents

  alarm reactions in, 232

  about bedwetting, 227

  function of, 37–39

  about illness, 312

  about premature children, 48–49, 350–51

Apgar scale, 23

Appendix, inflamed, 406

Articulation problems, 404

Aspirin and aspirin substitutes, 315–16

Assessment of children

  after cesarean sections, 7

  crying, 232

  fetal, 18–21

  newborns, 23–25

stages of development and, 244

walking, 152

Association for the Care of Children's Health, 301

Asthma, 219–21

Attachments, shifting, 163–64, 211–12

Attention deficit disorder (ADD), 183, 309

Auditory evoked responses (AER), 399

Auditory processing disorder, 188

Autism, 249, 250

Babinski reflex, 28

Babkin reflex, 33, 66

Baby talk, 189

Bandura, Albert, 411

Bates, Elizabeth, 186

Bathing babies, 100, 122

Bathtub, fear of, 156–57

Bayley, Nancy, 244

Bed, family, 92–94, 159, 381, 386–88

Bedwetting (enuresis), 227–230
  as child's vs. parents' problem,
    227
  parental help for, 229–30
  readiness of children to
    control, 228–29
  toilet training and, 203–4, 416
Behaviors, repetitive. *See* Habits;
    Self-comforting behaviors
Bettelheim, Bruno, 325
Bilingual children, 188, 403
Bilirubin lights, 42
Birth
  labor companions *(doulas)*, 6,
    39, 424
  preparing for, 5–8
Birth order, 378–79
Birth weight, 57
Biting, 149–50, 174–75
Blind children, 51
Block building, 146
Bonding, 39–40
Bottle-feeding
  bowel movements and, 72
  breast-feeding vs., 8–10
  cautions about, 46
  milk allergies and, 70, 221
  nursing bottle cavities, 94–95
Bowel movements, 46, 56–57,
    71–72. *See also* Toilet
    training
  constipation, 192–94, 205–6,
    406, 415–16
  flushing of, 191
Breast-feeding
  allergies and, 221
  bottle-feeding vs., 8–10
  bowel movements and, 70–72
  experience of, 288
  working mothers, 86
Breathing, obstructed, 313
Bruner, Jerome, 186, 244
Bullies, 439–40
Burping, 45–46

Caregivers, 443–50
  child care at home, 446

choosing and monitoring,
    448–50
day-care centers (*see* Day-care
    centers)
grandparents (*see*
    Grandparents)
home day care, 446–47
kinds of, 446–48
letting children adjust to,
    102–4
nurturing environments and,
    444–46
preschools (*see* Preschools)
schools (*see* Schools)
separation and, 443
Causality, concept of, 128, 147,
    161, 182
Central nervous system
    disturbances, 231–32
Cephalhematomas, 41
Cesarean sections, 7–8
Challenger space shuttle
    explosion, 328–29
Charren, Peggy,
    409
Cheating, 342
Chess, Stella, 106
Child care. *See* Caregivers
Child care at home,
    446
Child development
  assessment of children and,
    244 (*see also* Assessment
    of children)
  cognitive development (*see*
    Cognitive development;
    Learning; Play)
  concept of touchpoints,
    xvii–xviii
  crying as part of, 236–38
  disabilities (*see* Developmental
    disabilities)
  discipline and stages of, 255–58
  doctor–parent relationships
    and, xxi–xxii
  doctors and, xx (*see also*
    Doctor(s))

fetal development, 16–21
friend relationships and sta
    of, 440–42 (*see also*
    Friends)
motor development (*see* M
    development)
organization of this book
    about, xiii–xix
parents and, xx–xxi (*see al.*
    Families; Parents)
patterns, xix–xx
pediatric training in, xxii–x
    452, 453
self-esteem and stages of,
    365–66
speech and stages of, 401–2
    (*see also* Speech)
Choking, 313
Circumcision, 10–11
Cognitive development. *See c*
    Learning
  at ages
    six to eight weeks, 79–8
    beyond three years, 213–
  causality, 128, 147, 161,
    182
  delays, 246–47
  development of self-image,
    175–76
  imagination (*see* Imaginati
    and fantasy)
  object permanence, 114–15
    127, 145, 160, 246–47
  person permanence, 115–1
    127, 145
  sense of humor and empat
    208–9
  storage concept, 146
  stranger awareness, 101–4,
  two displacements, 160
Colds, 317–18
Colic, 62–64, 233–35
Colitis, 407
Communication
  at ages
    newborn, 44–45
    three weeks, 57–59

six to eight weeks, 74–76
four months, 95–96
seven months, 114
rying (see Crying)
peech (see Speech)
mpetence, 181
mpetition
vith caregivers, 443
omparisons with other
    children as, 50–51, 97–98
etween grandparents and
    parents, 430–31
etween parents, 4–5, 424
ngenital disorders, 42
nsciousness, states of, 19, 24,
    59–62
nstipation, 192–94, 205–6, 406,
    415–16
ntraception and nursing, 392
ntrol vs. independence, 201
nvulsions, 313, 316–17
leeping, 92–94, 159, 381,
    386–88
mer, Bertrand, xx, 41
wling, 110
wling reflex, 33–34
eping, 110
icism and praise, 363–64
up, 318–19
ising, 137
ing, 231–38
inds of, 42–43, 60–61
anguage of, 231–33
s part of development, 236–38
rolonged or fussy (colic),
    62–64, 233–35
t six to eight weeks, 72–73
tural rules. See Manners
tody, joint, 266–67

k, fear of, 280–81
/-care centers, 447–48. See
    also Child care at home;
    Home day care;
    Preschools
hoosing, 449–50
eparation and, 367–70

Deaf children, 398
Death, 328–35
  in family, 329–31
  fear of parent's, 281–82
  learning about, through
      Challenger explosion,
      328–29
  of other children, 332–35
  of pets, 331–32
  sudden infant death syndrome
      (SIDS), 29
De Casper, Anthony, 18
Dehydration, 315–16, 317
Depression in children, 239–42
Depression in parents,
      postpartum, 37–39, 53, 54,
      235
Development. See Child
      development
Developmental disabilities,
      243–51. See also
      Hypersensitive and
      hyperactive children
  assessment of, 244
  attention deficit disorder
      (ADD), 183, 309
  delays in cognitive
      development, 246–47
  delays in emotional and social
      development, 247–50
  delays in motor development,
      244–46
  expectation of failure and,
      129
  later developmental concerns,
      250–51
  recognizing, 244–51
Diarrhea, 319–20
Diet, minimal, 141, 202, 290
Disabilities. See Developmental
      disabilities
Discipline, 252–60
  at ages
      nine months, 121–23
      beyond one year, 148–49
      fifteen months, 154–56
      eighteen months, 168–170

beyond eighteen months,
    178–79
conflicted parents and, 252–53
crying and, 237–38
finding appropriate, 258–60
love and, 149, 252
for lying, cheating, and
    stealing, 336–42
promoting self-, 253–55
punishment vs., 149, 166–67,
    253, 258
spoiled children, 73, 118,
    135–36
stages of development and,
    255–58
Divorce, 261–68
  helping children adjust to,
      263–66
  joint custody, 266–67
  parental responsibility and,
      262–63
  stepfamilies, 267–68
Doctor(s), 451–61
  as advocates for children,
      11–13
  anticipation of issues as
      function of, xxi–xxii
  changing, 454
  child development and, xx
  choosing, 452–54
  determining when to see,
      321–22
  office visits (see Office visits)
  pediatric training of, xxii–xxiv,
      452
  relationships with children,
      185–86, 456–61
Doctor–parent relationships
  building, 454–56
  initial, during pregnancy,
      21–22
  problems, 451
  sharing responsibilities,
      461
Dogs, fear of, 280
Doulas (labor companions), 6,
    39, 424

Drink, refusal to, 317
Drugs
   doctor–child relationships and
      questions about, 460
   giving, to toddlers, 178
   during labor, 6–7
   during pregnancy, 13–15
Dying. See Death

Earaches, 315, 320–21. See also
      Hearing problems
Earliest Relationship, The
      (Brazelton and Cramer),
      xx, 41
Early intervention, 353
Eczema, 70, 219–21
Egg allergies, 222
Emde, Robert, 126
Emergencies, recognizing and
      handling, 313
Emotional development, delays
      in, 247–50
Emotional manipulation, 269–75
   beginnings of, 270–73
   at four months, 95–96
   as normal to parent–child
      relationship, 269–70
   responding to, 273–75
Empathy, 208–9, 210
Engel, George, 249
Enuresis. See Bedwetting
      (enuresis)
Erikson, Erik, 374
Evaluation. See Assessment of
      children

Failure
   expectation of, 128–29
   fear of, 283
Failure to thrive, 98, 286–87
Falling, fear of, 32–33, 276,
      281
Families. See also Divorce;
      Fathers; Grandparents;
      Mothers; Parents; Siblings
   cosleeping in, 92–94, 159, 381,
      386–88

deaths in, 329–31
planning (see Spacing of
   children)
single-parent, 11–12
step-, 267–68
Fantasy. See Imagination and
   fantasy
Fathers
   changing roles of, 421
   children's reactions specific to,
      79
   circumcision and, 10–11
   comparing penis size with, 194
   competition of, with mothers,
      4–5, 424
   including, at office visits, 55
   newborns and, 424–26
   shared parenting and, 422–23
   value of, as models, 426–27
Fears in children, 201, 276–85
   at ages
      one year, 147
      fifteen months, 156–57
      three years, 206–7
   of aggressive children, 283
   allergies and, 219–21
   of bathtubs, 156–57
   of being molested, 282
   of dark, monsters, witches, and
      ghosts, 280–81
   of dogs and biting animals,
      280
   of failure, 283
   of falling, 32–33, 276, 281
   of heights, 281
   helping children deal with,
      284–85
   of hospitalization, 298
   of invasion, 133–34
   of loud noises, 280
   of mutilation, 301
   of parent's death, 281–82
   of strangers, 102, 278–80, 282
   types of, 280–84
   universal, 276–78
   of war and nuclear disaster,
      283–84

Fears in parents. See Anxiety
   parents
Febrile seizures, 316–17
Feeding
   at ages
      newborn, 43–46
      three weeks, 56–57
      six to eight weeks, 69–72
      four months, 85–90
      beyond four months, 98–
      seven months, 111–12
      beyond seven months,
         117–18
      nine months, 125–26
      beyond nine months, 129
      one year, 140–43
      fifteen months, 157–59
      eighteen months, 170–71
      two years, 190
      three years, 201–3
   allergies and (see Allergies)
   breast vs. bottle, 8–10 (see
      Bottle-feeding;
      Breast-feeding)
   experience of, for children,
      286–88
   independence and, 291–92
   minimal diet, 141, 202, 290
   schedule for, 88, 288
   self-esteem and, 365–66
   solid food (see Solid food)
   stages of development and,
      288–91
   stomachaches, 240, 360, 40
   sucking, 30, 43–44
Fetal development, 16–21
Fever, 313–17
   convulsions, 316–17
   dehydration, 315–16
   refusal to drink, 317
   taking temperatures, 314–
Fine motor competence, 182
Finger feeding, 140, 289
First aid guides, 45, 313
Fixation of behavior, 293
Flop-jointed children, 138–3
Fontanels, 41, 120

erg, Selma, 158, 244, 338
ds, 437–42
gression and, 438–40
llies, 439–40
aginary, 323–27
f-esteem and, 366
ges of development and,
440–42
sing, 439
evision and peer pressure,
411–12
three years, 209–10
crying (colic), 62–64,
233–35

nt reflex, 33
ner, Howard, 244
keeping, 4
er differences, 182, 377–78
er identification, 180–81,
210–12
l, Arnold, 244
ral speech, 145, 186
ts, fear of, 280–81
ear, 399
dparents, 428–36
npetition with, 430–31
orce and, 264–65
delines for, 434–36
nners and, 345–46
t parenting patterns and,
428–30
ue of, 431–34
span, Stanley, 244
See Death

s, 293–97. *See also*
Self-comforting behaviors
sturbation, 195–96, 294–95
biting, 295–96
elf-comforting measures,
293
ond three years, 212–13
296–97
uate, ability to, 25
edness, 181
-to-mouth reflex, 33, 66

Headaches, 240, 360, 407–8
Head growth, 152–53
Hearing problems, 188, 398–400.
See also Earaches
Heights (falling), fear of, 32–33,
276, 281
Heimlich maneuver, 313
Hiccups, 46
Hitting, 149–50, 174–75
Home day care, 446–47
Hospitalization, 298–304
helping children after, 303–4
helping children during, 301–3
preparing children for, 298–301
Housework, children's help with,
197–98
Humor, sense of, 208–9
Hypersensitive and hyperactive
children, 305–11
crying, 234
helping, 307–11
identifying, 305–7
learning to walk, 139
newborns, 26–27
play, 160, 183–85
temperament, 76–77

Illness, 312–22
colds, 317–18
convulsions, 316–17
croup, 318–19
dehydration, 315–16
diarrhea, 319–20
divorce and, 264
earaches, 320–21
fever, 313–17
hospitalization, 298–304
nosebleeds, 321
recognizing and handling
emergencies, 313
refusal to drink, 317
taking children's temperatures,
314–15
when to see the doctor, 321–22
Imaginary friends, 323–27
importance of, 323–25
responding to, 325–27

Imagination and fantasy
humor, empathy, and, 208–9
lying, stealing, cheating and,
336–37
television and, 325
Imitation
at ages
newborn, 31–32
one year, 146–47
play and, 173–74, 182, 438
toilet training and, 177
Independence. *See also*
Negativism; Temper
tantrums
control vs., 201
feeding and, 291–92
at one year, 132–36
sleeping and, 385–88
Individuality, 164–65, 376–79,
397. *See also*
Temperament
Infant psychiatry, 235,
244
Infants and Mothers (Brazelton),
xxi, 76, 107, 232
Intussusception, 406
Invasion, fear of, 133–34

Jaundice, 42
Joint custody, 266–67

Kagan, Jerome, 78, 244, 277
Kaye, Kenneth, 44
Kennell, John, 39, 424
Kindergartens. *See* Preschools
Klaus Marshall, 39, 424

Labor companions *(doulas),* 6,
39, 424
Lead paint, 143–44
Learning. *See also* Cognitive
development; Motor
development
at ages
four months, 96–98
seven months, 114–16
nine months, 126–29

Learning (*Continued*)
  one year, 145–47
  eighteen months, 173–76
disabilities, 129
environments (*see* Caregivers;
  Schools)
fetal capacity for, 18–19
by imitation (*see* Imitation)
interference of, with feeding,
  88–90
through play (*see* Play)
rote vs. complex, 213
Lester, Barry, 20
Loss. *See* Death
Love
  discipline and, 149, 252
  falling in, with children, 83–84
  feeding experience and, 286–88
Loveys, 171–72, 389
Lying, 336–39
  imaginary friends and, 325–26

MacKeith, Ronald, 228
Mahler, Margaret, 89
Manipulation. *See* Emotional
  manipulation
Manners, 343–49
  conveying the pleasure of,
    346–47
  as cultural values, 343–44
  learning about, 344
  rudeness, 347–48
  social rules as, 345–46
  swearing, 348–49
Masturbation, 195–96, 294–95
Mead, Margaret, 396
Meals. *See* Feeding
Measles-mumps-rubella shots,
  154
Meconium, 46
Medication. *See* Drugs
Meltzoff, Andrew, 32
Meningitis, 314–15
Migraine headaches, 408
Milk allergies, 70, 221
Molestation. *See* Abuse
Monologues, 186–88, 189

Monsters, fear of, 280–81
Montagner, Hubert, 446
Montessori, Maria, 109
Moore, O. K., 213
Moro reflexes, 32–33,
  276
Mothers
  children's reactions specific to,
    79
  competition of, with fathers,
    4–5, 424
  drugs during labor, 6–7
  drugs during pregnancy, 13–15
  shared parenting and, 422–23
  as single parents, 11–12
  value of, as models, 426–27
  working, 12–13, 80–82
Motor development
  at ages
    six to eight weeks, 78–79
    beyond four months,
      100–101
    seven months, 108–11
    nine months, 120–21
    one year, 136–39
    fifteen months, 157
    eighteen months, 172
  creeping and crawling, 110
  cruising, 137
  delays, 244–46
  fine motor competence, 182
  pincer grasp, 109, 112, 289
  rolling over, 97
  walking (*see* Walking)
Moving, helping children handle,
  372–73
Mutilation, fear of, 301

Nail biting, 295–96
Narcotics, 13–15, 27
Narratives from the Crib (Nelson,
  et al.), 186
National Association for the
  Education of Young
  Children (NAEYC), 447
Negativism, 257. *See also*
  Temper tantrums

at ages
  beyond one year, 147–48
  two years, 196–97
  developmental delays and
    absence of, 250
Nelson, Katherine, 186
Neonatal Behavioral Assessm
  Scale (NBAS), 7, 24–2
New Child Health Encyclopea
  (Boston Children's
  Hospital), 45, 131, 313
Night terrors, 189
Night waking. *See* Sleeping
  patterns; Sleeping
  problems
Nightwalking, 171–72
Noises, fear of loud, 280
Nosebleeds, 321
Nuclear disaster, fear of,
  283–84
Nurse practitioners, xxii, 13,
  322, 451
Nurseries. *See* Day-care cent
  Preschools
Nursing bottle cavities, 94–9

Object permanence, 114–15,
  145, 160, 246–47
Office visits
  at ages
    three weeks, 53–56
    six to eight weeks, 68–6
    four months, 83–85
    seven months, 105–7
    nine months, 119–20
    one year, 132–36
    fifteen months, 151–54
    eighteen months, 166–6
    two years, 180–81
    three years, 200–201
  first, during pregnancy, 3–
Otitis media, 399

Pacifiers, 47, 64–67,
  143
Paint, lead, 143–44
Parallel play, 173–74, 438

ents, 421–27. *See also*
    Fathers; Mothers
nxiety in (*see* Anxiety in
    parents)
hanging roles of, 421
ompetition between, 424
ivorce of, 261–68
amilies and (*see* Families)
eeding problems and hangups
    of, 287
nodeling of feeding patterns
    by, 202
f newborns (*see* Parents of
    newborns)
ast parenting patterns, xx–xxi,
    428–30
elationships with doctors (*see*
    Doctor-parent
    relationships)
hared parenting, 422–23
hifting of children's
    attachments between,
    163–64, 211–12
eeping with children, 92–94,
    159, 381, 386–88
alue of two models, 426–27
ents of newborns, 37–52
djustment of, 53–56
abies as teachers of, 47–48
onding with babies, 39–40
iscovering real baby, 40–41
arly care of babies, 43–47
xamining babies, 41–43
ostpartum anxiety and
    depression of, 37–39, 53,
    54, 235
tarting out with premature
    babies, 48–52
iatricians. *See* Doctor(s)
kaboo games, 116, 127, 146
r relationships. *See* Friends
is size, 194
son permanence, 115–16, 127,
    145
s, deaths of, 331–32
nylketonuria (PKU), 42
obias. *See* Fears in children

Phototherapy, 42
Physicians. *See* Doctor(s)
Piaget, Jean, 244
Pincer grasp, 109, 112, 289
Play
    at ages
        newborn, 44–45
        beyond four months, 100
        fifteen months, 159–61
        eighteen months, 173–76
        two years, 181–85
    imaginary (*see* Imaginary
        friends; Imagination and
        fantasy)
    parallel, 173–74, 438
    self-esteem and, 365
    symbolic, 153, 160, 182, 336
    therapeutic, 302
Pointing, 145
Postpartum depression, 37–39
Posture, toddler, 157, 172
Potty chairs, 191
Praise and criticism, 363–64
Precocious children, 213, 363–64
Pregnancy, 3–22
    breast vs. bottle, 8–10 (*see also*
        Bottle-feeding;
        Breast-feeding)
    doctor as advocate for baby,
        11–13
    drug exposure, 13–15
    fetal development, 16–21
    first office visit, 3–5
    parent-doctor relationship,
        21–22
    preparing for birth, 5–8
Premature children, 350–54
    assessment of, 26–28
    parental responses to and care
        for, 48–52
    recovery and growth of,
        351–54
Preschools. *See also* Day-care
        centers; Schools
    choosing, 214–15, 355–56
    separation and, 370–72
    toilet training and, 176

Protective reflexes, 29–30
Punishment vs. discipline, 149,
    166–67, 253, 258. *See also*
    Discipline

Rashes, 222
Reading, teaching, 213
Referencing, concept of, 126–27
Reflexes, 28–34, 79
Regression, periods of, xvii–xviii
Rehydration, 317
REM (rapid eye movement)
    sleep, 1, 59–60, 91
Resonance (speech) problems,
    404
Reye's syndrome, 316
Rocking, 123–24
Rolling over, 97
Rooting reflex, 30
Rosen, Mark, 268
Ross, Hildy, 173
Rudeness, 347–48
Rules, social. *See* Manners

Sadness, depression and, 240–41
Safety
    at ages
        seven months, 110–11, 118
        nine months, 122–23
        beyond nine months, 131
        beyond eighteen months, 179
    and lead paint, 143–44
Schedule, feeding, 88, 288
Schools, 355–61. *See also*
    Preschools
    children's readiness for, 356–58
    choosing, 355–56
    preparing children for, 358–61
    role of, in helping children deal
        with fears, 333
Scratching, 149–50
Self-comforting behaviors. *See
    also* Habits
    crying and, 236–37
    loveys and, 171–72, 389
    pacifiers and, 47, 64–67, 143
    rocking, 123–24

Self-comforting behaviors
  (*Continued*)
  sleeping and, 74
  thumb sucking, 64–67
Self-confidence, 181
Self-discipline, 253–55
Self-esteem, 362–66
  balancing praise and criticism,
    363–64
  bedwetting and, 416
  boosting, at different ages,
    365–66
  encouraging positive
    self-images, 362–63
Self-exploration, 176. *See also*
    Masturbation
Self-image
  development of, 175–76
  encouraging positive, 362–63
  (*see also* Self-esteem)
Separation, 367–73
  at ages
    beyond nine months, 131
    one year, 145–46
    eighteen months, 172–73
  caregivers and, 443
  day-care centers, 367–70
  divorce, 261–68
  hospitalization, 298–304
  moving, 372–73
  nurseries and preschools, 370–72
  schools, 358–61
  working mothers and, 12–13,
    80–82
Sexuality. *See also* Abuse;
    Gender differences;
    Gender identification
  doctor–child relationships and,
    458–60
  masturbation, 195–96, 294–95
  beyond three years, 210–12
Sharing, 210
Shoes, 121, 157
Siblings. *See also* Spacing of
    children
  accepting rivalry between, 199,
    374–76

age and birth order differences,
    378–79
  divorce and, 264
  fears and rivalry between, 206
  gender differences, 377–78
  helping children adjust to new,
    199, 395–97
  tattling and teasing, 378
  valuing individuality of,
    376–79
Sickness. *See* Hospitalization;
    Illness
Silver nitrate, 41–42
Sitting, 101, 108
Skin rashes, 222
Sleeping patterns
  at ages
    three weeks, 59–62
    six to eight weeks, 73–74
    four months, 91–94
    beyond four months, 99
    seven months, 113–14
    beyond seven months, 118
    nine months, 123–25
    beyond nine months, 130
    one year, 139–40
    fifteen months, 159
    eighteen months, 171–72
    two years, 189–90
Sleeping problems, 380–89
  divorce and, 263
  guidelines for managing,
    388–89
  learning independence and,
    385–88
  patterns of night waking,
    383–85
  understanding sleep cycles,
    381–83
Small for gestational age (SGA)
    children, 50
Smiles, 74–75
Smoking, pregnancy and, 14,
    27
Social development, delays in,
    247–50
Social rules. *See* Manners

Solid food
  allergies, 87–88, 98–99, 222–2
  introducing, 86–88, 98–99
  minimal diet, 141, 202, 290
  swallowing, 71, 288–89
Sound spectrograph, 236
Spacing of children, 390–97. *Se*
    also Siblings
  affirming individuality, 397
  considering second child,
    391–92
  developmental stages and
    questions about, 390
  guidelines for family plannin
    393–95
  helping children adjust to
    siblings, 395–97
Speech
  at ages
    one year, 144–45
    fifteen months, 161
    two years, 181, 186–89
  development, 401–2
  problems, 400–404
  swearing, 348–49
Spitting up, 45, 70–71
Spoiled children, 73, 118, 135,
    237, 254, 379
Standing, 100–101, 120
Startle reflexes, 32–33
Stealing, 339–41
Stepfamilies, 267–68
Stepfathering (Rosen), 268
Stern, Daniel, 186
Stomachaches, 240, 360, 405–7
Storage, concept of, 146
Stranger anxiety, 102, 147,
    278–80, 282
Stranger awareness, 101–4, 11!
Stress
  of birth, 26–28
  stomachaches and headache
    as symptoms of, 405
  of television viewing, 410–1
Stuttering, 188–89, 402, 404
Style. *See* Temperament
Success, expectation of, 128–2!

king
utritive and nonnutritive,
43–44
flexes, 30
den infant death syndrome
(SIDS), 29
gery. *See* Hospitalization
aring, 348–49
mmer's ear, 320
mming reflex, 33
bolic play, 153, 160, 182, 336

trums. *See* Temper tantrums
ling, 378
sing, 378, 439
thing
t four months, 94–95
t one year, 143–44
vision, 409–13
s behavioral influence, 409–10
ars and, 207
nagination and, 325
mits on viewing time, 412–13
eer pressures and messages of,
411–12
resses of viewing, 410–11
eyond two years, 198–99
nperament
t ages
newborn, 34–36
three weeks, 55–56
six to eight weeks, 76–78
ssessing, 106–7
ight waking and, 383–85

Temperature, taking children's,
314–15
Temper tantrums. *See also*
Negativism
at ages
beyond one year, 148
beyond three years, 212
first, 154–56, 257
meaning of, 136
Thomas, Alexander, 106
Thumb sucking, 64–67
Thyroid difficulties, 42
Tics, 296–97
Toilet training, 414–18. *See also*
Bedwetting (enuresis);
Bowel movements
at ages
two years, 190–95
three years, 203–6
constipation, 192–94, 205–6,
406, 415–16
danger of too much pressure
for, 414–17
training pants, 203–4
waiting for readiness
beyond nine months, 130
beyond one year, 149
beyond fifteen months, 162
beyond eighteen months,
176–78
Tonic neck reflex, 30–31
Touchpoints, concept of,
xvii–xviii
Training pants, 203–4

Tranquil period, 200
Two displacements, 160

Ulcers, 407
Unconsciousness, 313

Voices, recognition of, 34–35
Vomiting, inducing, 111
Vulnerable child syndrome, 237,
351

Waking. *See* Sleeping patterns;
Sleeping problems
Walking
assessing, 152
beginning, 136–39
at night, 171–72
posture and, 157, 172
Walking reflex, 29, 137
Wallerstein, Judith, 261
War, fear of, 283–84
Weaning, 125–26, 170–71
Weight, birth, 57
Wheat allergies, 222
Winnicott, D. W., 37
Witches, fear of, 280–81
Working and Caring (Brazelton),
81, 104
Working mothers, 12–13, 80–82
Writing, teaching, 213

about the
author

T. Berry Brazelton, M.D., founder of the Child Development Unit at Boston Children's Hospital, is clinical professor of pediatrics emeritus at Harvard Medical School. Currently professor of pediatrics and human development at Brown University, he is also past president of both the Society for Research in Child Development and the National Center for Clinical Infant Programs. Dr. Brazelton is the recipient of the C. Anderson Aldrich Award for Distinguished Contributions to the Field of Child Development, given by the American Academy of Pediatrics.

A practicing pediatrician for over thirty-five years, he introduced the concept of "anticipatory guidance" for parents into pediatric training. The author of over 200 scholarly papers, Dr. Brazelton has written twenty-four books, for both a professional and a lay audience, including the now classic *Infants and Mothers* and *To Listen to a Child.* The Brazelton Neonatal Behavioral Assessment Scale is in use in over 500 hospitals in the United States and in twenty-five other countries.

photography credits

Steven Trefonides, pages xxi, xxiii, 1, 7, 13, 24, 45, 47, 61, 107, 131, 160, 168, 187, 202, 207, 245, 259, 271, 296, 302, 306, 332, 356, 385, 406, 432, 433, 444, 453
Janice Fullman, pages 85, 103, 116, 117, 121, 144, 145, 183, 213, 217, 234, 241, 265, 318, 324, 340, 347, 393, 422, 427, 441, 447
Dorothy Littell Greco, pages 17, 65, 152, 155, 281, 403, 423
Alexa Trefonides, pages 128, 223

Samuel Bell III, page 240
Beth Burleigh, pages 253, 415
Elizabeth Carduff, pages 58, 95, 124, 135, 429
Nancy Kricorian and James Schamus, page 31
Debra and Barclay Rockwood, pages 175, 287, 289, 364
Lisa Treacy, page 371
Samantha Welsh, page 40
Susan Fiske Williams, page 36
Barbara Wood, pages 314, 411